Beer in the Middle Ages and the Renaissance

Beer in the Middle Ages and the Renaissance

Richard W. Unger

PENN

University of Pennsylvania Press
Philadelphia

10 9 8 7 6 5 4 3 2 1

Published by
University of Pennsylvania Press
Philadelphia, Pennsylvania 19104-4011

Library of Congress Cataloging-in-Publication Data

Unger, Richard W.
    Beer in the Middle Ages and the Renaissance / Richard W. Unger.
        p.   cm.
    Includes bibliographical references and index.
    ISBN 0-8122-3795-1 (cloth : alk. paper)
        1. Beer—Europe—History—To 1500.   2. Beer—Europe—History—To 1500—16th century.
3. Brewing industry—Europe—History—To 1500.   4. Brewing industry—Europe—History—
16th century.   I. Title.

TP577.U54   2003
641.2'3'0940902—dc22   2004049630

For Barbara Unger Williamson
and Clark Murray Williamson

Contents

Illustrations

Tables

Preface

The mention of the history of beer always brings a laugh or at the very least a snicker. The history of beer for most people is not a serious topic of study. It seems to them frivolous and hardly worth more than a few diverting minutes of anyone's time. Beer, after all, is a drink for leisure, for young people, generally men, and associated with sports and student life. That perception of beer is a case of historical myopia, of an inability of many people at the beginning of the twenty-first century to conceive of a world different from their own. The prevailing presentism makes it difficult for many to comprehend a world where beer was a necessity, a part of everyday life, a drink for everyone of any age or status, and a beverage for all times of the day from breakfast to dinner and into the evening.

The popular conception of beer and ignorance of the place it enjoyed in medieval and Renaissance Europe are major obstacles but not the greatest ones to writing a history of beer, its consumption and production, and the brewers who made it. The greatest hurdle is the immense size of the history itself. Because of the scale and scope of the industry and its pervasive nature, much of the record of the past is part of the history of beer. The involvement of public authorities in the making of beer and its distribution, already in evidence six thousand years ago, opens up not only another extensive dimension of the history of beer but also created a mass of surviving documentation that is difficult to master even if the investigator imposes strict limits on the time and place to be studied. Many people—amateur and professional historians inspired by an interest in the economics of brewing, the techniques of brewing, the government income from brewing, or simply the taste of beer and the conviviality which accompanied its consumption—have tried their hands at writing about the history of beer. Success has been limited, the task simply too much.

Rather than attempting a comprehensive history of brewing, a work that may be impossible to produce, this effort is primarily descriptive and to a limited degree analytical. It establishes some categories which isolate features of the organization of brewing as well as significant and influential technical advances. It also discerns and offers some overarching patterns in the development of beer making in medieval and Renaissance Europe. The resulting framework may prove to be a basis for others to develop effective discussions of what happened to beer and beer drinkers in the years before 1650. Broad general trends are identified, but only through the compilation of many examples taken from different sites spread across northern Europe. Many other more sensible historians have chosen to concentrate on one town or one region during a limited period of time. It is from their studies, carried out over the last century and before, that the outline of development is drawn. The tables in this work constitute the most obvious cases of compilations where the value of some data may not be obvious. Singular figures or small groups of figures from one town in the tables may not be central to the thrust of this work, but they may, in a larger context or in relation to other questions taken up here, have a useful function. Many cases have been missed so more could easily be added and counterexamples could be found. There is always the chance in such an enterprise of missing yet one more piece of information. That certainly has happened here and will, of necessity, happen in any work on beer in medieval and Renaissance Europe.

This study relies heavily on my own earlier and deeper examination of the brewing industry in Holland. This book, however, is more than just an elaboration on that theme and involves more than placing Dutch brewing of the period into some larger European context. The Low Countries still receive the lion's share of attention along with Germany and England. Brewing, of course, went on in many other places, and inadequate consideration is given here to Poland and the rest of eastern Europe as well as to the Celtic fringe of the British Isles and to northern France. Brewing also went on in classical Greece and in rural Spain under Roman rule. How long beer making in the countryside continued in southern Europe in the Middle Ages and beyond is a question not considered here and, like so many other issues, must be left for others to tackle. Nonetheless, no similar effort has been made to draw together the body of research on European brewing before 1650—that perhaps is the primary value of results offered in this study. If this book serves in any way as a guide to the future work on beer making and drinking, and given past experience there will be a good deal of future work on those topics, then it will have served its purpose.

The language of beer creates another significant problem in writing about the history of the drink. In general the word beer is used generically in this work. It is also used to mean the drink made with the addition of hops. Ale is used to describe the drink without hops in which some other additive or additives were put into the drink during brewing. The distinction is kept especially for discussion of English practices. The etymology of the various words used in different languages to identify the drink and the process of making it is taken up in the text along with some of the language used in dealing with other drinks that were substitutes for or alternatives to beer. The many names used to describe the various types of beer made and drunk in Europe, especially during the sixteenth century, are also explored. Confusion, as with the description of the development of brewing, is difficult to avoid though extensive efforts have been made to minimize it here.

A book of this scope cannot be produced without extensive assistance, in the first instance financial. The Social Sciences and Humanities Research Council of Canada funded the earliest excursions into the history of brewing. Subsequent support from the John Simon Guggenheim Foundation made possible the expansion of the study to include a greater range of questions and a wider geographical area. The University of British Columbia supplied technical support. Most recently the Netherlands Institute for Advanced Study, librarians, staff and fellows, have been extremely helpful in bringing this long-term project to a conclusion.

A number of individuals over the years have offered help and information to add to the mass of information which is to some extent boiled down in these pages. Citations to and the loan of valuable works have come from Caroline Barron, Richard Hoffman, Diane Newell, Mark Peterson, and Hugh Thomas. The work of Max Nelson on classical brewing, Lydia Niehoff on Bremen brewing, Gerald Stefke on Hamburg brewing, Raymond van Uytven on Belgian brewing, and Richard Yntema on Dutch brewing have proven especially helpful as has their supplying me with products of their own research. Jessica Warner gave me valuable bibliographical assistance. Jan Woleński showed me the way through the maze of Polish orthography. Judith Bennett guided me to extremely useful English sources and, through her criticism, guided me away from a number of errors. Erik Aerts has been extremely helpful, not only as a source of information about brewing in the southern Low Countries, but also as an example of how to carry on the study of brewing even under difficult and trying conditions. I am also appreciative of Maryanne Kowaleski's many continuing and keen observations about the project. Jocelyn Smith read an earlier version of the manuscript, and for her comments and those of the anonymous reader for the University of Pennsylvania Press I am grateful, as I am to reviewers of my earlier book on Dutch brewing who pointed to errors or potential for error. Jerry Singerman of the Press has been patient through a project that took much longer than either of us planned or wanted. Angela Jansen at the Netherlands Institute for Advanced Study provided extensive support in the completion of the work. I am indebted as well to the many organizations that have allowed me to speak about brewing over the last two decades and to the audiences that have listened attentively and offered critical suggestions, many of which are incorporated in this book. Material published earlier in the *Deutsches Schffahrtsarchiv*, the *Journal of*

European Economic History and a Festschrift in honor of my long-time colleague and friend Janos Bak is subsumed in the text. My apologies to anyone who has the sense that he or she has seen some of the examples at some point before. I have relied on my colleagues in Medieval Studies and in the History Department at the University of British Columbia for support and for comments on the whole project as well as on some specifics.

This book would not have been possible without the patience, good humor, grace and kindness of my family, my close family in particular but also my extended family. I am indebted to all of them for their help. Equally the book would not have been possible without the extensive assistance of librarians, especially those at the University of British Columbia including Diana Cooper, and those at a number of libraries across North America and in Europe. That disappearing cohort of research librarians with unique skills and extensive experience created the opportunity to carry on a study like this which brings together a wide range of sources from different places in different languages. In this case, as in so many others, they have been critical to any success people doing research have enjoyed. They introduced me to material that otherwise I would not have known. Any mistakes I may have made in using it are entirely my own.

Abbreviations

ARa	Algemeen Rijksarchief, Brussels, Belgium
G. A.	Gemeente Archief of the town in the Netherlands
N. A.	Nationaal Archief, The Hague, the Netherlands
PRO	Public Record Office, London, U.K.
R. A.	Rijksarchief of the province in the Netherlands
Sa	Stadsarchief of the town in Belgium

Chapter 1

Introduction: Understanding the History of Brewing

Beer at the start of the third Christian millennium has little in common with the drink that carried the same or variant names through the European Middle Ages and Renaissance. It is true that beer was and is an infusion of germinated grain, made to ferment after being cooled, and then by some means clarified before consumption. This definition shares some features of that given by Louis Pasteur, the great chemist and one of the fathers of modern brewing, writing in the 1870s. He, however, placed much stricter limits on what could be called beer.[1] The word is generally used for any undistilled, fermented malt beverage of relatively low, but widely varied, alcohol content. Not even malt, or for that matter grain, is absolutely necessary as a principal component of the raw materials for beer. During Pasteur's lifetime beer became a more standardized product, and as a result of his own research, it was to become even more consistent throughout Europe and ultimately the rest of the world. Little consistency existed in the Middle Ages.

Nowadays beer is associated with inebriation, young adults, sports, and student life. It is typically produced by large, often international corporations. It is placed in the same category as all alcoholic beverages as a source of altered behavior and potential danger. The image of beer, the drink that is beer, and the methods of production are all products of the nineteenth century. The great transformation of the brewing industry depended first on its industrialization, the extensive use of machinery, and nonmuscle power to do work in the brewery. Second, the transformation depended on the adoption in most of the world of what was known as Bavarian or Pilsner brewing which relied on a specific type of yeast to get a lighter, clearer drink. Third, the transformation depended on the scientists' invasion of the brewery. Louis Pasteur started a trend when he took up research on beer in Clermont where he was exiled by the Franco-Prussian War. His work, which continued after his return to Paris in midsummer 1871, led to the use of microscopes in breweries to examine yeasts for infection. His book on beer, first published in French in 1875, took up many questions about effective brewing and led in time to each brewery having its own laboratory, testing the beverage at each stage of the production process, measuring a series of variables, and experimenting with different chemicals to produce desired results.[2] A by-product of the scientists' invasion included institutes and university departments devoted to the study of beer making and the training of students in the skill. Fourth, the transformation is linked with the rise of and changes in the temperance movement. As early as 1851 the state of Maine outlawed the sale and distribution of beer, lumping it with all other alcoholic beverages. The extreme Maine position did not prevail and for much of the nineteenth century brewers were the close allies of temperance forces. More beer consumption was expected to cause a fall in the drinking of spirits. A change from drinking gin and whisky to drinking beer was one favored by most temperance supporters for health as well as social reasons. By the early twentieth century, though, beer had lost favor and it was classed with all dangerous alcoholic drinks.

The precision of modern scientific brewing, the ability to produce, preserve, and distribute beer in massive quantities, and the popular, public reaction to the drink are simply not relevant for the centuries before 1700. Medieval brewing and the medieval drink were a world apart from the modern industry. Though it is difficult to escape contemporary ideas about beer and brewing, it must be done in order to understand what beer meant to the people of medieval and Renaissance Europe. Production units were of a different scale, yet production levels were still impressive. By the 1980s worldwide annual commercial beer production reached close to 100 billion liters.[3] Though estimates for earlier periods are notoriously inaccurate, the figure is more than ten times the production of all types of beer by all types of brewers in Europe in the fourteenth century. Certainly the amount of beer brewed in the twentieth century is much greater than that of any previous period, but contemporary brewing supplies a much larger population and a much wider geographical area. Consumption per person has gone down significantly since the sixteenth century. That late medieval brewers could reach even 10 percent of production at the close of the second Christian millennium is astounding, given the very different technologies and levels of investment. What makes it even more surprising is the difference in the character of the production units. Most beer in the Middle Ages was made at home in small quantities. Even the largest commercial brewers shared many of the practices of domestic brewers. Those thousands of brewers together were able to supply a smaller public with what were massive quantities of beer.

Alcohol in general, and beer in particular, "was the ubiquitous social lubricant; every occasion called for a drink" in medieval and Renaissance Europe.[4] Drinking was a social activity looked on by people of the day with neither suspicion nor awe. The society did not know about alcoholism. The concept simply did not exist. People thought alcohol therapeutic and a normal part of life, that is except for the very poor. Excessive drinking did exist and was frowned on, but moralists complained about overeating in the same sentences that they complained about too much alcohol. It was a society in which food was far from plentiful, so drink, especially beer, was perceived as an integral part of the diet, a source of nutrition and good health, rather than as a drug taken for recreation. Beer often had a low alcohol content and was taken at meals which consisted of sizeable proportions of carbohydrates that would have slowed absorption of alcohol and also mitigated its effects. Among alcoholic drinks beer was the standard beverage for breakfast. People drank at home and in public places, from morning throughout the day until well into the evening. In fact alcohol consumption was so normal that society depended on it to maintain cohesion and so function effectively.[5] It was a standard drink for all who could afford it from the laboring poor to the richest. Beer drinking went on throughout Europe, though the extent of the region where beer was the preferred drink moved and shifted over time with changes in brewing methods and changes in taste.

Brewing in medieval and Renaissance Europe went through a transformation. Although it was not on the same scale as that of the nineteenth century, it made the process of making the drink and selling it very different from the past. The medieval developments created an intermediate phase, a type of industry typical of the early modern period and one which offered a foundation for much of the development of the Industrial Revolution. Understanding the history of brewing is important because it affected the lives of many Europeans both as producers and consumers. The development of brewing is also important as a stage in the long-term development of industry. It passed through a series of phases in which production methods and organization were mixed, old ways continuing on in the presence of new ones. Its development is a mirror for the development of a broad range of other economic activity. The history of brewing, finally, is important as an indicator of the character of the social structure and social order in Europe up to and through the seventeenth century.

Making Beer

Historically the terms used to describe different drinks made from grain have been less than precise. Moreover, the purposes and uses of the names have varied and have often changed meaning over time. That makes following the history of brewing difficult but also indicates that brewing technology was far from static. The drinks brewers produced had varied purposes, names, definitions and were of different types. Brewers, through experience, learned of different ways to influence the nature and character of the final product. Despite all the possible permutations in the process there were certain steps in brewing which always remained the same. Well before there were even written records of any sort brewers knew that making beer involved a series of distinct, essential, constant, and unchanging stages to get to a drinkable final product. The first stage is to malt the grain and then grind it very coarsely. The second is to pour hot water over the malt to create the mash. Wort is the liquid extract taken off from the mash. The second stage can be repeated creating even more wort albeit with a lower concentration of vegetable matter. In the third stage the wort is boiled, usually in the presence of some additive or additives. In the fourth, after clarification and cooling, the boiled wort is fermented by yeast. In the fifth and final stage, after maturation and clarification, the beer is packaged for delivery in anything from a simple bowl for immediate consumption to a truck to be pumped into another vessel some distance away.[6] The changes in the biochemistry of the complex solution that is beer are many and varied and it is precisely those changes that all brewers have to try to promote and control.

To malt the grain, germination is started by spreading the grain out over a floor at a depth of about 10–15 centimeters and then covering it with water, which is then drained off after twelve to twenty-four hours. The temperature of the grain is then kept in the range of 15–25°C. Under those conditions the grains open and grow small rootlets. To get uniform growth, the malt is turned at regular intervals using wooden shovels and thrown into the air in a process called forking or raking. Water is sprinkled on the grain as needed to maintain the pace of growth. The malter stops germination by drying the modified grain in a kiln. Moisture content in kilning drops from 45 percent to 5 percent or less. The process uses low temperatures at the outset so that enzymes do not get destroyed, but once moisture content is down to around 12 percent, temperatures can rise to 38°C or higher. After curing, the malt has a moisture content ranging from 2 percent to 5 percent.[7] The malt is dried so extensively that it takes up moisture rapidly. If the level gets above 5 percent problems arise with grinding. The solution is to grind the malt immediately. The optimal time between drying and using malt turns out to be about three weeks,[8] one of many facts that medieval and Renaissance brewers would have been able to discover through experience. The miller tries not to break the husks, so the grist he makes is gritty. Too fine a malt becomes thick and spongy during mashing. If the husks are the right size, they go to the bottom of the mashing vessel. Then it is easy to draw off the wort, the husks acting as something of a filter in the process. If they are too small, they can clump at the bottom of the vessel and make it hard for the wort to flow out.[9]

For the second stage, mashing, the grist goes into a vessel and is covered with water already heated to about 65°C. Soft water is, in general, better for extracting vegetable matter; but a number of elements and compounds are included in any water, and they can add to or inhibit the mashing process. Brewers have always known that the quality of the water mattered to the quality of their final product, but it is only in the last 150 years that they have been able to identify the components they want and do not want. During mashing, various enzymes gradually make soluble some of the vegetable matter that is in the ground malt. The wort, when it is drained off at the end of mashing, is rich in carbohydrates and nitrogenous material. Repeated mashings lower the carbohydrate content in the resultant wort, and at some point concentration is so low that it is not worth continuing. At the end of mashing there are two products: wort—a colloidal solution of sugars and proteins—and draff—spent grains and about 80 percent water. The nutrients left after mashing are typically saved by feeding the draff, typically in a dried form, to animals. Animal feed has often been an important by-product of brewers, and into the nineteenth century piggeries were a common feature of even big urban breweries like those in London. In late eighteenth-century Paris brewers' leftovers went to feed dairy cows, while in London the operation was so large that brewers and distillers combined to fatten something on the order of fifty thousand pigs and cattle each year. The quality of the meat may have been poor relative to that of animals fattened from other sources, but costs were lower.[10]

Brewing, that is boiling the wort typically in the presence of additives, stabilizes the wort, sterilizes it, and stops enzyme action. The longer the boil, the less water is left in the solution. The wort is boiled in a kettle often called a copper since, though virtually any material can be used for the kettle, copper has long been preferred. The volume of the copper has to be the same as, or slightly more than, the volume of the fermenting vessels where the beer goes after boiling. The mash tun, on the other hand, can be a bit smaller than the kettle. In some cases, especially in the early Middle Ages, the same vessel was used for both mashing and boiling.[11] Since the fifteenth century the standard additive for beer has been hops. Boiling serves to extract hop resins, their principal function being to keep beer from contracting diseases. The type of hops and the quantity used have profound effects on taste and aroma. Though hops were used as an additive for centuries during the Middle Ages and Renaissance, there were competitors. Beer was often made with other herbs which gave it a very different character and taste and even a different name.

The next stage, fermentation, depends on yeast, a plant which cannot survive at temperatures over 40°C. The wort has to be cooled rapidly since it is vulnerable to infection before yeast is introduced. The growth of the yeast plant produces carbon dioxide and alcohol. Though the absence of air is not necessary to get the desired result, less exposure to air creates a stronger beer. Yeast is a living culture and runs the risk of invasion from a wide range of microorganisms. For example, if beer is exposed to air in the presence of acetic acid bacteria, it turns to vinegar. In some cases that was a desired result but most often an unfortunate and expensive accident.[12] There are some 350 species of yeast which fall into two large categories: one type floats on top of the wort during fermentation and the other falls to the bottom of the vessel. The latter type, while known in the Middle Ages, was used only in a highly restricted region in and around Bohemia. It produced Pilsner, which was to be the dominant type of beer in the twentieth century. Bottom yeast requires a lower and more consistent temperature to function than the other type of yeast, and until mechanical refrigeration became practical in the 1870s, its use was restricted to colder seasons of the year and regions where cooler temperatures could be expected.

Fermentation can take place in vessels and then be clarified by adding finings to coagulate the yeast and any remaining protein particles, which then settle out of the beer. The rate at which the yeast settles out of solution depends on the variety of yeast and on the reaction between the yeast and the composition of the wort. Some yeast needs to stay in the beer to carry out a secondary fermentation and convert any remaining fermentable matter. That secondary fermentation also diminishes the chance of the beer being infected by some bacteria.[13] At its most simple, the final processing of beer can mean simply delivering it straight from the fermenting troughs to consumers since it is ready to drink. The use of additives before delivery, things such as finings, along with other actions, such as filtering, can produce a higher-quality product with a longer shelf life. Isinglass, the dried swimming bladders of sturgeon, was and is popular for clarifying beer, at least from the sixteenth century on when Dutch traders brought the good from Russia. It replaced a similar dried substance from codfish. Getting the right combination of finings to work effectively with the yeast has always been difficult. Filtering, instead of using finings, eliminates many such problems and has the advantages of no loss of carbon dioxide, no oxidation of the beer, and little danger of infection.[14] The traditional package for beer was a wooden cask of which oak was known to be the best wood. Brewers often coated the interior with a thin layer of brewers' pitch so that the beer did not come in contact with the wood, thereby reducing chances of infection. Another way to prevent infection was to wash the casks with hot water before reusing them. Though they might be the best vessels for shipping and keeping beer, wooden casks were expensive, took up space, and required a large number of strong people, relative to the number of other brewery workers, to handle them. The final packaging stage might present the fewest biochemical problems to the brewer, but presented and continues to present a number of difficulties which translate into a significant share of the costs of operation.

Sources for the Study of Brewing

Knowledge of medieval and Renaissance brewing is based on a surprisingly large body of information. It is often repetitive and seldom gives direct answers to tantalizing questions about techniques or the economics of brewing. Nevertheless, the sheer quantity of material guarantees some understanding of what happened in breweries. It was not until the seventeenth century that writers put down on paper what they knew about the technology of brewing. Incidental information does predate 1600. The earliest recipe for beer making in the Low Countries, for example, comes from fourteenth-century Ghent. The first treatise which discussed how to brew did not appear until well into the sixteenth century, rather late considering the antiquity of the industry. Even eighteenth-century works on brewing were few and more practical than theoretical. In all cases, no matter date or place of origin, the works on beer show contemporary thinking about brewing but unfortunately do not necessarily describe the practice.

Anthropological studies of brewing technology have problems as well but of a very different sort. Odd Nordlund has made the most comprehensive effort to use the methods of anthropology to find out about brewing.[15] His survey of twentieth-century home brewing by farmers was carried out to document a tradition that was being destroyed by urban commercial brewers in his native Norway, just as it had been destroyed in the more urbanized parts of Europe in the Renaissance. Using questionnaires filled out by farmers and personal interviews, all from the 1950s, he concluded he was getting some idea of practices which had been established in the years around 1860. He could make that argument, he claimed, because he found such a high degree of stability in brewing. Since making beer was so deeply integrated into peasant society, he decided, as have other ethnologists, that it is possible to extrapolate back in time to an earlier period.[16] Matti Räsänen's study of Finnish brewing techniques is similarly based on a series of three questionnaires, stretching from 1933 to the 1970s. Though the number of informants in each case was small, he also found consistency, suggesting he was recording long-established practice.[17] Sources of information about traditional brewing carried out in the countryside in the Middle Ages and the Renaissance are virtually nonexistent. The temptation is great to accept the contentions of ethnological studies and to extend over ever greater geographical and temporal areas the conclusions about past practice based on recent traditional methods. Still, it seems almost impossible that the practices in remote Norwegian valleys in the 1950s were exactly the same as practices there and in the rest of northern Europe one thousand years before.

There may be indications not so much of brewing practice but of drinking practice from various manifestations of popular culture. Literary works are filled with mentions of beer drinking. Works of art depict drinking and drinkers. These, in turn, suggest something about the product that came from breweries and what consumers thought of that product. With visual art, though, the artist may have wanted to show something more than simply the drinking of beer. There may have been some more complex meaning in the act which contemporaries would recognize immediately but which is hard to fathom centuries later. Drinking was also a topic of songs and ballads.[18] In a few cases they, like paintings, offer some hint about the place and role of beer in the society of the day.

By far and away, though, the most common, the most consistent, and the most valuable sources of information about brewing techniques and production come from governments and their longstanding efforts to regulate brewing. Governments became interested in brewing by the tenth century at the latest. They realized that the price consumers were willing to pay for beer was significantly more than the cost of production. That realization opened the door to taxation, the level being determined by the ability of brewers to lower costs and by the consumption levels of customers. Officials found in beer a reliable source of income, one acceptable for moral as well as economic reasons. As a result, the archives of public authorities—local, regional and national—typically have extensive records of taxes collected on the production and sale of beer. The amount of income that entered the coffers of governments depended not just on the tax rates set but also on the honesty of producers and suppliers in paying taxes. To ensure governments got the share they wanted, they regulated brewing. The extent of regulation increased over time. The mass of controls created problems for brewers but also a mass of evidence on the industry that makes it possible to trace some of the developments in brewing with a degree of accuracy unique among industries or any form of work in the period. The origin of the regulation and its purpose does give something of a distorted view of the industry, however, since government interests were narrow and specific.

Regulations, on the other hand, can reveal a great deal about common practice in the trade. Governments in general, and especially urban governments, were concerned with maintaining the quality of consumer goods. They did so in order to protect their own citizens but also, if there was any potential for export, to insure a good name for their products in foreign markets. Towns often left to guilds the supervision of production in skilled trades. Those institutions, given legal status and authority by urban governments, regulated their trades while also offering a social and, in some cases, a religious focus for the lives of members.[19] Craft guilds were typically a product of the high Middle Ages, but brewers were often late in getting a guild both because of the character of the evolution of the trade and also because towns thought regulation of brewing too important to leave to guilds of brewers.

Beer was often a critical component of the food supplies of towns, and brewing was often a major employer. The heating needed for drying malt and for boiling made the trade a source of danger from fire. As early as the fourteenth century, for example, in the county of Holland in Haarlem and somewhat later in Amsterdam, the towns set limits for equipment used to dry malt in order to minimize the danger of fire.[20] The town governments, in those cases as in many others, regulated brewing for the general welfare of citizens. The competing and often overriding consideration, though, was in all cases the potential income from taxing the production, distribution, and sale of beer.

Governments increasingly restricted and regulated brewing through the high and late Middle Ages. Among the reasons was the increasing ability to control price and collect taxes. The English government as early as the thirteenth century set beer prices, relating them to the price of grain. They were followed by many other jurisdictions so that by the sixteenth century price fixing was common. Governments were committed, for tax reasons, to keep prices stable and high relative to costs. Even when grain prices fell, beer prices remained the same. When grain prices rose, brewers made a weaker drink to keep the price the same in what was probably a vain attempt to convince consumers that the product had not changed. Brewers, for their own gain, conspired with governments to levy taxes, in the process enhancing their chances for commercial success. At Liege in the southern Low Countries in 1241, for example, the town stepped into a dispute between the brewers and the clergy, taking for itself one-third of the brewers' profits.[21] From that date until the taxing structure was dismantled at the end of the eighteenth century, both brewers and the town government shared a joint interest in keeping up the profits of brewers. The Liege case is an overt example of the mutual dependence of brewers and governments and their common interest in the success of the industry.

Governments typically liked increases in output. Greater production of beer meant greater tax income. Such increases also meant more opportunities for tax evasion. Greater regulation of the making and selling of beer to inhibit evasion increased the volume of surviving sources for the study of brewing. Once in place, the bureaucracies for the collection of taxes typically grew. Even more than growth in output, technical change in the production of beer was a threat to tax income. At the very least, brewers would only introduce a new procedure if they could institute some saving in costs and so enhance their incomes. The owner of superior knowledge might well be able to capture more profit to the disadvantage of the public authority. Governments were especially fearful of technical change which caused some adjustment in the taxed inputs or taxed outputs. For the sake of efficiency, taxes were often highly specific. A new kind of beer, which did not fit an existing tax category or which used fewer taxed inputs, could mean a serious loss to the public purse. To deter such changes, government regulations often decreased the possibility of brewers developing or adopting new techniques. Since successful innovation tended to increase regulation, good new methods sowed the seeds of their own destruction or at least their own containment.

Governments tried a wide variety of methods to create and maintain monopoly profits, that is to keep beer prices above what they might be at competitive levels. The extra profits could be partly or wholly swept away by the government in taxes. Over time, the systems to maintain profits became more complex, the arrangements more confusing, but the basis stayed the same. Brewers typically were pleased with protection for themselves. The limitations laid down by governments made markets more transparent and so decreased the risks to producers. All the biochemical problems brewers had to confront constantly made them happy with almost any device to avert risks. While government legislation might make their lives simpler, brewers also sought to retain some of the profits generated by regulation. Thus brewers found themselves almost invariably at odds with governments. On the one hand, they wanted to promote and extend protection accorded them, which would increase the surplus of revenue over expenditure. On the other, they wanted to decrease the control over their own actions so that they could retain a larger portion of that difference between revenue and costs.

The common interest in the gains from brewing generated close links between the government and the brewing industry. In many cases brewers were part of government, or at least of civic government, in northern Europe from the fourteenth century on. Town councils in almost every sizeable town in northern Europe would have typically counted at least one brewer among their number. Brewers were habitually important figures in town politics as members of the magistracies, as executives, and as tax collectors. The frequency of brewers taking such positions can be explained by their prosperity and by their being tied to the town, not traveling. In part, though, the frequency of public service must also be explained by the mutual interest of public authorities and brewers in the profits of selling beer. As early as the eleventh century, brewers had close connections with government authorities. Brewers constantly found themselves lobbying, negotiating, and bargaining with government. That did not change, regardless of the fortunes of brewing. It is that relationship which is most fully documented and which generated even more official material for the study of brewing in the Middle Ages and Renaissance.

Stages of Development in Brewing

In the transition which went on from the so-called Dark Ages of the sixth, seventh, and eighth centuries to the complex and prosperous commercial economy of the sixteenth, brewing passed through certain stages of development. It is always difficult to describe with accuracy any wide range of complex events, especially over a long period. Yet a number of domestic industries which moved from the home to the international stage in that period did pass through identifiable phases. The first industry to become commercialized in medieval Europe was the making of pottery. D. P. S. Peacock, the Roman archaeologist and historian, has isolated eight stages of development, or rather types of production, which appeared over time in that industry. Peacock fully recognized that constructing a hierarchy of the modes of production, as he called them, from the simplest to the most complex meant the imposition of a conceptual framework which would never comprehend all potential variants or circumstances.[22] Despite obvious difficulties, his descriptive set of steps appears as applicable to brewing as to the making of pots. Pottery and brewing proceeded historically in many similar ways, and though brewing began the process of transition after pottery, in some cases it changed more quickly. For Peacock, the modes of production are defined by the scale of units, the methods used, the volume of production, the responsibilities both in and outside the industry of the people involved, and the skills needed by those directly engaged in making the good. The different stages always existed side by side. The pattern of change or transition to the next stage was similar, but by no means the same, in all places at all times. Still, the categorization does seem to apply to beer making and does help in understanding the long-term evolution of brewing in most parts of northern and western Europe.

The first category in the hierarchy is household production, in this case making beer for domestic consumption. Production is typically sporadic and the task is classed as a chore, like cooking or cleaning. Household production seems to have been the common form for all crafts and trades in the early Middle Ages. It may well be that since the job was classed with domestic chores it was generally done by women. Household production did not disappear, and even when British brewing was approaching the highest stage of production in 1850, something like 20 percent of all beer was still made privately.[23]

The second category is household industry in which the craft is performed by specialists, with production in the hands of a small number of skilled artisans. There is some permanent equipment devoted to the trade. The craftsmen carry on the trade only part time, and income from it serves to supplement family income. As a secondary economic activity, it can be and often is carried on by women.[24] Such was the case, for example, in one English village in the fourteenth century where at least 25 percent of the women in the village were definitely engaged in making beer, but more than 60 percent of production came from only about 12 percent of those making beer, and all of those large-scale brewers were women. They were obviously brewing and selling beer to augment and diversify household incomes.[25]

The third category in Peacock's scheme is the emergence of individual workshops with some commercial activity. The distinction between this and the previous level is slight and at times difficult to establish. Instead of the trade being a by-employment carried on throughout the year, the tendency is to concentrate energy on it during one part of the year, typically using the rest of the time for farming, gardening, or other agricultural pursuits. The equipment is in general more extensive than in the earlier stages. Producers may be isolated and may direct their production to more lucrative markets. At this stage the job is usually done by men.

More distinctive is the fourth category of nucleated workshops in which "individual workshops are grouped together to form a more or less tightly clustered industrial complex."[26] They are brought together at one site by the easier access to raw materials, labor, markets, or any combination of the three. This is clearly a different level of production. The competition among workshops generates better quality goods, and producers cooperate among themselves, even to the point of joining in cooperative schemes to invest capital in equipment they can all use. Since scale is larger, the market is larger and middlemen often appear to handle the distribution of output. In this stage the trade is practiced almost exclusively by men. The move from something like household industry to a system of nucleated workshops may well have occurred already in Mesopotamia almost four thousand years ago. In the old Babylonian period, women were associated with making beer and their disappearance from brewing by the mid-second millennium B.C.[27] may coincide with the emergence of this next stage. It would not be until the high and late Middle Ages perhaps, and then only in some places, that such nucleated workshops of beer makers emerged in western Europe and had the similar effect on the employment of women in brewing.

The fifth of Peacock's categories is the manufactory, the stage in which many artisans work together in one building or at a single place making a specialized product on a relatively large scale. Brewing did not reach the manufactory stage until the seventeenth century, and then only in some places in the Low Countries, parts of England and a few sites in Germany and Scandinavia.

Such organization preceded the development of the true factory system which appeared in Britain in the eighteenth century. In the manufactory, the production process is divided into constituent steps with workers specializing in each step. The difference between the manufactory and the next, or sixth category, the factory, is that in the latter there is machinery powered by something other than human or animal muscle power. The substitutes were wind, water, or steam energy. With additional power, production was larger. That, in turn, meant that both the scale of production and the area of distribution were much greater. A smaller number of major producers were able to reach international markets on what was, by earlier standards, a massive scale. This last stage was, and is, rightly, associated with the Industrial Revolution. It can be achieved only with extensive technical change in the making of the good itself and in the design and making of the more complex equipment used. While Peacock makes no claims about what might be called progress, it is clear that the factory is historically, technically, and economically the most advanced level of production and one not achieved by brewing until the middle of the nineteenth century at the earliest.

Peacock adds two other categories which do not fall in any way into a historical evolution but which do have unique characteristics. He includes a seventh category, estate production, ". . . because of its importance to the Roman economy."[28] Large Roman estates tried to be self-sufficient. It was even more true of the late Roman Empire as traditional production in urban workshops and the distribution system began to break down. As their ability to produce goods increased, estates sold surplus outside their boundaries. For brewing, such estate production remained important not only in the Middle Ages and Renaissance but up to and through the nineteenth century. The large country houses of aristocrats, as well as religious foundations, generally had their own breweries and often reached levels of output which far exceeded those of many commercial brewers. The last of Peacock's categories is military and other official production. Official production was distinguished by the small size of the work force since the men involved had other more pressing things to do. The work was highly planned, extremely well organized, used the best methods available, and, as a result, was relatively efficient.[29] Though military and other official production applied to the making of pottery in the late Roman Empire it does not appear relevant to brewing, with the possible exception of certain royal breweries in Scandinavia in the Renaissance. They seem, however, to have had more in common with the breweries of aristocratic houses on which they were presumably modeled.

The categories, or stages, devised by Peacock serve as a guide to the evolution of industry in medieval and Renaissance Europe. The categories indicate tell-tale signs, markers to look for in studying the history of brewing. They also serve to make studying brewing comparable to studying other industries. They indicate the economic and especially the social implications of changes in brewing practices. The categories and divisions set out by Peacock offer, at least, a first approximation of developments in brewing and also a way to distinguish different types of enterprises.

Chapter 2
Early Medieval Brewing

Beer Before the Middle Ages: Mesopotamia and Egypt

Brewing was important to society long before there was even the idea of Europe. It found a prominent place among early settled agricultural regimes. It is not likely that those settlements were started to generate grain for making beer. Other more compelling reasons existed for abandoning at least part of the hunting and gathering life, but it was not long after settling down that people began to make beer. A site in the Zagros Mountains of western Iran has yielded the earliest botanical evidence of beer making, dated to about 3500 B.C.[1] Two-branch barley was cultivated in northeast Mesopotamia as early as 7000 B.C. After 6000 B.C. it moved south and changed into six-branch barley. A residue of six-row barely turned up in a vessel, dated to the late fourth millennium B.C., from a Lower Mesopotamian site. It, along with emmer, a type of wheat, was the principal ingredient of beer. The first pictograph for beer from around 2800 B.C. looks something like a jar of 25–30 liters, suggesting that already at that early date there were jars dedicated to storing beer. A complex that may have served as a brewery and the first mention of the trade of brewer are dated to the mid-third millennium B.C. There are contemporary cylinder seals depicting beer drinkers, shown at banquets or during sexual intercourse.[2]

Beer was thought to have both magical and medicinal powers. There were recommendations on what to add to beer to gain medical benefits.[3] In the *Gilgamesh* epic, from Mesopotamia and dated to about 1800 B.C., beer is said to make the drinker warmer, happier, and more cheerful. The connection of beer to religion is even more indicative of the status of the drink. Some brewers appear to have had an official function, wore certain specified robes of office, and were associated with temples. The gods themselves had their own pair of brewers, and beer seems to have played a significant role in offerings made to the gods at altars. There was even a goddess of beer, Ninkasi. A hymn to her, describing the process of brewing, survives in a cuneiform tablet dated to the era of Hammurabi around 1750 B.C. The goddess gained what status she had from having given the art of beer making to humankind. Though Ninkasi appears to have been a minor figure the gods in general were thought to enjoy their beer.

There was extensive private beer making alongside any official brewing associated with the temples. Temple brewers were probably all male, but private beer producers and barkeepers may well have often been women, or so the regulations from a Babylonian stele indicate. There are cases of elementary brewing equipment being given as part of a dowry, suggesting an enduring connection between women and beer making.[4] The frequency with which beer appears in sayings and idioms, the extent of language dealing with beer and beer making, and its complexity by the fourth century B.C. in Mesopotamia suggest widespread production and a vibrant drinking culture. So, too, does the presence of taverns which were licensed and taxed by the government. The state already seems to have been concerned with the connection between drunkenness, prostitution, and beer drinking.[5] It was also concerned with the potential income from taxing beer consumption.

While there is abundant evidence for beer making and drinking there is almost no evidence, archeological or written, to indicate growing grapes or making wine in central or southern Mesopotamia. Wine making existed in the north, in the Zagros Mountains, as early as the sixth millennium B.C., well before the production of beer, but it appears to have been limited geographically, with production never moving and consumption rarely found to the south. Beer making and drinking dominated the region of ancient Sumer, Akkad, and Babylonia, the so-called cradle of civilization.[6]

Methods of making beer among Mesopotamian brewers prior to the Christian era are hard to establish because of the combination of the richness of the language and the paucity of documents. Brewers could make beer from malt or from unmalted grain. To malt barley, they soaked it and buried it in the ground or dried it in the sun for up to three weeks. They appear to have been prevented by the climate from malting in the heat of the summer. Malting needs temperatures of about 15°C, so except for the months from October to April it was probably too hot. After germination, brewers heated the malt in kilns. The malt was next crushed and, in some cases, but certainly not always, sieved to get out the hulls, using sieves of varying sizes made from reed, rush, or palm.[7] Next the brewers made a beer bread, *bappir*, from malted barley, though they sometimes added emmer to produce a different kind of beer. Next they crushed the *bappir* and added water, the proportion depending on the kind of beer to be made. They heated the mixture slowly with occasional stirring. They then cooled the resulting mash, adding various sweeteners to increase fermentable sugar and so get faster and more intense fermentation. Honey, wine, or the juice of dates were popular choices. One type of mash tun used for heating the mixture had holes in the bottom so the wort could be filtered through into a vessel set underneath it. Brewers discovered early on that they could add water a second time to the mash tun and get a weaker beer from the same grain. Brewers transferred the wort to a vat where heavier matter settled out and fermentation took place. The yeast used rose to the top. Since they may have relied only on airborne yeasts to infect their containers, different strains of yeast could appear in those containers. At some stage, during fermentation or perhaps earlier in baking the bread, spices seem to have been added to give different tastes. Alternately they may not have been baked into the bread. The goddess Ninkasi was said to mix *bappir* with sweet aromatics, such as the root skirret, which tasted like licorice, and honey to help fermentation. The sweetener may not have been honey but a date syrup, since apiculture developed only slowly in Mesopotamia.[8] From the fermenting containers the drink went into cleansing containers something like pottery jars where it was allowed to settle, or it was put directly into medium or small sealed jars for consumption. Beer could also be made with dates in place of grain, but that was a later variant, probably common from the eighth century B.C. on.[9] The sediment left in the beer must have been extensive given that drinkers commonly used a tube, a kind of straw. One surviving tube runs to a length of ninety-three centimeters and has an L-shaped end to keep sediment from clogging the end. Other devices, like built-in sieves in small drinking vessels, were used in the first millennium B.C. to keep the residue left in the beer out of the drinker's mouth.[10]

The results were a great variation in beers over time and in different districts. A list survives of some seventy different sorts of beer and one document from around 400 B.C. gives names for at least fifteen different types of beer. There was a general word for beer, *ka* in Sumerian, but there were also words to indicate the different types of beer that ranged from old to strong, fine to dark, bright to normal, brown and red brown, among many others. Oddly it appears that most of the technical terms of Mesopotamian brewing were of foreign origin.[11] A number of recipes or statements indicating the contents of beer survive. One calls for about 18 liters of spelt (27 percent), 30 liters of malt (46 percent), and 18 liters of a dough made of barley malt (27 percent) kneaded with water. Another calls for 60.4 liters of emmer (30 percent), 60.6 liters of beer bread (30 percent), and 80.8 liters of malt (40 percent). The combination was to produce 168 liters of beer. Regardless of the precise combination, the resulting beer must have been rather acidic with a low vegetable content. It could at least be made quickly almost anywhere with limited equipment. A stipulation of the Code of Hammurabi said that if 30 liters of beer was supplied on credit, then the lender had the right to 25 liters of grain from the new harvest. Since there is no source to indicate prevailing interest rates, it is impossible to be accurate about the implied grain content of the beer, but at least it can be said with certainty that brewers were using less than 0.83 liters of grain to make a liter of beer and probably considerably less than that figure. The regulation was put in place for reasons of efficiency, to get as much beer as possible out of scarce grain. Ratios of input to output were similar to, or higher than, those of the Renaissance and the beer was probably weaker, so Babylonian brewers were not as efficient as brewers four thousand years later.[12] The regulation was also put in place to maintain the quality and consistency of the product, a pattern of regulation which would dominate in the late Middle Ages and Renaissance as well.

Brewing existed in Egypt by around 3500 B.C. but probably did not start earlier than brewing in the valleys of the Tigris and Euphrates. The standard grains in Egypt were emmer and barley. In Egypt, women typically did the brewing,[13] and people at all levels of Egyptian society drank beer, apparently in sizeable quantities. Beer was a source , probably a significant source, of calories as well as certain vitamins. The drink was very much a part of daily life and also the after life judging from the beer containers buried with the dead and pictures of brewing on the walls of Egyptian tombs. Though beer was not connected to temple traditions as in Mesopotamia, public authorities did take an interest in brewing. The Egyptian state insisted that specific quantities of beer be handed over to officials, probably the first recorded case of government taxation of brewing. At some point, brewing may have even been a government monopoly.[14]

For many years it was thought that the standard Egyptian beer-making method was to let grain germinate, sieve it to eliminate most of the husks, and then make a lightly baked bread from the resulting malt. Brewers then, it was thought, put the bread in large vessels in water, exposed the solution to airborne yeasts, though possibly adding some yeast from a previous brew, and put in various additives including wheat, herbs, spices, or other seasonings like dates, orange peel, or safflower, poppy, or carob seeds. This view of Egyptian brewing came largely from tomb illustrations and the questionable translation of a number of words. The illustrations show the processes of beer making but do not necessarily show them in order. The depictions are often difficult to interpret. The understanding of Egyptian brewing was also based on a description of beer making by Pseudo-Zosimus Panoplitanus who wrote in Greek in the third century A.D. It was also based on descriptions of the making of a malt beverage called *bouza*, produced in modern Egypt and first described by an early nineteenth century traveler.[15] No source provided direct and reliable information on ancient Egyptian brewing.

Examination of the microstructure of residues from Egyptian beer from one site suggests that bread was not an intermediary phase in the brewing process. Instead brewers used a two-part process. They mixed coarsely and lightly ground malt or grain, well heated by sitting in hot water in jars, with malt that had been sitting in cold water. Chaff and coarse grain fragments on the remnants of brewers' jars suggest that the process of extracting vegetable matter by soaking in hot water was inefficient. The mixture was presumably taken from the jars, filtered to get rid of the spent grains and chaff, and then allowed to ferment. The spent grains may well have been squeezed to get out as much vegetable- and starch-rich liquid as possible. Yeasts could have been airborne or left over from the last brew, saved either in the fermenting vessels or separately, and then added at the right moment. The residues in brewers' jars, incidentally, turn up very few additives, so there may have been only light or no flavoring in Egyptian beer. The structure of the molecules in the residues makes it clear that Egyptian brewers did not use bread to make beer. The evidence from the residues is, however, limited in time and location, so it remains possible that Egyptians used a number of methods to make beer, including one starting with bread as is indicated by some illustrations.[16]

Breweries in Egypt as in Mesopotamia could be sizeable. A site identified as a brewery excavated at Hierakonpolis is estimated to have had a capacity of more than 1,200 liters per week so output was for more than domestic consumption. A brewery in Syria from around 1500 B.C. had stationary vessels with a capacity of up to 350 liters, so its production, assuming brewing two to three times per week, was somewhat less but on the same order of magnitude as the Egyptian brewery. There were even breweries on Egyptian vessels traveling the Nile or going to Syria. The beer, given the climate, could become undrinkable quickly, so typically production had to be kept close to sites of consumption, even when traveling by water. If beer was to be shipped, the containers were covered inside with a thin layer of clay to preserve the drink better. Baking and brewing, it appears, went on in shared quarters on the estates of Egypt, presumably because the two used the same raw materials and similar equipment. It would be a pattern repeated in the Middle Ages on large estates and in monasteries.[17]

The names Egyptians used show that they produced numerous kinds of beer, some distinguished by color or taste, and imported others. Medical papyri report no fewer than seventeen different kinds of beer including "joy-bringer" and "heavenly." The many possibilities created by varying the quantities of grain and malt and the types of malt would explain why there were so many different types of Egyptian beer. A myth relates that the sun god, Ra, sent the goddess Hathor/Sekhmet down to earth to punish disrespectful humankind, and she went at it with a vengeance. Ra relented and sent down red beer to cover the fields. Hathor/Sekhmet saw her reflection in the beer, was beguiled, drank the beer, became inebriated, fell asleep, and so forgot about her campaign of vengeance.[18] The story suggests beer was, if not a common drink, a commonly known one.

Brewing in Provinces of the Roman Empire

Presumably it was during the Babylonian Captivity that Israelites learned about beer and brewing from practices in Mesopotamia. The Babylonian Talmud talks about beer using the Aramaic word *šīkrā*. Whether the drink they referred to was made with barley or with dates, the Israelites took the novel skills of beer making back to the Holy Land. It is impossible to establish how extensive beer drinking was there. The Hebrew Bible uses the synonym for *šīkrā*, *šēkār*, for any alcoholic drink that was not wine, so written sources are of little help in establishing production and consumption of beer in Palestine.[19] When Palestine was a Roman province, people made beer there as they did apparently throughout the eastern part of the empire.

The fifth-century B.C. Greek historian Herodotus claimed that since grapes did not grow in Egypt, people there produced a kind of wine made from barley. The drink, he said, was the ordinary one of Egyptians. The earliest mention of beer in Greek sources is by Archilochus in the seventh century B.C., commenting on Phrygians or Thracians drinking it at parties. Later writers also associated Thracians with beer drinking. Greeks were impressed with the intoxicating powers of beer. A character in Aeschylus's *Lycurgus* gets drunk on strong beer, and Aristotle wrote that other intoxicants make drinkers fall in any direction, but beer drinkers always fall backward. He did not say how he determined the fact, nor did he give an explanation. Many other Greek authors from sixth, fifth and fourth centuries B.C. minor writers like Hecataeus of Miletus, Hellanicus of Lesbos, and Theophrastus as well as well-known figures like Aristotle and Xenophon mentioned beer.[20] Latin writers from Columella to Strabo to Athenaeus mentioned beer, though they rarely distinguished the type of beer. Some of them even wrote positively of the qualities of beer, and Diodorus went so far as to say that some kinds were scarcely inferior to wine.[21] Apparently Greeks learned to make beer from Egyptian practice, and though known in Greece, beer was not commonly drunk there. For Greeks, as for most others in the Roman Empire, drinking alcohol meant drinking wine. When classical authors did mention beer, it was often to relegate it to the provinces in the west and north, to mention some medicinal value, or to comment on its inferiority to wine.[22] Wine certainly was a common drink; by implication, beer was less widely made and consumed. There may also have been a difference in levels of consumption between the northern and southern parts of the empire, although it is possible that such a distinction is simply reading back into the past a later development.

No matter the literary evidence, by Roman times beer had become a commonly known drink and producers had acquired extensive knowledge concerning how to make it. Archeological evidence for malted grain has turned up in a number of Roman sites in northwest Europe. Officers and men stationed along Hadrian's Wall in the north of Roman Britain regularly consumed beer. The soldiers doing the drinking may well have been from the Low Countries. Some Romano-British sites have revealed ovens that could have easily served for drying malt. In general, Romans probably roasted their malt to stop the malting process, to make it easier to grind, to increase the content of sugars, to promote fermentation, and to enhance flavor. Roman practice was a step beyond Egyptian practice since brewers there resorted to adding only a little water to the grain to ease the work of milling.[23] Roman brewers certainly had one great advantage over their Egyptian predecessors in that they had wooden barrels. Strabo first mentioned casks about 21 A.D.[24] so it was the first century A.D. when the Celtic invention came into use in the empire. The casks made brewing, packaging, and shipping much easier.

Brewing in the Roman Empire may have been of two general forms, one like that of Egypt and the other taken over from Celtic practice. Linguistic, literary and archeological evidence suggest a distinction along those lines. In an edict of 301 setting prices in the empire the emperor Diocletian distinguished between the beer of Europe which he called *camum* and *cervesa* and the beer of Egypt which he called *zythos*, already an old word for the drink. The distinction by that time may well have been old as well and it may have referred to two rather different drinks, *zythos* being like the more modern *bouza*. In Latin *celea* and *ceruisa* or *cervisia* were typically used for the drink produced from grain suggesting that form was significantly different from Egyptian beer. *Celea* and *ceruisa* were apparently loan words from Celtic and Gallic languages respectively.[25] Though the Romans may have used a Celtic word for beer, it seems unlikely that the Celts were their source of beer-making methods, though it is certainly possible. Celtic tribes in Gaul knew of beer, calling it *ogre*. Pythius in the fourth century B.C. said beer was the common drink in Gaul, something later confirmed in the first century A.D. by Pliny the Elder. The latter said that brewers in Spain used the froth, the yeast that rose to the top, as leaven in bread making. The practice, also known in Britain and Gaul, made a lighter bread than what was common in Greece and Rome. Polybius in the second century B.C. mentioned a Spanish ruler who had the reputation for keeping large quantities of beer available in his palace. Posidonius, around 100 B.C., said that among the Gauls beer was the drink of the common folk and wine of the chieftains. For Celts, brewing was a domestic occupation and, like the baking of bread, was typically handled by women though there may have been a guild or society of professional beer makers in Roman Gaul. Celts used the word *brace* for malt which may be the origin of the French word *brasser* (which appeared already before 1175) and perhaps the German word *brauen* meaning, in both cases, to brew. In the early fifth century, Orosius said that beer was the typical drink of those living in the high plains of Spain and, in all likelihood, the peoples of Celtic origin in that part of the Roman Empire continued the practice of brewing throughout the Middle Ages as did many others in the lands once ruled from Rome.[26]

Beer drinking was identified with Germans, including those who lived on both sides of the northern limits of Roman rule. The description of daily life among Germans in *Germania* by the first-century Roman historian Tacitus gives a documentary basis for the connection. A law of one German tribe, the Alemanii, set a contribution of beer to be made annually to a temple, so the drink may have had a religious function among the Germans. It could be that as German immigrants spilled into the Roman Empire, first along its Rhine and Danube borders, and then later spread out across the western half of the empire, beer drinking displaced wine drinking. The degree of that displacement cannot, however, be measured.[27] Brewing probably declined in the later Roman Empire as the economy contracted, despite German immigration which presumably had a positive effect on consumption. Some time would pass before brewing recovered in terms of total production. The process of recovery was a slow one which went on, virtually undocumented, through the early Middle Ages. Brewing soon took on different forms and by the ninth century it undoubtedly had extended beyond the scale and scope that prevailed in the Roman Empire.

Mead, Ale, and Monastic Brewing

References to brewing in the early Middle Ages in northern Europe may be few, but they certainly support the impression that beer making was widespread. In Old Norse sagas two drinks are mentioned, *alu*, the drink of the people, and *bior*, the drink of the gods. The word *bior* or *beor* most likely is not from the Latin *bibere*, to drink. References in German and closely related languages suggest beer was a superior drink. The word ale, *alu*, *öl*, *olut*, and other variants may come originally from the word for mead with spices.[28] By the ninth century, though, ale meant the drink made from boiling wort that had been produced by mashing malted grain. In Viking mythology the heroes of Valhalla got beer, a proper reward for the powerful and strong. Their leader, Odin, enjoyed beer in the beer hall, but he also had both wine and mead.

Mead, made from honey and yeast, probably had a lower alcohol content than beer.[29] It was the drink of the poor and of slaves on the south shore of the eastern Baltic according to one ninth-century traveler who was surprised that there was no ale made among those people. His claim may have been exaggerated since early medieval documentation in Poland suggests that mead was the drink of the rich and noble, and typically the drink for weddings or feasts. It was even considered worthy of being a charitable gift. One possible explanation for his statement may have been that he was reporting to the king of England, and heavy drinking of mead was not common in his lands.[30] In neighboring Wales, on the other hand, mead appears to have been valued above ale, with a weaker drink called *braggot*, possibly made by adding honey to ale, falling between the two. *Braggot* did not disappear and continued to be popular for festive occasions into the late Middle Ages, at least in England.[31] In the eleventh century, the Welsh court had an officer responsible for making mead and for looking after the vat, a vessel that was big enough for the king and one of his officers to bathe in. The use of mead to reward members of the court attested to its importance, but even so, ale was a more common drink.

Mead continued to be popular in medieval Scandinavia and Prussia, areas where honey was abundant. The drink enjoyed its status more for its ability to intoxicate than for its food value. Consumption of mead declined as beer drinking spread, though drinking mead continued into the eighteenth century in parts of the north where raw materials were easy to get. Mead also survived in many different forms and variants as a drink for the sick. An aging Parisian in the 1390s, writing a book of instructions to his significantly younger wife, described a honey drink with spices added after some brewer's yeast had caused fermentation. The concoction was supposed to cure ills. The fact that the man offered a recipe and mentioned no other honey drinks for the household suggests that mead in its various forms was known but not common or widely sold in the towns of high and late medieval Europe. He called it *bochet*; other writers used other words for mead including *medo* and *mellicrattum* in Latin and mede in English and German. In the first half of the sixteenth century, the English writer Andrew Boorde talked about a drink made from honey, herbs, and water called metheglyn which he claimed was more wholesome than ordinary mead. It could well be that mead drinking declined among aristocrats through the high and late Middle Ages not only because of the improving quality of other drinks, but also just because mead was said to be so good for the drinker's health, a recommendation which might have restricted consumption to the sick.[32]

Ale was known in the British Isles as well as on the Continent. Ale in Wales retained the name *cwrw* and in some parts of Ireland retained the name *courmi* into the eighteenth century, evidence which certainly indicates the drink was there before any German speakers arrived in the islands. Pytheas, the Greek explorer who sailed to and possibly around Britain around 300 B.C., called the drink the residents made *curmi* so the term, and the drink, enjoyed a long lineage. Saint Patrick was said to have had a brewer in his household in fifth-century Ireland. The man was a priest as well. The Angles and the Saxons who migrated across the North Sea to Britain certainly knew about and brewed ale. The laws of King Ine of Wessex from the end of the seventh century mention the drink.[33] Anglo-Saxons apparently thought it had significant health advantages and recommended it as an ingredient in many remedies. In eleventh-century medical texts ale turns up often, relative to other drinks. It is mentioned in various forms so Anglo-Saxons knew about a variety of ales and expected them to be available. Anglo-Saxons produced something called twice-brewed ale, a weaker drink with possible medicinal advantages presumably made from a second or third mashing. Ale, and for that matter malt, appear on occasion in documents from pre-Conquest England as gifts, dues, rents, or even payments for penalties. William of Malmesbury, writing much later in the first part of the twelfth century, and no less a figure than Pope Innocent III, at the start of the thirteenth century, spoke of the English drinking to excess. Such complaining may have been a long tradition. Comments from two prominent eighth-century churchmen from England, Saint Boniface and Alcuin, suggest that ecclesiastical drunkenness was a continuing problem.[34] In the tenth century, King Edgar (959–975), influenced by the reforming monk Dunstan, ordered the closing of many alehouses and allowed only one for each village. Both of them were worried about intemperance; Dunstan also tried to use church law to diminish drinking. There may have been some truth to the fears since, by the time of Dunstan, Anglo-Saxon brewers knew how to make a very strong ale by mashing grain not in water but in ale. The powerful drink was known as double beer and may have had precedents in Roman times. Brewers are referred to in the 1086 Domesday Book so the brewing of ale continued in England on through the Norman Conquest without apparent interruption.[35]

In the Low Countries in the fifth, sixth, and seventh centuries—as elsewhere in thinly populated northern Europe in the few small collections of houses—farmers, herders and fishermen carried on traditional brewing. Archaeological evidence shows that brewers made ale in the region of Namur in the third and fourth centuries, after the Romans had left.[36] According to Nordlund, "Ale brewing is an activity deeply integrated in peasant society,"[37] and there is no reason to believe that the collapse of the Roman government changed that custom throughout the Low Countries, Britain, northern France, and much of northwestern Europe. The traditional practice of the two groups living in the region, indigenous inhabitants descended from neolithic-age set-

Figure 1. A man holding two drinking vessels, one a horn and the other a bowl, one of which was probably for beer. From a historiated initial in a calendar from St. Albans, c. 1140. Courtesy of The Bodleian Library, University of Oxford, MS. Auct. D. 2, 6. fol. 7r.

tlers and the new German immigrants, guaranteed the drink would be produced. Brewing continued as well in the homelands of the immigrants into the Roman Empire, in northern Germany and Scandinavia. Icelanders, the most adventuresome of German emigrants, once settled on their island were known to import malt for ale brewing. They and their Viking contemporaries drank beer from cups as well as from drinking horns (see Figure 1) and followed a trend of smoking the grain and malt before brewing. That custom may have implied little more than using the smoke of fires to dry malt, but certainly reports of such practices show brewing was probably common throughout Scandinavia around the end of the first Christian millennium. Sagas and other Old Norse works suggest the drink had the name *öl*, with *mungát* used for stronger brews. While Icelanders imported mead from the British Isles, it appears that most farmhouses on the island could produce their own malt-based beverage and even the stronger version.[38]

In the early Middle Ages, Europe knew virtually nothing other than household production. If there were tendencies toward household industry, they are essentially impossible to discern from the surviving records. On the other hand, there existed estate production, production which continued, and perhaps even expanded, in the early Middle Ages. The first large-scale production of beer in medieval Europe took place in the monasteries which emerged in the eighth and ninth centuries. In those institutions the first signs of a new level of beer making included using more and better equipment and the best of techniques, as well as having artisans who developed special skills to produce beer. The political revival of the eighth and ninth centuries associated with the Carolingians, and especially with the reign of Charlemagne, was critical in promoting the development of estate or official production.

Brewing was common in the Frankish kingdom, the kingdom which Charlemagne converted into a universal Latin Christian empire. The success of the Carolingians, their desire for order, their increased literacy, and their military victories contributed to the generation and survival of a broader range of evidence of the widespread practice of brewing. The *Capitulare de Villis*, a set of regulations for the proper administration of a landed estate dating from shortly before 800, mentions brewers in the forty-fifth chapter as among the skilled workers the steward should have in his service. It implies ale consumption in a number of other chapters.[39] There were breweries not only on landed estates, both secular and monastic, but also in some of the protourban centers promoted by the Carolingians, such as Regensburg and Constance. A document of 866, though a copy of an original from the seventh or eighth century, mentions a brewery, presumably as a separate institution. In 778 Charlemagne himself said that he was going to have a brewer at his court so that the quality of his beer could be maintained. He appears to have enjoyed drinking beer, for example, at a feast celebrating victory at the battle of Paderborn against the Saxons in 777. Alcuin, the leading writer and thinker of the day whom Charlemagne recruited from England to join the court, complained about the bitterness of continental ale. He was not alone. Contemporary Irish scholars in Cologne and Liege complained about the low quality of the continental drink compared to what they knew at home. Church councils in 868 and 895 discussed when a spiced beer could be drunk, so there were at least two types of beer, the spices in the one presumably there to combat the bitter taste of common beer.[40]

Large monasteries were institutions typical of the Carolingian Empire, and they were nearly always centers of brewing. Monasteries have left much more evidence, written and archaeological, about all aspects of early medieval life than any other institutions. Beer was important in monasteries, thus their records may exaggerate the place of beer in society. Monastic breweries probably existed even before the Carolingian period. Jonas of Bobbio, in his *Life of Saint Columbanus* written around 665, mentioned beer as an alternative to wine but also notes it was not liked in a number of places. Monasteries were the only institutions with quantities of surplus grain on any kind of scale, so they were alone in having resources which would allow large-scale brewing. They also had the capital to build the necessary facilities.[41] Carolingian monastic records indicate that certainly by the ninth century, and possibly earlier, northern Europeans had mastered brewing on a large scale. According to the art historian Walter Horn, "Before the twelfth and thirteenth centuries when brewing first emerged as a commercial venture, the monastery was probably the only institution where beer was manufactured on anything like a commercial scale."[42] Most beer was undoubtedly still made at home, typically by women, as part of the regular household chores of preparing food. The beer of monasteries might have been similar, but the scale and character of production were very different. Monks introduced a new form of organization to brewing and the new form served as a model for later developments and for the long-term evolution of the industry.

The rule of St. Benedict, promoted by the Carolingians, called on monks to live within their own community and, through their own labor, be self-sufficient; it also required them to offer hospitality to travelers. Both expectations forced houses of monks to produce beer for their daily diets. They could have kept to milk and water, as was the case at the abbey of Lindisfarne, England, in its early days. The monks there as elsewhere, however, shifted to beer and wine when given the opportunity. Maintaining the lives of monks and guests was not the sole reason to take an interest in beer. For monks and nuns, beer had spiritual and medicinal functions which may date back to the ninth century. Hildegard of Bingen, the twelfth century abbess of Rupertsberg, urged the use of beer made from barley or wheat in the treatment of lameness. Wine was preferred, but in its absence beer would do. If there was no beer, then water boiled with bread and strained through a cloth was the next best alternative. Hildegard recommended beer as a better drink than water for the winter when the dampness of the earth made water more of a threat to health. She was concerned, though, that beer caused tissues to become fatter and caused drinkers to have flushed faces.[43] She, and presumably her contemporaries and predecessors, assumed beer to be a part of the diet, one which, in some cases, could be beneficial to health.

The St. Gall Monastery Plan, drawn up about 820, offered a model for Carolingian religious administrators to follow in spreading reformed Benedic-

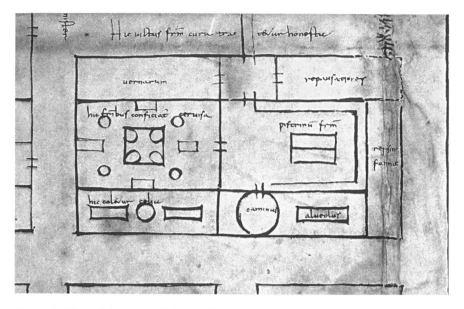

Figure 2. Plan of the monks' bake and brewhouse from the St. Gall Monastery Plan, c. 820, with the brewery on the left indicated by the label *hic fribus conficiat ceruisa*, that is, "here let the beer for the brothers be brewed." Reprint from Walter Horn and Ernest Born, *The Plan of St. Gall: A Study of the Architecture and Economy of, and Life in a Paradigmatic Carolingian Monastery*, 3 vols. (Berkeley: University of California Press, 1979), 2: 254.

tine monasticism, an essential part of the political program of Charlemagne (see Figure 2). The Plan lays out all the features essential to a monastery and prominent among them are three breweries, the oldest in Europe about which anything is known. One brewery produced beer for the guests, a second for the brothers in the monastery, and the third for pilgrims and the poor. The guests, noblemen, and royal officials got a better beer, made from wheat and barley, while the others had to be satisfied with beer made from oats. The design of the three brewhouses was essentially the same, but there were differences in size. The brewery for the pilgrims and paupers was only a little more than half of the size of that for the brothers. Each brewhouse was divided with a hearth room for brewing and a smaller cooling room. In each, there were four ranges for heating water and boiling wort. The design of the stoves in the breweries was exactly the same as that of the stove in the monks' kitchen. Around the stoves were four wooden vats, or possibly metal cauldrons, for mashing. There were two vats along an aisle for cooling the beer once brewed and, presumably, also for fermentation. After cooling, the beer went into barrels and was moved to the cellar. A kiln for drying malt was also sketched on the parchment of the Plan. There was a mill, very possibly powered by water, near one of the three breweries and so handy for the grinding of malt. There was also a brewers' granary which may also have served for malting grain. The breweries were next to the bakehouse. The similarities in the processes of making beer and making bread were not lost on the designers of the ideal monastery. The ability to share the generally higher ambient temperature and a yeast culture which had to be kept at about 30°C, even in the winter, were probably the deciding factors in placing one next to the other, as they were on Egyptian estates and in early modern English country houses.[44]

The St. Gall Plan may have been idealized, but other evidence strongly suggests that it did reflect components of reality. At a church synod in 816, it was agreed that shortages of wine in monasteries were to be made up with beer. The same 816 synod at Aachen also required that the brothers had to work in the bakehouses and brewhouses of monasteries. Apparently they liked to work there if not for the warmth, then for the aroma of baking bread and fermenting beer. Using as a guide the beer ration for paupers proposed by Adalhard, the ninth-century abbot of Corbie, per capita consumption of beer was more than 500 liters per person per year. To satisfy all needs for guests, paupers, and brothers, a monastery the size of that in the ideal St. Gall Plan would have had to produce on average some 350 to 400 liters of beer each day. While many monasteries never reached that level of output, they all faced problems of maintaining production throughout the year and problems of storing beer while it finished its fermentation in the barrels in cellars.[45]

Monastic brewing was not limited to the borders of the Carolingian Empire. Through the early Middle Ages it spread widely in the British Isles, to many parts of Germany, and to Scandinavia. The English abbot Aelfric in a tenth-century work has a novice answer the question of what he would drink with the following response: beer if I have it and otherwise water. At the abbey of Bec in northern France at night monks were to have water or beer if they were thirsty. There, as at other monasteries, it was a matter of choice between the two. At the monastery of Selje near Bergen in Norway, which dates from just after 1100, a brewery was built next to the kitchen with a connecting doorway. It was not the only monastery with such an arrangement. At Vadstena in Sweden around 1380 the bishop ordered that the bakery be attached to the old brewery, so the pattern represented on the St. Gall Plan was used in Scandinavia as well.[46] Making beer in a nunnery was also apparently a common practice and even abbesses were known to make small or weak beer. In one case, the head of the nunnery was so saintly that her small beer was alleged to have miraculously changed into wine.[47] In the early days of the Cistercian reform movement around 1100 the monks, aware that wine was allowed by the rule of St. Benedict, were too poor to drink much of it and so had to settle for beer or just water. In the thirteenth century, Clairvaux, the most prominent of Cistercian abbeys, had extensive vineyards so wine drinking increased but brewing and breweries did not disappear. The rule of Aachen, which applied not to monks but to canons, was modified shortly after 1000 to make the life of its followers more like that of the nobility and less like that of monks. The authors of the rule accepted the drinking of beer occasionally, that is if wine was in short supply. Wazo, the bishop of Liege early in the eleventh century, was a very devout man. One sign of his asceticism and dedication to self-mortification was that during Lent he drank beer and even water instead of wine.[48] Early medieval churchmen both inside and outside of monasteries may have preferred wine but it seems certain that they commonly drank beer.

Gruit

Indisputable evidence that monks made beer in the Carolingian Empire comes from grants awarded to monasteries of the right to use *gruit*. The state had the power to control the use of *gruit*, which was, by far, the most popular additive for ale throughout the early and the high Middle Ages in most of northwestern Europe. Brewers commonly used it in the Low Countries, the lower Rhine Valley, Scandinavia, and even in northern France. The term, in its many forms, appears all the way from Bayonne on the Bay of Biscay, along the coast, and in coastal regions to Gdansk in Poland.[49] The exact origins of *gruit* and its first use are not known. As early as the ninth century, governments apparently played a conspicuous role in fixing *gruit* as the predominant additive for beer brewed in monastic and other religious establishments. Governments in the wake of Carolingian expansion extended their taxing power and found a way to take a share of the satisfaction consumers enjoyed from drinking beer. Their method of extraction of income from beer drinkers depended on the specific technology which prevailed in brewing around the year 1000, a way of brewing that governments came to prefer and promote because of the ease of tax collection.

Exactly what was in *gruit* is now something of a mystery. Discussion and differences of opinion about its exact composition date back to the early nineteenth century. Since by 1800 *gruit* use had all but died out, only ambiguous written records remained to give an indication of what was in it. Part of the confusion over the meaning of the word may come from brewing practice. In the early and high Middle Ages, rather than mashing malt in a separate vessel and then taking off the wort to boil it in another, the two procedures regularly took place in the same vessel. Water and malt were poured in together and heated along with any additives the brewer thought would help. After boiling, she or he put the resulting liquor in wooden troughs or barrels to ferment.[50] If the malt went directly into the brewing vessel, then additives were probably often mixed with the grains first, so surviving documents might leave the impression that *gruit* was related to grain. The assumption of separate mashing and brewing processes could be one reason for uncertainty about the nature of *gruit*. A greater source of confusion is the imprecise language of medieval documents. The additive traveled under a number of different names, both in Latin and in vernacular tongues. The difficulty understanding the term is compounded by the fact that the sources are legal ones and little concerned with the art of brewing. The common Latin term *materia*, or various corruptions such as *maceria*, *magaria*, or *maiera*, were used in different regions to describe what was know in the vernacular as *gruit*. Alternative names included *scrutum* or *fermentum*. In Scandinavia the additive carried the name *pors* and in Westphalia *porsche*. As early as 999 in German-speaking regions, the word was *grut*. Whatever the name, many documents make it clear that *gruit* was an additive meant to give taste and some preservative qualities to beer.[51]

Gruit must have been a combination of dried herbs, including wild rosemary, with the most prominent ingredient being bog myrtle. Bog myrtle (*miricia gale*) is not *mirtus*, that is common myrtle, but rather is probably most closely related to the willow. Bog myrtle grows as a bush, often in clumps, and can reach a height of 1.5 meters. It flowers in late spring or summer. It does best in swampy ground so is often found along the shore or, more likely, close to rivers. Picking the leaves, drying them, and then crushing them to make the additive for beer would have been a relatively simple process. *Gruit* gave beer a specific and unique taste, a specific smell, and some resistance to spoilage. A 1068 act used *pigmentum* as a synonym for *gruit*, which suggests that it added color as well.[52] That document and others from the southern Low Countries show that brewers considered the addition of *gruit* necessary to maintain the quality of their product. That, in turn, made the additive valuable to them and worth their paying for it.

Urban accounts, as well as a few rural accounts, suggest that in addition to bog myrtle,the principal component, wild rosemary, other plants such as laurel leaves or the resin from an unknown plant called *serpentien* were included in *gruit*. There is no chemical indication that beer made with bog myrtle was any more intoxicating or that the herb combination had a narcotic effect, though some contemporaries may have thought otherwise. *Gruit* beer has a certain sharp taste.[53] Bog myrtle is bitter and astringent. This characteristic has led to its use in tanning. In France it is used in a medicine which promotes abortion, and, in China, it is used in a tea which settles the stomach and aids digestion. There seems little doubt that beer made with *gruit* would have had a distinctive and probably potent taste.

Gruit was only the beginning of things that went into ale. Both rural and monastic brewers added all kinds of plants when the wort was boiled to give specific flavors and other attributes to the drink. Types of additives varied with local conditions and the availability of raw materials. Some of those were later condemned because of their detrimental effects to the health of the drinker. Some were even poisonous. Though there might be locales where no additions were made, such instances were rare. Ginger, anise, and cumin were used in beer in Germany and various other things including laurel, marjoram, mint, sage, and acorns were used at one time or another in addition to *gruit*.[54] Traditional practices in Norway included pouring boiling juniper extract over malt or using alder or juniper branches or twigs to make up strainers to filter mash. Brewers used alder bark not only for taste, but also because it was thought to have certain preservative qualities. Brewers in the Low Countries town of Deventer in the Middle Ages used laurel to flavor beer, possibly importing it from southern Europe. In Anglo-Saxon England brewers used things called brionia and hymele, though exactly what they were is not known. In Norway yarrow, which also turned up in the Netherlands, and caraway among other spices were known to have been added in the making of *pors* ale. Anglo-Saxon works on medical treatments mention beer additives as varied as ground ivy, bog myrtle, carline thistle, yarrow, rosemary, heather, alecost, wormwood, tree bark, sycamore sap, and even spruce with a great deal of sap being used to make beer stronger.[55]

The government of the Carolingians never had a monopoly of beer brewing nor even the sole right to brew on their own lands.[56] But the government of the Carolingians, or more correctly their successors, asserted the exclusive right to dispense *gruit* as a specific imperial right vested in the emperor and based on his authority over and control of the benefits from unused land. In the Latin Christian empire created by Charlemagne, the ruler was able to establish a royal right to power over unexploited land and it was uncultivated land from which bog myrtle came.[57] Thus the emperor was the ultimate source of *gruitrecht*. In 974, Emperor Otto II, while granting a church in the district of Namur in the Low Countries to a certain Notker of Liege, also granted rights of toll, market, minting, and *gruitrecht*. It is clear that the emperor considered the monopoly of trade in *gruit* to belong with his other major regalian rights. The emperor, in making such grants, reaffirmed the public character of the right and his ownership of it. The recipient, usually a count or bishop, got the income. Emperor Otto I had made a similar grant to the monastery at Gembloers, perhaps as early as 946; the grant was reaffirmed by Otto II in 979. A grant by the youthful Emperor Otto III to the bishop of Utrecht in 999 put *gruitrecht* clearly among powers which came from public authority. Otto III gave the bishop the town and district of Bommel and with that came toll and mint rights as well as the right to all trade in *grut*. The lands around Bommel south of the river Maas it seems were good for growing bog myrtle. Such districts became known as sources of *gruit* and potential sources of income to officials.[58]

Grants of *gruitrecht* could go to towns as well. The imperial city of Dortmund got *gruitrecht*, in that case presumably directly from the emperor. Fearful that the bishop of Liege might usurp his established *gruitrecht* for the town of Dinant, Count Albert II of Namur—some time between 1047 and 1064—had a written statement of his power drawn up. Over time, grants were made to laymen, like the grant of the count of Flanders to a Bruges citizen in 1226 of *gruitrecht* for the town of Rodenburg. In 1045, Thierry II, bishop of Metz, granted *gruitrecht* to the monastery of Saint Trond, west of Maastricht; it applied to use at the monastery and also in the surrounding town. The monastery was empowered to build a house in which the *gruit* would be prepared and from which it could be distributed. In renewing the grant in 1060, Bishop Adelboro III said that before the beer had been bad but under the new arrangements it was much improved.[59]

By the high Middle Ages the supply of *gruit* to brewers was a right held firmly by the counts of Holland, Flanders, and the other counties in the Low Countries, in Westphalia, the Rhineland, and by the bishops of the lower Rhine region like those of Liege and Utrecht. The power to control the sale of *gruit* was in effect a right to levy a tax on beer production. It was a lucrative power and one which they jealously guarded. Landlords' power over the sale of *gruit* did not come into their hands because they were lords of their manors or because their tenants had to make payments to them as compensation for some capital investment. Fees, such as those for the use of mills or communal baking ovens, fell into the latter category. *Gruitrecht* was very different. It was not a seigneurial right but a public one, and holders were agents of public authority. Once granted *gruitrecht*, public figures, whatever their secular or religious authority, tried to extend and expand that power. For counts, it meant trying to tax the use of *gruit* throughout their entire domains. It also meant insisting that all makers of beer use *gruit* supplied by them or their agents or those who had bought the right to distribution from them.[60] The weakened authority of the emperor, made even weaker in the course of the late eleventh and early twelfth centuries, increased the ability of local figures to extend their control over *gruitrecht*. Over time, what had been a public right increasingly took on the appearance, character, and legal status of a seigneurial right, a customary right of the lord, even though its origins were very different from those of seigneurial rights. In the twelfth century one result was increasing litigation over the amount and extent of such taxes.[61] Though the legal status of *gruitrecht* may have changed, as far as brewers were concerned and no matter where they lived, *gruitrecht* meant a tax on their production of beer, a tax that was virtually unavoidable since they were required to use *gruit*.

Monasteries and Improvements in Brewing

Monasteries conceivably had a positive effect on the quality of beer making. Their relatively large scale of production and their bigger and often better equipment may have offered a constructive example to brewers in nearby settlements as was the case with the monastery at Saint Trond in the eleventh century and the monastery at Selje near Bergen in Norway. By the end of the thirteenth century Saint Trond was the most important center for the production of beer in the entire region. By 1250 the town and surrounding area boasted about thirty brewers.[62] The increase in the number and size of monasteries in general, but also their spreading out across Europe, reaching previously unsettled areas in the eleventh and twelfth centuries, presumably promoted beer brewing. As monasteries were set up throughout the Middle Ages, they soon got breweries. Some abbots preferred to rely, at least in part, on beer received from tenants on their lands, the beer serving as tithe payments for some of them. Abbeys could avoid or postpone setting up their own breweries that way. Levels of consumption, though, often made them choose to use tenant payments only as supplements to what they could produce in their own breweries. At Prüsening in Bavaria near Nuremberg, for example, the abbey is first mentioned in 1109 but its brewery not until 1329, so for some time external sources of beer predominated.[63] Monasteries could also buy beer from nearby domestic producers to supplement their own production. The brothers would have expected the beer they bought to be of at least the quality of their own product and so would have pressed their suppliers to maintain standards. Once started in brewing, abbots sometimes sought permission to sell their own surplus beer. The earliest case in Bavaria is from 1143, and the practice offered an example for other beer makers. Commercial sales of beer by monasteries, well known in Germany, were uncommon in other places, for example in the Low Countries. One exception in that region was the monastery at Maastricht.[64]

Monasteries were not the only religious establishments with breweries (see Figure 3). Episcopal households, though typically smaller than monasteries, did have resident populations of regular clergy who consumed beer. The people around the bishops produced their own beer and presumably the same technical influence on local brewing would have existed in episcopal households as in monasteries, if on a lesser scale. Many of those episcopal breweries probably dated from the Carolingian period as Charlemagne tried to install a

Figure 3. The brewer Herttel Pyrpreu, one of the twelve members of the *Mendelsche Zwölfbrüderstiftung*, which was a home to old, feeble, or sick craftsmen. The brothers dressed alike in a grey habit with cowl. The illustration can be dated to 1425 or 1426. *Hausbuch der Mendelschen Zwölfbrüderstiftung*. Courtesy of Stadtbibliothek Nürnberg, Amb. 317.2°, f. 20v.

pervasive system of bishops and archbishops within his empire. The chapter of the Strasbourg cathedral, for example, was required to produce beer in the tenth century for specific feasts. Donations of the 960s suggest an annual production there of an impressive 145,000 liters.[65]

Since bishops' canons brewed in cities, there was always the danger of conflict with the urban brewers when the latter became established. By the twelfth century, monasteries in Poland even operated taverns in the countryside, outlets for their own production and sources of profit.[66] Such cases were almost unheard of in northwestern Europe, partly because monasteries were always relatively less important to the economy than in the east and partly because monasteries, along with bishops' brewers, could, and on occasion did, face litigation from urban brewers. That typically did not come until late in the thirteenth century, usually when the urban industry had outstripped its monastic counterpart. Complaints from commercial brewers about monastic competition did not go away. They showed up even in the sixteenth century, for example, in Dresden in Germany. The duke of Lorraine as late as the sixteenth century still got his beer from a monastery, though at the start of the seventeenth century he finally changed over to having beer produced by his own household.[67] In the Low Countries conflicts between monastic and commercial brewers appear to have been uncommon, at least after 1300. By then the overwhelming majority of the urban populations relied on supplies from the urban brewing industry—a product of rising population, rising total production, government policy choices, and the adaptation of rural methods in light of monastic examples. Monastic brewing did not disappear but in the Low Countries, as elsewhere later in northern Europe, urban commercial brewing expanded rapidly and in the end dominated the making of beer.

Chapter 3

Urbanization and the Rise of Commercial Brewing

The pattern of change in commercial brewing in late medieval and sixteenth-century northern Europe falls into six loosely defined phases or periods. First, there was a period of preparation typified by development of a market for the good and development of a production base. Second, there was product innovation, the introduction of a superior product, a variant on the original, based on technical change. Third, there was a shock from some external source, sometimes a sharp shock, which promoted the introduction of the superior product. Fourth, there was a period of acclimatization of the new technique to local conditions and acclimatization of local markets to the new variant product. Fifth, there was full mastery of the new technology by local practitioners, yielding an industry which can be called mature. Sixth and last, there was a period of process innovation in which, by improving ways of making the better good, producers found ways to exploit fully the opportunity created by the product innovation. Those six different phases appear, admittedly in differing degrees, in late medieval brewing in Holland, the southern Low Countries, France and England. The first and last of the phases were drawn out while those in between occurred in relatively short periods of time. The era of preparation, the first of the phases, went on through much of the high Middle Ages and was closely connected with a broad range of other social and demographic changes of the period.

Only slowly were the northern Low Countries, the British Isles, northern Germany, and Scandinavia integrated into western Europe religiously, economically, politically, or even technologically. The integration brought other significant developments for brewing. As population and production rose, settlements became larger. This created new urban communities with a market for beer which, over the long run, would prove different from that in the countryside. The expansion of towns in the eleventh and twelfth centuries created new possibilities for brewing and a somewhat different kind of industry. In some places in northern Europe, Flanders, the valley of the Seine and southeastern England, towns came to dominate economic and, to some degree, political life. Urban growth required the assent of existing governments. In some cases it came with government support and even active promotion. Not all efforts to promote urbanization were crowned with immediate success. Still the result by the thirteenth century was to create a very different landscape and a very different market for beer in northern Europe.

The Roots of Urban Brewing

In towns in the southern Low Countries where bishops lived and where episcopal households were found, brewing certainly existed by the eleventh century. In 1068 the bishop of Liege granted to brewers at Huy the right to use *gruit*. He granted privileges to the brewers of his episcopal seat sometime in the 1070s, a privilege confirmed in 1215. In England, the bishop of Durham in the twelfth century had rents paid to him in equal quantities of wheat, oats, and malt, the last being principally for beer making. In Amersfoort in the bishopric of Utrecht, an industry was already in place when the overlord granted the town civic rights in 1259. But bishops were not a necessary prerequisite for commercial beer making. Normandy had professional brewers by the eleventh century. In Holland, Dordrecht had some brewing by the eleventh century, and it is clear there were beer brewers in Leiden before the fourteenth century.[1] Without question, urban commercial brewing, independent of any church connection, was found in many places in northwestern Europe by the end of the thirteenth century and often had significantly earlier roots.

The source of the urban brewing industry was not the presence of brewhouses in monasteries or episcopal households, regardless of the technical influence such establishments could and did have. It was rather the transfer of traditional brewing practice from the countryside to the cities by rural migrants, the people who formed the population of European towns in the twelfth and thirteenth centuries. Brewers continued in towns the same practices that they had followed in the countryside, at least initially. Among rural brewers, even before urbanization, some specialization had already started. Making beer took time. It involved a number of processes with varying intensity of effort. It was not easy to integrate beer making into the daily operation of a farm. That was especially true if, as was usually the case, malt had to be made first. A few village residents seem to have taken on making larger quantities of beer and then exchanging or selling the surplus to their neighbors. If they had the spare time, extra help in the form of servants, superior equipment, or a special talent for avoiding mistakes in producing beer, then they might have generated a household industry. Brewing was more common among rural dwellers than baking, since more households had the equipment for beer making at hand.[2]

Landlords in the countryside, seeing in brewing a potential source of income, began from the eleventh century promoting the establishment of breweries on their estates. Seigneurs would make any necessary capital investment, given the investment was often beyond the financial capabilities of their tenants. Landlords thought the presence of common facilities in the countryside would promote beer production. They also expected some return from charging tenants for use of the capital goods. Tenants often found their own equipment or found ways to make their own beer of a sufficient quality. Despite the efforts of the landlords, domestic brewing predominated in much of the rural Low Countries as well as in England. While there was a tendency toward specialization in beer production, in the countryside it was incomplete. The better-off tended to brew. Tax records from rural England show that while a very large proportion of villagers might make beer, a small share of them produced the majority of the beer. That share of the population, involved in what can only be described as commercial brewing, was neither especially wealthy nor especially poor, but the individuals did pursue brewing for sale for a long time. The bigger producers were often women though brewing in general, and commercial brewing in particular, was done by the whole family, often organized by the wife.[3]

Greater specialization in labor was a common feature of the twelfth and thirteenth centuries. This led to new understandings of work, leisure, politics, and social organization. Even though there was specialization and some brewers were clearly better at the task than others, that did not mean that they understood why they were better at it or that they escaped from the belief that there was something magical in the process. Abbot Aelfric in tenth-century England was scandalized by the shameful sorceries, which were presumably pagan practices, that foolish men used in brewing. As late as the twentieth century in Norway, brewing was approached with a certain religious earnestness and a belief that the brewing process had to be protected from potentially dangerous forces, such as the little people. Various signs and symbols, such as the sign of the cross on barrels, showed up in parts of northern Europe in an attempt to keep evil magic from contaminating the beer. During fermentation there was supposed to be quiet and peace in the house, no banging of doors or loud noises, since otherwise the result would be poor. Natural phenomena, such as the position of the sun, were also thought to have an effect on the outcome. Unique or especially important brews, such as Christmas ale, seemed to have called for even more extreme measures to prevent spoilage. The two weeks before Christmas were considered bad for brewing and that made precautions even more critical.[4] Though the new more professional urban brewers may have relied increasingly or even exclusively on beer production for their incomes, it did not mean that they had escaped the rural origins of brewing, both in the technology used and in their understanding of it.

Specialization and Urban Brewing

In the twelfth century, new words began to appear both in Latin and in vernacular languages to mean brewery, an indication that the institution was maturing. The words appear especially in urban records, strongly suggesting that a separate group of specialist brewers was emerging in towns. The reasons for moving toward specialization in brewing were stronger in towns than in the countryside. First, there were problems of space in the more densely populated urban centers. As towns grew, few residents had the room for kettles, troughs, and storage room for barrels in addition to an open space to use as a malting floor. Lack of room converted many new immigrants into being simply consumers of beer. Their being thrown onto the market translated into larger sales for those with the space to brew. That, in turn, translated into a tendency toward larger units with greater output, greater investment in bigger and better equipment, more workers, and greater division of labor among those workers.[5]

A second force for specialization in urban beer production was pollution. More people and more industry in a small area led to the fouling of water supplies. Since good water was absolutely necessary for the production of drinkable beer as well as for cleaning equipment and barrels, those with access to something like pure sweet water enjoyed a great advantage in towns. From the beginnings of urban brewing the breweries were located on waterways in order to guarantee water supplies and give easy access to raw materials and markets for the final product. At Haarlem and Delft in Holland, as at Huy in Brabant and at Hamburg, brewers found themselves clumped together along major streams in the town.[6] Brewers were always of two minds about the problems of pollution. They wanted clean water but also the ability to get rid of waste in the easiest way. They were polluters themselves, dumping the residue from cleaning into the water. They produced smoke and ash from the wood or peat they used for heating. Town governments appear to have been conscious of the danger of pollution from brewing. In England at London, Bristol, and Coventry, brewers were not allowed access to public water supplies.[7] Regulations on pollution increased over time, though the first regulations and the first direction of brewers into a common neighborhood, presumably to restrict pollution, date from the urbanization of the twelfth and thirteenth centuries.

A third force promoting specialization was the tax system. Urban govern-

ments were interested in gaining advantage from the sale of beer. To
in the Netherlands they controlled the supply of *gruit*. There were savings in
time and capital from buying the needed *gruit* in larger units that could give
an advantage to the specialist brewer. On the Continent and especially in what
by the late twelfth century had become the Holy Roman Empire, taxation was
local, determined and collected by local authorities. The fact that taxation took
a different form in England may help to explain the slower evolution of brewing there. In England, King Henry III established a national system of taxation
in 1267 through the Assize of Bread and Ale which regulated brewing throughout his kingdom. The law fixed the quality, price, and measures to be used in
the production of ale. The price of ale under the rules depended on the prices
of grain and of malt. The general purpose was to maintain the quality of beer.
Local authorities added their own regulations on the same topics—in London
in 1276 and in Bristol in 1283. Few people avoided violating the regulations, so
governments charged almost everyone who made beer in England, in effect
turning regulation into taxation of brewing. The *Assisa panis et cervisie*
remained in place in England from the thirteenth century until the sixteenth
and in some places even later. Local courts and local officials, aletasters, monitored production and enforced the rules. Each time a batch of ale was ready
the beer maker was required to call an aletaster to come and check the product
for quality and price before it could be sold. There was little consistency in the
application of the regulations other than that they became more regularized
over time.[8] The highly local and personal nature of enforcement created no
potential for saving by consolidation or specialization as did the application of
gruitrecht on the Continent.

A fourth source of the tendency toward specialization comprised problems of and potential gains from capital investment. The larger size of the
urban market increased possible advantages for bigger and more expensive
breweries. Regulations to reduce the danger of fire, like those of London of
1189 which forced brewers to use only wood for heating and not reeds, straw,
or stubble or like those forcing all alehouses not built of stone to be licensed
also increased the capital needed to enter the trade.[9] Various arrangements
mitigated against rising capital requirements. Two brewers could also own a
brewery together, as for example at Hamburg and in the Netherlands, each
operating his or her own business, brewing separately, and selling beer independently. In some towns in the Low Countries and in Germany, there
appears to have been a common site where grain was mashed with the resulting wort then distributed to individuals for brewing.[10] Town governments in
some cases supplied common equipment to ease the capital constraint on
potential brewers. The town, like a lord of a manor, owned the building and
the equipment, renting them to users for short periods and so getting the

investment back from fees for the use of the kettles and the tuns. In a number of inland towns in Germany, there were public brewhouses in the Middle Ages and Renaissance. In some of those places a brewer managed the equipment and helped citizens make their beer. His and any of his assistants' services were subsumed in the rental charge. Such brewers were almost like town bureaucrats. Lier in Brabant in 1390 set up a town brewery with a mill. Not only did the building allow residents or their servants or friends to make their own beer, but also it broke the monopoly of sales enjoyed by the few specialist commercial brewers. The town maintained the alternative source of beer for political as well as economic reasons. Production in the town brewery proved rather stable through the later Middle Ages. Bruges had a similar brewery for use by anyone who had their own raw materials and who paid their excise tax in advance.[11] The variety of strategies to find the capital needed to start a brewery indicates the value of greater investment to the success of enterprises and the pressure in towns toward consolidation of brewing.

One of the reasons for the increasing capital requirement for twelfth- and thirteenth- century brewers was the increasing use of copper kettles. Those produced better beer, potentially in larger quantities, and, in the long run, at lower cost than earlier wooden or pottery ones. Originally copper kettles may have been made just from copper bands soldered together and so had trouble when heated for long periods. But metalworkers got better at producing good copper kettles which made them even more worth having. Boiling wort in a copper kettle made it possible to decrease loss in boiling, to cut the amount of fuel needed, and to make the whole brewing process go more quickly. Kettles were undoubtedly the most valuable single pieces of equipment in the trade. All kettles had to have an opening near the bottom for draining off the beer which created a weak point. That limited the earlier pottery kettles to capacities of 100 to 150 liters. Copper kettles probably ran to over 1,000 liters by the late thirteenth century and possibly to 4,000 by the fifteenth. It became common to have these larger copper kettles sit on a circular, solid brick oven. Copper kettles could have flat bottoms, unlike their pottery predecessors, so they could sit firmly on a grate or supports over the fireplace. The first mention of the production of beer in Finland notes that a kettle was used.[12] The kettle may have been a sign of the development of brewing and also of the making of better-quality beer in a region on the technological periphery of Europe. With better and bigger copper kettles, mashing and boiling probably took place in separate vessels. By the thirteenth century, some urban brewers added hot water to the malt in a wooden mash tun and then took off the resulting wort to boil in a copper kettle. At that time specialist urban brewers probably had a copper kettle for boiling water and wort, a mash tun, wooden troughs for cooling and fermentation, and a number of barrels.[13] The number of barrels depended on production levels and the size of those barrels, the exact measures often already regulated by government. All the equipment added up to a significant capital investment, well beyond the reach of most urban dwellers.

By 1300, making beer was a viable occupation in towns in northern Europe. Not everyone could be a brewer since there were requirements of skill at making beer, at organizing a business enterprise, and of access to capital. Still, many individuals did take up the trade, not just to supply domestic needs but as a commercial venture. The most celebrated case, though it was not isolated or unique, was that of Margery Kempe, an English woman living in King's Lynn. In the later fourteenth century she, "out of pure covetousness, and in order to maintain her pride, . . . took up brewing, and was one of the greatest brewers in the town of N[orwich]. for three or four years until she lost a great deal of money, for she had never had any experience with that business. For however good her servants were and however knowledgeable in brewing, things would never go successfully for them. For when the ale had as fine a head of froth on it as anyone might see, suddenly the froth would go flat, and all the ale was lost in one brewing after another, so that her servants were ashamed and would not stay with her."[14] Taking this as a sign of God's punishment, and seeing her investment disappear, she abandoned brewing. Problems of stalled fermentation like Kempe's or failed fermentation because of yeast infection must have been periodic, if not common, phenomena. Her experience was probably not that different from many others who earlier during the growth of towns in the twelfth and thirteenth centuries tried their hand at brewing and did not succeed. Still, many brewers did survive and even prosper.

Towns and Taxation

Towns took over the *gruit* tax in the twelfth and thirteenth centuries. The owners of *gruitrecht*, counts or bishops, granted, leased, or sold the taxing power to towns. The count, as at Leuven in the southern Low Countries, often had an officer responsible for collecting the fees. By turning the tax over to the town, the count could eliminate that official. At Bruges in 1190 the count of Flanders, short of money, loaned *gruitrecht* to a noble in exchange for cash. The noble recouped his payment to the count by selling the right to collect the tax on the additive to prominent people from the town. At Zutphen in the eastern Netherlands, church officials owned the *gruitrecht* and leased it either to canons in the chapter of the church or to various individuals until 1326 when the city finally bought the tax outright for a lump sum. At least, they bought the right for part of the town. It would be 1479 before the town had purchased the tax for all neighborhoods. The earliest outright sale was possibly the grant to Dinant of *gruitrecht* by the count of Namur in the southern Netherlands between 1047 and 1064. Towns bought the tax and even paid a premium for it because they preferred the indication of political independence which collecting their own taxes gave them. Owning the tax on *gruit* also gave them authority over a growing industry, one with great potential to generate tax income. Access to *gruit* was so universally valued that to promote the development of new towns, lords might even grant residents the right to make the additive themselves, free of any restriction or any tax. The count of Flanders in 1289 gave that right to the people of his planted settlement, Nieuwpoort.[15]

In some jurisdictions, especially those outside of the region of rapid urban growth, public authorities were more jealous of their *gruitrecht*. In 1268, for example, the bishop and chapter of the cathedral at Münster in Westphalia agreed that they would keep the right to tax *gruit* and not transfer it to towns. The bishop of Cologne was very slow to release *gruitrecht* to any town in his jurisdiction. At Cologne itself the art of making *gruit* was kept secret. In 1420 the town council directed a knowledgeable woman to teach a certain brewer, and no one else, how to make it. Despite resistance in some jurisdictions in the lower Rhine Valley, over time more and more towns got power over the tax. In Rotterdam, for example, the count of Holland had borrowed money from the town and rather than pay it back he granted his right to tax *gruit* to the town, but that came only in 1402. Amsterdam was among the slowest to acquire the right, finally buying *gruitrecht* for the town from their new monarch, Philip II of Spain, in 1559.[16]

Towns, once they had the power to tax brewing, often and increasingly farmed the tax; that is, they auctioned off taxing powers to private individuals. The towns lowered administrative costs dramatically and also got a lump sum immediately.[17] The tax farmer tried to collect more than he gave the town so he could profit from the transaction. Since the towns lost some potential income, not all of them farmed their taxes but collected part or all the fees themselves. There was an obvious source of antagonism between brewer and tax farmer, one which persisted and created conflict, and even violence on occasion, so long as tax farming remained in place. The system survived well into the eighteenth century in much of northern Europe and often until the reforms in the wake of the French Revolution.

Towns controlled and regulated the supply of *gruit* in order to collect monies due. If all brewers had to use *gruit*, then a simple monopoly of supply guaranteed efficient and full collection of taxes levied. In the region where *gruit* dominated, the towns typically handed the job of making the combination of herbs and of selling it at fixed prices, including the tax, to an official called a *gruyter* or *gruiter*. In Latin, he was the *grutarius* or in some cases the *fermentarius*.[18] A few towns even had a building designated for the storage and sale of the herb called a *gruithuis* or *gruthuse*. The building may have had vessels for measuring and packing the herbs which had to be crushed, compressed, and then measured out before being handed on to each brewer who came to collect them.[19] The *gruyter* was typically a tax farmer, and often a brewer, who not only sold the herbs from but also brewed in the *gruithuis*. He might have been a salaried town bureaucrat, though it is not obvious how common that was. In Bruges in 1252, the holder of the *gruuthuse* tried to prevent retail trade in imported beer from England or Germany, fearful that sales would reduce the income from fees due him. He tried to use his political influence to enhance the income from the tax. Not surprisingly the men who held *gruitrecht* or in one way or another farmed taxes on *gruit* were often already in the thirteenth century wealthy and important figures in their towns, enjoying a measure of political influence and power.[20]

Practice was not uniform. There were variations depending on local conditions, economic and political. In Dordrecht in Holland, the *gruithuis* was mentioned in a 1322 document. Two years later it was made the only source of supply in the southern part of the county, presumably making farming *gruitrecht* extremely valuable to the *gruiter* but creating inconvenience for brewers in other towns who needed to buy *gruit*. Deventer in the eastern part of the Netherlands had a *gruithuis* at least by 1339. That was the year when the town first farmed the tax from the bishop of Utrecht, and detailed records have survived of the operation of the establishment. *Gruit* there was sold in units, one unit presumably being enough for a brew, so the system of taxation tended to set the parameters for brewing.[21] At Magdeburg in Germany there was, as in so many other towns in the region, a *gruit* office, but in the thirteenth century it was in the brewery of the archbishop. Not surprisingly, local brewers fought long to be free of the requirement of going to that brewery for their *gruit* since a competitor was in a position to dictate their rates of production. Requiring brewers to go to the *gruithuis* to mix their malt with *gruit*, which did occur in some instances, may have been a way to guarantee the brewers used an adequate amount of grain and did not try to brew thinner beer to boost profits. It may also have been a way to keep secret the exact composition of *gruit*.[22] Still, if brewers mashed and brewed in the same vessel, then mixing the *gruit* with the malt would save trouble and also assure even distribution of the flavoring. Once brewers mashed and brewed in separate vessels, any advantage to them from mixing dry ingredients was gone.

Presumably the use of *gruit* for brewing through much of northern Europe was virtually universal and only gaps in the surviving evidence leave any impression that some places escaped making beer flavored with bog myrtle.[23] The concentrated nature of urban brewing and the tendency toward specialization all played into the hands of the tax collector. By 1300 *gruit* and *gruit* taxes, though perhaps treated differently in different places, were a common feature of life in towns throughout the Netherlands as well as up the Rhine Valley. Conditions were to change. At Leuven by the end of the fourteenth century, the town had abandoned all pretense, gave up taxing *gruit*, and simply levied a fixed fee on each barrel of beer produced. Brewers were left free to go out into the country and pick whatever they liked to make their *gruit*.[24] Such freedom could have been possible only if *gruit* was, as is suggested by many sources from before that date, a mixture of herbs, and only if towns and governments in general were willing to accept that their goal was income so they could leave the flavoring of the beer to the brewers. The trend over time was for governments to pay less attention to the technology of brewing and to concentrate efforts on tax collection.

Taxes on beer were the origin of a general system of excise taxes on sales. The levying of a fixed fee on the purchase price of any taxable item started as early as 1122 when the abbey of Saint Trond was collecting money from people who engaged in business on their lands. The monks also levied an excise tax in kind, making brewers supply a fixed quantity of beer each week (see Figure 4). In 1141 another Low Countries monastery, Crepin, got the right to collect a beer tax which had nothing to do with *gruit* or *gruitrecht*. In most towns in Brabant there were excises by the early thirteenth century. Leuven, for example, had an excise on beer by 1365, if not well before. In Flanders by the last quarter of the thirteenth century, excise taxes were already long standing and well established. Beer was one of the most popular goods to be subject to excise, and by the fifteenth century many towns in the Low Countries had made the tax on *gruit* into an excise tax on beer.[25] In the shift to excise taxes on beer, Netherlanders were quicker than their German counterparts. At Wismar, for example, beer did not fall under excise until 1427, and the town only collected the excise on beer sporadically over the next century. After that, it became a standard of the town's taxing portfolio. Farther to the east in Prussian towns, excises on drink, which without question included beer, started in the period 1428–1457.[26] Though such taxes did present some constitutional problems everywhere, once in place they tended to stay, increase and become more complex.

The Freedom to Brew

The tax system was not a system of licensing. Everyone had equal access to *gruit*. All that was needed was the ability to pay the price, albeit purposely

Figure 4. A cellarer testing his brew, from a manuscript illustration, thirteenth century. Courtesy of The British Library, Sloane MS. 2435 f. 44v.

inflated, of the herb mixture. Everyone in towns had the right to brew beer. At least that was the law when brewing started in the new urban centers. In a number of places the towns and townspeople asserted the right. Some towns in the East Frankish kingdom got the free right to brew beer for residents as early as the reign of King Henry the Fowler (919–936), a right that remained in force typically well into the thirteenth century. The first Paris brewing regulation from 1268 exemplified the legal status of brewing in most European towns. Anyone could brew beer. There were no apprenticeship requirements, no monopoly rights, no limitations on entry into beer making. All any brewer had to do was follow established rules and customs of making beer. The only restriction at Paris, an extremely light one compared to thirteenth-century regulations of other crafts, was a requirement to belong to a trade organization with a chief and two assistants as officers who maintained surveillance on the additives used in making beer.[27] In 1246 the count of Holland told men living in Delft that they could not stop their wives from brewing the volume they liked, that is if they were used to brewing. It was a statement repeated for the town of Medemblik by a successor in 1288.[28] In that case too the tendency was to reassert the freedom to brew. At Nuremberg, as in a number of towns in Franconia, all citizens enjoyed the *Allgemeines Braurecht*, the general right to brew beer At Hamburg in the fourteenth century, as in so many other places, the only requirement to become a brewer was town citizenship.[29]

Over time, town governments limited the freedom to brew. By the fifteenth century the limitations in many cases were so extensive that the right had been all but taken away. The process was gradual, the steps down the road toward restriction sometimes being minor and seemingly inconsequential. Often the ostensible reason was the need for the town government to guarantee adequate supplies of good quality beer or to prevent fire. Hamburg prohibited brewing from one district of the town around 1301 for the latter reason. At Munich the cause for restriction was the former. The first report of brewing in Munich is from 1286, about the time the territorial lord, the duke of Bavaria, asserted his right to legislate on brewing. He insisted that he alone could grant permission to brew in the town. He did that if a brewer could show both competence and ownership of the necessary equipment. The Munich rules were not strict, though brewers who failed to give full measure had to donate their beer to the poor. In that case, as at Augsburg which had regulation of brewing beginning in 1155 and at Ulm which had ordinances for brewing by 1255, the rules asserted the power of the government over the trade. At Nuremburg, regulation began to take shape in the early fourteenth century with restrictions on the composition of beer, the brewing time, when and where it could be sold, and how it was to be served. Brewers were required to give an oath annually that they would abide by and uphold the ordinances. Town officials could visit any brewer at any time should suspicion arise about his abiding by the rules.[30] Eventually such limits would become the norm for urban brewers throughout Europe. The rules made it ever harder to enter and to stay in the trade.

At Hamburg the town tried to guarantee as many individuals as possible the ability to brew. In so doing they increased the regulation of brewing which, over the long term, had the opposite effect. The town had to grant permission before anyone could brew and that created, in essence, a licensing system. Already in 1381 a brewer planning to make beer for export had to get approval from the town council, so by then the government had established that the right to brew was in its power and not a right of citizens. By the mid-fifteenth century, the town had virtually outlawed brewing at home for household use. At Hamburg, Bremen, Wismar, and a number of other north German towns, no one was allowed to use a brewery except the owner. Leasing a brewery for a short or long term was illegal. The restriction sharply limited entry into the trade, raising the minimum capital needed even to make beer for personal use. At Hamburg, brewers had to make their own malt and only as much as they would use in brewing, no more and no less. After a crisis in 1410, the Hamburg government decided to decrease production of beer by refusing licenses to brew to some existing brewhouses and by prohibiting the building of breweries in certain parts of the town. In many north German towns by the fifteenth century, the right to brew, granted by the town government, was held by an individual but also held by the site so brewing could be practiced only on certain specified properties.[31]

In English towns the right to brew also came to depend on permission being granted by civic authorities. At Norwich and Chester, among other towns in the thirteenth century, a fee in beer, a *tolsester*, the sester being a measure of volume, had to be paid if a citizen wanted to brew. Sharp regulation, well known in Germany by the fifteenth century and increasing in England, was extreme even at that late date in the Netherlands but the tendency there was in the same direction. At Utrecht, for example, in 1442 the town had prohibited brewing at home for one year, and by 1493 the prohibition on brewing in and for a household had become permanent. The expectation was that the restriction would help the local brewing industry find a market. A common first step was for Low Countries towns to tax home brewing, as was the case in Amsterdam in 1484 and Haarlem in 1498, at a fixed rate for each brew.[32] To the south, Hasselt set a maximum of about 150 liters that an individual could brew in a year to prevent anyone from going into business secretly as a commercial brewer and, in the process, severely limited the right to brew. For Amsterdam below the threshold of twenty barrels annual production, home brewers were free of a tax on each barrel brewed, but they still had ley were reminded in a bylaw of 1492, a small fee for each brew. itions remained in place until 1573 when home brewing was out- pletely in the town, a prohibition reaffirmed in 1581.[33] In the 1580s iment of Holland outlawed home brewing throughout the province, and the rule was repeated in regulations on beer taxes through the seventeenth century.[34] The action of government recognized the long-term decline in home brewing, a trend which started in the thirteenth century. The prohibition did decrease the danger of fire, but that was not the reason for the law. The province wanted to be sure that revenue did not escape the tax collector. The same was true of the final act of limitation in England in 1637. From that date on, and with only minor changes through the subsequent Civil War, alehouse keepers, publicans, and victualers could not make their own beer and had to buy it from a common brewer. The legislation was part of a new tax levied on all beer sales.[35]

Town governments imposed the extensive regulation and restrictions on private domestic beer making because of pressure from professional brewers. Those townspeople who specialized in brewing and earned the overwhelming majority of their incomes from making beer wanted to be freed of competition. Restrictions to entry served to give them some monopoly power. Towns imposed regulations because they wanted to minimize the effort and cost in collecting taxes on brewing. The authorities could increase their tax income by allowing the remaining brewers to increase their prices. The logical next step was to fix prices, something done in England in 1267 in the Assize of Bread and Ale and in Austria as early as 1320 and at Nuremberg at about the same time.[36] The tax system and regulation in general hindered small-scale brewing and promoted the development of an urban industry increasingly dominated by professional brewers.

Distribution

By 1300 those increasingly professional brewers were making progress in creating and commercializing a distribution system for beer as well. Taverns were connected to brewers, often even in the same buildings as the brewery, or were supplied on some regular basis by certain brewers. The 1189 regulation in London of places selling ale shows that at least in England's largest city there was a system for licensing public houses. As time went on more towns developed rules for the operation of drinking establishments, such as fixing the hours and requiring clear signs indicating an alehouse was an alehouse. By 1309, London, with a population perhaps of 80,000, had 354 taverners, but they were more closely associated with the wine trade. There were at the same time over 1,330 brewshops which sold ale, one of them for every sixty inhabitants. Presumably by the early fourteenth century alehouses had spread throughout England, and drinking establishments like them probably existed in most towns in northern Europe. Many English taverns were kept by women. That was certainly the case in the countryside, but as the fourteenth and fifteenth centuries wore on it became less true, especially in the few large towns. By 1329, London taverns had to close at a specific hour. English taverns also had signs proclaiming their status, but unlike the signs of all other crafts those of taverns had nothing to do with the trade being practiced. Even before the Norman Conquest, a pole or broom was an indication of an alehouse open for business. Whether or not the sign found its origins in a bush used to stir beer in the fermenting trough and then hung out to dry in front of the house is far from certain. In any case, that type of sign appears to have been unique to England.[37] Continental taverns used different identifiers.

In fourteenth-century Hamburg, the town formalized the connection between brewery and tavern, ordering that beer could be served for the public only in the house where it was brewed. Such extreme restrictions were rare. Tavern keepers who were not brewers were often poor and had to get credit from their supplier. Tied by debt to a certain brewer, they also became tied as the seller of that brewer's beer.[38] Since taverns were continuing institutions and often in convenient locations, next to markets or on harbors, they became places to meet and to do business. Tavern keepers were generally legally free businessmen and businesswomen, often invested with certain public functions including the collection of tolls and of taxes, and not just on beer. In Poland, law courts and even moneyers operated, on occasion, in taverns. Polish tavern keepers enjoyed higher status as a result of the varied functions of their institution. Tavern keepers usually operated on what amounted to a licence from a lord who let the tavern operate on payment of a fee. Outside of Poland, taverns may not have played such a prominent role in the local and regional economy, but taverns were, at least by the thirteenth century, a common part of life in much of northern and eastern Europe. By the thirteenth century, Polish taverns, as their numbers increased and the economy developed, became more like taverns in England and the Low Countries, existing less as centers of business and administration and more as meeting places for the amusement of farmers and peasants.[39]

The product of urban brewers might be made with the same ingredients and in the same way as the product of country brewers, but there was apparently a significant difference in the quality of the beers. Urban brewers could produce better beer, and by 1300 they were finding a market in the countryside for their superior product. Access to better raw materials and better equipment, the economies of larger-scale production, and better distribution methods all worked to their advantage. Presumably specialist urban brewers had more chance than did their rural counterparts to practice and to experiment. Rural brewing did not disappear, and, in fact, in the Low Countries, for example, may have benefited from the rising production of raw materials for brewing. In England as in the Netherlands, brewing remained almost universal.[40] Urban brewers, however, did prove able to distinguish the beer they made from the traditional drink, creating a new market. The urban product was superior, but it was also more expensive, as much as 50 percent more in England in 1272.[41] Though distribution to the countryside might be possible, price differentials limited sales there.

In 1300, in Dutch and English towns there was no sign of innovation in the production of beer. The technology urban brewers used was very much like that which their rural counterparts used. Brewers in the growing population centers had taken a domestic chore, increased the scale of production, and commercialized distribution of the product. The household industry of the countryside was replaced in towns first by the stage of individual workshops and in some of the large towns by nucleated workshops where brewers lived and worked next to each other in the same neighborhood sharing, if nothing else, information. There were as yet no signs of cooperative schemes among producers but there was competition, part of the reason presumably for the relatively higher quality of the product.[42] Urbanization in northern Europe in the twelfth and thirteenth centuries made possible and promoted the commercialization of beer making. Changes in the scale and in personnel were not mirrored in changes in the product or the biochemistry of producing beer. As late as 1300, despite the larger scale and wider distribution of beer produced in towns, shipment of both supplies and final products took place over short distances. Brewers got their raw materials locally and sold their beer to consumers directly in the same town or the nearby countryside, and they sold it quickly. The industry changed dramatically in the closing years of the thirteenth and in the course of the fourteenth century with the introduction of a new kind of drink, a beer made not with *gruit* but with hops. The use of hops would start the second phase in the long-term development of northern European brewing, marking the transition from the period of preparation to that of product innovation.

Chapter 4

Hopped Beer, Hanse Towns, and the Origins of the Trade in Beer

Europeans cultivated hops (*Humulus lupulus L*) for centuries before hopped beer became a trade good and then became the beverage of choice for brewers and drinkers in the Low Countries, France, and England. The word *hops* had Ural-Altaic as well as Turkic origins. It appeared first in Slavic languages before it surfaced in north Germanic ones. In addition, "It may be true that beer-words and intoxication-words are linked with hop-words in Old Slavic, Estonian, Letic, Finnish etc., and not in Germanic or Romance languages."[1] The mention of hops in the folklore of northeastern Europe combined with the linguistic evidence connecting hops with intoxication suggests that cultivation and use of the plant spread from central Asia west and south. For the Greeks, hops was a wild plant but Romans raised hops in vegetable gardens, using it for flavoring. Pliny the Elder recommended hops as an aid for liver problems, and Strabo mentioned medical benefits from eating hops.[2] Romans considered wild hop tendrils a delicacy, eating them as people now would eat asparagus and, perhaps, even using the word *asparagus* for hops. Isidore of Seville, writing in 624, mentioned hops.[3] A Renaissance translation of a work by John of Damascus (777–857) includes a description of hops arguing for their value as a purge and as a sedative. No one, however, said that hops might be valuable in making beer, not even Pliny, though it is often claimed that he did.[4] Apparently Celts, who certainly brewed ale, did not even know the plant since they had no word for it. It is all but certain that preclassical and classical brewers did not use hops to flavor their beer. If they did, it was only rarely.

Hops and Making Beer

Carolingians made beer with hops. The principal uses of the plant at least in the early Middle Ages appear to have been medicinal. In 768 *humolariæ*, hop gardens, are listed in a document describing a gift from Charlemagne's father,

Pepin the Short, for the church of St. Denis. The abbey of St. Germain-des-Pres had hops brought into the monastery from a number of estates. A late ninth-century document from the abbey of St. Remi also mentions hops, apparently being moved in sizeable quantities. So hops were widely known in western Europe by the eighth century, raised at the very least in the gardens of monasteries. At the abbey of Freisingen in Bavaria from 859 to 875 and onward, the annals mention orchards with hop gardens and from the mid-ninth century tenants had to pay dues in hops at certain French monasteries such as St. Remi, Lobbes, and St. Germain.[5] There was even trade in hops, some turning up as part of a cargo of a mid-tenth-century vessel excavated along the coast of Kent in England. The type of hops and where they were found in the boat indicate that they were cargo and presumably being imported. Hops have been found in excavations of York in England, both from before and after the arrival of the Vikings. And at Hedeby, the principal port of Viking-Age Scandinavia in the western Baltic, archeologists found traces of hops dating presumably from the tenth, or at the latest the early eleventh, century. Hungary at about the same time had already gained a reputation for raising hops.[6]

Direct evidence of the production of hopped beer before about 1200 is scant, but there is enough to indicate that ninth-century brewers and their successors knew about and used hops. Archeological evidence of hop finds across western Europe tends to support the extremely sparse written evidence from the ninth century on. Hops cultivation and the use of hops in beer spread to many locations. It appears that hopped beer brewing, at least on a large scale, began in the big monasteries of the Carolingian era. The prominent Carolingian abbot Adalhard of Corbie in 822 laid down detailed methods for the preparation and distribution of hops in the context of brewing *cervisia*. Abbot Ansegis of Wandrille (c. 830) talked about beer made with hops. Making beer with hops may have been common in large establishments in England by the tenth century.[7] Hops grew in monastic gardens in Germany in the eleventh century and in England in the first third of the twelfth century. Hops grew in what is now Austria certainly by 1206 and probably by 1180. Hops appears in Danish sources from the first half of the thirteenth century and in Norwegian law at about the same time. The first specific mention of hops in Sweden comes from 1296, the cultivation of the plant possibly introduced by Cistercian monks. Raising hops first turns up in records from Finland in 1249 at a monastery in Turku, but linguistic evidence supports the view that it was cultivated by 1000 and probably much earlier in that part of Europe.[8] Archeological finds of hops from the years before about 700 range over a large area of northern Europe, but they are few and typically small in quantity. The number jumps in the early Middle Ages and then increases even more in the years after 1000.

The frequency of finds in the high Middle Ages in the Netherlands, northern Germany and the Czech Republic suggests those were places where hopped beer brewing was more common. Not all finds are associated with beer brewing, but the quantities at some sites leave little doubt.[9]

Advice from the medical practitioners and teachers of Salerno from around 1060 indicates their belief that hops functioned as an effective diuretic, and according to one author, the best results came from drinking beers heavily hopped. The passage is one of the earliest explicit statements about the use of hops in beer making. In the southeastern Low Countries explicit mention appears only in the twelfth century, well after hops were being raised in the region. The first times hops are mentioned in Nuremberg town records, that is in 1303, they are associated with regulations on brewing.[10] In general, specific statements about the use of hops in the making of beer typically postdated those about raising the herb, often by some significant time. While hops had been known before and throughout the early Middle Ages, it is possible to say that by the thirteenth century they were widely cultivated throughout northern Europe and had different uses, among them replacing *gruit* or other herbs in the making of beer.

Hops gave beer greater durability. Certain hops resins, extracted during boiling, helped to prevent infection of the wort and beer by various bacteria. Hops keep beer from contracting diseases. Since hopped beer could last longer it traveled better. Not all export beer was necessarily made with hops, but hopped beer was more likely to survive transportation over any distance.[11] In the absence of hops, the way to contain bacterial growth had been to raise the alcohol content. So beer with hops could be less strong than its predecessors. The alcohol level of beer is dependent on the quantity of sugar in the wort available for fermentation. With lower alcohol content, hopped beer could be made with less sugar. Therefore, it was not as sweet and took less grain to make since grain was the source of material for fermentation. That implied lower production costs but also implied a lighter and thinner drink. Preservation of foods was one of the greatest problems of pre-nineteenth-century Europe. The addition of hops in the brewing process made for a significant change in beer. It now joined the few foods that would keep for months without becoming inedible.

If hopped beer was so superior, it is surprising that it took such a long time for brewers to adopt the new additive and use it widely. There were some good reasons, technical and commercial, for the delay. The attributes of hops can be assessed by appearance, feel, and smell and the aroma can give some sense of the aroma of the final product.[12] Yet it was not until the eighteenth century that there was recognition of the different types of hops. Hops have to be picked around the first of September to get the most from them. They have to be dried as quickly as possible and then kept cold to retain their characteristics. How much hops to use depends on the quantity of nonmalted grain in the mash tun and the sulphate content of the water. The quantity of hops can be reduced if the hops are ground, but the grinding can also harm the taste of the beer. How long the wort is boiled with the hops can vary depending on the character and strength of the wort and the quantity of the hops. Spent hops can be a source of infection and need to be removed from the wort as quickly as possible.[13] Medieval brewers knew few, if any, of those facts except for what they might pick up by trial and error. Brewers had to find out a number of things to get the optimum advantages from hops and to prevent problems. Only after a number of tries would they have been able to predict what to look for and how to use hops and be able to pass that knowledge on to others.

If mashing and boiling took place in the same container, as was still common as late as the thirteenth century, then the addition of hops would originally have taken place in the presence of the malt and might have even been mixed with the malt before mashing began. Such circumstances could have only confused brewers about the contribution hops made to the final product, as well as increasing the chance of infection. Using hops may, in fact, have promoted the separation of the two tasks of mashing and boiling so that the herb could be added in the later stage and its role more carefully monitored. With two vessels, one for each operation, boiling was no longer the phase for extracting vegetable matter but the phase for stopping the work of certain enzymes, of getting the most from the hops, and of sterilizing the brew. Two vessels meant greater capital investment and that constraint may have slowed the adoption of hops. In Finland, brewers apparently added hops after the wort had cooled but such practice was rare. More commonly it was during boiling that hops were put in the kettle, either directly or after being softened in some of the heated wort or in hot water. In some cases the hops were lowered into the boiling wort in a sack or something in the form of a hamper made of straw, as at Haarlem, which solved the problem of getting the hops out quickly. Otherwise the wort was filtered to separate out the hops and other unwanted material. The strainer in the simplest form could be some twigs which could also give the beer some flavor, the exact flavor depending on the type of twigs used.[14]

Producers had trouble with hops and apparently so did consumers. Drinkers took time to acquire a taste for hopped beer. The drink had to compete with beer made with *gruit* which was more than acceptable, well known, easier to make, and served the purpose of an alcoholic beverage of some purity and good taste. *Gruit* proved durable in areas where bog myrtle grew, that is near the coasts of western and northern Europe. The philosopher Albertus

Magnus mentioned the use of *gruit* in Holstein for making beer in the thirteenth century, and a number of archeological sites in places as distant as Lin-
coln in England, northern Frisia, and Ribe in Denmark suggest the durability
of brewing with *gruit*. Initially brewers, in trying to get the proportions of
hops, malt, and water right, probably produced heavily hopped beers. The
excess was insurance against error but yielded higher costs and prices, as well
as a dramatically different taste from what consumers found normal. Hopped
beer was probably made for some time and in places as different as monasteries along the Rhine and taverns in Poland before it became a commercial
product. Brewing hopped beer may have started in monasteries since they produced relatively large quantities of beer at any one time and so had more reason to worry about preservation. Though it was Carolingian abbots who talked
about making beer with hops, not all hop finds by any means are associated
with monasteries. Monastic brewers were certainly not alone in understanding
the use and value of the plant.[15]

Commerce in Hopped Beer

The novelty of the years after 1200 was that brewers in Bremen, Hamburg,
Wismar, and elsewhere in northern Germany made hopped beer for export.
They could sell the better product in their own urban markets and found that
their beer could compete successfully against locally brewed beers in distant
ones. It was possible to stockpile the more durable hopped beer and to produce it when it was convenient or efficient rather than just when the beer
could be sold. Producers were no longer directly tied to consumers, nor did
they need to attach themselves to one group of buyers to assure them of some
market before the beer went bad.[16]

   Not just beer but hops itself became a commodity of trade. As early as
the 1250s Wismar had hop gardens and at least four breweries to use the hops
raised in them (see Figure 5). The town government, incidentally, taxed the
gardens. By the fourteenth century, the town imported hops from villages in
Poland. Lübeck at about the same time also had to look outside the town for
supplies, importing hops from as far away as Thuringia. By the middle of the
century, Nuremberg had a market in hops, overseen by two sworn town officers. Fairs were even devoted to the sale of hops, and town governments on
the north German coast laid down regulations for the hops trade. Over time
sources of supply expanded geographically. Hops became an export good for
Sweden in the fifteenth and sixteenth centuries, important enough that they
formed 14 percent of total exports by value in 1491.[17]

   Port towns in north Germany, members of the Hanseatic League includ-

Figure 5. Hop garden on the edge of Rostock, from the Vicke Schorler's scroll, 1578–1586. By that date urban hop gardens were common in north German towns. Vicke Schorler, Warhaftige Abcontrafactur der hochloblichen und weitberumten alten See- und Hensestadt Rostock Heuptstadt im Lande zu Mecklenburgk, 1578–1586. Courtesy of Archiv der Hansestadt Rostock, 3.02.1.1.15000.

ing Bremen, Wismar, and Rostock, but, above all, Hamburg became the export centers for hopped beer. Shipping beer over land in the late Middle Ages added from 25 percent to 70 percent to the selling price for each 100 kilometers it had to travel. The wide variation depended on the terrain the beer traveled over and on any unavoidable tolls that had to be paid. Shipping beer over water was cheaper. High transport costs explain why port towns dominated the beer trade and why towns such as Lübeck and Wismar got regulations on brewing earlier, in 1366 and 1399 respectively, than did inland towns such as Hannover, which in 1434 had only a vague statement about brewing. Breweries —houses designed with wide cellars, roomy floors, and high ceilings to accommodate the trade—were almost invariably on some waterway in all the port towns. Brewers built houses to suit the trade, for example, as they did at Hamburg as part of a rebuilding program in the wake of the devastating fire of 1284. That disaster became an opportunity to establish a foundation for the export trade which grew rapidly in the fourteenth century. Wismar also had a lively export trade in hopped beer in the fourteenth century, one which started well before the first written evidence of distant sales appears around 1327. Wismar and Hamburg, like many other German towns, were able to avoid effective legal authority of some member of the nobility so brewing evolved under the influence not of a governor but, rather, of the potential for international trade.[18]

Beer from north Germany found markets throughout northern Europe, but the biggest and most lucrative market from the start of the trade in beer was in the Low Countries. Beer from Bremen was an export good by 1220. It was mentioned in a Bruges privilege of 1252 and appeared on the north Netherlands market in 1274. Hamburg beer is mentioned in Gouda in 1357, though it certainly was being sold in Holland well before that date. Emperor Charles IV in 1364 praised what he called the new kind of brewing, the *novus modus fermentandi cervisiam* which had brought a thriving industry to the northern part of his lands and especially to Hamburg. The town was known, at least to one writer as the *"Brauhaus der Hansa."*[19] Hamburg had access to grain supplies from the Elbe Valley, to hops from small towns around the Baltic, and to beer markets throughout northwestern Europe by sea. The town of Bremen seems to have been first to identify the potential export market in the southern Low Countries but was superseded as the supplier of hopped beer by Hamburg in the course of the fourteenth century. By 1374 Hamburg beer had improved and so was being called "Bremen beer" and replacing the Bremen product in different markets including the Flemish one. It could be that internal political disruption in Bremen meant that oversight of beer making had deteriorated, and as a result, so had the beer.[20] Bremen beer exports may have been first to reach Groningen and the towns in western Friesland and those along the River

Ijssel in the northern Low Countries. Over time, Hamburg beer tended to replace it, and traders shipped so much Hamburg beer that only grain was a more frequently carried good. While Wismar beer turns up in import records in the west Frisian town of Enkhuizen in 1448, it rarely appears after that, presumably because it too was swamped by Hamburg beer.[21] By the fifteenth century, imports from Hamburg were so common that Hamburg beer was a generic term for all beer from northern Germany.

Hamburg and the Beer Trade

It is difficult to estimate the scale of beer production in Hamburg in the thirteenth century when it became a center of brewing. By the mid-fourteenth century it is possible to make a guess at production of about 25,000,000 liters per year for both export and domestic use. Figures for export before that period and for total production in subsequent years are more reliable (see Table 1). They indicate how big the industry was in Hamburg and also how important export was to the industry.

In a survey of 1376, lost in a fire in 1842, 175 Hamburgers stated their trade and of those 457, or 43 percent, said they were beer brewers. Of the 457, 126 said they were brewers for Amsterdam while 55 worked especially for Stavoren. Even those impressive figures understate the importance of the beer trade to Hamburg. Not all of the brewers were identified in the survey. The listing does, however, suggest that by the third quarter of the thirteenth century there was a clear division between brewers for local use and brewers for export, a division which later regulation would institutionalize. A number of Hamburg export brewers were known in the town as suppliers of Amsterdam and a few

TABLE 1. HAMBURG BEER, PRODUCTION AND EXPORTS, 1360–1540, IN LITERS

Date	Total Production	Total Exports
c. 1348		8,700,000
1360s		5,600,000 (to Amsterdam only)
1369		13,260,000
1375	24,000,000	
1410	37,500,000	9,000,000 (to the Low Countries only)
1417		18,250,000
1420	30,000,000	
1480	37,500,000	10,000,000
1530s	28,000,000	

Sources: Huntemann, *Das deutsche Braugewerbe,* 11, 18, 46; Stefke, "Die Hamburger Zollbücher von 1399/1400 und '1418'," 31.

as suppliers of Stavoren.[22] The latter was a small port in Friesland,which Amsterdam completely eclipsed by the fifteenth century. Hamburg merchants paid only a very light tax on beer brought into Holland. Their customers paid no duty and the German merchants also were free of tax on some other items if sales were in large quantities. Hamburg traders shipped so much of their beer through Amsterdam and concentrated so much on the beer trade that they remained aloof from the organization of Hanse merchants at Bruges in Flanders, maintaining a separate and much smaller organization. Using the proportions of the survey, 47 percent of Hamburg exports went to Amsterdam, 20 percent to Stavoren, and the remaining 33 percent elsewhere in northern and eastern Europe. Eighty-four of the Hamburgers stating a trade in 1376 said they were merchants dealing principally with Flanders. Another thirty-five said they were merchants dealing principally with England. Both groups would have relied on the beer trade extensively as a source of goods for exchange. In 1376, Hamburg had no less than 104 master coopers.[23] Many of them produced barrels for the brewers and so relied on the thriving brewing industry, as did the many merchants and other tradespeople in the town.

Records of an Amsterdam import toll on Hamburg beer which dated from 1323 give some indication of the total volume of fourteenth-century Hamburg beer exports. The average annual shipment from Hamburg to Amsterdam by the 1360s was almost 32,000 barrels, or at least 5,600,000 liters. That was more than 20 percent of total Hamburg output in 1375 and probably more than half of all Hamburg exports (see Figure 6).[24] The count of Holland chose to funnel beer imports through Amsterdam and he accomplished that goal by the way he set tolls. His decision does not explain why the town became so important, but in her early years in the fourteenth century the beer trade must have made an important contribution to her commercial development. The income to the count from the toll charged on Hamburg beer made a sizeable contribution to his coffers. And the income may have risen after 1374 when Hamburg brewers shifted from exporting dark beer to a lighter one of higher quality.[25]

Shippers had to move about 5,600 tonnes of beer along the coast to Amsterdam on average each year. The vessels Hamburgers used in the trade were approximately 40 to 50 tons, that is in the middle range of ocean-going ships of the day. The biggest of ships from the north German ports would have gone directly to Flanders, carrying beer to the larger and more prosperous towns in that county. Given the size of vessels used in the trade, even with multiple voyages more than twenty ships would have been fully employed to move beer alone. Ships did not sail in the winter and the shipping season was short, some six months for the year 1352 to 1353. The season lengthened, but not by much, over the rest of the century. Some skippers and ships obviously

Figure 6. The waterfront at Hamburg. At the right, shippers are paying tolls and, at the left, a crane loads barrels onto ships. From an illustrated manuscript of the Hamburg charter, 1497, plate 18. Courtesy of Staatsarchiv Hamburg.

specialized in the coastal trade to Amsterdam, showing up repeatedly in the toll records. In the twelve months from February, 1369, to February, 1370, beer made up fully one-third of all Hamburg exports by value. Almost half, 47 percent, of beer exports went to Amsterdam.[26] A significant share must have found its way to the Low Countries, either through Stavoren or Bruges. There were distinctions among Hamburg brewers, some having relatively large operations and often concentrating on the Amsterdam market. A few produced over 2,000 barrels in a year, and many more made over 1,000 barrels of beer. From 1352 to 1354 there were still some small brewers and small traders involved in export to Amsterdam and their names turn up on the list of shippers, but they were obviously a disappearing breed. Export brewers appear to have produced to order for Low Countries markets, making an entire brew which then was loaded on board a specific ship which carried virtually only that beer and went directly to Amsterdam.[27]

Hamburgers in foreign ports had factories or, more frequently, organizations of their own for merchants involved in the beer trade. The groups at Amsterdam, Bruges, and Stavoren even had their own regulations and statutes granted by Hamburg.[28] At Amsterdam, where in 1365, seventy-two of the seventy-eight beer importers came from Hamburg, the group formed its own legal organization or *hanze* before 1358. The members maintained a chapel for their benefit.[29] The Hanseatic League eventually required that only German merchants could act as agents in Holland for traders from their towns. The legislation thus prohibited joint ventures between Germans and Hollanders. In 1418 the League made clear that no goods, including beer, could be sent to non-Hansards in Flanders. Such rules were strengthened throughout the fifteenth century, but they had their origins in earlier arrangements like those of Hamburg brewers with their agents or *liggers* living in Amsterdam. The agents were usually relatives of the brewers back home who relied on the family connection to insure honesty and reliability. The agents were principally dealers in beer and, in some cases, exclusively so. There was cooperation among agents overseas, in one case an agent looking after the estate of another, all done with permission of the city government of Amsterdam, granted at the request of Hamburg.[30]

Tolls from 1399/1400 and 1417/1418 of goods leaving the port of Hamburg show that the principal export commodity remained beer. It continued to go to the traditional markets of Holland, Friesland, and the southern Low Countries, with Hamburg beer turning up in 1418 in toll records from the lower Scheldt.[31] The fifteenth-century Hamburg beer trade was increasingly handled not by those who were exclusively associated with brewing, but by merchants who dealt in a range of goods and could better finance the long-distance trade in beer. In the fourteenth century, some 40 percent to 50 percent of total income in Hamburg could be attributed to the brewing industry. Hamburg exports rose between 1369 and 1417, but compared to the previous century beer brewing was probably of less importance to Hamburg. After the second decade of the fifteenth century, internal difficulties and wars disrupted the Hamburg economy, affecting brewing. But as late as 1417, and even well beyond that date, Hamburg brewing was still prosperous.[32] The 457 professional brewers of 1357 increased to some 520 in the fifteenth century. Though that figure was high, reflecting Hamburg's position in the beer trade, other north German towns had a large number of people making beer. At Bremen there were 300 brewers in the early fifteenth century, Erfurt had about 250, Wismar and Leipzig some 200 each, and Lübeck 180.[33] A significant number of those in port towns, like their Hamburg counterparts, brewed for export.

Beer Sales in Flanders

Though merchants and shippers from the Hanse towns might sell beer in Groningen, Friesland, and Holland, their real goal had always been the large urban centers in Brabant and especially Flanders to the south. In 1252 and 1253 the count of Flanders granted privileges to Hanse merchants at Bruges, and the number of visitors rose sharply, including merchants from Bremen who brought beer. Others from towns like Wismar and then Hamburg followed them, supplying a growing market.[34] The Hansards trading to Flanders were subject to a tax on beer they sold, as were all foreigners. The tax was called *gruitgeld* but their beer had hops and not *gruit*. Hansards were always required to sell their beer in bulk, with retail sales allowed only in their own houses. The beer Bremen and Hamburg shippers brought to Flanders was heavy, strong, and expensive. It was not a product for the poor, but it was a product that could generate profits.[35] People bought Hamburg beer because it was better, or at the least they thought it was better. It was a matter of taste. What was not a matter of taste was the fact that it lasted longer. Ale made with *gruit* was a drink for the poor and the sick. Beer was something of a luxury good and so could sustain a certain tax level. The optimum level was something governments in the Low Countries regularly explored.

One result of the experiments with taxation was sporadic political conflict between the Hansards and Flemish authorities, a common feature of the fourteenth century. In 1360, for example, when Hanse merchants, because of differences with the count, boycotted the Flemish market, special attention was given to beer from Hamburg and Bremen to be certain that none of it was delivered to buyers south of Holland. In a long list of complaints the German merchants had about the Flemings, probably dating from 1379, the thirteenth was the import tax of one *groot* that they had to pay on each barrel of beer. A decade later the German merchants were attacking the additional excise tax they had to pay at Sluis, the port of Bruges, and in Flanders. They wanted it fixed at no more than eight *grooten* per barrel and wanted each jurisdiction to have the power to set the rate, presumably thinking that they could use their bargaining power in some ports to drive down the tax. In 1391, at least, they got the excise set at a maximum of eight *grooten* per barrel. In the autumn of 1393, Hamburg asked that her merchants no longer be charged *gruitgeld* of two *groten* for each barrel they brought into Bruges or Sluis, claiming it was a local tax for local beer so their imports should be exempt. They said that Hollanders did not have to pay it, though they appear to have been wrong. Only Bremen beer and *aale de Angleteerre* were exempt from the fee. The Hamburgers' appeal in 1393 worked, though, and they did get a year free from the tax.[36] However, it did not end the almost continuous efforts of Hamburg and the Hanse to get lower taxes.

Hanse merchants never fully exercised the option of carrying beer directly from Hamburg to Bruges. Certainly some beer did avoid the tolls in Holland by going straight to Flanders. In the 1370s probably less than 10 percent of Hamburg exports went directly to Flanders. There was some increase after that, with Hamburgers moving more beer all the way to Sluis without intermediate stops. That would explain the establishment of an organization of agents at Bruges, like the one at Amsterdam, in the closing years of the century, and it would explain the decline in income from the toll on Hamburg beer at Amsterdam.[37] Improvements in the design of ships in the fourteenth century may have made sailing directly to Flanders easier and safer. The direct voyage also had the advantage of avoiding tolls, of avoiding intermediaries in Holland, and of having Flemish cloth easily available to carry back home. One English observer of the early fifteenth century said beer went straight to Flanders but that was beer from Prussia, brought along with bacon which Flemings also very much liked. The Prussian beer was probably heavier and stronger but the writer of *The Libelle of Englyshe Polycye* said it was not expensive. Prussian beer from Gdansk also found a market among Amsterdam merchants, though they may have shipped it on to buyers farther south.[38]

Despite some shift to direct shipment after approximately 1370 the carriage of beer along inland waterways certainly did not disappear. To bring beer to Amsterdam first, and then by rivers and canals to Flanders, was probably always safer than going by sea. The counts of Holland in the thirteenth century promoted the *binnenvaart* through the county by investing toll income in the improvement of sluices and locks like those at Spaarndam and Gouda, and so kept the relative cost of moving beer through Holland low. In the fourteenth century, to help pay for the wars which brought Friesland under his control, the count of Holland had burdened the trade with taxes and even embargoes but on 14 August 1403, Count Albert gave Hamburgers freedom from tolls and *grutgeld* in his lands for fifteen years. They did have to pay a fee for each sixty-four barrels imported and no more than 1 percent in tolls as they passed through his lands. The count also set a maximum charge that the towns around the Zuider Zee could levy on Hamburg beer. He appears to have supported Hamburg shippers in disputes about the ownership of beer, putting in place an appeal procedure, and allowed Hamburgers to maintain their own trade organization. His avowed goal was to keep the trade in beer funneling through Friesland, Holland, and Zeeland and in part at least he succeeded.[39]

Beer Sales in Scandinavia and the Baltic

Through the fourteenth and fifteenth centuries many north German towns expanded their export markets and even institutionalized their connections with consumers in different places in northern Europe. Nearby Scandinavia was a logical outlet for beer from Hanse towns along the North Sea and also the Baltic coasts of Germany. First contact of Bremen with the Baltic was in the twelfth century and that may be true of many German towns, following in the wake of a general offensive in the region led by Henry the Lion, the founder of Lübeck in 1158. Since beer was the standard drink on board ship among German travelers at the time, the traders' vessels carried beer and so brought it into the region. Riga was founded by missionaries and knights in 1202 as both an episcopal seat and a trading center with necessary foodstuffs traded there, including beer. In the thirteenth century, a Bremen brewer began producing in Riga for local consumption, and he probably sold some beer beyond the town walls. Other towns in the Baltic soon developed their own brewing with larger ones like Gdansk, Lübeck, Rostock, Stralsund, and places in Prussia certainly having their own industries. The Livland towns of Riga, Reval, and Dorpat all had breweries by the fourteenth century. Local breweries in the new and many of the older settlements with immigrants from Germany were able to supply drinkers and that deterred imports from farther west, making the eastern Baltic market less promising than that in Scandinavia.[40]

The north German port towns tended to specialize. The division of export markets dates back to the late fourteenth century, if not earlier. Wismar established an early foothold in the north. Other Hanse towns typically did not shift to the Scandinavian market until the fifteenth century when other export markets, such as the ones in the Low Countries, tended to close to them. On the other hand, Rostock was already known for exports to the north in the fourteenth century. Beer from Lübeck, and also from Lüneberg on occasion, even got shipped through Hamburg to the north. Meanwhile Gdansk was the supplier for the eastern Baltic. German merchants were in Novgorod by 1184, and probably before, and by the first years of the thirteenth century they were certainly carrying beer to Livonia.[41]

In Scandinavia in 1351, King Magnus of Sweden granted toll freedom for Wismar beer at Kalmar, but Denmark proved a more difficult market to enter. There, in 1283, King Eric issued a prohibition against the import of any German beer. The massive herring fishery along the southwest coast of what is now Sweden in the province of Scania appears to have been only a very minor outlet for beer even though during the fishing season it was a market for a wide variety of trade goods sent from Lübeck. The fishermen's camps along the shore near Falsterbo were legally inside the kingdom of Denmark, and that fact may have been enough to keep out German beer. By 1466 the Danish prohibition on beer imports had been changed to a heavy tax. Bergen in Norway proved to be an important market for Wismar beer well before 1400. Consumers were mostly the German merchants in the sizeable colony there. Shipping beer to them and to other Bergen consumers from north Germany went on throughout the fifteenth century, despite the presence of a brewery there in the thirteenth and fourteenth centuries.[42]

Merchants from towns of the Hanseatic League used political, military, and commercial pressure to dominate trade to Scandinavia, but their position was slowly eroded in the last years of the Middle Ages. In 1284 German merchants had already put an embargo on the export of grain flour and beer to Norway to force King Erik Magnusson into concessions. A famine the following year convinced the king, and so those merchants came to control trade into the principal Norwegian port, Bergen. The Hansards tried the strategy repeatedly throughout the fourteenth century. They were regularly successful. With the trading links established and effective relatively low-cost transport available, beer was easily added to the cargoes going north. In the fifteenth century, the quality of beer for export seems to have gone down. In 1481, for example, the town government of Bergen complained to their counterpart in Wismar that brewers had over time decreased the quantity of malt used to make each brew. About 1400, Wismar exported some 10,000,000 liters each year, but by the end of the fifteenth century overseas sales had fallen to between 3,000,000 and 4,000,000 liters. The town council even legislated against the breaking up of breweries, many being forced to close in the face of falling sales.[43] The decline in traffic was a reflection of the declining political power of the Hanse. The League could no longer force trading conditions on Scandinavian governments, but it was not for any lack of effort. The Hanse prohibited the export of beer to Denmark in 1363, 1367, 1368, 1422, 1464, 1477, and 1490. In the fourteenth century the restrictions were combined with military action and led to success. In the fifteenth century little came of the embargoes. In 1466 Denmark imposed a duty of four shillings per barrel on German beer and set the sale price at eighteen shillings per barrel so the tax was 22 percent of the selling price. At the same time the Danish king prohibited import of German beer into certain towns. Later, in 1489, Denmark prohibited the sale of foreign beer at the Malmö fall market, and in 1491 another set of regulations and restrictions on imported beer followed.[44] The Hanseatic League by the end of the fifteenth century found itself incapable of stopping the Danes from visiting serious damage on their beer trade.

It is difficult to estimate the volume of beer German shippers sent to Scandinavia or to any markets for that matter. Imports into Scandinavia may possibly have risen overall in the fifteenth century compared to the previous one hundred years, but there were variations and some decline toward the end of the century. In the sixteenth century the volume increased, despite the growth of brewing in towns throughout Denmark, Norway, and Sweden. The growth in population in the sixteenth century and the increased urbanization which accompanied that growth created an improving market for both domestically produced and imported beer. Consumption of beer per person appears to have risen in the second half of the sixteenth century, another reason for German beer exports to have continued. The Scandinavian market remained the preserve of the Wendish towns, though Bremen made some inroads in the sixteenth century as its beer was driven out of other markets. From 1577 to 1578 over 93 percent of beer imported into Bergen came from Hanse towns along the Wendish coast. Bremen sent just over 4 percent of the total. In 1550, Bergen imported 11,400 barrels of beer; by approximately 1580, the figure was down to 5,400. After that the trend appears to have reversed. Wismar still had fifty brewers in 1560, but with a lowering of the Danish beer excise by 1592, the number was up to 120. Production rose from an annual average of 8,000,000 to 9,000,000 liters in the period 1560–1600 to between 10,000,000 and 12,000,000 liters per year by 1618. The number declined through the rest of the seventeenth century though. In a 1579 statement, Wismar said it was its task to supply Norway, Denmark, and Sweden with malt and with beer. That function did not disappear. Even in the seventeenth century Wismar still set the dates for exporting of beer to coincide with the peak of activity in the Scania herring fishery. Wismar exports to Sweden appear to have risen in the seventeenth century, aided by reductions in tolls. In 1610, though, 55 percent of Stockholm imports came from Rostock, 33 percent from Lübeck, and 8 percent from Greifswald. How much of that beer was produced in Wismar and then reexported from the other ports cannot be known. Imports to Stockholm in 1620 were about 565,000 liters, up from the approximately 115,000 liters of 1550. There was also a rise in exports to Scandinavia from Gdansk.[45] There was increasing competition from locally produced beer and competition among north German towns in Scandinavian markets in the late Middle Ages and Renaissance. Still, even in the seventeenth century, the old Hanse ports sent significant quantities of beer north.

Urban Regulation of Brewing in North Germany

Over the course of the thirteenth and fourteenth centuries, the government of Hamburg, in the face of the growth and prosperity of the brewing industry, instituted a long series of regulations covering many aspects of the trade. Similar regulation followed elsewhere, especially where brewers exported a sizeable proportion of the beer they produced and where town governments could make the trade serve the general economic policies of the town. The enduring and unchanging goals were the maintenance of both town tax income and the share of the export market. The extensive regulations and rules on brewing at Hamburg indicate, among other things, the importance of exports to the industry. To keep markets overseas it was clear that the quality of beer had to be maintained, without fail.

As the biggest export industry in Hamburg, brewing was organized differently from other trades, and government legislation was very different from that for other trades. Brewing and baking were regulated together in the thirteenth century, presumably because they were carried on in the same place or even by the same people. As both became more specialized that commonality of regulation declined. For those entering the brewing trade there was no learning period. That was somewhat surprising given the growing apprenticeship requirements in other trades and the extent of other regulations of brewing. Brewers could not make beer for export before St Peter's Day (22 February), at least from 1358 and probably earlier. This restriction was another reason the shipping season was short and certainly the reason that no beer arrived in Amsterdam until the middle of March. The volume of exports rose in April and continued through to mid-November. In 1372, the date of 22 February for the start of making export beer was dropped but not the requirement that no brewer could make beer for export without getting permission from the town government. That rule dated from 1359, if not before. It was the start of what evolved into a system of licenses to brew for export and then to brew at all. Legislation was designed in the first instance to benefit merchants who exported Hamburg beer to the Low Countries. The export brewers were not allowed to sell their product in the home market, so presumably natives could not buy the best beer brewed in the town. Unlike export brewers, those producing for local sales faced a restriction on the maximum amount they could brew each week, at least from 1372.[46]

From 1381 on, no one could start up a brewery for export without permission of the town council. Export brewers could produce beer in one house and one house only, though that rule was relaxed slightly in 1435 and more extensively in 1471. In 1411, restrictions on exporters were expanded, in essence introducing a licensing system and also, by revoking the right to brew of some producers, decreasing the number and increasing the average size of breweries. In the same year the town also set a minimum time between brews. In effect, the government limited output for export. The government was so interested in keeping up the quality of export beer that in the fifteenth century offices were set up near the entrance to the harbor for testing beer, with an officer of the town trying it before it left. After 1411 the town punished brewers who tried to export bad beer. In other north German towns, as at Hamburg, there was often specialization between brewers supplying the domestic market and those making beer for export. Lübeck brewers were divided into one group that produced for local consumption and one that produced for export. By the end of the fifteenth century, there were rules not only in Hamburg and Lübeck, but also in Reval and Wismar against combining production of beer for sales outside the town and retail sales through the brewer's own outlet.[47]

The brewing towns controlled prices, setting maximum prices, but often they were more interested in keeping the minimum at a certain level. Hamburg showed a great interest in maintaining minimum prices in its factories in the Netherlands and used its legislative powers to keep prices from falling. It kept up revenues from the sale of beer overseas but that was not the only reason for the extensive regulations. Town governments did not want to have the profits of brewers and their own tax income squeezed, either by falling prices of output or by rising prices of raw materials. Hamburg imported grain both from nearby regions and also from the northern Netherlands. As the export brewing industry grew, potential problems of grain supplies for the town were one source for the increasing regulation of brewing. That may also be one reason for the much more restrictive legislation of 1411. The restrictions in general may also have been an effort on the part of government to prevent overproduction and limit the wide swings in output so typical of export industries in the period.[48] By 1458 the amount of grain that could be used in the production of each fixed quantity of beer also came under town regulation. About the same time, Hamburg acted to prevent brewers from developing a sideline as grain traders. Brewers could only buy and sell as much grain as was needed for their brewing. Presumably the government wanted to prevent any one brewer from gaining an unfair advantage. Similarly, Hamburg insisted that hops be sold only on a market controlled by town officials with no more hops sold than was needed for the making of beer. The purpose was to give all brewers equal access to raw materials and to prevent speculation in what could be a critical commodity.

Hamburg brewhouses could lose their licenses since the license was attached to the house and not the brewer. That was not true everywhere. At Riga, for example, brewers, rather than brewhouses, were licensed. Hamburg brewers could work only in their own breweries and could not allow anyone else to use their equipment. They were also required to use only their own malt, which they made themselves. Independent malsters could be an advantage to brewers but town regulations, especially at Hamburg, tended to prevent the development of a separate trade. Hamburg brewers could make no more malt than was needed for making their beer, and they could not do it in anyone else's house. In towns in the Baltic, where there was an export trade in malt, separate malteries with specialized tradesmen developed earlier, but only with the permission of town governments.[49]

Hamburg regulated its brewers. It also taxed its brewers. Brewing kettles were treated as fixed property, like real estate, and taxed as such. The grating and other ironwork which supported the copper kettle was treated in the same way. That was true in Lübeck and Wismar as well. The Hamburg government either by omission or commission succeeded in making brewing a profitable trade with returns ranging from 20 to 30 percent on expenditure in the first half of the fifteenth century. That put brewers among the most prosperous of townspeople. Though those profits had halved by the close of the century, despite the efforts of the government, brewers still did well comparatively.[50]

At Bremen, another major export center of north Germany, regulation increased dramatically in the fourteenth century but even more so in the fifteenth century. It was presumably in reaction to the relative decline of exports, Bremen beer being supplanted by the Hamburg product. In the fourteenth century, Bremen shippers, in search of cargoes, carried foreign beer and even imported beers from other towns for consumption in Bremen. Competition from Hamburg beer was so intense that finally, in 1489, the town prohibited imports to protect local brewers, though beer imported from the small town of Einbeck and from Wismar was still allowed. To improve the quality of Bremen beer and to get back some share of the market, the town, in 1450, issued new regulations on brewing, including a prohibition of brewing after the fourth Sunday before Easter. There were also maxima and minima set for the amount of barley malt to be used in making a brew with provision for the substitution of oats if necessary. The revised regulations of 1489 did not mention such substitution, but the requirement that any beer for export had to be tasted first was finally instituted. Violation of the rule led to the serious penalty of prohibition from brewing for a year. Also no beer for export was to be brewed after St. Urban's Day (25 May). How that fit with the earlier prohibition of brewing after a certain date in Lent is not clear.[51] What is clear is that Bremen town authorities saw increased regulation as a way to regain some portion of an export market for beer which they understood as very important to the economy of the town. Many regulations mirrored those in Hamburg.

At Wismar the town government developed even closer regulation of brewery operations. As early as 1322, the government set the wages of beer workers and beginning about 1420 the wages of the supervisor of those workers. Fearing the potential for undue influence, the town forbade brewers from giving a morning meal to the deliverymen who came to the brewery to pick up beer for shipment to pubs, homes, or to the docks for export. The beer ordinance of 1332 set a minimum of fourteen days between brews for those making beer for taverns. In 1399 and thereafter, the period was reduced to one week. Since brewing decreased during the warm summer months when the chance of spoilage sharply increased, the number of times brewers produced beer in each year was typically much less than the level implied by regulations on the frequency of brewing. Beginning about 1350, no one could brew or make malt in a brewery except the owner of the house and equipment. Each brewer had to brew alone. Individuals could always brew at home as long as the beer was for their own use. In 1399 the town set an entry fee for the trade and no one could get permission to be a brewer without having paid the fee. In that same year Wismar laid down regulations on the quality of beer, regulations probably based on earlier rules and regulations which would be repeated again and again. By 1400 the quantity of malt that could be used in each brew was fixed by town ordinance. The amount increased in 1417 and again in 1480, in each case in response to requests from brewers. At Kiel in 1425, brewers were required to keep the beer in closed casks for two nights before it could be sold. Such regulations were also common in other towns like Wismar, all as part of the effort to maintain quality. Wismar brewers had to give an oath, promising among other things to make good beer. It was not until 1494 that a town officer was appointed to test beer for quality. If rejected by the officer, the beer could not be exported but could still be sold in town, though at a reduced price. The town fixed the price of beer sold in taverns as early as 1353.[52]

Brewers producing for local consumption got help from common regulations that fiercely restricted imports. The most extreme protectionist measure at Wismar was the prohibition of the import of foreign beer by sea, a regulation that dated from 1356. Some exemptions over time were allowed, but the principal of protection, developed in the fourteenth century, remained. The size of casks was regulated at Wismar as well. Brewers could not use the old casks of other brewers so, after use, barrels had to be returned to the source after being drained. Using barrels of the same size as barrels used in other towns enhanced the risk of imports taking part of the domestic market. But a common barrel could also mean lower costs overall. In 1375, Lübeck, Wismar, and other towns in the area agreed to use the Rostock barrel as the standard measure for beer. Even though the casks might have all been the same size, they were still distinctive because they carried unique marks. As early as 1419, Lübeck had strict rules about the marking of casks, in large part to prevent brewers from using the old casks of other brewers. It was not until 1480 that Hamburg gave up its own size of barrel and joined in using the common measure, resisting for so long perhaps to protect its own brewers.[53] The units of measure in brewing, especially barrel size, always remained a topic of government regulation to prevent unfair competitive advantage as well as to protect consumers from fraud.

The similarity in rules that developed in Hamburg, Wismar, and other north German towns in the course of the fourteenth and fifteenth centuries would be matched over time in other parts of Germany, the Low Countries, and, to some degree, in England. The timing varied and so, too, did the exact nature, stipulations, and severity of the regulations. The variations that did exist were generated by variations in the scale of brewing industries and in the character of urban governments. The most critical factor, however, in generating those variations seems to have been the relative size of the export sector. It was the importance of export in Hamburg and other Hanse ports which drove them to the early development of regulations and also the methods of enforcing them.

In the fourteenth and fifteenth centuries, brewing developed into one of the most important export industries in Hanse towns.[54] The ability of the Hansards to invade overseas markets depended on maintaining quality and cost control at home, on the ability to keep foreign governments from erecting insurmountable barriers to imports, and on the ability to keep shipping costs down. The large and increasing body of regulations was a critical factor in what success the Hansards enjoyed. With exports to the Low Countries, the Hanse towns always had difficulty. With Scandinavia they more often had success. Scandinavia in the early Middle Ages up through the sixteenth century was technologically backward compared to western and much of central Europe. That was certainly the case with brewing. The ability of Hanse traders to sell beer in north German and Scandinavian markets was in sharp contrast to what happened elsewhere. The technological gap remained sizeable between Hanse towns and Scandinavia, but not between Hanse towns and western Europe. At the outset of the thirteenth century, north German beer makers held a commanding position commercially and technically in Low Countries markets. However, in the fourteenth century, and more so the fifteenth century, they faced stiff and ultimately insurmountable competition from local producers in the region. There, too, the actions of government deeply influenced technical and commercial change.

Chapter 5

The Spread of Hopped Beer Brewing: The Northern Low Countries

The first phase in the development of northern European brewing was achieved by 1300 with an urban brewing industry in place, and the breweries in towns producing beer for a commercial market. There was a distribution network and regulations at various levels of government covering production and selling. Consumers were familiar with and used to beer, beer of a certain type. There was a market prepared to accept variant types with the necessary structure to absorb different types of beer. The second phase, the development of a new product, had been accomplished by brewers in north German port towns by the thirteenth century. German shippers introduced that superior drink, beer made with hops, into other markets. The shock of imports of German hopped beer to the Low Countries precipitated the third stage in the development of northern European brewing.

Wine and Hopped Beer

The cultivation of grapes and the making of wine expanded in early medieval Europe. The ritual of the Latin Christian church made wine a necessity, so by the thirteenth century it was produced almost everywhere. As a commodity of commerce, wine was adopted a little more slowly. By the later Middle Ages viticulture was practiced throughout southern and western Europe, even in England, and through lands with German speakers. It reached eastern Prussia by the fourteenth century. The height of viticulture in the Low Countries did not occur until the later Middle Ages, just as the brewing industry began its dramatic expansion.[1] The wines produced in the Rhine and Moselle valleys were much better than those produced farther east and so were traded, but shipping them over any distance raised their prices. In Strasbourg wine cost about as much as beer while in Nuremberg, French wines were 2.6 times as costly as beer. In Hamburg the ratio was 14 to 1 and in Cracow 19 to 1.[2] Wines had problems of infection and deterioration and did not necessarily improve with age or travel so most wine had to be consumed when it was very young. In northeastern Europe beer enjoyed a price advantage over wine. The addition of hops which improved the durability of beer made the drink a higher quality product, able, some consumers decided, to compete with wine.

The development of quality beer with hops made possible not only the long-term growth of the brewing industry, but also the gradual erosion of the market for wine and the slow migration south and west of the border between the regions where wine was preferred to beer. A Goliardic poem, probably from the second half of the twelfth century, talks about a battle between wine and beer. By that date, and probably before, the two drinks were seen to compete and for consumers there was at least a theoretical question of choice. The poet said that in Germany, Hainault, Brabant, in Flanders, in the empire of Frederick Barbarossa, and Saxony, beer was widely consumed by all estates, classes, and groups of men. The implication was that in areas to the south and west beer was not a common drink. Even though beer was widely drunk, the poet makes clear in the half of the poem devoted to wine that beer came in second place in the competition between the two. Wine makes the old young, gives light to the eyes, and takes cares from the heart. As in two nearly contemporary poems by Peter of Blois, wine is said to have more positive effects on health than beer. The idea that beer was inferior to wine proved highly durable. The *Regimen sanitatis Salernitanum*, produced in southern Italy around 1050, claimed wine was better than beer because beer caused longer and less pleasant intoxication and because the fumes and vapors of beer were grosser than those of wine, hence it was harder to clear them from the brain. Farther north in the Italian peninsula, Aldobrandino of Siena in 1256 talked about beer made from oats, wheat, and barley claiming that beer made with oats and wheat was better because it did not cause as much gas. For him, beer made from rye or rye bread with mint and wild celery as additives was the best kind of beer. Whatever the ingredients, he nonetheless complained that beer harmed the head and the stomach, caused bad breath, ruined the teeth, filled the stomach with bad fumes, caused the drinker to get drunk quickly, facilitated urination, and made the flesh white and smooth. How accurate his observations might have been are not clear, but at least as far south as Italy the question of beer and beer drinking was worthy of discussion. In the second half of the fourteenth century, Francesc Eiximenis claimed that his fellow Catalans had the best manners in Europe. Proof of his point was that Catalans drank good wine and never too much of it, while English people and Germans drank beer, mead, or cider, drinks clearly inferior to wine. As to the French and Lombards, they drank wine but to excess. The highly opinionated French traveler, Eustache Deschamps (c. 1340–c. 1406) complained of Germanic food habits, and in Flanders and Bohemia he said he always suffered from the pervasive and sickening stench of beer.[3]

Whatever learned people might say, noblemen in the fourteenth century bought hopped beer for their households as a supplement to purchases of wine. By 1350, and probably even by 1300, beer was no longer just a drink for peasants or servants. The records of the household of the countess of Holland and Hainault showed that everyone in her court drank beer in the 1320s and 1340s. In 1319 they consumed about thirteen barrels of beer on average each week, a third of that coming from Hamburg. At that time Dordrecht was the commercial center of Holland, and wine and salt were the most important trade goods there. Wine had a distinct advantage on the Dordrecht market because so much came down the Rhine for sale in the town. Wine also did well for similar reasons in nearby Middelburg in Zeeland, the import center for French wines in the Netherlands as early as the thirteenth century.[4] By the mid-fourteenth century, mitigated in some cases by local conditions like those in the two port towns, the shift of preferences from wine to beer was making its way southward through Holland. A sign of the advance was Dordrecht traders selling wine in other towns to get beer.[5] That practice became more common over time.

In 1447 a Paris bourgeois bemoaned the fact that wine prices were so high that poor people were being forced to drink beer or even mead, cider, or perry, that is, until late June when new wine came on the market and the price dropped to a third of what it had been. They could then go back to their normal drinking habits. So in the fifteenth century, Paris was on the beer- wine border. Not much farther north, beer enjoyed greater success. By then prices of good wine and the better imported Hamburg beer were about the same in Flanders. The prices were even more likely to be close after 1494, the year the government raised taxes on Hamburg beer. If beer could compete when prices were similar, then it is not surprising that over the course of the fifteenth century as the relative price of beer fell, even in traditional wine-producing areas in Germany, it made further inroads in markets for drink.[6] Exports of wine from Bordeaux, intended for ports in southeastern England and the Low Countries, fell in the course of the fourteenth century. In the first four decades of the fifteenth century, they were at about 15 percent of what they had been in the first four decades of the previous century. The Hundred Years' War, which ravaged the wine-growing area of southwestern France, played the largest role in the decline of wine exports. A revival at the end of the fourteenth century did not make up for the loss, and imports into England never reached the level at the outbreak of war in 1337. From the mid-fourteenth century on, prices for Bordeaux wine were 50 percent higher than those in the early years of the century. The rising prices of wine led consumers to seek an alternative drink. Hamburg hopped beer was the most appealing choice. In the mid-thirteenth century the well-to-do in Flemish cities drank wine at meals. In the fifteenth century, they, like skilled tradespeople, preferred to have good quality beer. Hopped beer was not only the drink of prosperous folk but having it on the table in Flanders, as elsewhere in northern Europe, had even become something of a sign of status.[7]

Over the course of the fifteenth and sixteenth centuries, wine consumption declined in the Low Countries. Though a number of factors played a role in the change, the rise in beer consumption was one critical reason.[8] The consumption of mead, still a popular drink at Leuven in 1410, also fell off sharply in the first half of the fifteenth century. Mead was as expensive as high-quality imported beer thanks to the cost of the principal raw material, honey. As with the drop in wine consumption, the reason was a turn to beer.[9] In all cases the expansion in the quantity and geographical range of beer consumption was aided by the increasing ability to produce hopped beer, first in the county of Holland itself and later throughout northwestern Europe. Competition from that beer was a threat to sales of mead and sales of wine, but, more immediately, it was a threat to the sales of Hamburg hopped beer.

The Holland Government and Hopped Beer

The sales of high-quality beer from Hanse towns were sizeable enough to disturb the count of Holland and drive him to act, making hopped beer brewing illegal. In Holland the Count prohibited the production of the drink because he was fearful of losing income from existing taxes which he and other authorities levied on *gruit*. His resistance to the change to a new and superior product had no other apparent explanation. In 1321 the flood of German hopped beer led Count William III of Holland to forbid the import of Hamburg and eastern beer. Just two years later, in 1323, he lifted the ban but set restrictions on imports. In the future, he insisted, all beer for Holland would have to pass through either Amsterdam or tiny Medemblik. The latter quickly faded as a port of entry, and by 1351 only Amsterdam was mentioned in a renewal of the restrictions. The count also insisted that all beer entering Holland pay a tax, one which proved to be rather lucrative for the him and his successors.[10] Presumably the count rescinded the 1321 order because of public pressure, that is, because of the popularity of hopped beer and because of loss of revenue to him from a decline in the trade in beer.

Another change made by the count in 1321 was that he allowed the production of hopped beer in Holland. His goal was to create a domestic industry which would replace imports. He made his own interests clear by taxing hops and doing so in a way that would guarantee that his income from taxes on beer consumption would stay the same. If, after 1321, brewers made beer with hops, the count required them to pay just as much tax as if they made the same quantity of beer with *gruit*. In 1351 the count set the tax on hops at one-fourth the tax on *gruit*,[11] suggesting that brewers used four times as much hops by volume as they did the old additive. Medieval beers were typically heavily hopped, and perhaps very heavily hopped in those early days while brewers in Holland got used to making the new type of beer.

In the first half of the fourteenth century, a number of Holland towns received grants that allowed their brewers to make hopped beer. Obviously it was the urban industry that wanted the right, the industry that had developed through the high Middle Ages. The arrival of the new type of drink created the problem of what to call it, a problem reflected in the grants. At Dordrecht brewers made hopped beer already in 1322. The new product they called *hoppenbier*, the old one *ael*. The distinction was continued in England in the following century. The word *beer* turned up in the thirteenth century in Flanders, but not until the fifteenth in France where the old term, *cervoise*, declined in use, replaced by *bierre*. The new word was in guild regulations in 1435 at Paris and elsewhere in 1429.[12] In England the word *beer* was also adopted from German-speaking regions of the Continent in the fifteenth century despite there having been an Anglo-Saxon word *beor*. The old word had by that time fallen out of use. *Ealu* was certainly the word preferred by the Anglo-Saxons who used *medu* for mead and *win* for wine. So there were clear distinctions among drinks and a clear hierarchy among them as well. *Beor* in English, at least by the eleventh century, had taken on a very different meaning, very possibly referring to a fermented drink make from fruit juice sweetened with honey. The drink was almost certainly stronger than mead or ale, falling second just behind wine in the hierarchy and probably consumed in smaller quantities than ale. *Bjórr* in Old Norse by the eleventh century probably had the same meaning, that is, a drink made from honey, to distinguish it from *öl*, a drink based on grain. While German lost the word *ale* in any form, it survived in England and Scandinavia. When hopped beer appeared in Scandinavia the new drink got the old name, *öl*. In England the new drink brought with it a German name and so through the Renaissance the old drink without hops was ale while the new drink with hops was beer.[13] In the Low Countries it seems brewers made hopped beer before the new word first turned up. The delay in the adoption of the word *beer* there, as elsewhere, may have had to do with the variety of different names used for the drink and with simple inertia, drinkers being slower to change their language than their habits.[14] The product of the new technology was not so dramatically different, it would seem, that it demanded an immediate linguistic response.

Urban brewers in Holland did develop hopped beer production but not quickly. By 1326 the town of Delft, which would become a major brewing center in the following century, had regulations on producing beer in what was called the eastern style. The rules limited the production of hop or turf beer, as it was also called, to winter, which meant from 1 October to 1 May. The practice continued until 1340 when the town dropped the restriction. The limitation suggests that Delft brewers had difficulty in changing to the new technology. It is possible, though, that since it was difficult to store the older type of beer through the summer, the town wanted to have a supply of the longer lasting hopped beer on hand in the warmer months in case the usual production of *gruit* beer decreased or stopped for any reason. It made sense to produce hopped beer in the winter and store it for later use. The problems of the changeover at Delft were not isolated. At Bruges, taxes on locally made *gruit* beer supplied 18 percent of town income in 1332–1333. Nearly sixty years later, 1391–1392, the share was down to 6 percent. The tax on hopped beer, both local and imported from Delft, on the other hand, made up 25 percent of town income by the later date (see Figure 7).[15] As elsewhere, the change to making and drinking hopped beer took time.

Local producers throughout Holland had difficulty in replacing imports, at least immediately. The technical innovation simply meant the replacement of one additive with another at one isolated point in the beer-making process. No special equipment was required, nor were there any changes needed in working habits or working relationships. Yet Dutch brewers were slow to adopt the new method. There were apparently a number of constraints. Imported Hamburg hopped beer was still sold widely through the fourteenth and into the fifteenth century. *Gruit* beer was still widely made and sold, competing with the new drink. The chemistry of hops is such that incorrect quantities of the herb can yield a poor taste and not do anything to preserve the beer. It may have taken brewers in Holland towns some time before they found the exact combination of hops, grain, water, and boiling time needed to produce something of the quality of Hamburg beer. Brewers could overcome the problems of adopting a new technique only slowly through experimentation. Government restrictions on the industry, in general, and low levels of production in individual breweries limited experimentation. The strong competition from imported Hamburg beer must have dampened enthusiasm for trying the new kind of brewing, but, more important, it must have decreased the chances brewers had to try out the new method and make mistakes from which they could learn. As hopped beer brewing spread through northwestern Europe, it proved necessary in each case to make some adjustments in order to acclimatize the new technique to local conditions. It appears that brewers in north German towns made hopped beer long before they started exporting the prod-

Figure 7. The home of the family of van Brugghe-van der Aa, Bruges, begun 1420.
The family was known as the lords of van Gruuthuse because they had the right to
sell *gruit*. They began building the house just as brewers were giving up the use of
gruit. There was a passageway into the neighboring Church of Notre Dame. Courtesy
of Stedelijke musea Brugge.

uct to the Low Countries. That suggests a period of slow development followed by mastery of the novel technique, a pattern repeated in Holland and elsewhere. For brewers, the interest in changing to hops depended not only on costs, which were often in the hands of the makers of tax legislation, but also on the ability to sell the new product to consumers. The sluggishness of brewers in changing to the new technology cannot be explained entirely by delays in getting government authorization. Competition from other drinks, the nature of hops, and consumer tastes must have created some difficulties.

Availability of hops was no constraint on producing hopped beer in Holland. The plant had long been known in the region and by the fourteenth century was grown widely in the northern Netherlands. Some Holland farmers found that they could grow hops commercially, selling them to the increasing number of local brewers. Hops were raised in town gardens like the *hoppecruydthoven* in Leuven, but such gardens could not meet the growing needs of the brewing industry, as was the case in the north German towns when the brewing industry expanded.[16] By the 1380s, Dordrecht was already a lively market for hops. Dordrecht traders sent hops to Haarlem and elsewhere in northern Holland, as did traders in Breda in the fifteenth century. When Dutch brewing expanded, producers went further afield and the southern Low Countries became a supplier of hops.[17] By the fifteenth century, hops for brewing in the northern Low Countries typically came from Brabant or from the Land of Heusden near Gouda in Holland where the soil was especially suited to the crop. The rise of hopped beer brewing was reflected in changes in farming patterns in the Heusden district. By 1391, if not earlier, hops were being grown as a field crop, replacing grain. Areas under hops were always small, absolutely and relatively, but cultivation was intensive and many villagers had their own small hop gardens. By the early fifteenth century, Heusden farmers were paying the lord of the district for measuring quantities of hops and were making contracts to supply fixed amounts on a regular basis to a nearby urban market. Producing the needed quantity of hops might not have been a problem, but maintaining quality was apparently a constant one as a dispute as early as 1340 at Delft showed. Regulations about the packing of hops to stop adulteration in 1643—322 years after hopped brewing was legalized in the county—show that maintaining quality continued to be difficult.[18]

Holland Hopped Beer Production

In Holland the great advances in beer production did not come until the end of the fourteenth century, some seventy to eighty years after the brewing of hopped beer became legal in the province. Beginning about 1390 the industry enjoyed rapid growth. Total beer production of the three biggest producing towns in Holland—Gouda, Delft, and Haarlem—may have already reached more than 11,000,000 liters at some point during the fourteenth century. The increase in production in the late fourteenth century in Holland was due not to breweries producing more beer, but to there being more breweries. Gouda in 1367 had at least twenty-six breweries and probably more since between 1367 and 1370 at least eighty-five different individuals were charged with violations of brewing bylaws which suggests more than eighty-five breweries. Before 1494, Delft had more than 200 breweries, Gouda 157, and Haarlem up to 112. All of them were small firms.[19] Those Dutch breweries in the fifteenth century supplied not only the domestic but also a number of foreign markets. For example, in the 1430s 55 percent of Haarlem production was sold outside the town. By the 1460s, in the face of competition from a number of other towns, that proportion was down to around 30 percent, but at the end of the sixteenth century, in the 1590s, the share was back up to about 65 percent of output. For Gouda, exports were even more important. Around 1500 only 10 percent of beer brewed in the town was consumed there, putting exports at about 15,000,000 liters per year on average.[20]

Evidence for a gradual shift to the production of hopped beer in the fourteenth century in Holland comes from the taxes levied on beer production by the towns. The old tax on *gruit*, the *gruitgeld*, gave way to *hopgeld* or *hoppegeld*. Another way for governments to maintain taxing levels in the face of the technical change was to convert the *gruit* tax to a tax on beer of any type based only on quantity, not on type or additive. To the south in the rural district around Bruges in Flanders, in 1380 *gruitrecht* changed into a charge per barrel.[21] Such fees, despite shortcomings, were to be typical of the future. The first tax on hops was levied at Delft in 1340 at a fixed fee for each ten barrels brewed. Similar taxes emerged in town after town throughout the county over the next one hundred years. One potential advantage of the change for towns was that monasteries and other institutions which had long enjoyed freedom from the *gruit* tax might have had to pay the new one.

Taxes on *gruit* disappeared in the course of the early fifteenth century. The income from the tax must have become so small as to make it simply not worth administering. On the other hand, hop tax income unquestionably rose, slowly in the fourteenth century, until the closing decades or decade, and then sharply. The increases were sustained. The *gruit* tax may have disappeared, but beer made with *gruit* did not. The old technology remained in place for some time, perhaps to satisfy conservative demand or to satisfy poorer consumers who could not pay for the better quality, but presumably more expensive, hopped beer. Many brewers obviously still made *ael* so there continued to be some income from holding the right to sell *gruit*. At Leiden in Holland (1343–

1344) the *gruit* tax brought in four and a half times as much as the tax on hops and in the following tax year almost eight times as much, but over the rest of the century the tax on *gruit* gradually disappeared. At Deventer in the eastern Netherlands in the 1340s, there was a *gruithuis* for the sale of *gruit*, but hops were already being grown in the area in 1325 and imported from as far away as Thuringia in 1348. By 1421, and probably well before that date, the men selling *gruit* also sold hops. At nearby Arnhem the first mention of a hops tax comes from the 1361/1362 accounts, and by the 1376/1377 accounts the old *gruit* tax was combined with and absorbed by the hop tax. In 1404 a bishop complained about the decline in income on the *gruit* tax at Zwolle not far away. The tax collector in Gouda commented in his accounts for 1468–1469 that the tax on *gruit* used to bring a sizeable sum, but it had not for many years because no one produced "*gruytebier*" anymore. On the other hand, the income from the tax on hopped beer had risen steadily since around 1360.[22] At Gouda and Delft, both export centers, by the 1470s *gruit* had largely disappeared from tax rolls, so it appears that the more beer that was sold at a distance the more hops were used.[23] Because authorities retained the old *gruit* tax in some cases long after hops had come to dominate the technology of beer making and because in some cases they rolled the old tax into the hop tax, it is often difficult to tell how long *gruit* continued in use. Still the general pattern of change in taxes in a number of towns in the northern Low Countries suggests that *gruit* remained in widespread use until the closing years of the fourteenth century and from then on, hops rapidly swamped its use.[24]

Towns in Holland also added to their taxes higher levies on beers from elsewhere to promote their own industries. The first signs of protection appeared soon after the adoption of hopped brewing. One reason probably was the great success of a few towns, Delft, Gouda, Haarlem, and Amersfoort, in producing hopped beer which flooded the Holland market and threatened, in the first instance, local producers in other Holland towns. Towns increasingly made distinctions in their accounts between beer brewed domestically and that brought from outside, another sign of growth in the exchange of beer. Towns were likely to be strictly protectionist. The count of Holland did, on at least one occasion, try to counteract that tendency. In 1411 he decreed that no town in Holland or Zeeland could levy any tax on imports from Delft over and above what they charged their own citizens. Beer was specifically the target.[25] The rule seemed to address an established and continuing problem. The count wanted to allow freer trade, to let the more efficient producers expand, and so, in the end, generate economic growth. In trying to break down the apparatus of protection he had only partial success. Towns imposed bans on imports not only as a way to promote their economies, they also exploited them as signs of their political independence from their overlords. No matter the source of protection, the result was a captive market for local brewers and an opportunity for them to increase sales.[26] It was a pattern that emerged in north Germany and one repeated in the northern Low Countries in Holland and in lands to the east of Holland. At Zutphen there was a direct tax on imported beer already in 1376, if not before, and Zwolle in 1370, and Tiel in 1371. The protectionist taxes in those towns, not far from places like Delft and Haarlem, coincided with the development of the export industries in Holland towns.

Towns and Beer Tax Income

What emerged in Holland—and over time in the rest of northern Europe in the wake of the development of the hopped beer brewing industry—was a system of excise taxes. The levies were on both the production and consumption of beer. The system, if the loose collection of different charges could be called a system, only became more complex over time. Back in 1274 the count of Holland granted Haarlem the right to levy an excise of a fixed amount for each brew produced in the town. In 1422, Haarlem brewers asked that the fee, called *brouwgeld*, be abolished. The answer was no and they were still paying the tax, at a higher rate, at the end of the fifteenth century. An excise at Dordrecht may well have predated the one at Haarlem. It appears that such early taxes were often temporary, but they were renewed, revived, and then often made permanent. They were not exclusive to beer or wine either. The 1274 grant to Haarlem included excise taxes on a wide variety of goods such as herring, grain, textiles, salt, and even services, such as carpentry work on boats. At 's-Hertogenbosch in Brabant, the town levied an excise tax on wine, beer, mead, and other special drinks sold at retail in 1445. The tax was to pay for a program to subsidize conversion to tile roofs. The idea was to decrease the risk of fire so the benefits were widespread among the townspeople. The town included a higher tax on beer coming from export centers, that is Haarlem, Hamburg, and Wismar.[27] Reactions like that of the town authorities in 's-Hertogenbosch to a short-term need for cash over time increased the incidence and frequency and variety of taxes on beer. Through the ensuing centuries, excise taxes would be a constant source of difficulty between brewers and governments. Finding the correct level was a small part of the problem. Administering the collection of the tax was another part that would prove a productive field for bureaucratic experiment.

    The transformation to brewing hopped beer brewing generated rising tax income for Low Countries towns. It also made towns dependent on, almost addicted to beer taxes because they became so important to urban finances.

The share of income which came from all taxes on beer increase
in the fourteenth century and even more so in the fifteenth
greater importance of beer and brewing to the budgets of tow..
greater interest on the part of urban governments in beer and brewing. On.
obvious and increasingly prominent result was greater town regulation of
more and more aspects of everything that brewers did. In the closing years of
the fourteenth century, town governments throughout Europe expanded their
competence. The increase in legislation was part of a general tendency, but it
was more extreme in the case of brewing. Brewing was probably the first trade
which faced limitations on its hours of doing business and on its standards of
production.[29] Certainly it was the first to be encased in a mass of legislation.
That pattern of regulation which first emerged in Hamburg and other north
German port towns, like the technology of making hopped beer, migrated to
other places to the west and south.

An essential part of legislation included restrictions to guarantee that all
excise taxes due on beer were paid in full. Regulations were to be repeated
many times. So, too, were rules on smuggling in beer without paying tax and
on serving beer outside the town walls, the effective city limits. Brewers were
typically prohibited from selling directly to consumers so officials could have
better surveillance of transactions and, thus, be sure that all excises got paid.
Brewers were allowed to keep a small portion of the beer they made tax free,
but that was only for their own consumption. The scope of the actions of officials responsible for the brewing industry increased as towns increased the
scope of regulation. Utrecht officials in 1392 already had the right to enter the
house of each brewer to check that the volume of beer being made was within
the law. At Dordrecht in 1401, the town laid down a series of regulations covering another important and recurring issue, the supply of barrels. The casks,
they said, had to be of the correct standard size and had to have the town
brand burned into them.[30] Schiedam brewers received a set of regulations on
the size and use of beer barrels as part of a general revision of bylaws in 1434.
Over time, the barrel of Delft would become the standard in Holland; other
towns, such as Hoorn, would insist that brewers use local barrels with local
marks but of the same size as those of Delft.[31] German port towns, not incidentally, were legislating on the use of casks in much the same way at about the
same time.

Beer and Dutch Economic Growth

The problems with taxes—their incidence, their varying rates, their avoidance,
and their being farmed—are reflected in the records of payments. Despite all

the difficulties with the sources it is still possible to say that output of beer in Holland rose in the fourteenth century and then rose sharply in the late fourteenth and through the fifteenth century. Tax data show a slow pace of development in hopped beer brewing in the fourteenth century and then rapid development in the fifteenth.[32] That followed precedents which were set in Hanse ports earlier and which would be followed later in the southern Netherlands and in England. Production had increased to such a degree that by 1450 brewing was by any measure of the day a big business and one of the great contributors to the rapid economic growth which Holland enjoyed, in contrast to so many other parts of Europe, in the fourteenth and the first half of the fifteenth century. The economy of Holland in general went through a broad range of structural changes in the fourteenth century. A massive number of often small reclamation projects undertaken over centuries meant that the peat bogs of the province had been extensively reclaimed and now were filled with dozens of settlements.[33] "In the period 1350–1400 Holland was completely transformed from a largely agrarian and rural society to an urban, commercial, and industrial one."[34] The most important export industry in that transformation was textile manufacturing, but beer brewing was undoubtedly in second place. The brewing industry was a significant contributor, as well as participant, in the emergence of Holland as the most important province in the northern Netherlands and in the rising income of the region. The traffic in beer may not have been the primary cause for the rise in economic importance of Holland in the fifteenth century, but it was certainly among the most important.[35]

Dutch breweries increased output in the century and a half preceding 1450 because they produced beer of high quality, or at least of a quality equal to that of imported German beer. Once Dutch brewers could match their competitors from Hanse towns, they could dominate their domestic market. Imports from Hamburg and the rest of Germany declined. Wars beginning in 1396 led to disruption of trade in the North Sea well into the second decade of the fifteenth century. Despite that and despite disputes between Holland and Hamburg around 1420, in 1421 an Amsterdam alderman still wrote in a letter about the group of Hamburgers in his town who carried on a lively trade in beer. The Duke of Burgundy became count of Holland in 1428. His powerful position in international politics and his successful conclusion of the Wendish War against the principal Hanse towns in 1441 finally brought a period of stability and peace along the trading routes of the North Sea. During that war the Estates of Holland had issued a prohibition of the import or sale of any beer brewed in any enemy town. Lübeck, Rostock, Stralsund, Wismar, and even Hamburg beer was included.[36] German beer exporters found it difficult to recover from that complete closing of the market. By 1445, with peace restored, the income from the Amsterdam toll on beer imports was nil. It did recover from that nadir but never returned to earlier levels. Hamburgers at a meeting in Utrecht to discuss trade, 1473–1474, blamed the decline of the toll on civic excise taxes in a number of Holland towns which discriminated against imported beer. Amsterdamers pointed out that exports of Hamburg beer for Holland and Zeeland were not, and had not for a long time, been directed exclusively through Amsterdam, so there had to be explanations other than the tax structure for the fall in Hamburg beer sales. Behind all the discussion lay the most important reason for the decline of the toll: effective competition from hopped beer brewed in Holland.[37] As the quality of Dutch beer improved, the quality of export beer from Hamburg and from Wismar went down, if consumer complaints from Flanders and from Norway are to be believed.[38] That decline helped Holland beer makers to win over consumers both at home and outside the county.

More important to Dutch brewers than sales in towns in Holland was success in export markets. After winning their own domestic markets next they turned to towns just to the east, like Deventer, where Holland beer was sold at fairs by the mid-fourteenth century. Next they turned to markets just to the north in Groningen and Friesland where there was little commercial brewing to compete with imports. Frisian traders by 1400 were carrying beer not from Hamburg to Holland, as they had for a century or more, but in the opposite direction from Haarlem to towns in Friesland and farther east along the North Sea coast. That was to become more common as the fifteenth century wore on. A sign of the change was negotiations between town governments in Friesland and Haarlem about such issues as the size of barrels.[39]

The making of, and the market for, hopped beer was urban. In the countryside there was virtually no market for the superior product, in part because of the higher price and in part because of the availability of beer made with other additives. In the fourteenth century, governments were not effectively able to regulate brewing by farm families. Hops grew wild in the woods or could be raised by farmers in small hop gardens, so the state could not control access to the plant. The authority of the counts was not pervasive. Much of the beer made in the countryside was never bought or sold. It was intended for domestic consumption or was bartered for other goods. So beer brewing prospered in the countryside in the fifteenth century. The cultivation of hops and also of barley, one of the principal grains used in brewing, increased.[40] It went on beyond the reach of regulation, taxation, and surviving records.

In general, changing real incomes in the late fourteenth century in the wake of the Black Death worked to the advantage of hopped beer brewers. A fall in grain prices not only reduced their costs and allowed the shift of food grains to industrial production from the making of bread but also increased the disposable income of many potential beer consumers in the towns. The extra money could be used to buy better and more varied foods like eggs, butter, cheese, meat, and beer. Though the gains in real income might be eroded over time, at least in the second half of the fourteenth and through the first half of the fifteenth century brewers could count on the price structure working for and not against them. The ability to experiment in a growing market made it possible by the close of the fourteenth century for brewers in Holland to produce the new type of beer as well as the experts, the brewers of Hamburg. By the early sixteenth century they were better at it. An Italian traveler in 1517 said of Holland, "The beer in these regions is better than in Germany and brewed in larger quantity."[41]

Brewing in the northern Low Countries in the fourteenth and fifteenth centuries changed from being dominated by household industry, as was the case in the early Middle Ages, and individual workshops, as was the case in the high Middle Ages, to being dominated by a new form of organization: nucleated workshops. The clustering together, especially in the export centers, of a large number of producers introduced greater efficiency through, if nothing else, easier access to raw materials. The brewers used middlemen or agents to handle the distribution of their products and could rely on specialists for getting their raw materials as well. Working close to one another the transfer of information, technical and commercial, was easier and even difficult to prevent. The competition among those brewers and in Holland among the towns which were so close to each other yielded ever higher levels of quality.[42] The brewers who experimented with hops in the fourteenth and early fifteenth centuries and finally figured out how to get the most from the new way of making beer, proved the source for the new form of industry and for its prosperity. From approximately 1380 through the middle of the fifteenth century, the brewing industry in the northern Low Countries grew rapidly in the wake of what was at first a gradual and then almost complete adoption of hopped beer brewing. This growth, together with the establishment of an extensive trading network supplying raw materials and giving access to markets for sale, laid the basis for the mature, large, growing, and highly competitive industry of subsequent years. It also brought hopped beer to other markets, inducing a shock similar to that experienced in Holland in the fourteenth century and resulting in the adoption of hopped-beer brewing in other parts of northern and western Europe.

Chapter 6
The Spread of Hopped Beer Brewing: The Southern Low Countries, England, and Scandinavia

Once Dutch brewers began to make hopped beer and sell it outside the county, the use of hops became popular, and even necessary, not just in Holland but also in nearby jurisdictions. The count of Holland made concessions on the use of hops rather early compared to his counterparts in the region of the lower Rhine where *gruit* was in widespread use. Changes in the law allowing brewers to use hops came in the second half of the fourteenth century in Flanders, Brabant, Utrecht, and Liege, all just to the south and east of the county of Holland. Changes in brewing practice followed, often slowly.

Shifting to brewing with hops was always done with the permission, if not the support, of the local and regional authorities. In 1364 the bishop of Liege and Utrecht acknowledged that over the previous thirty to fifty years a new way of making beer had become known which used an herb called hops. In the following year he levied a tax on hopped beer, with the permission of the emperor, and that was the first time he allowed people living in his lands to use the plant. He did insist that the tax paid be equivalent to what he had received before on the same volume of beer. As a result of the change, Liege brewers did so well that the town prohibited them from trading in money, that is in speculating in foreign exchange. In Flanders just a few years later, in 1380, the holders of the *gruit* tax even got the count to levy a new tax on imported beer, beer which was typically made with hops. The count's willingness to comply can be traced to the 50 percent of the new levy which he received.[1] In the same year Bruges got the owner of *gruitrecht*, Jan van Gruuthuse, to release brewers from compulsory purchase of *gruit*. The most important result was that they were then able to make hopped beer. In exchange, van Gruuthuse, whose family had gotten the name and wealth from ownership of *gruitrecht*, got a fee for each barrel of any kind of beer brewed in Bruges. In Brabant in 1378 the count agreed to the levying of a tax on beer made with hops at 's-Hertogenbosch. The grant appears to have applied throughout the county. At Diest brewers began to use hops at about the same time in imitation of German brewers but now also in imitation of Holland brewers. In the town, gardens formerly used to raise grapes for wine were turned over to hops. Though the *gruit* disappeared, the tax on beer retained the name *gruitrecht*. By the last quarter of the fourteenth century, brewers at Namur made beer with hops and early in the following century brewers in towns like Kortrijk and Lier made hopped beer in competition with imports from Holland.[2]

In general in towns in Westphalia, as earlier in Holland, Hamburg hopped beer had trouble making inroads because of the threat it posed to tax income for local authorities. They, in reaction, set up restrictions on imports. They also restricted or prevented local brewers from making beer with hops. Some German lords held out prohibiting the use of hops for a century or more after the count of Holland made his about-face. At Dortmund brewers still used *gruit* in 1447, but by 1477 they had gone over to hops.[3] As late as 1381, the archbishop of Cologne, since he held *gruitrecht*, tried to suppress the use of hops completely. Finally, in 1500 he did agree to take a rent in lieu of his right to tax *gruit* and then allowed the import and sale of hopped beer. It was not until the middle of the fifteenth century that a brewery outside of Nuremburg had taken up the use of hops which, along with evidence from Flanders and the Rhineland, suggests the new method of making beer only slowly worked its way south.[4]

Southern Low Countries Beer Imports

Flanders and Brabant had been the logical goals of Hamburg exporters in the years around 1300, and those were the logical places for fifteenth-century Dutch beer makers to find buyers for the hopped beers they produced. Flanders would remain the most important market for Dutch exports for some time. The replacement of German beer in the southern Netherlands in the late fourteenth century was a powerful motor for the expansion of Dutch brewing, for the shift in Holland from a local to an export industry and for the change from using *gruit* to using hops. Beer making in the southern Low Countries had already been an important source of welfare for townspeople there before 1350, but the industry declined in the late fourteenth and early fifteenth centuries in the face of competition from imports, principally from Holland but also from more traditional suppliers farther east.[5]

As late as 1411, Sluis, the port of Bruges, took some 9,000,000 liters of Hamburg beer. In fact, Hanse exports to Flanders rose more than tenfold from 1388 to 1411, moving from some 25 percent to about 90 percent of Flemish beer imports. The improvement was reflected in a growth in beer production in Hamburg. But the changed and heavy reliance on German sources for beer may have been more apparent than real. In 1392 the towns of Flanders suggested that the Hansards had been selling Dutch hopped beer and passing it off as their own so that it would enjoy their privileges.[6] That was the same year that the count of Holland gave Haarlem and Gouda permission to brew beer in the Hamburg style. The Dutch imitation at the end of the fourteenth century must have already been good enough to pass for the real thing. In 1392, two representatives sent by the Hanseatic League to Ghent met with the officers of the brewers' organization there to complain about beer from Holland being shipped to the town in casks from north Germany and sold in Ghent as "eastern" beer, much to the detriment of Hanse merchants and traders. The Hanse representatives asked the brewers and the Ghent town council if they had thought about the problem of counterfeit beer entering the town. The answer in both cases was a clear and unequivocal "no."[7] Dutch success in Flemish markets was not immediate, and Hanse exporters did hold on to a share of the market. That share declined markedly, however, in the first half of the fifteenth century.

The counts of Flanders had not always dealt favorably with Hamburg beer. In 1370 the count even issued a short-lived restriction on imports. In the following year, he prohibited the import of hopped beer and other foreign beers into Flanders, with the exception of Eastern beer and English ale, and in 1392, he extended the ban to the import of *des servoises de Hollande, appelez oppenbier*.[8] The prohibitions typically proved temporary. A much greater burden than those bans was the taxes levied on Hamburg beer, like those beginning in 1379. At Sluis in 1387, import duty was about 50 percent of the value of beer. The duty on Holland beer added a full 100 percent to its price, but even with that discrimination against it, Dutch beer still sold for less than other imports. The Dutch, being closer to Flanders than Hamburg, enjoyed lower transport costs. They also did not have to pay a number of tolls that Hanse shippers did when they brought their beer through Holland. In 1392, the year he stopped Dutch hopped beer imports, the count of Flanders set a maximum excise that could be charged on Hamburg beer and, subsequently, lowered the import duty as well. His actions must have lowered the price of Hamburg beer and made it better able to compete with Dutch beer, but any advantage gained was only temporary.[9] Rates of tax rose in the course of the fifteenth century.

Beer from Holland gained widespread acceptance rather quickly in the southern Low Countries. Dutch shippers had been carrying Hamburg beer from Amsterdam to the region well before hopped beer production began in Holland, so presumably it was easy for those carriers to replace the north German product with locally produced beer in their cargoes. Similarly, Hamburg shippers seem to have been able to carry Dutch beer in place of their own. In 1408, Lier, in Brabant near Antwerp, imported about three-fourths of its beer, and the imports came almost exclusively from Haarlem. Haarlem beer did well in the market because of the relatively favorable relationship of price to quality. Its alcohol content reached more than 7 percent and so was not cheap. It cost more than local beer in Lier but was half, or less than half, the price of imports from Germany.[10] In 1388, Bruges imported some 1,400,000 liters of Delft beer, three times the amount of mead and beer from Hanse ports combined. In that year Bruges brewers produced 6,549,900 liters of beer while all hopped and Dutch beer imports together totaled 2,577,750 liters. Dutch and other hopped beer imports were about 40 percent of local production, though that ratio dropped to just 10 percent in 1411. By 1397 there was even a broker for Holland beer at the port of Calais. In 1385 to 1386 Dunkirk imported more than 270,000 liters of hopped beer, mostly from Haarlem. In 1439 to 1443 the ratio of imports of Holland to Hamburg beer at Dunkirk was almost eleven to one. In Antwerp local brewers in 1418 to 1419 produced only 25 percent of the beer drunk in the town. Of the remaining three-quarters, 97 percent of the imports came from the town of Haarlem, a quantity of more than 1,500,000 liters. Antwerp authorities officially promoted local production of hopped beer in imitation of what came from Haarlem but, at least in the short run, they had little success.[11]

Hamburg exports to Flanders were burdened through the first half of the fifteenth century with increasingly higher duties. The reasons for levying them were financial, but the results made what was high-priced beer prohibitively expensive for many and made even wine a reasonable alternative. In 1435, Hanse merchants at Bruges complained that they were having to pay taxes in advance of sale, in a lump sum to the tax farmer. The merchants were not pleased with having to produce a large sum of money before they had a chance to get any income from sales.[12] In the 1450s, the Hanse was able to get some relief but it proved to be temporary. Taxes rose again in the last third of the century to even greater heights. While the counts of Flanders might levy such taxes for fiscal reasons, towns often did it to protect their own industries. The result was the same. For Hamburgers it was more and more difficult to find markets or even ports where they could trade in beer. In the 1470s, Hansards had complained to Ghent, Bruges, and Ypres about those three towns raising the charges on Hamburg and other eastern beers. After promising some relief, in 1478 Ghent raised the duties, contrary, the German merchants said, to their privileges and to an earlier commitment from the town. Another pledge to lower duties was not honored. What is more, Ghent prohibited citizens from buying Hamburg beer in large quantities. That forced the importers into the costly role of retailers, something they did not like. Ghent imposed a transit tax on Hamburg beer and insisted that an excise collector be present whenever such beer was sold. Ypres and Bruges also raised the tax on Hamburg beer, and they all insisted that the Hanse merchants pay the tax rather than the buyer, as was traditional. In 1493 the three towns agreed to a common and lower charge for each barrel of eastern or Hamburg beer imported, but by no means were all the other complaints dealt with and promises for further discussion appear to have led to nothing.[13] Hamburg tried in 1507 to get the Hanseatic League to lobby for a 50 percent reduction in the excise levied on her beer and all eastern beer in Bruges, Ghent, Ypres, Antwerp, Amsterdam, and all the towns of Flanders, Brabant, and Holland.[14] The plan succeeded no better than any earlier or later schemes to lower protection and open the door to German imports. The importance of Bruges as a port declined, not only because of the silting of the Zwin, but also because Hollanders supplanted Hansards in much of the carrying trade. The beer staple at Bruges declined with ships from Hamburg going instead to Holland, Zeeland and Antwerp. In Holland ports Hansards found little comfort. In the second half of the fifteenth century, Amsterdam increased taxes on Hamburg beer. When Hamburg threatened to move the beer staple, now very much in decline, there was no other town interested in offering tax advantages to Hamburgers to lure the staple. Three times between 1479 and 1504, Amsterdam made short-term prohibitions of the import of Hamburg beer altogether. Even so, in 1507 beer was the most important commodity carried by the thirty-three ships in the Amsterdam-Hamburg trade.[15]

Import Substitution in the Southern Netherlands

In 1485 Flanders imported beer at an annual rate of significantly more than 2,000,000 liters. Shiploads of beer from Holland made their way from Gouda, Delft, and Haarlem via Mechelen to Leuven in the early fifteenth century before Leuven brewers learned to imitate the hopped beer brought in from the north. Once they learned how, imports fell off markedly. Dutch sales to Antwerp and to markets in Flanders held up somewhat longer, in part because of the network of inland waterways.[16] The pattern in the southern Low Countries—gradual replacement of imports as local producers perfected the ability to make beer as good as that flooding in from other markets—was exactly like what had happened in Holland almost a century before. It was also similar in outline to what happened in England about a half century or more later and in Scandinavia and the eastern Baltic even later.

In Flanders and Brabant, production levels for hopped beer were slow to rise as had been the case in Holland. There was competition from old-style drinks. There were many variations on the traditional theme. Brewers continued to make a *gagelbier* which, presumably, was made with *gruit* and not hops. In Flanders when in making the beer or serving it, people could and did add various spices and honey or sugar to create a drink something like mulled wine with a pleasant color and taste.[17] More important in preventing, or at the very least deterring, the adoption of the new technique of making beer was the import of Holland hopped beer. Governments were also reluctant to allow hopped beer brewing. Resistance was greater the farther south and east the jurisdiction was from Holland. The final rise in hopped beer production in the Duchy of Brabant dates from second decade of the fifteenth century, that is about forty to fifty years after Holland had gone through the same change. Brewing had long existed in Brabant. In 1212, brewers were mentioned at Lier along with bakers and grocers as necessary to the people of what was then a new town, and a 1336 document refers to local beer, beer made with *gruit*. The first efforts at imitating hopped beer date from around 1365. The process spread slowly and unevenly, to Leuven in 1368, Mechelen and Vilvoorde around 1370, 's-Hertogenbosch and Helmond around 1380, Hoogstraten in 1391, Maastricht in 1394, Lier around 1400, and the biggest town, Antwerp, in 1408. Between 1400 and 1417, the imitation of Haarlem beer was officially encouraged in Antwerp, and at Mechelen in 1425 a local brewer set up a brewery to make beer in the Haarlem style.[18]

Leuven became the great center of brewing in the southern Low Countries. It was located near grain supplies and upstream from sizeable urban markets such as rapidly expanding Brussels. Leuven from the mid-sixteenth century sold its bright brown beer in increasing quantities in Brussels, Mechelen, Antwerp, and other export markets with the maximum level reaching some 1,950,000 liters a year. The Leuven industry was so successful that in the sixteenth century grape growing was driven from the nearby countryside as farmers went over to raising grain to supply brewers' malt. At Leuven as late as 1378, tax records show brewers made seventy-seven times as much *gruit* beer as hopped beer. In 1408 the volume of unhopped beer was still about four and one half times as much as that of hopped beer. By 1422 the relationship had turned around, and tax records show brewers produced 2.6 times as much hopped beer as *gruit* beer. By 1436 they were making only hopped beer.[19] Leuven production in 1372 was about 4,600,000 liters and it hardly changed over the next century, reaching 4,740,000 liters in 1472. In 1522 it had risen to 7,700,000 liters. This was still well below the Gouda total, which in the 1480s averaged 26,400,000 liters, or the Haarlem total which in 1514 was about 20,000,000 liters.[20] In 1524 production at Leuven had fallen again and so was hardly more than it had been in the late fourteenth century. There, as elsewhere, the industry was subject to substantial fluctuations from year to year. As in most other towns, the growth in beer brewing at Leuven had a massive impact on urban finances. Between 1348 and 1570 the share of taxes on beer in the town income tripled. During the same period, the share coming from taxes on wine fell by half.[21]

By the end of the fourteenth century brewing changed in Lier—and in a number of other Brabant and Flanders towns—from a domestic industry producing beer without hops to one which produced hopped beer for local drinkers. In 1380 the duke of Brabant changed the old *gruit* tax to an excise tax on each brew and each barrel of imported beer. The tax was neutral in that it applied to beer made with *gruit* or with hops. Hopped beer imported from Haarlem was the model for the first Lier hopped beer, that is, for the grains used and the mix of those grains. At first Lier hopped beer was of poor quality, so imports declined only slowly. Lier brewers asked town authorities for some kind of protection since they knew they could not compete directly with beer from Holland. In the first two decades of the fifteenth century, the town government complied with the request using all possible methods to improve and support local brewing. Anyone setting up a brewery received a tax rebate of 50 percent in the first year. From 1417 on, all foreign beers were taxed at a higher rate than local beer. There is no doubt the town set out to stimulate the local industry. Policy changed dramatically in 1424 and 1425, however. There were no more tax reductions for new brewers and a drop in taxes on imported beer. The action was presumably a response to complaints about the poor quality of locally produced beer. Beginning in the 1440s, though, the town was able to return to a policy of protection, raising taxes on imports faster than on locally produced beer. After 1440, when Gouda beer made great inroads in Brabant, Lier brewers imitated it as well and the town raised duties on Gouda beer coming in from Holland. As time went on, Lier brewers were able to make a good-enough imitation of Holland beers that imports were increasingly just luxury beers from Germany. In the first decades of the fifteenth century, average monthly imports from Hamburg and Baltic coast towns to Lier were between 2,000 to 4,000 liters and in 1474 to 1475 the figure was down to about 1,700 to 1,800 liters. Comparing production figures of 1408–1409 and 1473–1475 at Lier, the success of the local industry is obvious. Production per year on average went from 470,000 liters to 830,000 liters and imports fell from about 75 percent of total consumption to 25 percent and then to about 7 percent by 1500. Average production per brewery went from about 4,300 liters per year in 1408–1409 to about 9,800 liters per year in 1473–1475. Despite the growth in the Lier industry, it was still relatively small. The number of breweries remained low. In the 1470s there were still only six or seven, fewer than at the start of the fifteenth century. Growth slowed in the late fifteenth century because import substitution was virtually complete and because the tax burden on beer and everything else rose with the wars of the period.[22]

In the southern Netherlands it was not only in the bigger towns where hopped beer brewing expanded. In 1513 Leuven itself imported about 78,000 liters of beer from Hoegaarden, a small enclave of the bishopric of Liege in the duchy of Brabant, an enclave which was able to ignore rules of both Liege and Brabant about brewing, In 1541 Antwerpenaars consumed almost 170,000 liters of beer from Hoegaarden and the small village of Zoutleeuw. *Hoegaards* was drunk in Mechelen, Diest, Tienen, and many villages in Brabant as well as in Ghent and Veurne. Zoutleeuw exports to Antwerp began before 1519 and rose until 1555 when they hit a maximum of 1,300,000 liters. Zoutleeuw beer was relatively strong, which made it more durable as well as more valued. Another small town, Diest, exported beer in the mid-sixteenth century but not more than 130,000 liters a year, which was some 9 percent of production there. In Flanders the undistinguished town of Menen had 104 brewers around 1520, and Rijsel (Lille) had thirty large breweries in 1540.[23] The smaller centers enjoyed a measure of success in the sixteenth century because the ability to brew hopped beer was widespread, because there was a ready market for the product, and because the tax burden was lighter in villages like Zoutleeuw and Hoegaarden (see Figure 8).

Compared to Brabant, the Flanders brewing industry was always small even after taking on producing hopped beer. It is true that the county had significant local production, but it continued to rely on imports, first from Germany and Holland and then, in the fifteenth century, from the growing industry in Brabant. In the 1490s, the ruler of the day estimated imports to Flanders to be as much as a fourth of total sales. High-priced luxury beers from England and Germany continued to enjoy a steady, if very small, sale. At Ghent in 1520 beer imports made up about 20 percent of total beer consumption. From 1505 to 1542, the volume of imports ranged from 2,700,000 to 3,000,000 liters each year. Local brewers' continued growth in the sixteenth century, combined with the troubles associated with the Dutch Revolt, led to an ongoing drop in imports. By the first two decades of the seventeenth century at Ghent, beer imports had fallen to zero.[24]

The shock of imports generated a hopped beer brewing industry in Brabant and later in Flanders. The slow geographical expansion of the industry in the southern Low Countries—from central Brabant westward toward the coast—may, in part, be explained by problems of supplies of good quality water, always a concern for brewers and especially in low-lying regions. Across the North Sea it was not a problem with raw materials which slowed the growth in hopped beer brewing, but consumer taste and government regulation. The earlier success of traditional brewing in England in the fourteenth century made it less susceptible to the pattern of development that prevailed in the southern Low Countries.

Figure 8. Brewers weighing barrels of beer, c. 1500, with brewers at work in the background. This stained glass window by Arnold van Nijmegen from the southern Low Countries commemorates the importance of the trade in the town. Cathedral Notre Dame, Tournai. Reprinted from Jean Helbig, *Les Vitraux médiévaux conservés en Belgique, 1200–1500* (Brussels: Imprimerie Weissenbruch, 1961), fig. 142, p. 257.

Hops and English Brewing

English brewers produced good-quality ale for centuries before hopped beer appeared. English beer was good enough to be thought a worthy present for a king of France in the late twelfth century as part of a diplomatic mission. Still from the thirteenth and into the fifteenth century, a reputation for poor quality hounded the drink. At the later date it may be that English ale, made without hops, was perceived in France as not being up to the caliber of good beer.[25] The English brewing industry had enjoyed expansion and tendencies toward commercialization and concentration in the second half of the fourteenth century despite any perceived deterioration in quality. The economic impact of the Black Death, falling grain prices and rising consumption per person, increased profits. Commercial brewing expanded, especially in towns and especially in the southeastern part of England. The economic forces unleashed in the second half of the fourteenth century combined with a general tendency toward greater specialization to decrease the number of beer makers and to make brewing less likely to be done incidentally or in addition to regular household duties. The process was both accelerated and complicated by the introduction and slow advance of the brewing of hopped beer.[26]

It has been said, incorrectly, that it was the Dutch who brought hopped beer to England for the first time in 1400, to the port of Winchelsea. In fact, the export of beer from Holland and Zeeland to England existed throughout the fourteenth century, if not much earlier. Around 1289 a Norwich man was charged with selling "Flanders beer privily." The distinctive name suggests that it may have been hopped beer.[27] The English market was already a target for Dutch beer exports in the early fourteenth century before brewers in either place were familiar with the use of hops. The exchange was on a somewhat equal basis and, if anything, more beer went east to Holland than west to England. The exports of ale made without hops went from England to Zeeland and Flanders, as well as Holland. Though Lynn was a center for such exports, it was not the only destination for beer from the Low Countries. By 1380, or very soon after, Dutch beer was a common cargo for England. Ships coming from the northern Netherlands to east coast ports through the later fourteenth century carried beer almost incidentally. It was mixed in with cargoes of herring, wood, or floor tiles and went to Hull, Newcastle, Yarmouth, or London. Not all ships from Holland carried beer and few carried beer in large quantities, but frequently skippers filled out their cargoes with beer of varying value.[28] Some Dutch skippers got into trouble for failing to pay import duties levied on Dutch beer. Some got into trouble because English sailors seized their goods in what later might be called acts of piracy.[29] Dutch exporters may have also sent beer to England through Calais where they could trade it for English wool. More likely, though, they shipped beer directly to east coast ports. Over time, it became hopped beer they shipped. Yarmouth, in the twelve months starting on 1 May 1398, saw the import of 103,000 liters of hopped beer. Presumably one market for the growing quantities of the product was the alien population of southeast England composed largely of immigrants from the Low Countries accustomed to hopped beer. English beer imports seem to have fallen off in the 1410s, perhaps a first sign that brewers in England were beginning to produce hopped beer.[30]

Beer brewing, as opposed to ale brewing, was centered in London. The first mention of making hopped beer in England is in the London City Letter-books from 1391. Beer brewing started as an operation largely for foreigners run by foreigners. After 1400, alien beer brewers began to settle in other English towns but there were still very few of them outside of London. Beer brewers were able to prosper there because of the resident alien market, the lower prices at which they offered drink, and their ability to supply the army and the navy. In 1418 when the agents of King Henry V bought supplies for the English army besieging Rouen, they found that a barrel of beer cost only two-thirds as much as a barrel of ale. Low Countries immigrants dominated beer production and trade in England through the sixteenth century, with a complaint about aliens controlling the beer trade coming as late as 1607. Even in 1574 more than half of London's beer breweries were owned and operated by aliens. The "Dutch," as they were called, brought not only a new type of beer, but a larger scale of production and more complex systems of organiza-tion. Though in the Low Countries a large proportion of brewery workers were women, the immigrant population was largely male so men dominated hopped beer brewing.[31]

Resistance from public authorities delayed the adoption of hops in beer making in England. Opposition to producing the new kind of beer seems to have come principally from established ale makers who saw hopped beer and its brewers as threats to their livelihoods. English ale brewers feared, rightly, that the efficient brewers of beer would make inroads into their traditional market. In 1436 some breweries operated by Dutchmen were attacked. The sheriffs of London in response issued a writ saying all beer brewers should continue with their trade, despite attempts by locals to prevent natives of Hol-land and Zeeland, as well as others, from making beer by saying that it was poisonous, not fit to drink, and caused drunkenness. Not surprisingly, conflict over beer brewing was always greatest in the capital, where immigrant brewers made the most hopped beer.

When beer brewers started out, they were, unlike ale brewers, free from any official inspection or control so in 1441 King Henry VI appointed two men, with no experience of the trade, as surveyors and correctors of beer brewers throughout the kingdom. The inspectors received from the crown the power to take a halfpenny for every barrel that they or their appointees passed as good. In 1461 the London "mistery of berebruers," an informal group, was asked to elect two men to act as searchers to guarantee compliance with rules of good conduct. The group had obviously grown. In 1484 ale brewers had the City of London lay down restrictions on what they could use in making any ale, presumably to improve quality and so allow ale brewing to survive in the face of competition from higher quality hopped beer. The regulations reinforced and institutionalized the distinction between the brewers of true ale and those making beer. That clear distinction, established in the reign of King Edward IV, was to continue to the reign of Queen Mary I in the mid-sixteenth century. In 1493, probably in part as a reaction to the rules of ale brewers, beer brewers became a definite guild.[32]

The use of herbs instead of hops could be durable, judging from what happened in the countryside throughout northern Europe and especially in England in the fifteenth and sixteenth centuries. There ale, that is beer made in the old way without hops, remained popular especially for women and older drinkers and also for certain times of the year. Lambswool was Christmas ale made with roasted apples, nutmegs, ginger, and sugar. It got its unique name from the froth that floated to the surface. Other additives used to spice the ale included eggs and toast. Since tax records are silent about such a drink, presumably it was only made on a few festive occasions. Ale, without hops, still had its defenders in England as a superior drink and not just among the brewers who adhered to traditional methods. Despite the success of beer brewers in England in the course of the fifteenth century, there was a continued dislike of and agitation against hops. At Norwich, for example, its use, along with that of *gawle* which may have been an herb mixture, was prohibited in 1471. In 1519 Shrewsbury authorities outlawed the use of hops, calling it a wicked and pernicious weed.[33] The actions may have reflected more than xenophobia or resistance to novelty but, rather, a reflection of a desire to maintain the standard and quality of old English ale (see Figure 9). Andrew Boorde in his *Compendyous or Dyetary of Health* published in 1545 said that ale was a natural drink for Englishmen while beer was a natural drink for Dutchmen and much used in England to the detriment of many English people because beer makes men fat and inflates the stomach. That was his explanation for Dutchmen's fat faces and bellies. He also claimed that beer would kill those with colic. Accounts of an English noble house from as late as 1548 show that ale was still brewed for the sick, the young, ladies, and a few others who preferred the sweeter ale to beer.[34] A contemporary visiting jurist from Brandenburg said that in England the general drink was ale made from barley. He found it to be strong and intoxicating. In 1597 one English writer, arguing against the use of hops, suggested wormwood as a good alternative, but the idea never gained currency. On the other hand, in 1577 William Harrison in his *Description of England* spoke contemptuously of the old ale, saying it was thick and fulsome, calling it "an old and sick man's drink" and claiming it was only popular with a few consumers. He took the use of hops for granted. Beer had supporters, but the antipathy for, and fear of, the new product did not disappear even

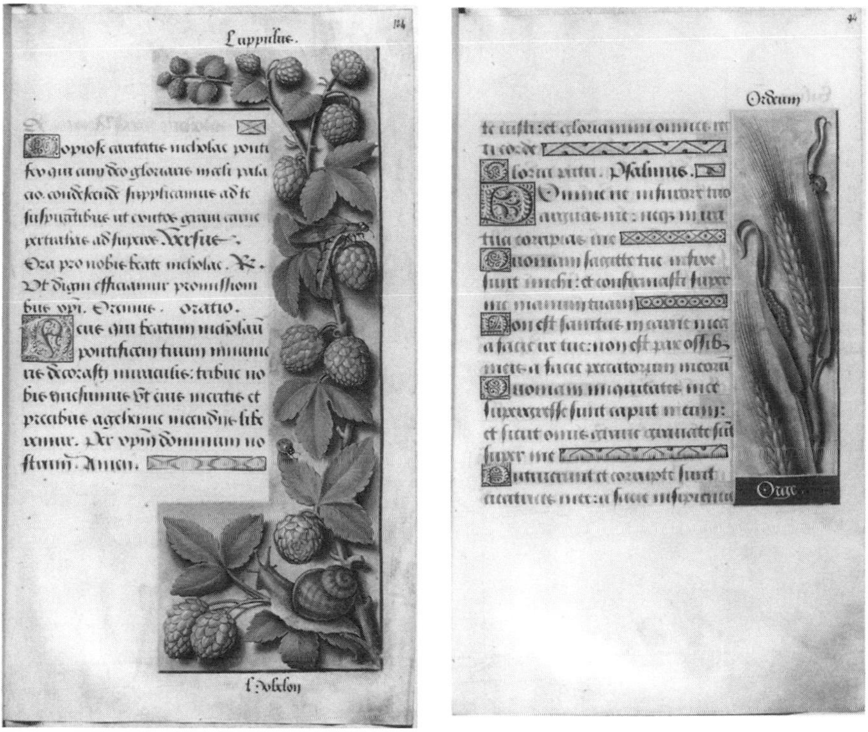

Figure 9. Barley (fol. 184) (*right*) and hops (fol. 94) from a book of hours of Anne of Brittany by Jean Bourdichon (c. 1457–1521). Tempera on parchment. Bourdichon was one of the greatest artists of his day. He decorated the margins of the 238 folios with various flowers, plants, and trees. At the time that English brewers wondered about hops, they were well enough known in France to be pictured in a book for a French queen. Courtesy of Bibliothèque national de France, Paris, Ms. Latin 9474.

after beer became well established as a popular drink. As late as 1662 in Derby-shire hopped beer brewing was remembered as an innovation within living memory so, especially in domestic brewing, the introduction of the novel additive in brewing came slowly. An early seventeenth-century writer claimed that a quarter of wheat would produce eight gallons of ale but eighteen gallons of beer.[35] Sheer economics in the end sealed the fate of unhopped beer, as it had elsewhere in Europe as much as four centuries earlier.

In the case of England, the import of the new technology was embodied in the brewers who immigrated into the country. It is the only case, it appears, in northern Europe in the later Middle Ages where in the first instance it was not domestic brewers who imitated the new method but rather skilled and experienced practitioners from elsewhere who transferred the technology to new surroundings. Almost all beer brewers mentioned in fifteenth-century

England had foreign names. In a tax levied on aliens in 1483, brewhouse masters were a separate category paying tax at a higher rate than common householders. Such men would typically have on the order of ten servants, aliens as well, working for them in the brewhouse. A 1531 act of Parliament said that alien brewers were exempt from penal statutes against foreigners practicing their trade in England.[36] In that case, as earlier, the government acted to protect beer brewers against actions by the defenders of the old technology. The government also recognized the continuing role and durable presence of foreigners in the making of beer.

In England, as in the Low Countries, it took time for the hopped beer industry to develop, for brewers to make the switch and acclimatize themselves to the new process. In the counties of Kent and Sussex, the first to be exposed along with London, to the influx of hopped beer from the Netherlands, the changeover to the new technique moved across the countryside from town to town to village. That march through east Sussex, it seems, was complete by the end of the fifteenth century. In 1520 the town of Coventry, in the Midlands and some distance from those early sites of beer brewing, with a population of 6,600 had sixty public brewers making hopped beer. It was not perhaps until the mid-sixteenth century, however, that hopped beer dominated English brewing and beer consumption. The acceptance of the beer barrel, four gallons larger than the ale barrel, as the standard for the brewing industry in that same 1531 act of Parliament which dealt with alien brewers was a clear sign of the dominance of hopped beer.[37] The sharp distinction between beer and ale brewers of the fifteenth century, once a distinction defended by the makers of ale and governments, had disappeared in the sixteenth century. By 1556, the beer brewers had absorbed the society of ale brewers of London in an umbrella group that covered all brewers. Presumably, ale brewers by that time formed such a small portion of the total brewers, or produced such a small portion of total drink, that there was no need for them to maintain a separate organization. By the 1570s the largest ale brewers in London produced only about as much drink annually as the smallest of the beer brewers.[38]

Hops were in ever increasing demand as the English hopped beer industry developed. Through the port of Antwerp, and also through Bergen-op-Zoom, high-quality hops from Brabant and the Land of Heusden made their way across the North Sea. Exports to England began around 1438. Quantities were originally small but grew significantly over the course of the fifteenth century.[39] As late as 1563, the chronicler John Stow said that the failure of the hop harvest in Zeeland forced English brewers to go over to using bayberries or broom instead to flavor their beer. Hops were not grown in England until early in the sixteenth century, so as hopped beer production rose in England so, too, did imports from the Low Countries.[40] Once beer brewing was well established, domestic production of hops began to replace imports.

By the mid-sixteenth century despite resistance from government, consumers, and traditional brewers, the hopped beer brewing industry in England had achieved a maturity similar to that already known in Low Countries and Germany. An English writer on hops in 1574 simply said that his countrymen had given up ale for beer, so a victory had been won, but the war was not yet completely over. Pockets of ale making held out in England as they did elsewhere in northern Europe for some time. English beer brewing still showed its Dutch origins in the use of the word *gyle* to describe the fermenting wort, a simple adoption of the Netherlandish word *gijl*. The English variant of the word was certainly in use through the seventeenth century and probably later. A German visitor to London in the 1590s said that people there drank beer as fine and clear in color as old Alsatian wine, so obviously, whatever the language or its origins, by the end of the sixteenth century English brewers had learned to make high quality hopped beer.[41]

Beer and Hops in Eastern Europe and Scandinavia

In areas of Slavic speech, *pivo* was the word for hopped beer. The word seems to be related to the verb which means to drink and to have Greek roots. Using a noun for that higher quality beer (which meant little more than just a drink) leaves the impression of fairly common and widespread consumption. All other evidence, however, would seem to suggest the opposite. It is the case that people in Poland may have also known the drink in the early Middle Ages since hops turn up in some quantity in archeological sites from the period. Hopped beer may have been made first in Russia in the thirteenth century, supplementing lower strength and lower quality drinks like mead and *kvas*. Mead was certainly known and drunk in Poland around 1000 but it was not in the same category by any means as *kvas*. Despite its being better than the most common and easily made drink, mead was still understood to be inferior to hopped beer. That higher-quality drink no doubt appeared in Poland at just about the same time as brewers in north German port towns perfected the skill of making a hopped beer consistently good enough for export. The word *braga* even in the nineteenth and twentieth centuries, meant home-brewed beer, that is made without hops. The practice of making the drink almost certainly long predates 1800. *Braga* is presumably related to the Celtic word *brace*. It probably owes nothing to the English word *barkott* or *braggot*, a spiced ale, other than perhaps some common Celtic root.[42]

Kvas, on the other hand, may have sources in Sanskrit but presumably has no cognates in western European languages. The word appears in a number of Slavic languages to describe anything that had soured. The word could be and was applied to any item that was pickled. *Kvas* got its taste from infection by airborne lactic-acid bacteria, which would cause the beverage to sour, and infection by yeast, which would cause the beverage to have alcohol. A Lithuanian barley beer called *alus* appears to have been similar, though it may have had a higher alcohol content. The alcohol content of *kvas* was always low. It may, in fact, have been similar to the beer produced in ancient Mesopotamia. Flavoring with various roots and herbs might give it both a distinctive taste and a somewhat greater life expectancy. Barley was the traditional raw material for *kvas*, but it was made from almost anything that would produce the sugars needed for fermentation. *Kvas* was always produced in rural homes for domestic consumption. It was a peasant drink. The same was true of *oskola*, a beverage made in Poland flavored with sap from birch trees and other fermentable matter. Enough carbohydrates were used to get a relatively high alcohol content. Especially in towns along the Baltic it was hopped beer, rather than root beer, which enjoyed growing popularity at least from the thirteenth century on. *Pivo*, as the hopped beer was called, lasted longer and had a more consistent taste. Hopped beer drove domestically produced drinks, whether *kvas* or *braga* or mead, farther and farther east in the Baltic, Bohemia and probably in the Danube Valley in the later years of the Middle Ages. Even so the weaker beers flavored, if they were flavored at all, with various roots retained their place as day-to-day drinks in the Russian Empire and perhaps elsewhere long after the Middle Ages.[43] Hopped beer may have dominated many urban markets, but its inroads in the countryside in eastern Europe were less extensive than in the west.

With the necessary raw materials present, it is not surprising that commercial brewing of hopped beer began in Scandinavia. What is surprising is that records of the practice begin to appear rather late, that is in the sixteenth century. The records for Scandinavian brewing development are best for government enterprises, centers of official production. Gustavas Vasa, for example, set up a royal brewery at Uppsala, about 1540, to make beer in the Hamburg style and also to make Danziger beer. There was a brewery in Stockholm castle at an even earlier date. In 1554, it produced over 1,600,000 liters of beer, virtually all of it for the consumption of castle residents which included the court. There were private, that is nonroyal, breweries in the period as well but little information about them has survived. A campaign, beginning in the middle of the sixteenth century, against drink worked against the growth in beer sales. Gustavas Vasa laid down regulations for the production of beer in his Swedish kingdom in 1558, setting the types to be brewed, the proportions of ingredients, and the prices. Olaus Magnus in his *Historia de gentibus septen-*

trionalibus published in Rome in 1555 described the brewing process in the north. The regulations, the description of the process, as well as the changes made in brewing in Sweden and Finland in the sixteenth century, all indicate that the impetus for the rise of brewing and the technology used came from Germany and especially from north German towns which exported beer to Scandinavia.[44]

In Denmark, Copenhagen got a royal brewery to supply the court, the navy, the overseas trading companies, and to a limited degree the public, but it was not until 1616 that the extremely active King Christian IV set up the establishment. Another sign of changes in international production patterns was that the king did it with the help and advice of a master brewer who was not from Germany but Amsterdam. By the 1640s the brewery had a staff of thirty-five, including a swineherd to look after the pigs. Production in the single brewery could run up to around 3,200,000 liters per year, an impressive figure. It seems, though, that those levels of output were reached only after the brewers of Copenhagen leased the plant from the king in 1739 and after it was rebuilt in 1767 in the wake of a destructive fire [45] In the seventeenth century operations were on a smaller scale.

The comparatively long delay in Scandinavia in going over to commercially brewed hopped beer may have been a result of the success of domestic brewers through much of the Middle Ages. They still produced beer of reasonable quality and strength using other herbs and traditional methods. It could also be that the spread of beer brewing in Scandinavia was slowed by the poor internal communications which typify the region. Markets for all goods, including beer were usually limited. With almost no exceptions towns were few and small. Large-scale production often did not make economic sense; retaining traditional methods did. German traders had established themselves in seaborne commerce so it was difficult for Scandinavian beer producers to compete effectively. German brewers in Lübeck, Wismar, Rostock, and elsewhere had the capacity and the ability to produce high-quality beer in sufficient quantities to satisfy the Scandinavian market, and German shippers could deliver it to port towns. The developed grain markets of the Hanse ports and the shipping network they developed always meant German brewers could get barley or wheat more easily than their Scandinavian counterparts. Norway had to import grain in the sixteenth century from Hanse towns to make bread. It is unlikely that Norwegian brewers with ambitions to compete in urban markets could have gotten the grain they needed at prices anything like those paid by German brewers.[46] The small size of the market, combined with political and economic circumstances, worked to slow the pace of adoption of hopped beer brewing in Scandinavia.

Brewing in late medieval and Renaissance northern Europe became modern in that success came from adaptation to technical advance, to exploiting opportunities created by innovations in the product. Success was based on borrowing from others, on imitating practice elsewhere, and then improving that practice, even if slowly, once the new technology was adopted. Brewing also became like modern industries in that success, both technical and economic, was based on being part of a network of trading, of exchange of goods and information. That was most obvious in the case of Dutch brewing but, in fact, it was just as true for England and Brabant and probably Germany as well. Brewing was not modern, however, in the ways in which technology was developed and improved. Innovation was slow. Advances came, if at all, through painstaking trial and error, often, it would appear, with significant losses to brewers because of mistakes they did not understand. Brewing was modern but also medieval in the importance of government regulation to the development of the industry, both economically and technologically. Governments took an active interest in the industry which became an even greater interest when the brewers were more successful. Once fully in command of the new technique and with a mature industry, brewers throughout northern Europe carried on, both by design and by default, a series of experiments leading to innovations in the process of making beer, in order to exploit fully the opportunity created by the addition of hops to the brew. That was the sixth stage in the development of the industry in the fifteenth and sixteenth centuries. Experimentation to refine techniques and business practices would dominate the development of brewing through the Renaissance and in the process create technical, structural, social, and economic problems for brewers, town governments, and consumers.

Chapter 7

The Mature Industry: Levels of Production

The years from around 1450 to the early seventeenth century were a golden age for brewing. Though levels of output as well as the number and size of breweries varied—from Flanders to the Celtic Sea to northern Scandinavia to Estonia and Poland to Austria to the upper reaches of the Rhine River—brewing expanded in those years. It grew as population increased. In some places in northern Europe, it grew faster than the population. It enjoyed unprecedented economic success. Beer invaded new parts of Europe, claiming or reclaiming territory where wine was the preferred drink. The higher quality of hopped beer compared to its predecessors, the greater efficiency of producers over time, and improved distribution all combined to make beer an increasingly popular drink.

With acclimatization of the process of making hopped beer came signs of brewers gaining full mastery of the new technology. Figures for production and for export suggest that such mastery was achieved around 1300 in north Germany, around 1390 in Holland, around 1470 in the southern Netherlands, and after 1500 in England. The level of hopped beer exports is often the best indicator of maturity in dealing with the novel dominant technology. The level of regulation, the degree of institutionalization, and the refinement of ways of dealing with the new technique also serve as indicators of maturity, although such developments did lag behind growth in production and in exports. For Germany, the evidence comes almost exclusively from the level of exports. For Holland, signs of a mature industry appear in the first half of the fifteenth century and the principal indicator is exports, in that case exports to Flanders and England. In England the shift in both production and consumption from ale to hopped beer by the mid-sixteenth century suggests that brewers had command of the new technique. By that time there are also a number of references to export of beer from England. A 1543 act of Parliament prohibited the export of beer in anything larger than a barrel, and every beer exporter had to import an amount of wood equal to what he exported as a beer barrel. The goal was to protect wood supplies in the kingdom. No one expected those beer barrels would ever to return to England. The legislation indicates England exported a sizeable amount of beer by then. Enough beer went out of the country that some seventy-four years later English beer was famous in the Netherlands and lower Germany where towns prohibited the sale of English beer to protect their own brewers. In Delft one English traveler claimed brewers tried to imitate English beer but could not create anything comparable to the English because the sea voyage from his homeland gave the beer a better taste.[1]

Higher levels of production meant brewers could reduce costs with a larger scale of production. The investment in the brewery but also in the maltery could be spread across a greater volume of output. The doubling of the number of brews annually could be achieved with virtually no increase in fixed costs, at least in the short term. The rise in export volume implied scale economies in shipping services as well. Vessels could travel with holds nearer to capacity and at no increase in cost. When sales rose and returns to investment increased, brewers also discovered a potential for greater capital investment in the industry. With rising levels of output it became easier to capture all the advantages of specialization which had existed back in the twelfth and thirteenth centuries when brewing first came to towns.

The Victory of Beer

The beer border, that imaginary line between areas where drinkers more commonly chose beer over wine, moved south. The process, which started even before the invasion of German hopped beer in Holland in the early fourteenth century, was repeated again and again in the southern Low Countries, the Rhineland, and then in Bavaria and Bohemia. The milder weather in southwestern Germany had favored the production of wine, but changes in the relative prices of wine and beer combined with efforts by both governments and private individuals to raise beer consumption in grape-producing regions led to positive results over time for beer.[2] Wine became more of a luxury or festive drink while beer became the daily beverage, often for no other reason than price. Beer prices in Germany fell in the fifteenth century by about 50 percent over the one hundred years. In the following century, prices of both beer and wine rose, beer prices if anything increasing more rapidly. Consumers commonly shifted to drinking less expensive beers. Even if the price advantage of beer was eroded, the erosion was less in southern Germany than in the north, and beer was still, in terms of volume, much less expensive in most places than wine. From 1590 to 1620 in Nuremberg a liter of wine cost as much as 6.1 liters of beer and at Vienna as much as 4.5 liters of beer. At Strasbourg in the same period wine cost only 1.2 times as much as an equivalent quantity of beer, so beer had trouble penetrating regions to the west and into France.[3] Wine consumption fell in the Low Countries in the fifteenth and sixteenth centuries, in large part because beer was relatively inexpensive. The price of wine was such

that daily consumption was simply out of the question even for skilled laborers. That became even more true as governments typically increased taxes on
wine. In area after area, the improving quality of beer drove out marginal wine
and marginal wine producers.[4] If Flanders had ever belonged to the Mediterra-
nean world of wine drinking, by the end of the fifteenth century only historians resorting to myth would suggest that to be true.[5] Flemings by 1500 were
beer drinkers.

In 1487 Duke Albert IV of Bavaria issued a regulation for the making of
beer in Munich, saying that only barley, water, yeast, and hops could be used.
That *Reinheitsgebot*, first stated in Munich brewing regulations of 1447–1453,
was repeated in 1516 by Duke William IV and from that date applied to all of
Bavaria. It was repeated in a rule for the entire duchy in 1553 and again in 1616.[6]
The repetition suggests that enforcement may have been a problem, but it
would seem that at least by the early seventeenth century, most Bavarians
would have known that it was the law. More important the *Reinheitsgebot*
marked the victory of hopped beer in southern Germany. The rule was in part
inspired by a desire to guarantee effective taxation. If only hops could be used
in making beer, then the state would find it easier to get its share of income
from the sale of beer. Purity may have been less important than tax payments.
The production of white beer, *weisses bier*, in Nuremberg in 1541 or 1551 by a
Netherlander was one more sign of the advance of hopped beer (see Figure
10). The name was virtually a synonym for Hamburg beer. In 1602 the duke of
Bavaria opened his own *Hofbrauhaus* in Munich, another successful agent for
the spread of beer brewing and consumption. In the fifteenth and sixteenth
centuries, beer drinking and brewing in Germany, as a result of the spread of
hopped beer and changes in prices, enjoyed its greatest period of growth
before industrialization. By 1600 the industry had, like that in the Low Countries, reached a peak.[7] The brewing tradition of Bavaria and Austria, so much
a part of popular images of the region, was a product of developments in the
sixteenth century. The English traveler Fynes Moryson in 1617 claimed that
Germans drank a great deal and that at least in northern Germany, little Rhine
wine was consumed because of a preference for beer. He was impressed by the
strong heavy beer and even more impressed by a German fellow traveller who
had drunk too much beer and so vomited all over him in a coach.[8]

The victory of hopped beer in England, the southern Low Countries, and
Scandinavia dates from the same period as the success in southern Germany.
In the course of the sixteenth century there seems little doubt that the quality
of beer improved in England and elsewhere and increases in both production
and consumption followed.[9] Brewing was among the most successful industries of the fifteenth century in northern Europe in terms of technical accom-
plishment, productivity, and contribution to the development of local and

Figure 10. South German round disk showing a beer brewery, Nuremburg, sixteenth century. Reprinted from *Hermann Jung, Bier- Kunst und Brauchtum* (Dortmund: Schropp Verlag, n.d.), 103.

regional economies. Legal distinctions separating professional brewers from all others became more sharp as the professionals succeeded in making better beer in adequate quantities and in convincing governments to support them. Governments were even more enamored of brewers than ever because, as always, beer production and beer sales served as excellent sources of tax income.

Production and Tax Records

The continuity of taxation and the maintenance of tax records provide the greatest evidence for the pattern of growth in production during the Renaissance. The income that towns enjoyed from beer taxes may indicate the general tendency of production but the data do not yield a statement of the exact amount of beer brewed or drunk. Tax collectors produced an extensive body of surviving evidence, but the data are not always easy to interpret. Rises in income from beer taxes were caused by some combination of increasing consumption, rising rates of taxation, and the introduction of new types of beer subject to different levels of tax. Imports and exports were typically taxed differently. The system got so complex that in some cases taxes would be "composed," that is the brewer and tax collector would strike a deal, the tax collector getting a lump sum payment based on what the brewer might have had to pay for the period. The brewer got a discount for saving all parties a lot of trouble. Now and again, town governments urged agreement between brewers and tax farmers to make collection easier.[10] The most common reason given for new rules on brewing by any public authority was to stop tax fraud. With more extensive taxation came what appears to have been more extensive avoidance of taxes on beer. The extent of avoidance can only be guessed, so official reports understate production but by how much can never be known with certainty. Since there were different levels of tax on different beers, misrepresenting beer as being of lesser value could sharply reduce the incidence of tax. If taxes were "composed," that removed the brewer from regular over sight of the tax collector and created a wide range of possibilities for violating restrictions.

Some beers were free of tax and some people, because of their office, circumstances, or the occasion, were free of excise tax on the beer they drank. The list of those free of tax was often long and for towns it meant a loss, in the case of Lier probably something like 7 percent, of potential tax income. Brewing in monasteries escaped urban tax collectors. The Reformation eliminated monasteries in much of the beer-drinking region so that loophole was partially closed. Production continued in monasteries in Catholic Europe, as it had since the early Middle Ages.[11] The military could at times enjoy tax freedom. At Ghent in the 1550s while a new fortification was being built, Spanish soldiers, who got their beer without having to pay town excises, were billeted with local households. Those households, as a result, got tax-free beer too.[12] Beer of very low quality produced for the poor was free of tax. So, too, was beer produced for and drunk by shipbuilders at Amsterdam, Delft, and Wismar where not only ship carpenters but also house carpenters were free of excise when building. Beginning in 1629 at Wismar the mayor, aldermen, town physician, secretary, teachers, and others in some official or quasi-official capacity did not have to pay tax on the beer they bought.[13] At Schiedam in Holland before the Reformation, monks, beguines, other religious, inmates of the lepers' house, and ship carpenters building ships all drank excise-free beer.

The schoolteacher, a minor town official, got some beer each year tax free as a supplement to his salary. Each member of the Schiedam Popinjay Society, a guild of marksmen, got eight barrels of beer tax free.[14] In general, and not just in Holland, guilds often enjoyed tax freedom for the beer members drank at their annual meetings. In Middelburg in Zeeland, foreign merchants like those from Andalusia, England, Scotland, and Venice got concessions at different times from the government, including tax free beer for their own consumption.[15] Students at universities like Leiden, Leuven and many others in Europe got special tax consideration when it came to the preferred drink of young scholars.

Nobles also typically enjoyed tax freedom for the purchase of beer. Country houses of the nobility throughout northern Europe had their own breweries with all the necessary tools and often a specialist brewer as well.[16] The raw materials and the methods of brewing appear to have been much the same as was common in towns. A noble could usually find the needed capital. Once his or her household was over a certain threshold size, it was economically advisable to have beer made in the house rather than buy it on the market. If buyers could be found for any surplus, the idea had even more appeal. Free of many urban taxes noble households could often produce beer for less. As quality improved through the sixteenth century, so, too, did the competitiveness of the beer. In the sixteenth and seventeenth centuries in north Germany, where the aristocracy was more powerful, nobles tried to exploit their lighter tax burden, developing their own brewing enterprises to the detriment of the towns. Urban governments resisted but usually lost out to country breweries owned by nobles. In eastern parts of Germany and in Bohemia, towns found that production fell along with sales to the countryside as the nobility promoted brewing on their estates.[17] Capacity for brewing in noble houses could be sizeable. One English country house in 1552 put out over 83,000 liters of beer in a year, that is about 0.6 percent of the total output of the major exporting Holland town of Gouda at the same date.[18] Because it was tax free, production of noble households escaped urban record keepers so the contribution to total output is not known.

The repeated regulation of tax freedom and the numbers and variety of people who were able in one way or another to shake the burden of paying some or all of the excise on beer throws even more into doubt the reliability of tax records as an indicator of actual beer production. Even so, general trends are clear from government receipts. Other forms of both statistical and anecdotal evidence often confirm the trends. Typically those trends, with significant variations, were toward greater output and higher sales over an ever widening geographical area through the Renaissance.

Levels of Production and Export

In Germany, Hamburg remained a major center of beer production even though it was joined over the course of the sixteenth century by a number of other towns. Capacity in north Germany typically exceeded production. Around 1480, if demand was strong enough, Hamburg could produce some 37,500,000 liters of beer in one year. Around 1500, capacity was down to 28,000,000 but still above average output. Hamburg apparently made more beer than towns elsewhere in Germany. This was due in part to high levels of consumption in and around Hamburg, and in part to high levels of exports. The Amsterdam market took only about 600,000 liters of Hamburg beer each year in the mid-sixteenth century. It was enough to make an impression on beer production statistics, and well above the approximately 160,000 liters sent on average in 1531 and 1532 from Hamburg to Lubeck, but well down from levels a century and a half before. In the second half of the fifteenth century, export markets for Hamburg beer shrank as alternate supplies and suppliers developed. Joint political action by Hanse towns to reverse the trend proved futile, and so Hamburg brewers shifted toward local markets. Sales of beer in Hamburg itself in 1549 equaled 6,800,000 liters. The figure, though large, was not large enough to sustain brewing on the scale of the export industry of the fourteenth and fifteenth centuries.[19]

Output growth in most German towns, as at Hamburg, relied on more local people drinking more beer. Such growth was most obvious in Bavaria. The best the port towns of northern Germany could hope for was to retain former levels of output. Most failed. Wismar and Lübeck certainly saw declines in output in the sixteenth century as production inland, at sites like Göttingen and Hannover, rose. While Hamburg produced beer on a scale with Antwerp, the great metropolis of the Low Countries, the ports of Wismar and Lübeck were comparable to the exporting towns of Holland. Gdansk, one of the largest beer producers in northern Europe in the fifteenth century and comparable to almost any town anywhere, suffered a sustained long-term decline into and through the sixteenth century.[20] The combination of increasing grain exports to western Europe, which must have increased the price of grain in the town, and the growing competition from other sources of beer must be a large part of the explanation for the drop in production there. Even so, in the early seventeenth century the town was still, by international standards, a major producer of beer.

The principal casualties of the spread of beer production to new places were German inland towns which specialized in export, places like Einbeck, Zerbst, and Schweidnitz. Even Hamburg had imported beer from Einbeck. Einbeck, near Hildesheim, was raised from a landed noble estate to city rank between 1203 and 1256 and had a monopoly of beer imports into Hamburg. Hamburgers late in the fifteenth century called the town hall where Einbeck beer was sold the *Eimbecksche Haus*. The cost of shipping beer fell in the fifteenth century, which helped all exporting centers and somewhat countered the negative effects for them of the spread of hopped beer brewing. From Einbeck to Munich, transportation costs added only 36 percent to the price of the beer for every 100 kilometers traveled by late in the century, well down from the previous 50 to 70 percent. By sea, costs were, of course, less. Taking beer from Lübeck to Bergen around 1600 added only 20 percent to costs. Einbeck beer even made its way to the eastern Baltic and Scandinavia, shipped out through the ports of Hamburg and Lübeck. It was also shipped to Holland, Italy, and even to the Orient. In the sixteenth century, faced with rising competition, Einbeck exporters reoriented the trade southward and, until the rise of hopped beer brewing there, Bavaria proved to be an excellent market. Einbeck beer was still so highly valued that in the late sixteenth century Munich imported brewers from Einbeck to make beer and train local brewers.[21] The improvement that those men brought to Bavarian brewing further damaged Einbeck exports. Schweidnitz probably suffered more than Einbeck. There output fell continually through the second half of the fifteenth century and into the sixteenth. The industry still produced a significant quantity of beer as late as 1610, comparable to many prominent towns in Holland and Brabant, but much reduced from earlier levels.[22]

In Holland in the late 1470s, brewers in the three towns of Haarlem, Delft, and Gouda made beer something like 32,000 times a year on average which generated a maximum of 100,000,000 liters. In 1514, total production may have been up to 110,000,000 liters and probably more. Of that only 7 percent was consumed in those towns. The rest of the beer was made for export.[23] In addition to the great exporting centers many other towns in Holland had breweries. Production levels throughout the northern Low Countries would remain high, probably even exceeding the 1514 level through the sixteenth and even into the seventeenth century.

Holland brewers continued to export sizeable quantities of beer to the southern Low Countries. Antwerp imports from the county just to the north reached a peak of 86 percent of town production in 1543. Figures closer to 75 percent were the norm in the 1530s. Imports for all Flemish harbors in 1485 were about 1,960,000 liters. Sluis brought in 83 percent more beer than local brewers made in the first nine months of 1478. Most of the imported 550,000 litres came from Holland. The annual average of Holland beer landed at Nieuwpoort, a small town, in 1487 and 1488 was more than 1,700,000 liters. People living in the Franc of Bruges, the rural district around the town, drank about 1,400,000 liters of Holland beer in 1485. Other foreign sources generated only 7,500 liters. In the 1540s, Holland beer exports to the region were higher, around 3,000,000 liters each year, and they continued to swamp all other foreign sources which accounted for between 4 percent and 12 percent of imports from Holland. Imports from Holland into the Franc of Bruges, Dunkirk, Nieuwpoort, and harbors along the Zwin were always much greater than imports from Germany, England, and anywhere else. That was true in the 1470s and 1480s and through the first half of the sixteenth century as well.[24] The southern Netherlands constituted a significant market for Dutch beer, but the share of total export from brewing towns in Holland going to the region was probably never more than 25 percent and often considerably less. Even so, the levels of export help to explain the health of Dutch brewing up to the middle of the sixteenth century and the shrinking output in some exporting towns after that.

Outside Holland in the northern Netherlands, brewing output was less impressive. Only Amersfoort in the province of Utrecht, a center of beer exports since the fourteenth century, could compare in number of breweries to the most successful of Holland towns. In 1614 a now-lost record mentioned that Amersfoort once had 350 brewers. The reference was apparently a general one and may have reflected the number of people who earned their living from brewing in the late fifteenth century rather than the numbers of breweries. Annual output in the fifteenth century could never have reached a level to employ that many breweries. Despite the lack of evidence and the impossible numbers, the reputation of Amersfoort for having many breweries has survived. By 1602, there were still thirty-one breweries in the town, certainly a sharp fall from 150 years before but how sharp simply cannot be known.[25] In the county of Friesland in 1511, only three commercial breweries were mentioned in a tax assessment, two of them in the town of Leeuwaarden. Much of the beer drunk in the province came from elsewhere or was brewed at home. Still beer was important to consumers. Differences over the proper regulation of brewing and the beer trade in Friesland led to violence in 1487 and to something approaching a civil war, the short-lived so-called beer war.[26]

In the city of Leuven in Brabant, in the southern Low Countries, production in 1500 was between 3,600,000 and 4,700,000 liters and by 1524 4,533,000 liters. In 1479, exports were over 3,000,000 liters but such high figures were not common. In 1518, the town sent out only 41,000 liters but such low figures were not common either. The norm was somewhere around 1,300,000 liters. At the end of the sixteenth century, 1595–1596, a report on daily output listed average annual production of all beer, including very weak beer, at just over 1,250,000 liters.[27] Diest was the other export center of Brabant but the earliest production figures, from 1625, show total output at over 1,750,000 liters. Of that, almost 750,000 liters were exported. At 's-Hertogenbosch in Brabant in

1568 there were twenty-two breweries but by 1601 the number had risen to at least fifty-one, the growth coming from an increase in exports which approached 1,000,000 liters by the later date.[28] At Lier, despite success in the fifteenth century in replacing imports with locally produced beer, the achievement was not sustained. Output in the 1640s, the start of a period of long-term growth, was still below even the 1408–1409 level.[29] Brabant exports whether from Leuven, Diest, 's-Hertogenbosch, or other smaller towns went mostly to neighboring Flanders.

Ghent in Flanders, larger than Leuven or Lier, was a center of consumption as well as production. Output there in 1511 was about 16,000,000 liters but went through a decline to slightly under 11,000,000 liters in 1527. Imports were at around 2,700,000 liters in the 1520s but they declined, too, down to something like 2,000,000 liters in the 1530s. The new lower level of domestic production, under 12,000,000 liters annually but above 10,700,000, was apparently maintained until the 1560s. Imports fell to something a bit above 650,000 liters per year in the 1560s. During the fighting of the 1570s and 1580s in the early stages of the Eighty Years' War there were sharp variations in production levels. They did later recover, though not to previous levels. By the 1590s production had stabilized but at figures around 8,000,000 liters each year, a level comparable to export centers in Holland. Consumption fell in other urban centers in Flanders as well. The residents of Bruges drank 8,400,000 liters of beer in 1477 and 12,378,000 liters in 1544, but after the political turmoil and population loss of the Dutch Revolt consumption went down to 3,680,000 liters in 1596, 4,250,000 liters in 1597, and 4,800,000 liters in 1598.[30]

The changes in total output at Ghent obscure significant changes in the composition of that output. The same to a lesser degree was true at Lier and, more or less, in many places in northern Europe. The amount of beer of different types fluctuated much more than the total levels. A significant portion of the fall in total production at the end of the sixteenth century can be attributed to a turning away from inexpensive beers at a time when grain prices were going up and brewers were looking for ways to increase their revenues. Governments resisted beer price increases, so brewers offered different and better types in order to charge more for each barrel.[31] Ghent brewers in 1573 introduced a new type, *dubbele clauwaert*, and they saw its production rise sharply to 1583. By the close of the century, brewers were making around 4,500,000 liters a year of the heavier, more expensive beer. By then that was something on the order of one half of total production. In the same years small beer, the weakest product, had shrunk from being 20 percent of output to between 6 percent and 7 percent.[32]

In Antwerp the population rose rapidly in the fifteenth and sixteenth centuries. Beer production rose too, but it lagged behind the growth in number of residents. The lag was caused by problems of water supply which were not addressed effectively until the middle of the sixteenth century. Even with poor water, Antwerp brewers produced sizeable amounts of low-quality small beer, and in the 1530s total output was comparable to that of Ghent or Gouda in Holland. Over time, the proportion of production devoted to such low-strength, less expensive beers declined as it did at Ghent. A sharp increase in production at Antwerp after midcentury, thanks in part to investment in water supplies, led to a fall in imports, from 1558 to 1560 down to some 40 percent of what they had been in the 1530s. At the same time exports rose from being only 5 to 7 percent of output in the first half of the century to 10 percent from 1558 to 1561 and about 25 percent on average after 1570. Antwerp beer was even exported to Amsterdam on occasion.[33] The industry in the southern Low Countries, despite serious political disruption through the sixteenth century, over time became competitive with Dutch brewing. By the early seventeenth century the industry in Brabant and Flanders had reached a point that in absolute terms matched Dutch production.

In England, total output rose with the spread of hopped beer brewing. In the small provincial town of Coventry in 1520 brewers produced over 2,860,000 liters of beer. In 1574 production of beer and ale at London, assuming approximately equal quantities of both were made, was 312,000 barrels and in 1585, London brewers produced 648,690 barrels, that is probably over 100,000,000 liters.[34] The higher figure for the latter year may reflect greater exports to the Low Countries where the Dutch Revolt was disturbing the economy. The two isolated figures, neither highly trustworthy, still suggest that by the late sixteenth century, London already was the greatest center of beer production in Europe. Levels of output could be similar to the Dutch exporting towns at their height, combined. In 1591 London exports to north Germany, the Low Countries, and France had reached about 4,330,000 liters, the exports coming from some twenty large breweries along the Thames.[35] Even though export was important to English brewers, most of the beer made in the kingdom, and even in London, was for local consumption.

A comparison of production estimates for the most important centers of the industry indicate reputations of local industries were not always based on how much beer was made (see Table 2). Hamburg might be the largest producer in north Germany in the sixteenth century but Wismar and Lübeck often made more than 50 percent of the amount of beer that came from Hamburg and Gdansk in Poland could even produce more. Dutch towns matched or exceeded Hamburg output in the first half of the sixteenth century, but, with the exception of Haarlem, they lagged well behind after the revolt against Spanish rule. Big towns in the southern Netherlands, the new urban centers like Antwerp and Brussels, were producing much more beer than Hamburg

TABLE 2. ESTIMATES OF BEER OUTPUT BY TOWN

Town	Year	Quantity in Liters
Gouda	1480	44,376,000
Gouda	1480s	26,400,000 (avg.)
Gouda	1545	29,303,400
Gouda	1550s	13,800,000 (avg.)
Gouda	1560	15,193,000
Gouda	1570	10,396,000
Gouda	1580	1,230,000
Haarlem	1514	20,000,000
Haarlem	1576	1,730,000
Haarlem	1592	8,700,000
Haarlem	1594	12,700,000
Haarlem	1595	11,000,000
Haarlem	1600–1620	57,000,000 (avg.)
Leuven	1372	4,600,000
Leuven	1434	3,625,500
Leuven	1472	4,740,000
Leuven	1500	3,600,000–4,700,000
Leuven	1524	4,533,000
Leuven	1560s	7,400,000
Bruges	1388	6,549,900
Bruges	1411	7,144,725
Bruges	1477	8,400,000
Bruges	1482	7,844,000
Bruges	1492	6,590,890
Bruges	1542	10,662,618
Bruges	1544	12,377,925
Bruges	1550	10,624,556
Bruges	1580	15,836,000
Bruges	1585	4,932,698
Bruges	1588	6,412,744
Ghent	1511	17,770,000
Ghent	1527	11,924,000
Ghent	1562	12,400,000
Ghent	1567	11,787,000
Ghent	1572	12,217,000
Ghent	1578	12,460,500
Ghent	1583	16,127,000
Ghent	1587	3,370,000
Ghent	1593	7,926,000
Ghent	1600	8,866,000
Antwerp	1531	10,620,000
Antwerp	1537	13,800,000
Antwerp	1543	13,407,000
Antwerp	1565	26,373,000
Antwerp	1570	36,425,000
Antwerp	1575	29,257,000

TABLE 2. ESTIMATES OF BEER OUTPUT BY TOWN *(continued)*

Town	Year	Quantity in Liters
Antwerp	1577	28,356,000
Antwerp	1580s	45,000,000
Brussels	c. 1500	20,868,000
Brussels	1617	35,520,000
Hamburg	1350	25,000,000
Hamburg	1401–1450	30,000,000 (avg.)
Hamburg	1451–1500	25,000,000 (avg.)
Hamburg	1501–1550	20,000,000 (avg.)
Wismar	1351–1400	17,500,000 (avg.)
Wismar	1401–1450	12,000,000 (avg.)
Wismar	1451–1500	6,000,000 (avg.)
Wismar	1560–1600	8,500,000 (avg.)
Wismar	1600–1618	11,000,000 (avg.)
Lübeck	1401–1450	10,000,000 (avg.)
Lübeck	1451–1500	8,000,000 (avg.)
Lübeck	1501–1550	7,000,000 (avg.)
Gdansk	1401–1500	25,000,000 (approx. avg.)
Gdansk	1501–1550	20,000,000 (avg.)
Gdansk	1551–1600	14,500,000 (avg.)
Elblag	1580	5,000,000 (approx.)
Malbrok (Marienburg)	1580	4,000,000 (approx.)
Göttingen	1401–1450	3,000,000 (avg.)
Göttingen	1470	2,500,000
Göttingen	1555	3,200,000
Schweidnitz	1451–1500	5,500,000 (avg.)
Schweidnitz	1501–1550	4,500,000 (avg.)
Schweidnitz	1610	2,500,000
Hannover	1600	6,000,000
Munich	1600	6,500,000
London	1574	51,060,000
London	1585	106,158,000

Sources: ARa, Papiers de l'état et de l'audience: 1665/1; Abel, *Stufen der Ernährung*, 52–53; De Commer, "De brouwindustrie te Ghent," 113–114, 118 (for Ghent the year in which the tax year ended is given); Houwen, "De Haarlemsche brouwerij," 4, 9, 11, 14, 16, 19–20, 27; Huntemann, *Das deutsche Braugewerbe*, 11, 48; Klonder, *Browarnictwo w Prusach królewskich*, 160; Löhdefink, *Die Entwicklung der Brauergilde*, 19; Loenen, *De Haarlemse brouwindustrie*, 45, 47; Pinkse, "Het Goudse kuitbier," 112, 114, 128; Soly, "De brouwerijenonderneming van Gilbert van Schoonbeke," 347, 1198; Soly, *Urbanisme en Kapitalisme te Antwerpen in de 16de Eeuw*, 312; Soly and Thys, "Nijverheid in de zuidelijke Nederlanden," 6: 47; Uytven, "Bestaansmiddelen," 155, 157; Uytven, "Stages of Economic Decline," 253–65.

by the early seventeenth century, and Flemish towns, like Ghent and Bruges, enjoyed significant recovery in output in the years after the Dutch Revolt. Despite expansion in many continental towns, no place in northern Europe could compare in the production of beer by the late sixteenth century to the burgeoning and prosperous English capital city.

The number of breweries might also reflect levels of output. Falling numbers of breweries indicate not only changes in production but also the increase in output per brewery typical of the fifteenth and sixteenth centuries. Declines in numbers, without question, indicate greater specialization and increasing professionalization in the trade during the period.[36] Governments sometimes acted to slow the fall in the number of breweries. At Ghent one reason the town gave brewers permission in the 1570s to produce the new more expensive *dubbele clauwaert* was the sharp fall in brewing operations. Even that action did not stop the continuing decline and not until the end of the century did the number of breweries grow again.[37] The total at Ghent was high compared to such Brabant export centers as Leuven and Diest but low compared to those of north German port towns such as Bremen, Hamburg, and Wismar which had long been involved in the export of beer. To the east, Elblag had twenty-one new entrants to the beer brewing trade in 1568 though the figures of nineteen for 1559 and 1562 appear more normal.[38] Even so, the indication is of a very large number of new brewers and breweries in what was no means the largest town in Prussia.

Often the surviving figures are not for the number of breweries but for the number of brewers or the number who had or gained the right to brew. While informative, such data are an even poorer proxy for variations in output. At Wismar in 1615, 125 brewers had the right to make beer but only 119 exercised it and of those only 76 fully. Eighteen used much of their right and 25 made less than two-thirds of the quantity of beer they were authorized to make.[39] At Hamburg the right to brew was taken seriously, and so the government tended to keep track of the number of people and properties which enjoyed that right. In 1376, 307 Hamburgers could brew and the number rose, mostly in the late fourteenth and early fifteenth century, to reach 531 by 1542. It stayed at that level until the nineteenth century though the number of breweries fell. Foreign merchants who came to Hamburg in the late sixteenth century needed houses with large cellars to store goods and so took breweries out of production when they bought or leased the buildings. By 1608, of the 531 legal brewhouses only 286 were in use.[40] Still, that was a large number of breweries by any contemporary standard. The decline and the rare increases in the establishments making beer did not move in the same direction or to the same degree as the changes in production, but the figures below (see Table 3) indicate if nothing else that brewers and brewery workers made up an obvious and

TABLE 3. NUMBER OF BREWERIES IN NORTHERN EUROPEAN TOWNS, C. 1450–1650

Town	Date	Number
Amsterdam	1505	9
	1545	10
	1557	11
	1585	16
	1620	15
Antwerp	c. 1550	22–23
	1578	38
	c. 1650	31–35
Breda	1422	15
Bremen	1500	300*
	1550	285
Bruges	1441	54
Coventry	1520	60
Delft	Fifteenth century	200
	1494	100
	1510	138
	1513	77
	1514	98
	1539	40–50
	1568	100
	1600	82
	1645	25
Diest	1625	9
	1637	14
Gdansk	1416	378
Ghent	1580	36
	1595	46
	1602	53
	1605	59
	1615	59
Goslar	1500	300
Göttingen	c. 1500	300*
	c. 1600	c. 400*
Gouda	1479	159*
	1480	172
	1494	157
	1504	156–157
	1509	141
	1510	152*

TABLE 3. NUMBER OF BREWERIES IN NORTHERN EUROPEAN TOWNS, C. 1450–1650
(continued)

Town	Date	Number
	1514	148
	1515	152*
	1539	115*
	1543	113*
	1545	97*
	1580	120
	1588	120
	1609	14
	1616	14
Hamburg	1374	457
	1500	520*
Hannover	1609	300*
Haarlem	1490	114*
	1494	120
	1495	115
	1496	112
	1503	95
	1511	84
	1512	81
	1514	77
	1519	78
	1538	53
	1548	45
	1563	20
	1576	7
	1579	11
	1589	15
	1590	19
	1596	19
	1599	20
	1600	22
	1607	30
	1608	33
	1610	37
	1612	44
	1623	54
	1629	54
	1634	50
	1640	49
	1650	55

TABLE 3. NUMBER OF BREWERIES IN NORTHERN EUROPEAN TOWNS, C. 1450–1650 (*continued*)

Town	Date	Number
Hasselt	1543	31
	1592	30
	1629	41
Hoogstraten	1550	25
	c. 1565	24
	1650	3
Leuven	c. 1420	50–60
	1476	61
	1477	72
	1512	59
	1516	73
	1518	70 (+4 outside the town)
	1519	70 (+4 outside the town)
	c. 1520	62
	1525	65
	1532	59 (+19 outside the town)
	1538	49 (+18 outside the town)
	1565	46
	1597	34
Liege	Sixteenth century	160
	1621	180
Lier	1408	9
	1470	7
	1599	6
	1610	10
	1630	9
	1650	14
London	1419	300*
Lübeck	1546	176
Mechelen	1472	111
Menen	1524	104
Munich	1400	c. 40*
	c. 1500	c. 40
	1560s	c. 45
	1600	c. 60*
Nuremberg	1402	56*
	1579	42

TABLE 3. NUMBER OF BREWERIES IN NORTHERN EUROPEAN TOWNS, C. 1450–1650
(continued)

Town	Date	Number
Oxford	1348	88*
	1351	33*
	1381	29*
Rostock	1572	360
St. Truiden	1250	36
Stralsund	1600	140
Wismar	c. 1460	200
	1465	182*
	1500	200*
	1560	50*
	1592	120
	1615	119*
	1629	96*
	1632	68
	1640	93*

Sources: ARa, Papiers de l'état et de l'audience: 1665/1; N. A., Archief Grafelijksheidsrekenkamer, Rekeningen: #1722; G. A. Haarlem, Archief van het Brouwersgilde: #27; Sa Leuven, Oud Archief: #2817–2820, #2922–2823; Aerts, *Het bier van Lier*, 93, table 24; Bennett, *Ale, Beer, and Brewsters in England*, 112–14; Bleyswijck, *Beschryvinge der Stadt Delft*, 735–36; Breen, "Aanteekeningen uit de geschiedenis . . . ," 75; Brugmans, *Amsterdam in de zeventiende eeuw*, 2: 209–10; Clement, "De bierbrouwerijen van Gouda," 67, 199–200; Dalen, *Geschiedenis van Dordrecht*, 1: 388–89; De Commer, "De brouwindustrie te Ghent," 157; Dillen, *Bronnen tot de geschiedenis van het bedrijfsleven*, 1: #608 [1620]; Dollinger, *La Hanse*, 282; Eeghen,"De brouwerij de Hooiberg," 46; Egmond, "De strijd om het dagelijks bier," 158; Eycken, *Geschiedenis van Diest*, 199; Eykens, "De brouwindustrie te Antwerpen," 90, 93; Hoffmann, *5000 Jahre Bier*, 59; Houtte, *An Economic History*, 170; Huntemann, *Das deutsche Braugewerbe*, 38–39, 73; King, *Beer Has a History*, 51; Langer, "Das Braugewerbe in den deutschen Hansestädten," 73; Loenen, *De Haarlemse brouwindustrie*, 61–62; Martens, "Bier en stadsfinancien te Hasselt," 251; Niehoff, "Bremer Bier im Baltikum," 15; Penninck, *Het bier te Brugge*, 11; Salzman, *English Industries of the Middle Ages*, 290; Santbergen, *Les bons métiers*, 164–165; Schultheiss, *Brauwesen und Braurechte in Nürnberg*, 32–34, 37; Sedlmeyr, *Die "prewen" Münchens seit 1363 biz zur Aufhebung der Lehensverleihung durch den Landesfürsten (1814)*, 244–47; Soly, "De brouwerijenonderneming van Gilbert van Schoonbeke," 346; Soly and Thys, "Nijverheid in de zuidelijke Nederlanden," 47; Techen, "Das Brauwerk in Wismar," 269–70; Ter Gouw, *Geschiedenis van Amsterdam*, 5: 437; Timmer, *De Generale Brouwers van Holland*, 1–3; Timmer, "Uit de nadagen der Delftsche brouwnering," 741; Uytven, "L'approvisionnement des villes des anciens Pays-Bas au moyen âge," 100; Uytven, "Bestaansmiddelen," 155–157; Uytven, "Bier und Brauer," 3, 10; Yntema, "The Brewing Industry in Holland," 44, 47.

*Number of brewers.

unavoidable component of the population of northern European towns in the Renaissance.

The data on the number of breweries suggest, as do the data on production, that a few German towns typically produced more beer than did those in the Low Countries and that some towns in the southern Low Countries produced more beer than towns in the northern counties. The effects of the spread of hopped beer brewing certainly appear in the numbers of brewers and of breweries. Throughout northern Europe, but especially in the northern Netherlands and especially after the middle of the sixteenth century, the production of beer appears to have been stable or, in a number of places, to have risen while the numbers of breweries and active brewers were stable or falling. The undeniable implication is that breweries got bigger. That change in scale along with the high levels of total output were clear signs the industry had become a mature one.

Chapter 8

The Mature Industry: Levels of Consumption

A certain sign of the success of the adoption of brewing with hops and perfection of the technique in northern Europe was the high level of beer consumption in towns. Consumption and production in most towns were closely tied, the exception being the few places that specialized in export. Consumption level data, that is data for per capita beer drinking, are just as sparse as are data for production and for the number of breweries. Figures are sometimes derived from known sales and not always reliable population data and sometimes from unique circumstances, such as practices in hospitals or monasteries. Since the sales figures are based on tax records, they run the risk of missing consumption by tax-exempt groups. At the very least, though, what survives does give an impression of the great importance of beer to the people of Renaissance northern Europe.

The figures of the absolute quantities of beer people drank can be misleading. Not all beer was the same. Small beer was much weaker and less nutritious than full beer or double beer. Export beers, like those that came from Einbeck and were shipped to Frankfurt and Bavaria or from Gdansk and shipped to the Low Countries, were even heavier and of higher quality in every sense. The amount of beer drunk from one year to the next might be stable, but the amount of grain used and the nutritional value of the beer might vary widely. In the sixteenth century, grain prices rose and with them the costs of brewing beer. The population increase, which was the principal cause of rising prices, brought more consumers, but with their declining real incomes as the cost of bread went up, they were less able to buy beer. Wars, the disturbances to the economy and the higher taxes that came with them, could also cause marked short-run fluctuations in consumption levels and obscure long-term trends.[1] Compared to Renaissance drinkers, modern consumers of beer fall far behind. In 1995 Belgians, among the most avid beer drinkers in the world, consumed on average 102 liters per person per year,[2] less than half the amount of urban populations in the late Middle Ages or the Renaissance.

Consumption Variations over Time and Place

Data from a broad range of towns in Germany and the Low Countries from the second half of the fourteenth century to the middle of the seventeenth show significant differences from one place to another and over time (see Table 4). The numbers do suggest that something around 300 liters consumed per person per year was near the norm with figures, if anything, rising in the fifteenth century and stable or even in a few instances declining in the sixteenth.

The sparse data on consumption show drinkers in the Low Countries to have been consistent but less avid than German beer drinkers while English drinkers kept pace with their German counterparts when both ale and beer are taken together. A general estimate for medieval England of between four and five liters each day for each person is reasonable but perhaps too high. More sensible and likely is an estimate of some 1.1 liters each day for each person. Members of better-off farm families in England in the fourteenth century may have consumed on average as little as half a liter of ale each day. At about the same time, members of aristocratic households probably had between 1.5 and 2.0 liters per day, a figure perhaps not incidentally similar to the supposed average consumption in contemporary Poland.[3] Under a revision of the Assize of Ale in 1283 some four liters of ale would have cost an English craftsman about a third of his daily earnings and a laborer about two-thirds. It was unlikely that people could earn enough to afford to buy five liters of beer each day, but many people had other sources of ale and did not have to buy it from brewers. Social groups like religious and craft guilds would buy ale for members for festive occasions, and very often employers, both urban and rural, supplied ale as part of compensation to workers. A hospital for lepers in the north of England in the fourteenth century gave inmates four liters a day, or at least that was the ration under the regulations. A London hospital in the 1570s, on the other hand, gave the more expected one liter per day with a supplementary half liter in the summer.[4] That still amounted to annual levels of close to 400 liters per inmate, an impressive level of consumption even by contemporary standards. A general figure for Antwerp of 415 liters per capita in 1543 suggests urban populations in better off towns drank more beer than did farmers but less than people in the country houses of aristocrats.[5] Sketchy but similar data from elsewhere in Europe suggest that seemingly high figures for consumption at specific sites and in certain institutions are, in fact, accurate. A Danish children's workhouse in 1621 was serving each inmate about 700 liters a year, something like half the common adult ration. At the Swedish monastery of Vadstena in the fifteenth century, each member of the household got about

TABLE 4. CONSUMPTION OF BEER PER PERSON PER YEAR, IN LITERS

Town	Date	Population	Estimates of Consumption Levels
Leuven	1372	16,500	277
Bruges	1387		250
Bruges	1411		310
Antwerp	1418	10,000	210
Lier	1418–1433	7,000	289
Leuven	1434	18,000	210
Hamburg	c. 1450		250 (hospital inmates)
Leuven	1472	17,000	271
Lier	1473–1475	10,000	177–179
Haarlem	1475	11,000	250
Hamburg	c. 1475	20,000	310
Alkmaar	c. 1475		237
Bruges	1477	42,000	200
Leuven	1500		275 (for adults)
Hamburg	c. 1500	25,000	320
Leiden	1514	14,000	228
Haarlem	1514	11,000	158
Leuven	1524	17,000	273
Hamburg	c. 1525	25,000	285
Antwerp	1526	39,000	369
Diest	1526		253
Ninove	1526		approximately 300
Antwerp	1531	50,000	369
Antwerp	1543		300
Leiden	1543	13,000	269
Mechelen	1540		335
St. Truiden	1545		250
Hamburg	1550	20,000	400
Bruges	c. 1550	35,000	263
Lier	c. 1550		approximately 310
Antwerp	c. 1550		550 (adults only)
Lübeck	c. 1550	25,000	400
Nuremburg	1551	30,000	300
St. Omer	c. 1560		56
Antwerp	1567		295
Antwerp	1568		346
Leiden	1571	12,500	267
Ghent	1580	50,000	202
Bruges	1584	26,000	190
Haarlem	c. 1590		300
Wismar	1600		1095 (hospital inmates)
Bruges	c. 1600	29,000	158
Ghent	1607		156
Antwerp	1612	54,000	259
Hamburg	c. 1615		700 (all types of beer)

TABLE 4. Consumption of beer per person per year, in liters *(continued)*

Town	Date	Population	Estimates of Consumption Levels
Antwerp	1618		400
Leiden	1621	45,000	301
Diest	1650		250

Sources: Aerts, *Het bier van Lier,* 89; De Commer, "De brouwindustrie te Ghent," 143; DuPlessis, *Lille and the Dutch Revolt,* 123; Eykens, "De brouwindustrie te Antwerpen," 90; Huntemann, *Das deutsche Braugewerbe,* 28, 58–60; Loenen, *De Haarlemse brouwindustrie,* 55, 58–59; Prevenier and Blockmans, *The Burgundian Netherlands,* 45, 87; Soly, "De brouwerijenonderneming van Gilbert van Schoonbeke," 349–351; Soly and Thys, "Nijverheid in de zuidelijke Nederlanden," 47; Uytven, "Bestaansmiddelen," 155, 157; Uytven, "Bier und Brauer," 14; Uytven, "Het bierverbruik en de sociaal-economische toestand," 26; Uytven, "Oudheid en middeleeuwen," 39; Uytven, *Stadsfinanciën en stadsekonomie te Leuven,* 327–35; Uytven, "Stages of Economic Decline," 263–265; Vandenbroeke, *Agriculture et alimentation,* 535–36; Yntema, "The Brewing Industry in Holland," 95.

three liters of beer each day, and at Stockholm Castle in 1558 the rate was 4.5 liters. In 1577 the rules at the castle were revised and aristocrats got 5.2 liters each day on average while tradesmen and working people got a mere 3.9 liters.[6] It is possible that where beer was easily available and where large quantities of low-quality beer were always at hand, such as in aristocratic houses, then adults at least did drink more than 4 liters a day, or more than 1,460 liters per year, on average.

The same was apparently true on board ship through the sixteenth and seventeenth centuries, that is so long as there was beer to be had.[7] In theory, crew members on warships were to have as much beer as they wanted. The facts may have been different. Sailors on ships of the Hanseatic League were to have 5 liters each per day. In 1340 Great Yarmouth in England was required to have a supply of 4.5 liters of beer for each man for each day on the ships fitted out for naval action against Flanders. The ration for sailors in the English navy in 1565 was 4.6 liters per day and for the Danish navy in the 1570s about 4 liters per day. Those figures were relatively high compared to consumption on land, but much of the difference can be explained in the relatively lower quality of what was called ship's beer. Through the fifteenth and sixteenth centuries, brewers thinned the beer used on ships as they did certain types of beers consumed on land. Even so, a significant share of daily calories for men at sea came from beer.[8] Crews, whether traveling on inland waterways or on the high seas, expected beer. That would remain true for naval and merchant vessels as late as the early eighteenth century. Navies had an interest in the presence of a brewing industry in ports where they had bases. If there was no industry, as at Stockholm, the admiralty set up its own brewery, that already in the sixteenth century, to fulfill the needs of the fleet. The beer for use on shipboard might be extremely weak but it could be, as in Sweden and Finland, a little stronger than the weakest beer sold in town.[9] No matter how weak the beer, at least there was a chance that it was drinkable. For sailors the weak beer was their trustworthy water supply and also a source of some, but not much, nutrition. When there was no butter for the hard biscuit of their breakfast, beer softened the bread. During wars against Denmark in the sixteenth century, seamen on Hanse ships are said to have received a ration of as much as 20 liters of beer each day, but that was, if true, extraordinary. The Dutch States-General in 1636 estimated per capita consumption on board merchant ships at 1.6 liters a day in the winter and 2 liters a day in the summer, putting the total for the year above 650 liters.[10] Those figures, and indeed all daily ration figures, are misleading for long voyages since the beer on board was drunk early in such trips before it could sour too much. When that was gone, beer consumption fell to zero. Crew members did complain, at least on Dutch naval vessels, about beer going sour. Presumably for long voyages, captains took on some better-quality beer which would have spoiled more slowly and still have been drinkable after the crew downed all the weaker beer.

Figures for average consumption are somewhat deceptive in that they suggest beer was the drink of the people. Many people drank no beer or only extremely weak beer. Averages also are deceptive because skilled workers and laborers kept the average high by drinking a good deal more beer than the poor or the rich. Averages are also deceptive because beer consumption could take other forms. Beer was used in the preparation of many dishes. Though cooking took a small share of total beer consumed, it was still a common ingredient in Renaissance kitchens and brewers needed to supply the cooks as well.[11] One thing that averages do give is a sense of the long-term direction of the market for beer.

In fifteenth-century Germany, the average of beer consumption was probably something on the order of 300 liters per person per year. The figure was a little higher in the north and along the Baltic coast, lower in the south. It rose over time, so that by 1600 it was in the range of 400 to even 600 liters per person per year.[12] The shift of the beer border southward and the wider distribution of beer over the course of the sixteenth century drove up the levels of consumption (see Figure 11). For the Low Countries, in towns which had a broad range of ages and of incomes some people could not afford beer so a figure for urban consumption something like one liter for each person each day was more typically the case in the sixteenth century. The general trend was stability or a slow decline through much of the sixteenth century, indicating no improvement and probably some deterioration in the welfare of urban residents. Already in a fourteenth-century poem, folk from Leuven and Lier were said to be renowned for drinking beer. In 1438 a Spaniard said that Lier had

Figure 11. A peasant dance with beer drinkers at a tavern, Pieter Brueghel the Elder, c. 1567. His depiction of peasants spawned followers in both the southern and northern Low Countries in the seventeenth century. Courtesy of Kunsthistorisches Museum, Vienna.

what seemed to him a high level of beer consumption. Production and population data suggest that around that time consumption was about 300 liters per year, a figure that was not high compared to other places in northern Europe and, if anything, seems to have been more like the norm. The figure fell over the fifteenth century so that by the last quarter it was down to about 180 liters per year, a relatively low number. Despite long-term decline, Lier could still boast, even as late as the 1720s, per capita beer drinking of about 220 liters per year, and Leuven in 1785 was at about 270 liters, both levels high for that period in the Low Countries.[13] Meanwhile in Germany, and perhaps Scandinavia, consumption levels rose; in England, too, beer drinking seems to have held up better than in the Low Countries. As late as the closing years of the seventeenth century, the statistician Gregory King said that on average every man, woman, and child in England drank a quart of beer each day or over 350 liters per person per year.[14]

Figures for per capita wine consumption are also sparse, but the few that exist indicate a general pattern of decline up to and around 1500 in reaction to rising beer drinking. In the Middle Ages the average for wine drinkers was about a glass a day equaling approximately 50 liters per person per year. Many people did not drink wine so that those who could afford it drank a good deal more than the 0.14 liters each day implied by the average. In the late fourteenth and fifteenth centuries consumption of wine in general went down. In England levels of 15 to 31 liters per person per year, reached early in the fourteenth century, had fallen to 4.5 to 6.0 liters by the mid-fifteenth century. In religious or quasi-religious institutions inmates often drank considerably more wine. A Ghent monastery in 1409–1410 gave the brothers 3.1 liters each day, a figure which fell to 2.5 liters a day, or over 900 liters a year, by 1432–1433, and it stayed at that level through 1467–1468. For the general population of the town, average annual consumption was much lower, varying from 44 to 15 liters and regularly under 25 liters. At Antwerp in 1543 the number was only a little over 19 liters. That year was abnormal so something more like 20 to 30 liters would have been typical.[15] In sheer volume, beer was always more important than wine. In Brabant in general, consumers drank twelve times as much beer as wine. At Lier in 1473–1475 the ratio was even higher with only 4 percent of consumption of the two drinks, by volume, being wine. A Lier mason with his daily wage could, in 1427, buy 13 liters of beer, but by 1452 it was up to 16 liters. When grain prices started to rise at the end of the century, local farmers gave up on grapes so cheap local wine disappeared. Drinkers were left to choose between beer that was slowly declining in quality and wine which was relatively even more expensive because it was imported from France and Germany and subject to heavy duties.[16] In general in the sixteenth century in the southern Low Countries beer prices never rose as much as wine prices.[17]

By the end of the fifteenth century, the poor, laborers, and to a great degree skilled workers did not drink wine. It was reserved for parties and celebrations, special occasions, and the tables of the rich. The same was true in the sixteenth century, not just in the Low Countries but in increasingly larger areas of Germany. The renowned Belgian medievalist, Raymond van Uytven, summarized the changes:

> In the course of the sixteenth century, and in parallel with the rise in the cost of living, there was a shift in the psychology of the consumption of drinks. Wine became the drink of a class; drinking wine became even characteristic of a higher social standing than it had been in the middle ages. At the same time beer consumption received a strong stimulus, in Brabant from the last quarter of the fourteenth century and above all in the fifteenth century. This region thus joined an extensive belt that extended across the whole of Germany, Holland and the countries round the Baltic, where Rhine wine rather than French wine was consumed as a luxury drink, while the everyday drink was beer. England resembled these countries in its higher beer consumption, but was distinguished from them by the dominance of French wines.[18]

Beer Consumption and Grain Supplies

The sheer volume of beer consumed had a direct effect on the economies of towns where brewers produced the drink. Brewers competed for access to raw materials; in most towns and in most cases, it was not a problem, except with regard to grain. Bakers were the other principal users of grain. Using grain to make bread or to make beer had different results. There is no doubt that the same quantity of grain in the form of bread was more nutritious than in the form of beer. There seems little doubt that even those with access to sizeable quantities of beer still got most of their calories from bread in one form or another. In the fifteenth century, one liter of good quality barley beer had from 400 to 800 calories. A kilogram of bread had 2,500. With prevailing prices in the Low Countries, it was possible to get nine times as many calories from bread as from beer for the same expenditure. The nutritional loss in making beer instead of bread out of grain was something over 75 percent in the sixteenth century. Making grain into beer instead of bread increased the requirements of transportation for grain and of land to raise the grain by a factor of as much as tenfold (see Figure 12).[19] Governments in the Low Countries and England from the fifteenth century on laid down restrictions on beer brewing in periods of grain shortage or high grain prices, so there was a clear understanding at the time of the burden placed on scarce resources from making beer. The growing interest in protecting urban food supplies, something started already in the high Middle Ages but increasingly common in the fif-

Figure 12. Tavern scene by David Teniers the Younger, c. 1680. Oil on canvas. Painters such as Teniers, Adrian Brower, and Adriaen van Ostade did a number of uncomplimentary scenes of peasants generally drinking beer and too much of it. They were a small group of artists, however. Courtesy of Memorial Art Gallery of the University of Rochester.

teenth century, led to more regulation of brewing during periods of grain shortages.

Contemporaries were certainly impressed with the demands beer placed on grain resources well before the late Middle Ages. According to Galbert of Bruges, Charles the Good, the count of Flanders, required that oats be used to make bread and prohibited the brewing of beer during a famine in 1125.[20] The archbishop of Cologne forbade brewing during a famine in 1220, as did the king of Norway, Magnus the Law-Mender, at the end of the thirteenth century. In the wake of a famine in 1315 London prohibited the malting of wheat to make beer, requiring that, in the future, other grains should be used in its place. Presumably this was a way to preserve wheat for making bread. London did not prohibit brewing but in September of 1316 the city set maximum prices for the poorest and the best ale with harsh restrictions on those who over-charged. Hamburg made the export of beer illegal on occasion in the four-teenth century and whenever that happened the town simultaneously prohibited the export of bread. There were stiff penalties for violation.[21] In the Low Countries when the Wendish War (1437–1441) disrupted grain imports, Count Philip the Good required that only so much beer be exported from Holland as could be made with the quantity of grain imported. Limitations on brewing during periods of grain shortage could and did lead to conflict between public authorities and brewers, especially in towns like Gouda with a large export sector. In England under the 1495 Beggars Act, two local justices could suppress ale selling where necessary, both an effort to control potentially disruptive institutions but also a chance to limit sale of drink in periods of high grain prices.[22]

At times in the sixteenth century, brewers found themselves unable to produce beer because of the constraints on their supplies. In 1555 the English government prohibited the export of beer to conserve grain supplies but the situation did not improve. In 1556, an especially bad year, the Holland government prohibited brewers from making the high-quality beer which used relatively more grain. The government ordered brewers to water down the beer and use wheat instead of barley since the latter would make more nutritious bread. By the end of the year, the county government told malters that they could use only the wheat not fit to eat. In England grain shortages in the 1590s and again in the 1620s led to complaints from both the Crown and local magistrates that beer sellers were diverting grain from making bread to making beer aggravating an already difficult situation.[23] By the fifteenth century there was a well-established and widespread tradition of regulating brewing in times of dearth for the public benefit. That tradition of regulating brewing for the defense of the people against shortages also served as an excuse for Renaissance governments to expand direction and control of beer consumption and production.

The grain demand for beer made up some 25 to 45 percent of the grain demand in towns. To supply a population of around 100,000, Antwerp brewers of the late 1550s needed something on the order of 17,250,000 liters of grain, not much under 14,000 tonnes, to produce their 25,500,000 liters of beer. Brewers needed a total of probably somewhere around 625,000 tonnes of grain each year for the entire Low Countries in the fifteenth century and significantly more in the sixteenth. Hamburg produced about 20,000,000 liters of beer around 1500, and brewers used 100 liters of grain to produce 145 liters of beer.[24] That put the brewers' grain requirement in the town at slightly more than 11,000 tonnes. By the end of the sixteenth century the population of the Dutch Republic was some 2,000,000 and beer consumption was about 250 liters of beer on average each a year, so total consumption was above 500,000,000 liters and the total grain demand created by making that beer was over 200,000,000 liters or 160,000 tonnes annually. The scale of grain demand

and grain imports needed to satisfy demands of beer drinkers were large for individual towns, provinces, or regions. They were large enough to have a deep effect on agriculture, transportation, and government action.

Quantities of grain used to make a fixed quantity of beer varied depending on the quality of the beer. Town bylaws often fixed quantities required. There was wide variation in the rules on grain requirements, and though the rules were subject to both change and evasion and though not all sources are consistent, it appears that production varied between 0.39 and 2.80 liters of beer for each liter of grain used. Both extremes appear to be exceptional with figures from 1.05 to 1.80 being more characteristic. In Bremen in the first half of the sixteenth century, brewers got only some two-thirds of a liter of beer from a liter of grain, but that figure was uncommon and could have been a result of the concentration on quality products for export markets. At Bremen brewers got 0.65 liters of beer from a liter of malt, those at Hamburg 1.30–1.50, at Lübeck 0.90–1.10, but at Wismar the levels were lower, more like those at Bremen, that is 0.60–0.80 liters of beer. A common figure for Germany and the Low Countries would seem to have been somewhere around 1.5 liters of beer for each liter of grain, but with the ratio lower more often than not in Germany.[25]

Aristocratic households in fourteenth-century England got from 0.77 to 1.16 liters of ale from each liter of grain.[26] The figures perhaps reflect the relatively greater efficiency of urban brewers compared to those working for nobles, but it could also be the figures reflect the lower quality of the commercial product. One noble English house produced some 5.5 liters of traditional ale, that is made without hops, from a liter of grain, an extreme case perhaps but an example of the production of low-quality beer in such breweries. A yield ratio more in the range of 0.92 to 1.22 liters of ale per liter of malt seems to have been the norm. Reginald Scot, writing in 1576, said that brewers got a bit more than 1 liter of ale from a liter of malt but 2.33 liters of beer. In 1503 Richard Arnold, the author of the earliest English printed book on brewing, said that 3.33 liters of beer could be produced from a liter of malt, a number which certainly seems inflated. Sporadic English records suggest that beer brewers needed about half as much malt to get the same quantity of drink as ale brewers. That was the ratio set down in 1601 legislation at York.[27] Low Countries regulations suggest that the makers of hopped beer often found themselves using as much grain as English ale brewers. The exact type of beer, that is the intended quality of the product, seems to have been the most important factor in fixing the range of grain used no matter where it was made in northern Europe.

There was, undoubtedly, a tendency to increase the amount of beer made with each unit of grain as grain prices rose in the sixteenth century. Typically beer prices remained stable in the fourteenth and fifteenth centuries, but in some cases the pressure was too great and brewers increased prices of even poor quality beer.[28] Through the Renaissance the problem for brewers in general was to get as much out of grain as possible. Data from various towns between the mid-fourteenth century and the early seventeenth, mostly in the Low Countries, suggests a trend but by no means a strong or irreversible trend toward more beer made from each liter of grain (see Table 5).

Beer Consumption and Heating Fuel

After grain, heating fuel was the raw material which placed the greatest strain on the economy and transportation network. The principal source of heat was wood. Brewers used 7–8 cubic meters of wood for each brew which, in the reign of Elizabeth I, translated in London to an annual burning of about 20,000 loads of wood. That drove up wood prices, not just in England. In the Low Countries and especially in Holland, the rapid growth of energy-intensive industries, including brewing, combined with population growth to put an intolerable strain on declining supplies of wood in the sixteenth century. Wood and charcoal had to be imported from Germany and, after 1550, from Norway. Brewers had long used peat wherever and whenever possible rather than wood. It took more than 20 kilograms of peat to make just 100 liters of beer—or something on the order of 22 cubic meters of peat to make a brew similar in size to the English one—so a shift to peat did not necessarily mean saving in space or in transportation costs. As early as 1514, Delft, the great brewing center, consumed almost 22,000 tonnes of peat each year.[29] The shift to peat from wood was aided by rising wood prices and similarly the shift away from peat was helped by rising peat prices in the second half of the sixteenth century, a rise created in part by brewers' increasing demand for heating fuel. Despite the construction of new canals in the sixteenth century to open untapped sources of peat, for example in Friesland, and despite the growth in peat digging, supplies still could not keep pace with demand. Brewers, as a result, experimented with the obvious alternative, coal.[30]

Town governments, especially in Holland, resisted coal burning within their walls. They were afraid that air pollution would damage other industries. Coal was long known as an air pollutant, and as early as 1307, brewers in London, along with other industrialists, were forbidden to burn the fuel. As late as 1578, a brewer in Westminster went to jail for using coal, but in the same year the London Company of Brewers, in a petition to the government, said that their members had turned to the use of coal. Despite what the organization said, many London brewers still used wood in the middle of the seven-

TABLE 5. BEER OUTPUT PER GRAIN INPUT, IN LITERS

Town	Date	Grain/Brew	Beer Produced	Ratio (Beer Produced to Grain/Brew)
Delft	c. 1340	3174	3725	1.17
Gouda	1366	644	1660	2.58
Utrecht	1404	1857	3100	1.67
Haarlem	1407	1698	1790	1.05
Utrecht	1433	2302	2480	1.08
Utrecht	1433	2418	2800	1.16§
Utrecht	1433	1842	2480	1.34
Utrecht	1447	2302	3100	1.35
Amsterdam	Fifteenth century	2104	3100	1.47
Utrecht	1451	1381	2480	1.80*
Amersfoort	1484	2698	2480	.92
Amersfoort	1484	1188	1920	1.60§
Gouda	1488	1140	1220	1.07
Gouda	1488	2603	3820	1.47
Haarlem	c. 1490	2600	3720	1.43
Utrecht	1491	2188	2480	1.13
Utrecht	1491	2417	3725	1.54
Amsterdam	1497	1750	2600	1.48
Leiden	1497	1830	5120	2.80
Leiden	1497	1569	4350	2.77
Hamburg	1500			1.45
Haarlem	1501	1698	1850	1.09
Haarlem	1501	2202†	c. 3600	1.63§
Gouda	1513	1210	1450	1.20
Gouda	1513	2500	3950	1.58
Zutphen	1515	2435	3100	1.27
Zutphen	1515	1991	4970	2.50§
Haarlem	1544	1237†	c. 4200	3.40
Bremen	1550			.65
Hamburg	1550			1.50–2.00
Haarlem	c. 1590	4600	3720	0.81
Holland	1633			2.58

Sources: De Clerck, *A Textbook of Brewing,* 1: 157; Doorman, *Techniek en Octrooiwezen,* 57, 96–98; Halbertsma, *Zeven Eeuwen Amersfoort,* 42–44; Houwen, "De Haarlemsche brouwerij," 30; Huntemann, *Das deutsche Braugewerbe,* 13, 75; Niehoff, "Bierproduktion und Bierkonsum," 170; Philpsen, "De Amsterdamsche brouwnijverheid," 7; Pinkse, "Het Goudse kuitbier," 100.

Note: Assume 1 liter of grain weighs 800 grams.

* Thin beer.
† Extensive substitutions possible, which would alter the total.
§ *Koyt,* a unique type popular in the fifteenth century.

teenth century. Rotterdam in 1615 prohibited the use of Scottish coal in brewing and other trades from the beginning of April to the end of October. Liege coal was acceptable, but no other. The town was responding to complaints from the citizenry, probably about pollution. Governments were afraid that a shift to coal would make fires more likely in their crowded and largely wooden town centers. Some governments were afraid a shift to coal would mean a loss of tax income, that is where towns had imposed levies on peat. Both governments and brewers were afraid that the use of coal would decrease the quality of the beer. When used to dry malt, coal could give the resulting beer a foul taste. That meant that malters stayed with wood longer than did brewers. The most common way for brewers to avoid potential contamination from coal was to use closed furnaces rather open grates under the kettles. Any dirty smoke was carried off through a chimney out of the brewery and away from the beer. Dutch inventors in the Renaissance were more interested in dealing with the problem of smoke and soot than in the improvements in the process of beer making if the evidence of patents is any indication of their goals.[31] How effective all those inventions and innovations were is impossible to measure. It may be that most potential gains for fuel saving had already been realized by the closing years of the sixteenth century, hence the search for ways to use cheaper fuel became more prominent.[32]

In the sixteenth century in Haarlem, coal cost about one-fifth as much as peat for making the same quantity of beer and presumably something like that ratio prevailed throughout the rest of Holland and much of northern Europe depending on proximity to sources of coal. Coal was not only cheaper, it had the advantage of producing higher temperatures and more energy than peat, about four times more heat for each unit of weight and volume. Coal took up less space and was easier for stokers to handle. A 75 percent decrease in the volume of fuel represented a considerable saving in effort, and coal supplies did not have to be replenished as frequently.[33] Over time, breweries increasingly came to prefer coal. A process which started in the fifteenth century continued through the eighteenth as more brewers used more coal more often.[34] The savings in volume from the change to coal decreased the amount of shipping needed, in part balanced by the greater distances which had to be covered to bring the coal to the breweries. Brewers who lived close to coal mines had no trouble with the change in energy sources and relied exclusively on coal. At Liege a number of the brewers in the sixteenth century invested in coal mines, presumably to insure supplies for themselves and to profit from the increasing industrial use of the fuel. For brewers in Holland and Brabant, coal had to come from Newcastle and Sunderland (along the northeast coast of England), Scotland or Liege (in the southern Netherlands). In 1608–1609 at Antwerp, brewers would have needed something on the order of 2,675 tonnes of coal to produce their beer.[35] If all that coal came from England and colliers averaged six trips per year between Newcastle and the Low Countries, then about five ships would have been needed full time to supply Antwerp brewers alone. Holland brewers may well have used four or more times as much coal and so required four times as much shipping capacity. Already in 1610, brewing in England was one of the industries identified where coal could replace wood, and in seventeenth-century England coal as in many parts of the Low Countries, was the brewers' fuel of choice.

Consumption and production of beer enjoyed a period of sustained growth in the fifteenth century and, in many places, continued growth in the sixteenth and early seventeenth centuries. The experience of brewing varied in different towns and in different regions through those years. Brewers in certain densely populated metropolises like Antwerp and London enjoyed greater comparative success. In parts of Flanders and Brabant in the sixteenth century, the economy defied general European trends and real wages actually rose. In any case, throughout the sixteenth century they did not fall as much as elsewhere in Europe which translated into favorable circumstances for beer sales. In Holland, in general, through the sixteenth and early seventeenth centuries, workers did better in terms of buying power than their counterparts in the rest of Europe. Cash incomes rose faster than prices as laborers put in more hours.[36] Increases in incomes of industrial and construction workers were the best possible turn of events for brewers since traditionally those men favored beer as a drink and were willing to spend spare cash on it.[37]

Another sign of rising consumption was the consolidation of the retail trade. In England, as elsewhere previously, the total number of ale sellers went down but those remaining did business on a more regular basis. Brewers had been and were expected to sell to consumers first and to retailers second, the rules being an effort to avoid unwarranted price increases. That might still be true but the rules did not prevent more and more retailers from increasing the scale of their businesses. Drinking establishments began to take on more fixed characteristics, became social centers and places for playing games, singing, and other communal activities. By the sixteenth century the drinking house had become an integral and essential part of the social world of ordinary people in England and elsewhere (see Figure 13). The English government took an active role in regulating the sale of drink from the middle of the sixteenth century. The licensing system for what would come to be called public houses was hardly a system and only sporadically effective, but records generated by the government requirement of permission to sell drink indicate that by 1577 the kingdom had one alehouse for every 142 people. By the 1630s, the number may have been of the order of one for every 100 people. If anything, those figures

Figure 13. A boy being asked to fetch some beer for an old man who is eating. Drinking beer at home meant not only missing the social life of the pub but also that someone, often a child, had to go to the nearby pub to bring back beer for the household. Frans van Mieris the Elder (1635–1681), *Domestic Scene in a Farmhouse*. Courtesy of Statens Museum for Kunst, Copenhagen.

are underestimates. There were, of course, more alehouses per person in towns than the countryside.[38]

Rising grain prices through the sixteenth and into the seventeenth century forced consumers to spend a larger share of their income on bread. That meant buying less of something else, and it appears that buyers, individual and institutional, were more willing to cut back on beer than on meat.[39] Even with, and in many cases despite, such pressures in many parts of Europe, beer drinking did not fall but actually rose. Even in regions where beer consumption declined, daily intake was still significant. By the late Renaissance, beer and beer drinking were a very visible part of the lives of virtually everyone. Though real incomes might fall in England or in parts of Germany, brewers seem to have been able, more or less, to maintain levels of production and drinkers, more or less maintained levels of consumption. The beer might not be the same as before and methods of brewing and raw materials might adjust to changing circumstances, but the results were more beer, more brewers, and more ships to carry the raw materials and the final product.

Chapter 9

The Mature Industry: Technology

Trying to identify and isolate the process innovation that formed the sixth stage of development in brewing in northern Europe is even more difficult than trying to establish when people mastered the new technique. At least it is certain that the pace of process innovation was slow. To get more from the earlier breakthrough, that is from the introduction of hops and all that went with it, brewers tried larger-scale production, even greater specialization, and more capital investment. The available evidence for what innovation actually did occur is limited at best and often ambiguous. It is by no means evenly distributed geographically, perhaps creating a false impression of where improvements were to be found.

Treatises on Brewing Technology

In the Renaissance, technical information about brewing could be and was communicated more easily than ever before. In distributing knowledge to other brewers sixteenth- and seventeenth-century writers created much better sources of information on techniques than any which exist for earlier periods. Books on estate management increasingly included advice about beer brewing. Treatises devoted exclusively to brewing and the handling of beer began to appear in the sixteenth century. Those from Germany and England suggest not only a general tendency toward greater interest in categorizing and comprehending nature but also a more systematic approach to making beer. The works may have been largely descriptions of how to brew but, by definition, they were also theoretical works. The first German book on drinking beer came out in 1505, just two years after Richard Arnold's *Chronicle*, that first printed book in English on brewing. As early as 1539, an anonymous author published a book in German on how to deal with serving beer, how to maintain its quality in the cask, and what to add to counteract deterioration during storage. Fresh eggs, salt, hops, a handful of ashes, and even a little wine at the right time could improve beer or save it from being undrinkable. The longer beer could be kept, the greater the need for some additives before serving.

Combinations of herbs and eggs and even linseed oil were suggested to preserve the drink and to improve taste before serving.[1] An English writer in 1594
suggested putting a handful or two of ground malt in the barrel and stirring it
around to revive beer that had started to go sour. He also suggested burying
the barrel for twenty four hours or simply adding some new strong beer to it,
or even putting in some oyster shells or salt. Presumably brewers and publicans in general drew on the well-established tradition of ways to deal with
wine to make sure their beer was and remained palatable.[2]

By 1549 there was already a book in German, *Über Natur und Kräfte der
Biere*, by Johann Brettschneider who styled himself Placotomus. He was a professor of medicine at the University of Königsberg, town physician in Gdansk,
and a friend of the reformer Philip Melanchthon. Placotomus pointed to the
increasing consumption of beer in Germany as one of the reasons for writing
the book. His principal concern was health: in general, he thought beer a good
thing for consumers. Ludovici de Avila, writing on proper diet, in Germany in
1553 said that if beer is not heated enough and then cooled too little, it is bad
for the stomach; while if it is heated too much, it causes wind. Barley and hops
were the ingredients he recommended and he warned against drinking beer
too soon after brewing.[3] His position was echoed by a seventeenth-century
anonymous writer who pointed to the disadvantages of drinking cold beer.
The author argued that in making beer the water should be heated but not
boiled. The argument was punctuated with quotations from Galen, Pliny,
Aristotle, and a broad range of classical writers.[4] Abraham Werner, another
professor of medicine but at the University of Wittenberg, in 1567 published a
largely etymological work on the origins of beer. He also endorsed beer drinking as being healthy. Thaddeus Hagesius published *De Cerevisia* in 1585 and
before that, in 1573, Basil Valentine in England published a book on brewing.
By the second half of the sixteenth century clearly brewing had become a topic
worthy of consideration by scholars.[5]

Jacob Theodor von Bergzabern, who called himself Tabernaemontanus,
was perhaps the most scholarly of the writers on beer. He was the personal
physician of the count of Heidelberg. In 1588, after thirty-six years of collecting
information he published a botanical encyclopedia. He included a broad range
of information about beer: how it was made, how to make it better, and what
should be avoided. While he did explain the process, for example, stating specific times that beer should be boiled to get the healthiest product, what interested him most were the plants used as additives. Hops were the standard but
he mentioned that the English often suspended a mixture of sugar, cinnamon,
cloves, and other spices in a sack in the beer. Flemings did much the same but
also used other sweeteners like honey. He accepted the use of laurel, ivy, or
Dutch myrtle—presumably bog myrtle—to keep the beer resistant to souring.

Henbane, on the other hand, he warned could cause insanity while chimney soot could dry out the lungs and liver and make the face red and ugly. Willow leaves—another possible reference to bog myrtle—in place of hops would, he said, cause the beer to cool too quickly and so cause cramps and colic. He did allow for variations in ingredients and recognized the potential for differences in the quality and potency of beers. His work produced a much more precise picture of the brewing process and of brewers' options than is available from any earlier time.[6]

All those works were precursors of the first extensive and comprehensive work on brewing, *Funff Bücher, von der Göttlichen vnd Edlenn Gabe, der Philosophischen, hochthewren vnd wunderbaren Kunst, Bier zu brawen* by Heinrich Knaust. It appeared in 1573, was reprinted in 1575 and again in 1614, the last edition being the most influential. Knaust thought beer a gift of God and beer brewing a philosophical exercise. There was some negative reaction to his view, criticism which he denounced in a foreword to the second printing. He relied very heavily on Werner and Placotomus, copying large sections from them. He brought together the contemporary body of thinking about brewing at length and in great detail. His principal contribution was to combine the growing theoretical literature with his own experience.[7] Too much should not be made of a scientific approach in any of his work, or that of any of the others of his day, or of the sixteenth century in general. On the other hand, there were clear signs of some systematization of knowledge.

Making beer was a topic for books on housekeeping like one from 1569/1570 written in Dresden, possibly by Abraham Thurmshirn. The author recommended making sure that the beer was neither too hot nor too cold. He also had thoughts on additives and suggested a number of different spices which could be used. Like the author of the 1539 book on pub management, he recommended eggs to help preserve beer but he suggested they be used in combination with wax, linseed oil, and some spices. Beer for him also had other uses, as in a recipe for preparing a goose and as a drink for hens which would make them lay year round. Similarly, in England books on household practice were the usual place to find comments on brewing. Gervase Markham whose book on housewifery first appeared in 1615, explained in gross terms how much water, malt, and hops to use and how the brewer should proceed. The description read like a cookbook with tips on how to know from appearance of the brew when to do what.[8] The few cookbooks and books on household management that appeared in the Renaissance had the dual problems of being directed solely to the urban middle class and of being far from trustworthy since they were idealized programs of what should be done. The readership was interested in social status and how food could enhance status. So books on household management may not accurately reflect what actually went on.

Cookbooks do, at least, indicate the extent to which beer could be used in preparing foods in the later Middle Ages and down through the sixteenth and seventeenth centuries.[9]

While works on brewing appeared in England and even more often in Protestant Germany, in other parts of Europe they were extremely rare. The Low Countries produced beer in significant quantities but did not produce theoretical works similar to the German ones. The absence of published works about brewing may be an indication of the traditional handicraft character of the industry in the Netherlands. Despite the efforts of the few writers on brewing, in the seventeenth century the famous Dutch scientist Constantijn Huygens could still say that the brewer had little understanding of what he did.[10]

Making Beer in the Sixteenth and Seventeenth Centuries

The equipment and processes for making beer were much the same in the sixteenth and early seventeenth centuries as they were around 1400. Even if the essentials of design and construction of the gear for brewing remained much the same, over time brewers found themselves in better buildings and using kettles, troughs, and other implements of higher quality. One long term improvement, begun in the fourteenth century or earlier, was the setting of the brewing kettle on top of an iron grate set on a furnace. Often made of brick, there were walls or platforms around the furnace so workers could stand over the kettle and stir the wort. By the sixteenth century, bigger and more complex versions had replaced earlier forms, often with closed chimneys to carry off fumes. Efforts to save fuel and prevent contamination by smoke from coal or other heating fuels dictated enclosed spaces for the fires and chimneys. The furnaces were limited in size by the space in the brewery, but they had to be big enough to hold the ever larger kettles. The more shallow the copper, the better it was which in turn dictated the form of the furnace.[11] The size of the kettles and the fixed places for them gave breweries the appearance of something larger and more permanent. By the early seventeenth century, bricked ovens under large kettles with some plumbing to move water and wort to and from the kettles were part of virtually all urban breweries. By the seventeenth century underworks to hold the kettle were common in country houses as well (see Figure 14).[12] One inventor in 1619 claimed iron kettles were better because they were less expensive and used less fuel to heat an equivalent quantity of liquid. Despite the lower price of iron, lighter weight and greater durability kept copper as the common choice for brew kettles in the Renaissance. The troughs and vats continued to be made of wood with hard and dry oak

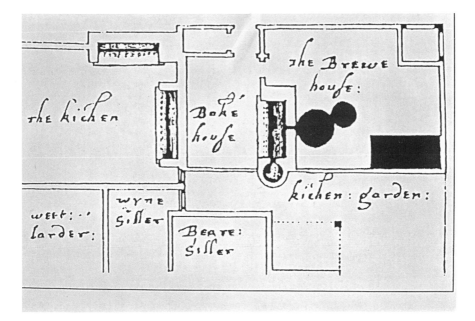

Figure 14. Plan of a 1618 brewhouse from an English country house at Houghton. It is next to the bakehouse and shares the flue. Courtesy of RIBA Library Drawings Collection, as found in Pamela Sambrook, *Country House Brewing in England 1500–1900* (London: The Hambledon Press, 1996), fig. 13, p. 28.

cut across the grain being preferred for the fermenting troughs, at least according to one Dutch author.[13]

A London will of 1335 left the heir with a brewhouse, three shops, and brewing equipment. To make beer there were two leaden vessels, a lead cistern, a tap-trough, a mashvat, a vat for letting unwanted matter settle out, a vat to hold the finished ale, tubs, and other utensils.[14] An English inventory of 1486 made some additions to that usual complement of equipment. There were no less than twenty small tubs of yeast and a loose wooden frame with small openings or false bottom for the mash tun.[15] The last was a common feature for keeping spent grains separate from the wort and allowing the wort to be tapped through the bottom or pumped out without interference from the spent malt or draff. Brewers used a variety of ways to attack that problem. In the fourteenth and fifteenth centuries, Dutch brewers used straw in the vat as a strainer. In the course of the sixteenth century, they replaced straw with a false bottom. That way they could let the wort run out a bung hole in the bottom of the mash tun or pump it out from the bottom of the tun. The other and laborious option, used earlier and continued in some breweries, was to bale the wort out using a bowl or ladles. The first mention of the use of a false bottom in an English country house comes from 1635, so the technique was also an option for domestic brewers by the end of the Renaissance.[16] Accounts for an English country house in the 1540s show equipment that is consistent with what little is known about contemporary breweries in towns like De Arent in Bruges which, in the sixteenth century, had a large brew kettle, a mash tun, a couple of cooling troughs, three small kettles which presumably could be carried, and some equipment for stirring. Breweries always had heavy oars for stirring the malt in the mash tun and stirring the wort while it was boiled. De Arent had stores of yeast but what the urban commercial brewery had that was often missing in private breweries was a stock of barrels and racks to store them, the number in the dozens and possibly even over one hundred in the bigger breweries.[17]

Brewing, Beer Drinking, and the Four Seasons

Brewing was still subject to significant seasonal fluctuations in the Renaissance. Despite that, the trend toward specialization did not abate and more individuals found themselves concentrating their full attention on brewing. By 1500 in some places in England there were efforts to regulate the supply of beer and to improve public order by making brewers brew in all seasons and at all times.[18] Government efforts, however, faced the limitations set by the existing technology so the variations from month to month did not disappear. Sixteenth-century brewers did seal casks. It may be that they understood the advantages of keeping down the amount of air to which beer was exposed during fermentation and so were making progress on decreasing seasonal variations in production. Whatever progress brewers made was, however, limited.

Town governments circumscribed the possibilities for producers to respond to changing technology by restricting the times that they could brew, both during the day and during the year. Restricting hours of brewing in German towns dated from 1310 when Munich fixed times. Such rules turned up later in other German towns like Nuremberg but were not as common in the Low Countries or England. In Flanders, the Ghent government allowed brewers to start brewing earlier in the summer, that is at five o'clock instead of six o'clock, the starting time which prevailed in the winter.[19] Brewers usually started work early, even before dawn, so that they could get the wort into the fermentation troughs in the cool of the evening and night. Those troughs would be in a place open to breezes. Later brewers even had hand-driven fans to push cool air across the top of the troughs.[20] Brewers had to give careful attention to the rate of cooling so that the yeast could grow. In Holland, brewing at night or even in the evening was prohibited, though the repetition of such regulation suggests that brewers violated the rules.[21] The goal of the brewers was to be as busy as possible, to get as much out of their capital investment as they could. Governments often shared that goal though they worried more about quality and about tax evasion than profitability.

Restricting the months during the year in which brewers could produce was more common than restricting hours. The argument was that malting and fermenting needed cool and even temperatures. That was why a number of places, such as Göttingen and Wismar, prohibited brewing in the summer, or, like Lübeck, limited brewing in the summer. More common were restrictions on malting in the summer, as at Rostock and Groningen in the northern Netherlands, and on the export of beer in the summer, as at Bremen where the latest date to brew for sales overseas was 25 May.[22] Though malters in sixteenth-century English towns produced malt all year round, it was still common knowledge that the best malt was made in the winter, and so in country houses the practice remained seasonal. At Norwich in the second half of the sixteenth and early seventeenth centuries, the town fixed beer prices, adjusting them several times a year, presumably in reaction to changes in seasonal production as well as to changes in the price of grain. The prohibition of malting before a certain date, as the one instituted at Wismar in 1587, was probably not so much to prevent a rise in the price of barley through the summer, but rather to maintain the quality of malt.[23] In many places in the summer months less malt was needed anyway.

As brewers in southern Germany turned toward using a type of yeast which settled to the bottom of the fermenting trough, the type which required temperatures from 6° to 8°C, restrictions on brewing in the summer increased. It was the policy in Bavaria from 1539 and reaffirmed in 1553 to limit brewing to the period from 29 September to 24 April. By the early seventeenth century, Bavarian brewers used yeasts that fell to the bottom in the winter but returned to those that rose to the top in the summer because it was too warm for their standard yeast to work.[24] The milder climates of the Low Countries, lower Rhine Valley, and of England made brewing with bottom yeasts difficult even in the winter. Such beers would get an unpalatable taste and would not last through the warm summer months even if kept in deep cellars.[25] Restricting brewing to certain months left brewers and their capital idle for almost half the year. Workers in Germany and the Netherlands, in some cases, turned to carpentry, bricklaying, or another trade in the summer as a seasonal occupation complementing brewing.[26] To compensate for the lack of summer production, Bavarian brewers in March produced a stronger beer with higher alcohol content and more hops. The so-called March beer was typically more expensive than the common winter beer and would last longer into the summer.[27] Antwerp citizens were allowed to buy one barrel of beer each year at half the normal excise, and they usually used the tax exemption to buy *Meerts* or March beer in the spring. Braunschweig brewers also produced a stronger March beer in the winter and in the summer something called *Farschbier*. It was of lower quality and had to be drunk soon after it was made. It was that weaker beer which kept brewers working occasionally through to September and October. Though there may have been seasonal production prohibitions in German towns, they seem to have been less common in the Low Countries. When hopped beer was first introduced in the first half of the fourteenth century, Delft brewers had been allowed to make it only between 1 October and 1 May. That restriction was short lived and by the middle of the century they produced hopped beer year round.[28]

Whether governments based the regulations on practice or practice was dictated by government action, the fact remained that brewers concentrated production in the months of October, November, December, March, and April. The spring months were the time when noncommercial brewers concentrated their efforts, often making more small beer of lower alcohol content for drinking in the warm summer months.[29] At Elblag and Torun, as at Wismar, output of beer was highest in March, April, and May, dropped through the summer months and then picked up again in November and December.[30] Larger brewers were the most likely to maintain something closer to the average level of production throughout the year. Smaller brewers were likely to abandon brewing entirely in at least one and sometimes both of the quarters when production went down.[31] Smaller brewers, with relatively less capital invested, did not face as big a loss if they let their breweries sit idle. If they could find other work for themselves and the rest of their small crews, then the choice of shutting down for a while was easier.

Monthly tax figures from Zwolle for the fifteenth century show what must have been the common pattern among brewers in the Renaissance with high levels of tax paid in February, March, and April with another lower peak in December. For the rest of the year the inidcation is that there was much less activity in the breweries. The timetable was only slightly different from that common a century or even two centuries before, moved perhaps a few weeks later. Restrictions on brewing in the warm months despite advances in technology still prevailed in England even in the eighteenth century.[32] It was only with the development of refrigeration equipment in the second half of the nineteenth century that brewers could control the environment inside their plants and so escape the discipline imposed by the seasons.

In most cases consumption did not show the extensive seasonal variation which production did. Many records from Holland suggest a consistent level of drinking throughout the year. In Flanders, consumption in the region around Bruges was always highest in the months of April through June. It remained at a relatively high, albeit reduced, level through September and then reached the low for the year during the trimester of October through December.[33] The consumption pattern reflected the lessening of grain supplies as the harvest approached, the problems of keeping beer during the warm summer months and production levels of breweries. Peaks of production came weeks, or even a few months, behind peaks of consumption. Consequently the value of using hops to preserve beer became even higher and probably helped in promoting their widespread use. The herb also allowed some, but as it turned out not great, flexibility for brewers in when they would make beer.

Additives, Yeast, and Fermentation

Hops, unquestionably, became the common additive by the sixteenth century. Even in England, certainly by the 1580s, it was taken as a matter of course that hops would be used in making beer, both commercially and domestically, and it was understood that hops made beer keep longer.[34] In Bavaria, thanks to the *Reinheitsgebot*, using anything other than hops was illegal. Brewers had used hops long enough that they realized different quantities were needed, depending on the time of the year and how long the beer was to last. Brewers had also developed a sense of how long to boil the wort with the additive to get the most from hops without destroying the taste. The practice of boiling for twenty, thirty, or even more hours to get a stronger beer did not disappear completely, but a period of around three hours was found to be optimal.[35] As to other additives, there is only the slightest evidence of *gruit* still being in use in the Netherlands in the sixteenth century. It is possible, though, that in the countryside, beyond the scope of the surveillance of authorities, farmers held on to the older and now outmoded practice of using the mixture of bog myrtle with other herbs. In rural western Norway in the 1950s brewers still used *pors*, that is bog myrtle. The survival of the practice was certainly exceptional since in the sixteenth, but especially in the seventeenth centuries, there were campaigns in central Europe to get rid of *grut* or *pors*.[36] There are many indications—including books on making beer—that, along with hops, some brewers added other things like sugar, honey, spices (such as cinnamon and cloves), and in one case powdered bayberries to give some beers a specific taste. Typically it was the dried stems, roots, leaves, and flowers of plants—rather than fruits or seeds—that found their way into beer, though brewers did use sweet fruits like cherries, sloes, and raspberries to get results similar to those they got with sugar and honey.[37]

Brewers resorted to a number of options to eliminate impurities and unprocessed vegetable matter. They tried a pig's or ox's foot but also burned salt, clean sand, lime, ground oak bark, and the more modern option of dried fish membranes as finings to make for a clearer beer. Bruges brewers skinned the feet of oxen and calves, boiled them to get rid of the hooves, and then hung them along with other items like berries or an egg, in a bag in the brewing kettle. The collection could last a month with twelve to fourteen oxen feet or twenty calves' feet required to make 10,000 liters of beer. Brewers also tried various methods of filtering the wort. Government rules on grinding malt, inspired by fiscal considerations, tended to improve the quality of work done for brewers and so improved the chances of their getting the roughly ground malt that acted as a filter. In 1606 at Wismar, brewers were using straw to filter beer, presumably after fermentation and before putting it in barrels. The straw became impregnated with nutrients in the process and so became valuable. One item caught after fermentation was yeast and brewers sold that yeast to other commercial brewers and bakers. The sale of the dregs of still-fermenting beer, used for leavening bread, is mentioned among the cries of Paris, so apparently bakers and householders bought yeast in that form on the street.[38]

The ways brewers dealt with yeast changed during the fifteenth and sixteenth centuries. A common option in the early and high Middle Ages was to let airborne yeasts infect the hot wort after boiling. That was the way fermentation was carried out with wine, cider, and mead. Relying on airborne yeasts, brewers virtually never got a distinctly high or low fermentation variety but rather something mixed. The method worked but was haphazard and raised the risk of infection from unwanted yeast strains which could ruin the beer. Some brewers did, it seems, recognize the possible infection of their brews by airborne yeast, a situation first mentioned at Munich in 1551. The realization was slow in coming, however. As early as the mid-fourteenth century a Flemish recipe book mentions adding yeast to beer, and it seems likely that already by 1300 brewers were using some of the foam skimmed off the top of the fermenting beer from the last brew to start fermentation with the next one. By the sixteenth century, brewers commonly added yeast to wort from cultures which they kept separate and which they controlled and maintained. Regulations in Harlem in 1519 and 1550 leave no doubt that brewers added yeast once the wort was in the fermenting troughs.[39] Storing yeast was a problem since the culture could become infected and excessive heat could kill the organism. Summer was the most dangerous time of the year for yeasts. One solution was to dry the dregs of the beer barrel and mix that yeast with flour to make cakes which would start to grow again when the brewer added water. The dregs could also be kept wet and then used to start fermentation in the next brew. Brewers could add some beer from a previous brew to start the process along.[40] They could alternately add some bread in which yeast had been growing. They simply could not clean the fermenting troughs very well, so there was always some yeast still in them. Brewers could not guarantee pure yeasts, as was possible by the end of the nineteenth century, but through selection and care in dealing with what they had they did gain some control over the product. Excess yeast, skimmed off the top of the beer in the fermenting troughs or run out of the casks, was valuable both for use in starting the next brew and also in baking. In sixteenth century Norwich brewers gave the yeast to charities. In later centuries brewers would be less willing to part with that valuable commodity for nothing.[41]

The typical yeast used in Europe in the Renaissance was the type that rose to the top. In 1420 a brewer in Munich got permission to use yeast that fell to the bottom and regulations from Nuremberg suggest that bottom yeasts which had been identified and to some degree isolated were already in use in the fourteenth century. It may be that the practice started in Bohemia since before 1485, Bohemian workers came to Munich to brew beer in what was called the Bohemian manner. In 1603, with the agreement of the brewers, the town council of Cologne outlawed the use of yeasts that went to the bottom. By then, obviously, brewers could not only distinguish the two, they could also choose which one grew in their beer. In rural districts it appears that both types of yeast were known and that both were used for baking as well as brewing.[42]

With bottom fermentation as it was practiced in Bohemia and Bavaria, the overwhelming majority of fermentation took place in ten to twelve days. Brewers then put beer in casks where secondary fermentation matured the drink. They left some space in the top after filling to accommodate foam. Barrels were stored where they were cooled by breezes around them which slowed the fermentation process. At least that was the practice advised in the second half of the sixteenth century.[43] Letting beer ferment longer, as was the case with yeasts that fell to the bottom, increased the alcohol content, but it rose no higher than the upper limit set by the vegetable matter available for fermentation. With the yeast which rose to the top, the period of fermentation was typically shorter, from one to three days. With those yeasts brewers could let the whole process take place in the cask. The yeast, bubbling up, filled the empty space and then was pushed out through a hole in the barrel where the brewer skimmed it off. He or she could speed the process of fermentation along by using smaller vessels which put more yeast surfaces in contact with vegetable matter. One option used was to move the beer into smaller containers, like barrels, after the first two or three days. Whether fermentation went on in troughs or in casks, one goal was to keep down the amount of air available to the beer. Pieces of rough paper put in the bung holes before tapping in the bungs kept air out of the casks. Another way to get the same effect was to use deep fermenting troughs so that only a small amount of the beer had a surface exposed to the air.[44] The increasing size of brews and the need to conserve space led to the use of larger and, therefore, often deeper troughs. Brewers got better results, but it is not clear if they appreciated why fermentation improved.

Brewers also adjusted the aging or the period of curing their beer. Governments laid down rules on how long beer had to stay in the brewery before delivery to consumers. As early as 1425 at Kiel, beer had to sit, stoppered, in casks in the cellar of the brewer for two nights before it was considered drinkable (see Figure 15). At Hamburg, a 1483 regulation required beer to be sent out of the brewer's cellar within eight days of being put in barrels and within three days in the summer. The rules were to guarantee that full and proper fermentation had taken place and also to be sure the beer was sold quickly before it went bad. At Wismar in 1574, it was expected that the beer would sit in the cellar for awhile, and since the beer would lose some liquid, brewers were allowed to make additions within strict limits. In all cases, the beer was to be stoppered within two hours of going into the cask. Brewers, in general, in Germany were expected to have cellars, cool areas for storage; in Nuremberg from 1380 the minimum size of the cellar was fixed in town bylaws.[45] Amsterdam regulations called for beer to sit in the brewery for four days before it could go on the market, three days in the warm months of June, July, and August. Beer for export out of the city, on the other hand, could be shipped from the brewery the same day. In order to maintain the quality and also the durability of her beer in the second half of the sixteenth century, Maastricht required that it sit in the cask for eight days, ten days for heavy beer. In London by the mid-fifteenth century, brewers had to let beer sit working in a vat for at least a night and a day before sale. At the least that gave time for some settling out of solid matter.[46] Hopped beers could last longer than English ales, so there was all the more reason for gaining any possible advantages by letting it sit for a few days before drinking.[47] After the process of aging in the cask in the brewery was finished, the beer could be moved. On delivery it would have to sit for a short time to allow any solid matter to settle to the bottom. Stronger, heavier beers could tolerate and even benefited from aging for longer periods.[48] In most towns, aging periods fixed by law reflected governments' desires to maintain the quality and the reputation of the local product as well as insure the health and welfare of citizens.

Restriction and Regulation

During the fifteenth century and even more in the sixteenth, town governments tended to circumscribe the technical possibilities of brewers through increasing legislation which dictated the methods brewers had to use. Nurem-

Figure 15. Sliding beer barrels into a cellar, by Matthäus Landauer, d. 1515. Miniature on parchment. Courtesy of Stadtbibliothek Nürnberg, Amb. 279.2°, f. 8v.

berg's first regulations on beer (dated 1303–1305, 1315, and 1325) fixed prices, the composition of the beer, the brewing time, and even the sale and serving times of beer, as well as requiring an oath of brewers and putting in place town officials to control the trade. Those rules remained in force until Bavaria absorbed the imperial free city in 1806. The level of restriction was extreme by standards of the early fourteenth century, but two hundred years later it was common. In Bavaria when brewing was still a minor industry and beer was not able to compete with wine, the duke laid down regulations for Munich brewers first in 1372, and again in 1409 and from 1447 through 1453. The avowed purpose was to benefit general welfare, and one way to do it was to require a license to practice brewing as well as payment of an annual fee, all that as early as 1372. Munich in 1310 had the first case in Germany of fixing the hours when brewers could make beer.[49]

In England regulation was less systematic and complete than it was in the Low Countries or north German towns. The origins of legislation for the entire English kingdom were local. Aleconners or aletasters, minor officials, were common in England by the fourteenth century. They were responsible for tasting beer, and if they found it too weak or otherwise lacking in some way, they had the right to set its price below the norm. London had regulations on the use of malt by the mid-fifteenth century. Oxford in 1434 directed brewers to set a rota so that at least two or three of them brewed two to three times a week, whatever the price of malt might be. Brewers there were under continuing surveillance. In 1449 the town found nine brewers guilty of making weak beer and forced them to take an oath to boil their beer longer.[50] It was 1532 when Norwich required a license from the city for the right to brew. York followed in 1562, Nottingham in 1566, and Leicester in 1599. The English licensing requirements, unlike the German, did not prove very durable, and new brewers were often able to break through the limitation.[51]

The greatest restriction on the ability of brewers to respond to changing circumstances was town legislation on the composition and strength of beer laid down in specific recipes which brewers had to follow. The regulations fixed the *pegel* or standard for beer production. They laid down fixed quantities of each type of grain brewers used. The *pegel* was probably effective not only because of the quality of enforcement, but also because brewers benefited to some degree from having a standard. Not all places adhered to strict regulation of the components of beer. Diest in the southern Low Countries, for example, relied on common practice or tradition. The rules setting the *pegel* were not always rigid. There were many opportunities for substitution of different grains. For rural brewers, availability of brewing material was always the critical consideration, no matter what preferences might exist. In towns the flexibility in the rules suggests that, even though there were preferred grains, brewers used first and foremost what they could get. The *pegel* could be complex. The confusion from imprecise and variable regulation helped brewers to evade or bend the regulations to their advantage.[52] That would interest them since the relative prices of the different grains were not stable.[53] Towns often made short-term changes in the regulations in response to a marked shortage of a certain grain. Towns also made changes now and again to accommodate long-term trends in taste. While the rules set proportions, they also, in many cases, set volume; so the rules dictated both the type and the strength of the beer. The government and the consumer were probably more interested in the latter than the former. In 1549 at Delft, it was agreed that rather than have fixed legislated proportions of grain, the town itself would, after consultation, decide on the best proportions for the next month.[54] Though there were civic rules, legislators could not address inevitable variations in the quality of grains used. Moreover some brewers were better at getting more beer from their malt mixture than others.[55]

Though beer could be made from literally any grain, the usual components were oats, wheat, rye, and barley. The combination of the four could be and was adjusted according to availability, price, season, and the desired results. By the late thirteenth century, the food grains the canons of St. Paul's Cathedral in London got from their manors were by volume 46 percent wheat, 46 percent oats, and 9 percent barley. Most of the wheat went to make bread and any left over, along with virtually all the oats and barley, was malted for making ale. Monks at Westminster Abbey, on the other hand, consumed by volume 31 percent wheat, 44 percent oats, 24 percent barley, and 2 percent dredge; the barley, dredge, and much of the oats went for brewing. Dredge was a mixture of barley and oats. In 1289 before Christmas, the household of an English bishop used wheat, oats, and barley together, but in the following March it was wheat and oats only. From 1412 to 1413 the household of an English noblewoman used equal parts of barley and dredge except in January and February when barely malt was the sole ingredient.[56] Placotomus in 1549 called beer made with wheat "white beer" and that with barley "red beer." The latter, he claimed, did not remain sweet as long as the former. In 1588 Tabernaemontanus said any two- or three-part combination of wheat, spelt, rye, or oats was best but conceded that any one alone would be fine. The results from different parts of northern Europe for the Middle Ages and Renaissance show the consistency of diversity, of prominent roles for wheat and oats and the slow move toward barley. Rye did not disappear entirely. It was used more in the north and east and even survived in Estonia as a raw material for beer into the nineteenth century.[57]

The historical tie of barley with beer was a product of the closing years of the Middle Ages and the Renaissance. The share of barley and dredge in total grain production went up in England before 1350, along with all of the cheaper bread grains, as consumers adjusted to rising prices. And ale was made more cheaply, that is increasingly with dredge and oats rather than with relatively more expensive barley. After 1350, however, English farmers sowed more arable land in barley and dredge and had a higher proportion of their harvest malted to make beer. Oats gradually disappeared from breweries, and dredge production went down while farmers grew more barley (in relative and possibly even absolute amounts) as cultivation spread to new parts of the kingdom. It may well be that more land was used to cultivate brewing grains in 1400 than in 1301 in England. Barley unquestionably predominated in beer breweries in sixteenth-century England as it had predominated in the making of ale in aristocratic English houses in the fourteenth and fifteenth centuries (see Figure 16).[58] Price data suggest that barley, typically the cheapest grain, was perceived by consumers to be an inferior good along with rye; if the buyer could afford it, wheat was much preferred. Wealthier individuals chose wheaten bread which left barley less in demand. The logical result was dampened price increases, making barley an ever better candidate for use by brewers. Over time, their demand raised the price of barley, so the difference between the prices of the two grains narrowed in the course of the sixteenth century. Barley prices fell less in southern Germany than wheat prices in the first two decades of the sixteenth century. The explanation may have been brewers' demand for barley.[59] The Bavarian *Reinheitsgebot* more or less drove all grains but barley out of the brewing process in the duchy, something accomplished at Nuremberg by law in 1290 and 1305. The Nuremburg restriction seems to have been unique not only because of the early commitment to barley, but also because it remained in effect no matter the relative prices of different grains. In the 1530s, brewers in Upper Austria used a combination of malts made from wheat, barley, and oats, but a government regulation of 1560 required that henceforth they could use only barley.[60] Their counterparts in Bohemia, an exporter of malt to Austria and Bavaria, used barley and wheat. Bohemian barley beer was heavier and more expensive and, presumably, of higher quality than beer made from wheat.[61]

Despite the general drift toward barely as the principal grain in brewing, there were some prohibitions on its use in beer in the sixteenth and early seventeenth century, largely in southern and southeast Germany. Breslau, for example, said brewers could no longer use barley in 1573 and again in 1622.[62] Such restrictions were typically short term and based on the price and availability of grain rather than on the type or character of the beer being produced. By 1650 such restrictions were rare. Any preference for wheat in beer had eroded by then as well. The *pegel* for different towns across northern Europe from the thirteenth to the sixteenth century suggests a drift away from wheat

Figure 16. The medieval brewhouse at White Castle, Monmouthshire, Wales. Photograph by C. M. Woolgar. Reprinted from C. M. Woolgar, *The Great Household in Late Medieval England* (New Haven: Yale University Press, 1999), 127.

TABLE 6. PROPORTIONS OF GRAINS FOR THE PRODUCTION OF BEER, THIRTEENTH THROUGH SIXTEENTH CENTURY, IN PERCENTAGES

Town	Date	Beer Type	Wheat	Oats	Barley
London	1286		17	66	17
Nuremberg	1305				100
Ghent	Fourteenth century		50		50
Lier	1440	*kuit*	43	35	22
Lier	1440	*hop*	20	60	20
Brussels	1447	*wagebaard*	27	46	27
Hamburg	1462		10		90
Lille	c. 1500		23	45	32
London	1502 (?)		14	14	72*
Bavaria	1516				100
Antwerp	1518	*kuit*	73	15	12
Antwerp	1518	*klein bier*	13	47	40
Lille	1521		12	70	18 ‡
Hannover	1526		33		67 †
Antwerp	1536	*kuit*	8	49	43
Antwerp	1536	*knol*	18	45	37
Antwerp	1536	*half stuuyvers*	18	40	42
Antwerp	1530s	*cleyn bier*	13	47	40
Antwerp	1530s	strong	20	40	40
Lille	1546			20	80 ‡
Hamburg	Sixteenth century	*Weissbier*	10		90

Sources: Arnold, *Chronicle (Customs of London)*, 247; Bing, *Hamburgs Bierbrauerei*, 254; Bracker, "Hopbier uit Hamburg," 29; Campbell et al., *A Medieval Capital and Its Grain Supply*, 205–6; DuPlessis, *Lille and the Dutch Revolt*, 124 n. 13; Löhdefink, *Die Entwicklung der Brauergilde*, 18; Maitland, *Domesday Book and Beyond*, 440; Peeters, "Introduction," in combined facsimile editions of Lis and Buys; Soly, "De Brouwerijenonderneming van Gilbert van Schoonbeke," 340–44; Uytven, "Haarlemmer hop," 345.

*Called "malte" by Arnold and presumably barley malt.
†Said to be in the Hamburg style.
‡Temporary restrictions to meet grain shortages.

for brewers and a decrease, though less dramatic, in the use of oats for making beer. Barley, as a result, was the most popular beer grain (see Table 6).

In general the mixture of grains was probably the most important determinant in fixing the type of beer. Barley, though perhaps the dominant grain, was still only one of many components of the mix of malt and grain used in beer making. Whereas unmalted grain may well have continued to be a component of the raw materials for beer as late as the early sixteenth century in Holland and in home brews in England in the 1570s, that practice had disappeared from commercial breweries by midcentury.[63] There were regional variations in the kinds of malted grains brewers used or governments allowed them to use. Oats remained popular with beer makers in the west of England. Augsburg brewers in 1430 were limited to the exclusive use of oats, though that may have been a temporary measure. Oats grew more easily than other grains in the damp soil of the Low Countries which may help to explain the popularity of the grain for brewing there. In the first half of the fifteenth century, the earliest period for which there is information, brewers at Lier used more than 50 percent oats to make both the standard beer and small beers. Holland lagged behind the general tendency in the rest of Europe toward greater use of barley in brewing. The presence of rye in recipes from the northern Netherlands also set the region apart from the rest of Europe. Leuven in Brabant was emphatic and never allowed the use of rye or oats in brewing. Spelt was acceptable at times, and when prices rose, even wheat was prohibited to brewers.[64] In sixteenth-century Antwerp barley and oats made up 80 to 90 percent of the grain used to produce beer. Wheat made up the remaining 10 to 20 percent. There was a move away from the use of oats toward barley in seventeenth-century Antwerp, though brewers added spelt and buckwheat to their mashings as well.[65] The preference in Poland in the high Middle Ages was apparently for beer made with wheat since in 1303 a prominent cleric declined the archepiscopal see of Salzburg when he was told he could not get wheat beer in Austria. Later, in 1470, an observer said that Poland's native drink was made from water, hops, and wheat, so tastes were apparently slow to change.[66]

The Jesuit houses in the southern Low Countries in the 1620s seem to have been old-fashioned using 25 percent unmalted wheat, 15 percent malted oats and 60 percent malted barley. The practice shows the continuing tendency to move from oats toward barley and a consciousness of the cost of wheat as a component. By not malting the wheat, Jesuit brewers could save money, although the result gave a different taste to the beer. Beer with wheat, at least according to some, caused disease, and so it was thought better to replace the unmalted wheat with 1.5 times as much malted barley for a better tasting and healthier drink. The wheat must have also given an extremely pale appearance to the beer, contrary to the typical amber hue of seventeenth-century beers.[67]

Profits

Many towns fixed beer prices. Many towns fixed the grains used. Some towns, such as sixteenth-century Wismar, fixed wage rates for workers, down to the smallest task.[68] Even if wages were not set, the prevailing combination of restrictions meant that brewers' profits were strongly influenced by the amounts of particular grains they used to make a quantity of beer. Since grain costs made up such a large proportion of total costs and made up the large majority of variable costs, a small change in the market price of grain could make a big difference in brewers' returns. In the sixteenth century, farmers could not keep pace with the rising demand for food grains which a growing population created, so grain prices rose.[69] In addition political troubles, and they were common, could drive prices up. At Ghent between 1527 and 1585, grain prices rose fourteen fold and the cheapest beers did not even double in price. Brewers were then faced with a long term price trend which worked against them and short-term fluctuations which could spell disaster. In order to keep profit margins up, brewers' solutions over the long term were to make high-quality beers which commanded much higher prices and to make weaker beer at a price that could be kept, more or less, constant. The latter choice meant using less grain for each barrel of beer and so lowering the alcohol content. The small or *klein* beer brewed in Lier in 1434 was 6 percent alcohol but by 1505–1508 it was down to 3.35 percent. Less alcohol meant beer was less durable and so less likely to be a trade good. Another way to degrade beer was to use substitutes like buckwheat, beans, or peas for the traditional brewing grains. As the century wore on and grain prices rose, it became more likely that brewers had to adjust the quality of their beer to maintain sales.[70] At Wismar from the second half of the fourteenth century to 1640, the amount of beer produced from the same quantity of malt increased threefold. At Nuremberg it increased twofold in the short period from 1521 to 1564.[71] It was not just in Germany that beer became thinner. Everywhere quality deteriorated, consumers were dissatisfied, and brewers were forced to seek ways of improving productivity to protect their threatened profit margins.

Legislated maximum beer prices usually depended on the type of beer. At Liege, as elsewhere, there were officers of the town to set those prices and to maintain the standards for each type. Towns could and did use imports of beer to keep down or drive down the prices of domestically brewed beer, as London did in 1478 and 1492.[72] Hamburg set maximum prices, too, but as an exporter, the town was also interested in maintaining minimum prices. Realizing the importance of brewing to the urban economy and the potential for trouble in the industry, Hamburg regulated the grain trade in the interests of brewers. For example, three times in the sixteenth century the export of barley was prohibited.[73] Such restrictions were no longer possible a century later when Hamburg became a center of the grain trade and so had to allow free movement of all grains in and out of the port. The same problem, being unable to regulate the grain market for the benefit of brewers, turned up for the same reason in Holland by the mid-sixteenth century, if not before.

Since towns set prices and since profits were threatened, brewers often petitioned the town government to do something about the prices at which they could sell beer. The pressure became greater as the sixteenth century went on. At Nuremberg, for example, between 1564 and 1620 half of the some 120 petitions made to the town government by the brewers had to do with the beer price. In some cases the brewers persuaded the government to allow increases for beer sold to drinkers in public houses and also for sale to homes, as at Leiden in 1604 when local producers got a small rise in the price of beer sold by the barrel to public houses.[74]

Price increases were the exception. Diluting beer was the way brewers typically passed on rising costs to customers. The practice could well damage brewers' chances for getting a price increase from the authorities. As part of their perceived public function, brewers were expected to continue to brew even if profits were squeezed or even if they lost money.[75] Town policy goals, together with the seasonal and annual wide swings in grain prices, made regulation of beer prices a battleground for governments and brewers. In England in 1597 several brewers were sentenced to prison for charging more than the legislated price. Their defense—that with rising grain prices they thought the authorities would allow them to charge double the legal maximum—did them no good. They believed, it would appear, as did many brewers, that the posted price was only the normal price, and that they would not be subject to prosecution for responding to rising prices. One option open to brewers to skirt the law on maximum prices was to export. It was extremely difficult to control export prices, and town governments generally preferred to let local brewers get as much as they could out of selling beer elsewhere.[76] The Holland towns with established export markets, at least in the late fifteenth century, could hope to pass on price increases to traditional buyers in other towns, but their position was not a common one. In the sixteenth century even their advantageous position eroded.

One solution to the brewers' problem, tried by government in England under the Assize of Bread and Ale, was to allow the price of beer to rise when grain prices rose and, by implication, to fall when grain prices came down. A similar scheme at Lille dated from 1474 and allowed fluctuation of beer prices within a narrow range. The formula, however, could yield a greater proportional drop in beer prices than in grain prices. In Wismar the town government checked twice a year, after 11 November and in January, to see what had happened to barley prices so they could make any necessary adjustment in price regulations for beer.[77] The policy was similar to the one which let brewers change the grains they used in response to changes in the relative prices of their principal raw materials.

The general tendency toward decreasing beer quality in the sixteenth century was often met by the production of a premium beer alongside the thinner beers, with prices fixed to keep them still within reach of most buyers. By the late sixteenth century, at least two kinds of beer were available to consumers. Imports supplemented the choice. Brewers and publicans preferred sales of the more expensive beers since, at least in the example of Ghent in the 1570s, the price differential between beers was more than the tax differential. Thus the greatest profit was to be had from the most expensive beer. Governments proved more willing to entertain price increases for the premium products. On the other hand, only with great reluctance did they increase the price of *klein bier* (small beer) since that had to be a politically unpopular move.[78] Towns then affected brewers' profits not only by the prices they set for the products, but also by the excise taxes they set, taxes which made up a large share of the selling price of the product.

Estimating the profitability of brewing is virtually impossible. The English regulations on price and information about grain use and prices from Oxford for 1310 indicate that in that year, depending on other costs and the range of output from the inputs, it was possible for a brewer of ale to have achieved anything from making extraordinary profits to suffering extraordinary losses. There as elsewhere in late medieval and Renaissance Europe, reality fell between those two extremes.[79] The change to making beer with hops in the short run may have improved profitability, but rising grain prices and tighter government regulation over time swept away the advantage.

An English household management manual of the mid-sixteenth century gave a breakdown of costs in making beer. For heat the expenditure was 7 percent of the total, for hops 2 percent, and for grain 91 percent. Another English description from the 1570s made malt only 48 percent of total outlay but included among the costs were not only wood for heating, 20 percent of the total, and hops, 8 percent of the total, but also the wages of servants doing the work at 12 percent and wear and tear on the brewing kettle at 9 percent. There were other incidental expenses.[80] So even for the domestic brewer, capital and labor costs could be significant. Commercial brewers faced distribution costs and tax burdens as well. Even with those additions, raw-material costs overwhelmed the expenditures and that was true for virtually all brewers everywhere. At Hamburg in 1589, grain and hops and fuel were 93 percent of total outlays and the biggest share of those were grain costs which in general ran from 70 percent to 80 percent of expenses. Labor costs seem to have been typically around 10 percent though possibly rising to 15 percent of total outlays. Often much of the crew was made up of family members, so it would have been difficult even for the brewer to identify the expenses for labor.[81]

The data on expenses and on profits, are sparse and so can easily be misleading. There does seem to be some consistency, however, in the breakdown of expenditures for sixteenth-century breweries. There are also indications of a profit rate in the range of 20 to 30 percent in some German Hanse towns in the early seventeenth century. It is impossible to follow the pattern of change over time or to find out how much effect taxation had on brewers' incomes. As always, both brewers and governments had interests in the success of the industry, a joint interest which was regularly tested when matters of profit came to be considered. Direct taxation on beer and indirect taxation on inputs and land were undoubtedly a heavy burden for the brewing industry. That burden increased through the sixteenth century to the point, at least in some German towns, where profits may have fallen to zero by 1600.[82] Brewing was critical to the financial health of governments. All of them retained a deep interest in the welfare of brewing and so adjusted taxes and regulations, but over the long run they always showed less interest in brewers than in their own incomes. Governments might tolerate extraordinary losses on the part of brewers but would not tolerate extraordinary profits for long. The interests of governments ultimately, through regulations, set limits on what brewers did and so, in the process, set limits on the technology of brewing.

Chapter 10

The Mature Industry: Capital Investment and Innovation

By the standards of the sixteenth century, breweries already involved a sizeable investment in fixed capital. Brewing, like leather working, was different from most contemporary economic activities on land in that it had a relatively high ratio of capital to labor, a fact dictated by the technology and by continuing efforts to exploit existing technology more effectively. Brewers felt pressure to innovate because people were often drinking less beer. In southern Germany, beer production and sales grew as it displaced wine, but in much of the rest of Europe, with few exceptions, the market for beer stabilized and in the seventeenth century in a number of places it declined. With the price of grain, the most expensive raw material, rising brewers went to all kinds of expedients to reduce their costs. Those included technical changes in heating, investing in more and better equipment, becoming involved in the coal trade and coal mining, becoming involved in the grain trade, forcing down wages of workers, increasing the scale of production, becoming more active in export markets, supplementing local ones, and, of course, asking governments to reduce the tax burden.[1]

Renaissance brewers reacted in a number of ways but the one which was most consistent, which promised the greatest savings, and which best exploited the potential of existing technology was to increase the size of the individual firm. The pattern of consolidation into a smaller number of units was consistent with the general tendency that had existed in towns and even in villages since brewing with hops began.[2] Growth in demand and the need to have access to hops had been important in promoting the early consolidation of brewing. Having a product that lasted longer increased capital requirements as brewers kept greater stocks on hand. The more durable beer allowed brewers to reach a wider market which made commercial and credit connections with buyers more important to success. The potential for gain from increasing the scale of production in any brewery was greater than ever before in the sixteenth century. Consolidation, however, immediately created political problems. Many smaller brewers saw the potential for their being driven out of business by bigger and expanding competitors. Rising grain prices and rising taxes increased the threat to smaller brewers. They turned to governments in the Low Countries, especially in Holland, to protect them by maintaining and enforcing existing legislation which limited the scale of brewing operations. In the end, the big brewers won the battle and if anything European governments, through the promotion of investment, contributed to the growth in the scale of breweries and the brewing trade.

Raw Materials and Official Assistance

Bigger brewers typically had better access to raw materials. Even with the most used and most ubiquitous raw material, water, bigger brewers had an advantage. About 85 percent of beer is water and in addition brewers needed large quantities of water for cooling and cleaning. Finding good, clean water was a constant problem for brewers. Having brewers close to each other made supplying water to them easier but also made the problem of getting clean water more acute—the larger the industry, the higher the levels of production, the more serious the problem.[3] Pollution forced the creation of joint capital-intensive schemes to give access to needed water. Such schemes increased the pressure for concentration, even though the schemes had only limited success.

The profession of water carriers, or transporters, was a product of the Middle Ages. In England when water supplies in London, Bristol, Coventry, and elsewhere became less reliable because of the multiple uses of streams, tradesmen apparently supplied brewers with the water they needed.[4] Lübeck from 1294 on had a system of conduits which brought water into the center of the town from a river that flowed along the walls. The water was for everyone but brewers were the ones who promoted the construction of what was the first of the waterworks constructed in Germany. Brewers were also the greatest beneficiaries. The Lübeck system served as the example for Bremen, Augsburg, Ulm, Hannover, and other towns when they built waterworks.[5] Brewers in Edinburgh, Scotland, in the early seventeenth century built a special reservoir to guarantee their supplies of water, and Wismar in northern Germany had a system of piped water that connected houses, including breweries, to a reservoir. In those cases users paid for the systems. In Holland such arrangements were hardly known. There brewers, as at Haarlem and later Amsterdam, organized the shipment of water by boat from sources away from the pollution of the rapidly growing towns.[6] As was the case with the wooden or metal pipes, such arrangements implied cooperation among brewers and often capital investment by them.

The one case in the sixteenth-century Low Countries of joint action with government support to create direct access to good water on a large scale occurred in Antwerp. The economic historian Hugo Soly has carefully and fully documented the cooperation between the town government and an entrepreneur, Gilbert van Schoonbeke, to revive and expand the brewing industry in the town through the construction of a system to get good water to one place. The project, implemented in the 1550s, owed as much to dreams of real-estate speculation as to the promotion of industry. The town had already, between 1486 and 1490, dug a new waterway to bring better water to the town. The quality still could not compare with that available in small towns near Antwerp. Van Schoonbeke, who had farmed the beer excise tax from 1551 to 1553, realized the potential of the brewing industry in the rapidly growing and prosperous town but also knew that the brewers needed fresh, sweet water and protection from competition from brewers near at hand. He created a new source of water which centralized brewing and had a deep and lasting effect on the industry.

In 1542 Antwerp expanded its city limits. A new district, aptly named Nieuwstad, was set up and beginning in 1548 the government tried to promote industrial development there but did not succeed. When in late 1552 van Schoonbeke came forward with a scheme to use a portion of the land for breweries, the town willingly agreed (see Figure 17). In 1553 the overlord, Emperor Charles V, approved the plan. The approval came after the developer agreed to turn over 31 percent of his beer excise-tax income to the emperor. Van Schoonbeke contracted with the town government to construct breweries on a site between two canals complete with windows, rooms, and cellars. The brewers got the premises rent free and some of the equipment. They only had to supply the remaining equipment and the barrels. The town agreed to close its own town brewery, and the brewers who moved their operations to the new site were exempt from certain taxes for twenty-five years for themselves and their families. The excise office was to be moved to the new district so brewers would not waste time traveling back and forth to pay taxes due.

Not all Antwerp brewers leapt at the chance, though, in part because of the excise tax they had to pay to van Schoonbeke and in part because they did not want to leave their old sites, old neighborhoods, and, most important, old and established clientele. It was typically the smaller brewers who did not accept van Schoonbeke's offer. Even so, within less than a year ten of the sixteen breweries planned for the Nieuwstad were filled with producers hard at work making both thin and double beer. In addition to paying a tax on each barrel they produced, brewers had to buy their heating fuel (peat or wood) from van Schoonbeke at fixed prices. Moreover, Schoonbeke had a monopoly on the delivery of their beer. He owned the mills where the brewers had to have malt ground. He had the right to rental income from the parts of their

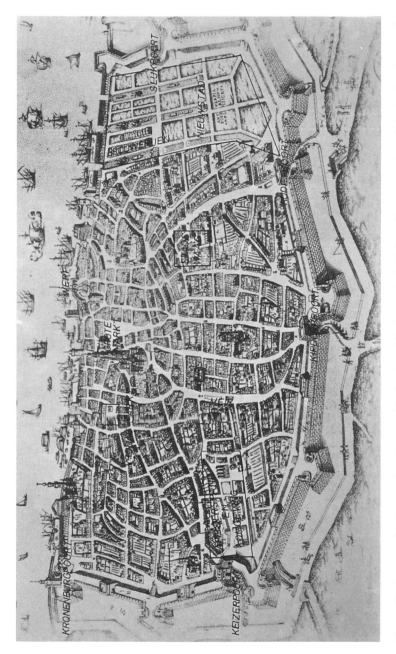

Figure 17. Antwerp, bird's-eye view of 1557, with the site of the breweries built by Gilbert van Schoonbeke in the Nieuwstad indicated in the upper right (*Brouwerijen*). Reprinted from Hugo Soly, *Urbanisme en kapitalisme te Antwerpen in de 16de eeuw: De stedebouwkundige en industriële ondernemingen van Gilbert van Schoonbeke* (Antwerp: Gemeentekrediet van Belgie, historische uitgaven pro civitate, series in-8°: no. 47, 1977), 201.

cellars and grain attics they did not use. As it turned out, those other charges were worth almost as much to van Schoonbeke as the direct excise charged on each barrel of beer. Brewers had to pay a minimum amount to van Schoonbeke which probably translated into a minimum level of production. Van Schoonbeke did not completely fulfill his part of the bargain, and the town government found itself insisting that he build all the breweries he had promised as well as some cellars. Originally the plan was to bring water to the new breweries by boat from out in the country but that proved to be too expensive. Van Schoonbeke instead constructed a conduit from outside the city walls to a central water house in the middle of the development, a mill powered by horses to raise the water, and a system of pipes to take water to each of the new breweries. The total capital investment in the entire operation—breweries, water supply, draft animals, wagons, and mills—was massive by contemporary standards.

In 1554 there were disruptions and demonstrations in the city against the privileges granted to van Schoonbeke. The threat to small business and to traditional supplies of beer led to the public outburst. Order was not restored until the following year, and even then the town government had to make concessions to the crowd. Van Schoonbeke lost some of his entitlements but was able to negotiate a new contract with the town in 1555. The deal gave him compensation for losses and restored some sources of income. It also installed inspectors who would guarantee the quality of the water supplied by his system so that the reputation of beer from the new breweries would not be damaged by rumor. It appears that van Schoonbeke enjoyed a return of about 11.4 percent per year on his invested capital, about twice the typical return in brewing, with virtually no risk. The town got a 14 percent return for its trouble, but after renegotiation and some repayment of capital from van Schoonbeke, the annual return rose to no less than 60.7 percent.

After van Schoonbeke died in 1556, legal difficulties plagued the project. From 1557 on the brewers themselves had the responsibility of looking after the water supply. They got a reaffirmation of their contractual arrangement and confirmation from government that their beer would not be taxed at a rate higher than any other type of beer in the Low Countries. To make the project prosper, the town tried to suppress brewing elsewhere in Antwerp, but brewers in the Nieuwstad had a different idea. Finding themselves far from their customers, they asked for permission to return to their old breweries. The town denied the request. The property development did not go as planned, and the town ended up owning the entire project by 1561. In that year a new contract with the brewers confirmed protection from competition. The town levied higher excise taxes on imported beer which helped the brewers in the Nieuwstad development but at the same time rescinded their monopoly within the town. Political opposition to the entire project finally proved too strong. In 1562 the town sold off the breweries and left itself owning only the water house and conduit which brought water there.

In one way, the project did succeed. The average production of the new breweries by the late 1550s was 52 percent above the minimum level van Schoonbeke had set for them and almost 70 percent above the average production of Antwerp breweries from 1550 to 1551. Total production rose as well. By 1570 more than 70 percent of all beer made in Antwerp came from the van Schoonbeke development. Between 1565/1566 and the early 1580s, total production rose by more than 50 percent. One of the original goals, to establish an export industry in Antwerp, was also achieved. Early in the sixteenth century only 5 to 7 percent of output was sold outside the town but by the 1570s the average was about 25 percent.[7] Production of beer rose rapidly at Antwerp thanks to the massive investment in clean water and new breweries. Bruges, not far away to the west in Flanders, in the same period had growth in beer production which was much slower. Total output there was always lower as well.[8] At Bruges, water quality was always a problem and one never solved. The relative experience of Antwerp and Bruges indicated the benefits of capital investment in brewing and government promotion of such investment.

Growth in the Scale of Production

The biggest new investment made by brewers in the Renaissance was not, however, to get water but to increase the scale of their operations. Specialization, commercialization, and professionalization had for centuries, ever since brewing moved beyond being a domestic task, been sources of increasing efficiency and profit for brewers. The most noticeable sign of process innovation, of larger-scale production, was the growing size of the brew kettle in northern European breweries from the fifteenth through the seventeenth century. Savings from making more beer in each batch came in lower capital expenditures per unit of output but also in lower labor costs per unit of output. Brewing in larger quantities was a way to use less increasingly expensive grain for each liter of beer produced. Larger-scale production could maintain quality as well as protect brewers' incomes.

If the scale of operations increased, all the vessels, and not just the brew kettle, had to be bigger. Since the other containers were normally made of wood and were in some cases divisible, it was not difficult to increase their capacity for mashing or fermentation. Above all, the investment in those vessels and in rakes, shovels, and stirring paddles could be made incrementally. With the brew kettle, only one unit was possible. Since the kettle was made of copper and typically sat on a furnace with an effective chimney, the investment had to be made all at once in a big lump. Wort contracts about 4 percent on cooling and since it is necessary to have about 30 percent so-called "head space" to allow for vigorous boiling, the copper had to be about 35 percent larger than the maximum amount of beer being made at one time. The bottom of the kettle had to be thicker than the sides, but not too thick, since that would slow the transmission of heat and so increase fuel requirements. Too thin a bottom, on the other hand, would not stand up for long.[9] The need for good workmanship in the making of the kettle increased its price as did the amount of copper used. For brewers to get a return on the sizeable investment in bigger kettles, they needed to make more beer each time they brewed. Often they faced legislation which limited their output, creating a source of conflict with governments and among brewers.

The *peil*, the maximum amount a brewer could produce at any one time, was typically set in the number of barrels that could be extracted from a single brew. By setting the *peil*, governments also set the optimal size of the beer kettle. Brewers could take two or three mashings in a single brew to get more beer from each brew but that only mitigated and did not overcome the upper limit on production set by the *peil*. Often town governments also restricted the number of times per week, per month, or per year that a brewer could turn out the maximum amount allowed under the rules. The result was an upper limit on what any brewer could produce. The first such regulations appeared in the early fifteenth century. They became more precise and extensive as time went on. The number of barrels allowed per brew did go up through the fifteenth and sixteenth centuries in the Low Countries and, very likely, in much of the rest of northern Europe as well.

Smaller and less efficient producers resisted the advance in the scale of brewing which could potentially drive them out of the trade. They often called on governments to maintain an upper limit for the size of the kettle. That happened in Holland in the sixteenth century and led to a protracted political dispute. The overlord of the county, Emperor Charles V, tended to favor larger kettles, siding with capital-intensive producers. Though backing those more aggressive entrepreneurs was an unpopular position, governments still typically supported the process innovation implied by larger scale.[10] There were advantages in simplifying tax collection and in the possibility of collecting more tax from the sale of each barrel of beer. As a few brewers became more prosperous from investment in larger operations and came to play an ever larger part in civic politics, governments were ever more likely to favor relaxing production limits.

Brewers sometimes found ways to get around the regulations. Governments' concerns over the problem of brewers' *drinckbier*, the extra beer produced for consumption in the brewers' household, grew in part from a fear that provision for that private consumption might prove a loophole and allow larger scale brewing. At Amsterdam in 1514, for example, brewers were allowed 3 percent of their production for drinking in their own household, not a large portion but worthy of consideration. Brewers also could avoid the limits by having another brewer produce for them at a fee. The subcontractor became little more than a wage laborer for the first brewer.[11] Production limitations became, in effect, a quota which had a value and could be, in a sense, sold. In some places where the *peil* was hard and fast, brewers could acquire other breweries to expand their scale of operation. They might not be able to reap savings from larger kettles but they could lower administrative and distribution costs. Owning a number of breweries also distributed risk. Expanding existing facilities and buildings always created the potential problem that income would not cover the increased capital costs but with buying breweries capital investment was at least predictable.[12]

Monastic breweries historically had large vats for the making of beer, but by the sixteenth century, commercial brewers had matched or passed them. At Vadstena monastery in sixteenth-century Sweden the largest vat could hold 1,200 liters, slightly more than two old kettles at the brewhouse in Kalmar but a little less than the new one installed there in 1545. At about the same time a Rhineland monastery had a kettle of 1,500 liters. Those monasteries could then produce eight to ten ordinary barrels at a time,[13] but that left them at half or less the capacity of the more aggressive German and Dutch brewers of the late sixteenth century (see Table 7).

The long list of legislated maximum brew sizes, whether in barrels or liters, indicated the long-term potential increase, the commonly larger scale of production in export centers, and the persistence in some places of smaller operations (see Table 8). The figures for kettle size in Germany generally appear to have been higher than contemporary levels in the Low Countries.[14] The trend toward bigger operations was by no means universal; in part it was restrained by government action. The higher figures over time in a number of places show there was potential for expansion in the size of units and that some brewers saw and reaped gains from larger investment. In some towns in Germany, there was mutual agreement among brewers not to produce more than a certain maximum. Such voluntary agreements were less frequent and less effective over time. The tendency in many German towns from the fifteenth century into the seventeenth was clearly toward making more beer from the same quantity of malt. To do so effectively, the work was typically done in larger batches with the quantity of malt increasing and the quantity of beer increasing even more quickly. At Bremen, brewers used about 1,125 to 2,250 liters of grain in 1450 to make a brew but that was up to a range of about 1300

TABLE 7. THE MAXIMUM SIZE OF A BREW IN TOWNS, FIFTEENTH THROUGH
SEVENTEENTH CENTURY

Date	Town	Number of Barrels	Restrictions
Fourteenth century	Hamburg	25	
before 1340	Delft	24	
Fourteenth century	Delft	36	
1366	Gouda	14	
c.1380	Hamburg	25	
c.1400	Lier	12	
1407	Haarlem	14	Hoppenbier
1407	Haarlem	25–26	Export *kuit*
1437	Lier	13	
1440	Haarlem	14.5	Export hopbier
1440	Haarlem	24	*Kuit*
1440	Haarlem	28	*Kuit* for Friesland
Fifteenth century	Amersfoort	18.5	.5 barrels for household use
Fifteenth century	Leuven	7–14 (avg. 11)*	
1442	Amersfoort	24	Exporters only
1450	Leiden	24	*Kuit*
1460	Hamburg	35	
Fifteenth century	Gouda	31	
1484	Amersfoort	25	
1484	Amersfoort	30	Exporters only
1488	Gouda	30	
c.1480	Delft	37.5	
1495	Gouda	31	
1495	Gouda	28	Beer for Bruges
1497	Amsterdam	20	
1498	Haarlem	30	*Kuit*
c.1500	Wismar	30	
1501	Haarlem	31	
1501	Haarlem	31	For export to the south
c.1510	Lier	16	
1514	Haarlem	30	
1518	Gouda	30	
1520	Haarlem	32	
1521	Liege	32	
1536	Antwerp	58	*Koyte* of the lowest quality
1540	Veere	40	
1540	Gouda	41	
1544	Haarlem	32	
1547	Gouda	41	
1547	Ghent	18–21	
1548	Haarlem	40	
1549	Holland	41	
1549	Holland	82	
1549	Delft	41	

TABLE 7. THE MAXIMUM SIZE OF A BREW IN TOWNS, FIFTEENTH THROUGH
SEVENTEENTH CENTURY *(continued)*

Date	Town	Number of Barrels	Restrictions
1549	Rotterdam	41	
1562	Leiden	33	
1570	Amsterdam	30	
1577	Liege	40	
1584	Liege	55	
1586	Liege	40	
1595	Haarlem	50	
1598	Flushing	20 (minimum)	
Sixteenth century	Haaselt	12	
1624	Haarlem	80	
1667	Delft	50	
1685	Lier	20	
1687	Haarlem	80	
1692	Haarlem	85	
Eighteenth century	Lier	28	
Eighteenth century	Leuven	27	

Sources for Tables 7 and 9: ARa, Papiers de l'état et de l'audience: 1665/1; N. A., Archief Grafelijks-heidsrekenkamer, Rekeningen: #1722; G. A. Amsterdam, Archief van de Thesaurieren Ordinaris, 'Rapiamus', G. A. Haarlem, Archief van het Brouwersgilde: #29; G. A. Delft, Eerste Afdeling: #954; G. A. Leiden, Secretaire Archief na 1574: #4337, fol. 25v; G. A. Veere, #311: fol. 96v-97v; Aerts, *Het bier van Lier*, 41, 92–94, 185; Bemmel, *Beschryving der Stad Amersfoort*, 2: 776–77; Bijlsma, "Rotterdams welvaren in den Spaanschen tijd," 79; Bing, *Hamburgs Bierbrauerei*, 244–45, 248; Bleyswijck, *Beschryvinge der stadt Delft*, 728–29; Clement, "De bierbrouwerijen van Gouda," 58–60, 70–71: Couquerque and Embden, *Rechtsbronnen der Stad Gouda*, 135, 160, 164–65, 278, 514; Dillen, *Bronnen tot de geschiedenis van het bedrijfsleven*, 1: #18, 15; Doorman, *De middeleeuwse brouwerij en de gruit*, 40, 96–90, Halbertsma, *Zeven eeuwen Amersfoort*, 43, Hoeksma,"Het Haarlems brouwersbedrijf," 3, 8; Houwen, "De Haarlemsche brouwerij," 4, 16, 24; Huizinga, *Rechtsbronnen der stad Haarlem*, 114, 119, 134–35, 196–97; Loenen, *De Haarlemse brouwindustrie*, 21, 36–45, 64–67, 103; Martens, "Bier en stadsfinancien te Hasselt," 249; Muller Fz., *Schetsen uit de Middeleeuwen*, 63–66; Philipsen, "De Amsterdamsche Brouwnijverheid," 7; Pinkse, "Het Goudse kuitbier," 102–3; Rootselaar, *Amersfoort 777–1580*, 2: 144–45; Santbergen, *Les bons métiers*, 236–37; Soly, "De brouwerijenonderneming van Gilbert van Schoonbeke," 342; Soutendam, *Keuren en Ordonnantiën der Stad Delft*, 160–72; Techen, "Das Brauwerk in Wismar," 294–295, 339–340; Timmer, "Grepen uit de geschiedenis," 360; Uytven, "Bestaansmiddelen," 154–57; Uytven, *Stadsfinanciën en stadsekonomie*, 326–35.

Note: Figures understate growth in output for Lier since barrel grew considerably in the period.

*The brew size depended on the type of beer made and the price of grain.

to 2600 liters in 1489, and by 1656 the norm was up to around 3,200 liters of malt. The increasing amount of grain reflected a sustained increase in kettle size and may well understate the increase since typically brewers were getting more beer from a liter of grain in the mid-seventeenth century that in the mid-fifteenth. A Wismar kettle in 1602, just short of 4,000 liters, weighed 406 kilo-

TABLE 8. SIZE OF BREWS AND KETTLES, FOURTEENTH THROUGH EIGHTEENTH CENTURY, IN LITERS

Date	Town	Brew or Kettle Size
1340	Delft	3,730
1400	Gouda	1,000–2,000
1400	Hamburg	6,125 (maximum)
1404	Utrecht	3,100
1407	Haarlem	1,790
Fifteenth century	Hamburg	4,200 (typical)
1470	Nuremburg	6,400 (one case)
1484	Amersfoort	2,760–3,600
1488	Gouda	3,820
1497	Leiden	4,350–5,120
c. 1500	Leuven	c. 2,500
1514	Haarlem	3,600 (maximum)
before 1530	Utrecht	3,400 (maximum)
1530	Utrecht	3,400 (minimum)*
1540	Hamburg	8,750 (maximum)
1550	Haarlem	3,840–4,800
Sixteenth century	Utrecht	2,500–2,900
Sixteenth century	Lier	2,400–2,500
1547–1606	Ghent	2,200–2,500
1568	Munich	4,700–4,800
1594	Haarlem	6,000
1602	Wismar	4,000
Seventeenth century	Poland, towns	1,200–1,700
Seventeenth century	Poland, rural	60–900
Eighteenth century	Lier	3,380
Eighteenth century	Leuven	3,250

Sources: Aerts, *Het bier van Lier*, 41, 92–3; Doorman, *De middeleeuwse brouwerij en de gruit*, 48, 65, 96–98; Halbertsma, *Zeven eeuwen Amersfoort*, 42–44; Huntemann, *Das deutsche Braugewerbe*, 74–75; Klonder, *Browarnictwo w Prusach królewskich*, 158; Langer, "Das Braugewerbe in den deutschen Hansestädten," 70–71; Loenen, *De Haarlemse brouwindustrie*, 45–47; Muller, Fz., *Schetsen uit de middeleeuwen*, 63–66; Pinkse, "Het Goudse kuitbier," 100, 108; Techen, "Das Brauwerk in Wismar," 333; Uytven, "Bestaansmiddelen," 154.

*In 1530 Utrecht required brewers to make no less than a fixed number of barrels from a fixed quantity of grain in each brew, the goal being to guarantee the number of taxable units for each quantity of grain.

grams, so it is no surprise that for a long time kettles were treated for tax purposes as immovable goods.[15]

For Holland the dates of process innovation are equally hard to establish, but it appears brewers started as early as 1450 to increase the size of their brew kettles. Dutch towns promoted the increase in the size of the brewing kettle by increasingly charging, in addition to the hop tax, a fixed amount for each time the brewer made beer. By making more beer each time, brewers could reduce the tax burden per barrel produced. The tax on each brew was supposed to be more equitable, but no matter the intention it had the tendency to promote the use of increasingly larger brew kettles. Dutch brewers never knew anything like the voluntary limiting of output to protect fellow brewers that appeared in Germany. The regulation of production by town governments had the same effect, but the continued lessening of restrictions decreased the protection of those smaller operators. By around 1600, Dutch brewers had coppers which could compare with the big ones in use in Germany. Brewers in Brabant, unlike those in Holland, may have been able to escape restrictions on the size of their brews, that is after some legislation by the duke in 1464.[16] However, figures from both Lier and Leuven suggest that kettle size in Brabant lagged well behind that in Germany and in Holland.

Brewing Frequency

In addition to increasing the size of the kettle, brewers, with government compliance, tired to increase the frequency of brewing, to get more out of the greater capital investment in vessels for brewing and fermenting. At Lier, for example, the rise in the size of the kettle along with more frequent brewing combined to increase average monthly production for a brewery from some 4,300 liters (1408–1409) to around 9,800 liters (1473–1475) to around 17,100 liters in 1600. That figure, in fact, started to fall, down to 16,300 liters in 1610 to approximately 14,900 liters in 1630 and about 6,700 liters in 1660.[17] The contraction was due to a decrease in brewing frequency rather than a change in kettle size. How often brewers made beer was highly flexible with only regulation establishing some rigidity and that just at the upper limit (see Table 9). There was wide variation in those legislated limits with somewhat higher levels in export centers, but little in the way of long-term increase.

In England, brewers in Oxford were exceptional. Beginning in 1353 they were under direct supervision of the university and so were more closely controlled than any others in the kingdom. The university fixed frequency of brewing. The strict rota that prevailed by the end of the fifteenth century meant that each brewer had to produce once every two weeks. Smaller brewers wanted the period lengthened so they could sell off all they made before brewing again. When in 1501 the period between brews was extended to eighteen or twenty days, beer shortages appeared in August and September, so the old period of fifteen days was restored, to the advantage of larger producers. Brewing at Oxford could go on only in designated brewhouses. In 1516 the university became even more restrictive by fixing the number of brewers who could

TABLE 9. MAXIMUM FREQUENCY OF BREWING IN TOWNS, FIFTEENTH THROUGH
EIGHTEENTH CENTURY

Date	Town	Frequency per Week	Restrictions or Remarks
Fourteenth century	Hamburg	1	
1332	Wismar	0.5	
before 1340	Delft	2	
1356	Wismar	2	
1399	Wismar	1	
c. 1400	Lier	0.5	
1407	Haarlem	3	*Hoppenbier*
1407	Haarlem	3	Export *kuit*
1407	Haarlem	3	Export *kuit*
1440	Haarlem	3–4	Export *hopbier*
1440	Haarlem	3–4	*Kuit*
1440	Haarlem	3–4	*Kuit* for Friesland
Fifteenth century	Amersfoort	1	
1442	Amersfoort	2	Exporters only
1450	Leiden	2	*Kuit*
1455	Leuven	1.08	
Fifteenth century	Gouda	2	
Fifteenth century	Haarlem	1	
1462	Utrecht	1	
1465	Leuven	1.08	
1470s	Gouda	0.5	Most common frequency
c.1480	Delft	4.1 (avg.)	
1483	Leuven	1.2	
1497	Amsterdam	2	
c. 1500	Utrecht	2 (maximum)	
1501	Haarlem	3	
1501	Haarlem	4–5	Export to the south
1514	Amsterdam	1	
1520	Haarlem	2.15 (avg.)	
1526	Leuven	0.96	
1521	Liege	1	
1540	Gouda	2	
1547	Gouda	1.4	
1549	Holland	2	
1549	Holland	1	
1549	Delft	2	
1549	Rotterdam	2	
1565	Leuven	1.73	
1574	Amersfoort	2*	
1592	Haarlem	3	
1595	Haarlem	0–4	
1598	Leuven	1.88	
Eighteenth century	Lier	3	

Sources: See Table 7.

*Before 1574 brewing was restricted to no more than once a week.

operate in the town. In 1534, brewers were prohibited from working or dealing in any other food trade. That further restricted the possibility of making a living as a brewer. On the other hand, the large market of thirsty young scholars certainly helped Oxford brewers, as did the doubling in student numbers between 1560 and 1640. By the late sixteenth century, English common brewers were producing beer at a rate that more than allowed them to dominate their own urban markets. In the 1580s, twenty-six London brewers made about 85,000,000 liters of beer in a year.[18] That made the annual average per brewery more than 3,200,000 liters, so the scale of firms was indeed large though by no means massive, that is in comparison to contemporary operations in the Low Countries.

At Wismar, regulations were somewhat different from those in England and Holland and the town, in effect, did deter innovation. Brewing rules set the amount of beer that could be made at one time with an implied, and sometimes explicit, regulation of the amount of grain used in each brew. In some cases the town might set the quantity of beer produced from a brew but decrease the amount of grain. The change yielded thinner beer without allowing the scale of operations to increase. Such regulations might keep a larger number of brewers in place but offered no opportunity for increasing productivity.[19] Wismar ordinances set maxima for brewing frequency but the reality was a great deal different. Even the most active brewers made beer on average little more than once a month (see Table 10). Wismar remained highly restrictive and continued to limit the maximum number of times a brewer could make beer in a year, though exceptions were occasionally granted. The number went down from fourteen times in 1480 to twelve in 1559 to ten in 1572 to eight in 1606. The pattern there was exceptional. More typically the size of brewing operations and the frequency of brewing rose in Renaissance Germany.

In France, or more specifically in Paris, the scale of production was large compared to other parts of northern Europe, but then Paris was the largest

TABLE 10. FREQUENCY OF BREWING ANNUALLY AT WISMAR, 1464–1465

Frequency	Number of Brewers
Once	8
Twice	10
Thrice	7
Thirteen times	8
Fourteen times	1
Fifteen times	1
Total = 182 brewers	Average brewing frequency for all = 8

Source: Techen, "Das Brauwerk in Wismar," 186–289, 294–96.

city in that part of the continent. Brewing frequency at Paris was regulated but very generously. Paris brewers in 1514 were restricted to no more than one brewing per day.[20] It is doubtful that any brewer made beer 365 times in a year, but even at half the maximum allowed, Paris brewers were making beer much more often than their counterparts anywhere else. The regulation suggests a scale already well beyond that even thought of among Dutch, German, or London brewers, and that even if Paris kettles were significantly smaller than those used in Germany.

The Scale of Production and Civic Politics

There were economies of larger-scale production for brewers to reap that did not come simply from spreading both fixed costs and labor costs across larger output. Larger firms could have more efficient connections with the markets for their output, either through direct sales to the houses of consumers or through sales to outlets such as inns and taverns. Larger brewers could also economize on administrative costs, so much so that smaller ones often preferred to subcontract work for larger ones. Those bigger brewers with greater access to capital could combine malting and the production of yeast with the making of beer and expand the potential for profit.[21] The upper limit of production was effectively set by two factors: the size of the copper brewing kettle and the frequency of brewing. As metallurgy improved and as it became possible to construct larger and larger kettles, the more aggressive brewers ran squarely into government regulations on the scale of their operations. Originally set to maintain quality and to give as many commercial brewers as possible a chance to carry on the trade, the rules on scale increasingly became a way to protect smaller brewers against their expansionary competitors. The conflict led to investigations, government regulation, court suits, and often bitter correspondence, all of which not only illustrate the changing character of brewing through the sixteenth century, but also the rifts opened in towns as the population and the economy grew.

By the late fifteenth century, towns in north Germany already showed a split among brewers. A few brewed often and held high social status. Many more small brewers made beer less frequently. The tendency through the sixteenth century was for smaller commercial brewers to be forced out of business by the rising scale of production. In England two decades after the Black Death, a distinction was made in London between brewers who used less than 1,450 liters of malt each week and those that used more. The tax on the latter group was twice as high and presumably the distinction was between commercial producers and domestic ones, the latter selling some beer only now and then. At about the same time in Lynn, Hamburg, and Haarlem there were distinctions made between greater and lesser brewers.[22] In 1484 at Amsterdam brewers making fewer than twenty barrels each time they brewed were considered amateurs and it seems that domestic brewers would rarely come close to such figures, even in large country houses.[23] Scale was used to identify professional brewers and the high threshold set at Amsterdam suggests that professionals were already producing at levels well above even small commercial brewers.

It was numbers rather than wealth that gave the smaller brewers political influence. Towns may have set out to give as many citizens as possible the ability and the right to brew, but they insisted on a clear separation between commercial brewing and brewing for personal use. The usual pattern in the period of expansion, that is in the fourteenth and fifteenth centuries, was for output to grow through an increase in the number of commercial producers. The rise in the number of breweries up to around 1500 in many places indicates the way brewing grew. For example, as production went up at Leuven so, too, did the number of brewers, that is until the 1520s. From 1526 to 1565 production continued to increase by 50 percent, but the number of brewers fell by 25 percent. The pattern was repeated at about the same time in Holland and England. In the Low Countries, the protests from brewers in a number of towns about the increasing scale of firms confirmed the general direction taken by the industry. A crisis at Ghent in the 1580s, caused by fighting during the Dutch Revolt, led to a sharp fall in the number of breweries as many small brewers had to give up the business. With the restoration of some order, a revival did follow and the number of breweries did rise, but few, if any, of the new establishments were small.[24] The average size of breweries there, as elsewhere, increased though rather from a sudden shock than gradual erosion of the position of smaller brewers which was the common pattern.

The trend through the sixteenth century was for limits on production to be raised. Governments, at all levels, proved more interested in improving their tax income than in protecting small brewers. The rising capacity of breweries and decreasing numbers translated into easier surveillance for tax purposes and a decrease in the danger from fire in the towns—two advantages discovered by governments throughout northern Europe.[25] The larger brewers, expanding, developing, and exploiting all the possibilities of new technology, became something of a political force. Small brewers sold out or became contractors or employees of large brewers. In some towns a juridical difference existed, as at Diest in 1556 and Leuven in 1569, between big brewers and small brewers-tavern keepers who just produced for their own local clientele in, and possibly around, town. In the sixteenth century, brewers formed a progressive faction in the politics of Liege. The smaller brewers, there as elsewhere in the

Low Countries, tried to impede the growth of the larger brewers. An effort to raise the number of barrels from thirty-two to thirty-six per brew was successfully overturned by conservative forces. Later, in 1586, the number was forced back to forty from fifty-five where it had been for only two years.[26] There were complaints regularly about brewers exceeding the set limits. Like the towns in Holland, in the sixteenth century Liege appears to have been a battleground between a small number of expansion-minded large brewers and conservative smaller ones. The efforts of the latter did not prevent the continued growth and success of the larger brewers nor prevent their own decline and often their disappearance.

The smaller brewers were always at a disadvantage because successful businessmen were the source of personnel for town governments, and the big brewers, were therefore, likely candidates. Brewers sat in town governments in Germany, the Low Countries, and Scandinavia from the fifteenth through the eighteenth century. Already in 1370 there was a brewer on the town council of Nuremburg. In 1465 at Wismar, twenty-one of the twenty-four members of the town council came from among the 182 brewers in the town. By the mid-fifteenth century, a Leiden brewer could become a mayor. The collection of excise taxes was typically auctioned in towns, and brewers often found it highly profitable to buy the right to collect the beer excise.[27] There was no perceived conflict of interest for a brewer to combine politics and tax collection with his trade.[28] Brewers' critical role in supplying tax income to governments not only made them popular with public authorities but also made them into a part of public authorities. The cooperation between government and brewers to increase public income, even as early as the fifteenth century, led to a merging of the profession and public power.

In the sixteenth century, brewers could afford to commission portraits of themselves and their wives. In Munich in 1610, 17 percent of brewers belonged to the highest level of tax payers, most of them settled in the middle range of wealth, and only one brewer was classed as poor.[29] At Lier in the seventeenth century, brewers were among the highest levels of the wealthy with assets equal to those of mayors of villages or small towns. The wealth, often acquired or maintained through marriage, was the basis for success in the industry and the success of the industry. The process of wealth concentration continued after 1600. In 1667 at Antwerp all thirty-two brewers belonged to the wealthiest 5 percent of the population. Government officials in Brabant in 1692 and 1702 found brewers had the most capital among villagers in the countryside, three to four times as much as other craftspeople.[30]

In many places the larger brewers did gain the political upper hand and so gained tolerance, or even government support, for their expansion and their eventual domination of the industry. The trend toward concentration was initiated by brewers responding to financial pressures. The avenues open to brewers were limited, and growth in size through investment was the simplest and most obvious strategy. It proved productive but also brought brewers even more into collusion with the governments which oversaw their trade. It made town governments vehicles for the promotion and, ultimately, protection of brewing on a large scale.

Chapter 11

Types of Beer and Their International Exchange

Over the course of the sixteenth century, the number of beer types increased and the number of names multiplied. Brewers, in response to rising grain prices, lowered the quality of many beers. As a result there were rising complaints about beer being thin, and not just in north German towns like Wismar.[1] Brewers also introduced higher-quality beers to replace those that were deteriorating. The adjustments in quality created more kinds of beer with an ever greater variety of names. The various designations do suggest some trends in the development of Renaissance brewing. The great number of names reflect extensive government regulation of all aspects of the brewer's trade. The more precise names and fixed distinguishing features for beer types made it easier for towns and counties to tax properly, so governments as much as, or more than, brewers promoted the use of different classifications. Typically in the sixteenth century urban governments tried to promote some accuracy in the production and the naming of beers. In the process those governments created confusion since there was no guarantee of uniformity from town to town or over time in the same town. Some names were unique to certain towns or districts, others enjoyed widespread use but the meaning of a name could and often did vary.

The names given beers were not always informative. At *Aalborg* in Denmark, for example, in 1553, Danish beer was divided into two categories: ordinary beer and worse-than-ordinary beer. Fortunately many names were more precise than that. Distinctions were made, among other things, on the basis of the additives used, the color, the time of year or day the beer was made, the intended customers, the price of the beer, the strength of the beer, the thickness or thinness of the beer, or the origin of the beer. Color, which depended on the heating of the malt, ran from black to white, brown, yellow, and, many times, red. Another method of differentiation was according to the grains used, the combination giving beer a unique hue and taste. At Nuremberg from 1531 brewers produced something called *weiss* beer or clear beer, made with wheat; it also got the name Dutch beer. The distinction and name lasted into the eighteenth century. Distinction by price, oddly enough, was uncommon until the sixteenth century.[2] Before 1500, the variety of names suggests that strength was a relatively unimportant criterion for distinguishing beers. Often it was origin that mattered. Beers from farther away were considered superior and not just because of the higher prices which reflected transportation costs. Stronger beers traveled better and their higher alcohol content also gave them prestige. Consuming them was something of a status symbol.[3]

In the sixteenth century under various names there were, in general, three types of beer: expensive and of high quality, cheap and thin, and another somewhere in between the other two.[4] Whether the beer came from the first mashing, the second, or possibly the third or the fourth deeply affected strength, value, and, presumably, the name brewers and drinkers gave the beer. Nuremberg offers an example of what often happened. In the fifteenth and sixteenth centuries there were three types: earlier, middle, and later beer. The distinction depended on when in the mashing process the wort was made. In addition there was a seasonal summer beer. It was lighter than its winter counterpart, with less grain used to make each barrel. It was also boiled longer. By the seventeenth century the special summer beer had disappeared, leaving the standard three types.[5]

The Names

Towns did what they could to maintain the fame of specific beers. Attaching a certain name could, in some cases, do the trick. Hamburg used terms like *rotbier, matber,* and *langbier* for the highest quality export beers. Names such as convent beer, *mol, knol, porter,* and *uytset* (that is export) also turned up. Very strong beers made for export were sometimes mixed with spices to make a festive drink intended for a wealthy clientele and then given an appropriate name. *Kermisbier,* though not necessarily for export, was a seasonal beer presumably made with some spices to add flavor and produced for celebrations before Ash Wednesday. In the southern Low Countries names like *geuse, lambic,* and *faro* appeared now and then. *Lambic* may have been a general term for the strong beer introduced in the fifteenth century and *mais* a term for small beer, with *faro* being a combination of the two. In addition, there were beers with herbs and spices which a sixteenth-century poet called "medicinal beers."[6] Beers, such as *salbei, wermut, schlehen,* and others mentioned in the fifteenth century belonged to that category.[7]

The expert Heinrich Knaust listed and described in detail about 150 different beers from Germany. For him Gdansk beer was the king of all barley and rye beers, and Hamburg beer was the king of the wheat beers.[8] The list for the Low Countries was probably about as long, and it was by no means static. In the southern Low Countries *goudale* was mentioned as early as 1223 and variants appeared in Flemish and Latin for two centuries or more. In France the name could also be *godale* and may have been derived from "good ale" in English. It was a strong beer made from barley and spelt and, possibly, without hops.[9] However, a 1521 writer used the word *goudale* to mean poor beer so its character changed over time. The reference to ale of any sort in the Low Countries after the thirteenth century was extremely rare if not unique, since even though English used the term ale through the Middle Ages and Renaissance, it had virtually disappeared from the Continent outside Scandinavia.[10] By about 1300 in England, there was already a distinction between strong ale and small ale based on the amount of grain used in producing it, though apparently at that early date the only way to be sure which category applied was to sample the drink. In English country houses even as late as the twentieth century, a distinction remained between much stronger ale and a weaker drink, made in exactly the same way, called beer. The terms which in the late Middle Ages were used to distinguish between malt beverages made with or without hops in Renaissance England were used to distinguish between drinks of differing strengths.[11]

The sixteenth-century Antwerp collection of types indicates how confusing the variety could be. In 1536, products included small beer and *halffstuyvers bier*. The latter and better quality beer was defined by price. In addition, heavier and more expensive *knol*, *dubbele knol*, *blanckxx bier*, *wit bier*, and a strong March beer came out of Antwerp breweries in the sixteenth century. In the 1620s, the breweries in Jesuit houses in the southern Low Countries made two kinds of beer: good and small. The difference was that half as much grain was used to make an equal quantity of small beer. The good quality was then a true double beer, a term often used in the sixteenth century. The proportions of different grains and, presumably, the taste was the same with only the strength of the two being different, the stronger beer having an alcohol content of about 5 percent and the small beer one of 2.5 percent. At nearby Lier starting in the mid-fifteenth century, the distinction was among *knolbier* of higher quality, small *bier*, and *buiten-bier* or imports. Occasionally there was mention of *bruwers biere*, the *drinkbieren* consumed by crews producing beer. The *knol*, which appeared in Lier before it was brewed in Antwerp, deteriorated in quality over time so that while in the 1560s it was still thought of as a double beer by the mid-seventeenth century it was a small beer. By that time *cave* was the best beer produced in Lier and one which quickly found buyers in other markets.[12]

Adjusting names was part of coping with changing circumstances for brewing. The town of Ghent introduced a new name for the strongest beer made in the town three times in the sixteenth century. The changes reflected the declining quality of beer, a product of rising grain prices and innovations to satisfy a market for beer of better quality.[13] High-priced *crabbelaer* of the first half of the sixteenth century was superseded by *enkele clauwaert* which, in turn, was first supplemented and then replaced by *dubbele clauwaert* from 1573 on. The last saw production fall in the 1580s when yet another premium beer, *dusselaer*, was brewed. By the close of the sixteenth century small beer had fallen from a 20 percent share of production, a figure that prevailed as late as 1571, to about 6 to 7 percent. From 1586 on, commercial brewers produced no more small beer, always defined as the bottom end of the spectrum, since it was of such poor quality, leaving only home brewers to make it. By that date *crabbelaer* had deteriorated so much that there was no more need to have small beer to meet the demand for an inexpensive drink. *Crabbelaer* fell from about 50 percent of sales around 1570 to 15 percent in 1577 but was back up to 43 percent in 1604. Consumers ended up drinking a beer with a different name even though it may have been of the same low quality as the small beer they drank before. *Enkele clauwaert* held almost 30 percent of the market in 1571 but little more than 2 percent in 1604. It was caught between the types above it and below it. In 1573, *dubbele clauwaert* came on the market and leapt quickly to 27 percent of production, rising to 49 percent by 1583, and in the 1590s it typically made up more than 50 percent of production. Sales did collapse in 1587 to under 2 percent of the total but that was because of the brewing of *dusselaer* in that year. *Dusselaer* took the place of *dubbele clauwaert* for a year, gaining almost 48 percent of the market, and then it disappeared for no apparent reason.[14] The variable fortunes of the different types and the different names of beers at Ghent was something which happened, though usually with less drama, everywhere in the Low Countries and much of the rest of northern Europe through the sixteenth century. The variations became more marked and the problems more acute toward the end of the century with the rise in raw material costs. The Eighty Years' War in the Low Countries only made things worse for brewers. Legislation was emphatic about the names and about fixing the prices of the different types. The towns insisted on proper marking of casks for the different types of beer. This meant, for example, at Ghent that after 1567 casks carried three marks: one for the brewery, one for the town and one showing the beer type.[15]

Tax authorities, like brewers, preferred the sale of heavier beers. A small increase in quality—reflected in an increase in the amount of grain used which, in turn, yielded a higher alcohol content—could generate a significant increase in price and allow both brewers and governments to take in more money from consumers. At times after the fourteenth century, some English towns required brewers to produce strong and small ale, the low-quality ale

being for sale to poorer citizens. The requirement suggests that brewers preferred to make stronger and potentially more profitable high-priced ale. To
make less expensive small beers like *kuit*, brewers first had to produce a
higher-quality beer from a first mashing.[16] Governments wanted to be sure
that brewers made the effort and reused the grain. Brewers may not have
always been convinced the extra labor to make small beer was worth it. Harder
yet was convincing them to produce beers of lower quality all on their own in
an entirely separate operation. Labor and heating costs were the same and
though the cost of grain went down since brewers used less of it, sale prices of
the product were also less. In 1536 at Antwerp *knol* cost three times as much
as a common type called *kuit*, but it took only 40 percent more grain to make
a barrel of *knol*, so brewers did much better with sales of *knol*. In 1541, the town
of Veere in Zeeland, downstream from Antwerp, realizing the possibilities of
raising tax income through the sale of higher priced beers, rescinded an order
of a year earlier and let the price of better beer be a minimum of 16 percent
higher than normal beer and even higher if the quality was superior.[17] In 1560,
repeating a 1552 rule, Queen Elizabeth I of England prohibited the brewing of
a very strong double-double which brewers seemed to prefer because of the
higher profit margins. She also insisted that brewers make as much of the
weaker single beer as they made of double.[18] Presumably the queen wanted to
protect less well-off consumers, making sure there was a beer on the market
that they could afford.

Stronger beer, not just in England, often went by the name of *dubblebier*
implying it was twice as good. But premium beers were called many other
things as well. A Cracow brewery produced a double beer called *potus marcialis*
in records. It was said to be good for invalids. At Antwerp when *knol* decreased
in strength, brewers produced a *dubbele knol* making *knol* the middle-quality
beer. The shift at Antwerp was just like that at Ghent from *dubbel bier* to
crabbelaer to *clauwaert* to *dubbele clauwaert*. At Middelburg in Zeeland in 1536,
the town gave brewers permission to brew something called *dobbel bier* which
was to taste like English beer and so was presumably stronger than the normal
domestic beers which could be sold alongside it. At Middelburg the term *knol*
may have applied, at least at the start of the sixteenth century, to a double
beer. The *kluunbier* of Groningen was probably a true double beer with double
the amount of grain used to make it compared to the local thin beer and, as
with a number of stronger beers, Groningen *kluun* seems to have enjoyed
some popularity in markets outside the town itself.[19]

Small Beer

The polar opposite of expensive double beer was small beer or, as it was called
in the northern Netherlands, *scharbier*. Governments were conscious of both

the market and technology for *scharbier*. It was thin and extremely weak, satisfying the simplest type of demand for beer. Consumers bought it more for its purity than for its nutritive or inebriating qualities. At Groningen the town council insisted that such beer should have its full proportion of hops so at least the drink would have the strong taste of its more nutritious predecessors through the mash tun. At Leuven there was an inexpensive brown beer that brewers claimed was not worth making, but the town insisted that they continue to produce it and conceded in 1422 that brewers would pay no tax on that beer type. In Germany, the weak and cheap beer was called *kofent* or *kovent*, suggesting a connection with religious houses.[20] The cheap beer appeared as early as 1405 at Lübeck and turned up in a number of other German towns. Other names for it included *pfennigbier* and *blaffertbier*. Beer sold as *kovent* may have even included the water used to rinse out the brewing copper. By the early seventeenth century, there were complaints in Germany about its quality. It was brewed too thin and it was undrinkable, or such were the claims. By that time in Antwerp the small beer was so weak that it was called, derisively, reboiled water.[21] The low-quality beer carried an extremely low price because it was free of tax. Governments had an interest in seeing that everyone knew the composition of the tax-free beer and that no other beer be considered to be taxfree. Governments hardly ever stopped the production of low-quality, low-priced beer, even in times of grain shortage. They even forced brewers in some cases to continue to make it if they wanted permission to produce higher-quality beers since small beer was considered by many a social necessity to meet the needs of the less well-off.[22]

There was a beer even weaker than *scharbier*, *scheepsbier* or ship's beer, designed for use on board.[23] Herring beer in Holland appears to have been just like other ship's beers except that it was put in small casks which, once emptied by the crew at sea, could be filled with fish. A regulation from Emperor Charles V in 1549 limited the brewing of the low-quality beer to the four months after 1 October, but brewers at Delft petitioned him to extend the season to 1 June. They claimed the short period hurt their industry.[24] Presumably they wanted to supply vessels setting out in the spring, or at least after 31 January. At Stockholm the least expensive beer was called *skeppsöl*; the term meant not beer of the worst quality or beer for shipboard use, but rather just small beer. It had 42 percent of the market in 1561.[25] The figure of about 40 percent of total taxable sales of beer is consistent with the pattern of small beer in the Low Countries. It at least had some substance to it, was stronger than the tax-free version, and probably enjoyed better sales. But since the ship's beers and very thin beers were beyond the tax collectors' jurisdiction, they also fall beyond the records of governments, that is unless some publican tried to pass off a taxable small beer as the tax-free drink. The concern for such tax evasion, which turns up repeatedly in urban regulations, suggests that it did happen.

Imported Premium Beers

In addition to the locally produced beers of varied names, consumers could buy, generally at great expense, imported beers. Their range in name and type was even greater than that for domestic beers, but their range in quality was by no means as great. Weak beers did not travel well so only the strongest beers, called *seebiers* in some north German towns because they were shipped by sea, made their way into international exchange. In terms of volume, though certainly not in terms of value, beer traded was, with a few highly notable exceptions, of little importance. Imports into Holland, for example, most of which came from Germany, probably never in the Middle Ages and the Renaissance formed more than 5 percent of consumption. Even after 1600, when signs of decline began to appear in Dutch brewing, imported beers were less than 2 percent of total sales in most markets. At Mechelen and Lier in the southern Low Countries from around 1500 to 1750, when the local brewing industries were firmly in place, imports seem rarely, if ever, to have gone above 8 percent of consumption. At Leuven in the sixteenth century, annually something like an insignificant 15,000 liters came into the town. They were all premium beers from German ports like Hamburg, Lübeck, and Gdansk, as well as ale from England which was first imported in 1503. In the first half of the sixteenth century at Ghent, imports were on average a very high 15 percent of total consumption, despite their carrying a heavier tax burden than local beer. The 15 percent, however, included massive quantities of low quality *kuit* which came from Gouda. In addition to that beer, in order of importance the imports were Eastern, Hamburg, *Joopen*, and English beer. In a rare move, Ghent lowered the taxes on premium imports in the 1590s, but taxes were lowered from a very high level in the 1580s. Even with the reduction, those taxes were high compared with the excises levied on locally produced beers.[26] There were times when imports rose in volume to become significant, for example, in Holland around 1300, in the southern Low Countries around 1400, and in England around 1450. In those cases, local producers responded by making beer good enough to replace imports of lower and middle quality. Nowhere and at no time could they fully replace the premium quality beers.

Imported beers were consistently subject to rather high levels of taxation. In 1494 at Bruges, imported Hamburg beer was taxed at a rate 75 percent higher than local good beer and more than ten times that of small beer. Other Low Countries towns even added a surcharge on Hamburg beer, always in the spirit of protecting local producers.[27] The result of the tax policy and prohibitions on imports was to force exporters in north Germany as early as the fifteenth century to seek other potential markets, to concentrate on only the most expensive types, and to develop some genuine luxury beers. The defensive legislation in Scandinavia against imports from Einbeck, Hamburg, and Prussia in the fifteenth and sixteenth centuries attests to the success of German exporters in the north and to the diversion of their efforts in reaction to high taxes in the Low Countries.[28] A market share for imports, even if small in volume, was common since such beers were unique, had distinctive tastes, and consuming them was a sign of affluence. Even though quantities were not great and imports often satisfied a different and special market, it did not stop governments from worrying about the potential threat to their own brewing industries from exports nor did it stop governments from taking measures to protect their own industries.

At Hamburg, that great export center, problems with imports forced the government to take defensive action, just as governments in the Low Countries and Scandinavia had earlier in the face of imports from Hamburg. Beginning in 1381, the town council set a tax on foreign beers and the rate could be as much as four times that on domestic beer. The most popular imported beer in the fourteenth century was *gosa*, a beer from Goslar. In the fifteenth century it was beer from Einbeck and in the sixteenth *mumme* from Braunschweig.[29] In the sixteenth century, Hamburg importers also brought in a *Preussing*, a high-quality beer originating in Gdansk. Oddly the town was an important buyer of those luxury beers since it used them as diplomatic gifts to guests and superiors. In Hamburg as elsewhere when barriers to trade in beer increased, quantities of beer exchanged went down and the quality of traded beer went up.[30] Hamburg was a favorite market for beer from the small town of Einbeck. It was so successful as a beer exporter to so many places that by the beginning of the seventeenth century 700 of the 1,200 houses in the town were breweries or brewhouses. The beer from Einbeck proved very popular in Munich and got the name *bokbier* in Bavaria. It also found a market in the north in other beer-producing German towns, but its popularity, like that of many export beers, waxed and waned in different places over the sixteenth and seventeenth centuries.[31]

There was without doubt a family of high-quality beers, good enough to warrant shipment and sales to distant markets. Placotomus, the mid-sixteenth-century writer on beer, spoke about red beer from Gdansk as the best followed by other beers from Prussia. His list included *israel* from Lübeck and a summer, or light, barley beer from Einbeck, but these did not exhaust his choices for notable beers. By the seventeenth century, writers in Germany identified a few towns as important centers of brewing producing certain specialty export beers. Some produced beers with a lower level of hops such as Minden. Braunschweig produced *mom* or *mumme*. Hannover produced *broihan*. Goslar produced *gosa*. Darker beers for the summer came from Zerbst, Bremen, Hamburg, Rostock, and Gdansk among others.[32] The popularity of such specialty beers changed over time in a market that was highly sensitive to reputation and fashion. When a translator at Antwerp dealt with a list of premium wines in a Spanish story in 1550, the text, as well as the language, was changed to suit local readers. In the Dutch translation numerous beers were added to the wines given as gifts to flatter a lady. The Dutch translation, among all sixteenth-century translations of the story, has the longest and most cosmopolitan list of wines. The beers, appended to that list of wines, included *Joopen*, Hamburg, *mom*, English, March, Bremen, Leuven, Hoegaard, and similar types.[33] Leuven and Hoegaard beer came from brewing centers in Brabant and enjoyed a market in larger towns such as Mechelen. The *mom* was presumably Braunschweig *mumme*. *Joopen*, *mom*, and English beers were the most important luxury imports to the Low Countries, it would appear, in terms of volume and value in the sixteenth century. English beer was good enough to command a market at Königsberg in Prussia, a town that made its own export beer. The top Antwerp imported beer in the sixteenth century was English "ale" followed by Eastern beer (a general term for the products of north German towns but including Baltic ports) and then lastly Hamburg beer.[34]

The success of London beer brewers in the sixteenth century appears to have been in part related to their good fortune in the Low Countries export market. A toll charged downstream from Antwerp showed imports of Hamburg beer, and even Wismar beer, through the fifteenth century, but the records increasingly mentioned English beer. By the sixteenth century the latter had a more prominent place than its German counterpart.[35] The increasing numbers of English merchants coming to Brabant to sell their cloth may have contributed to the market for English beer at Antwerp and Bergen-op-Zoom where the major fairs were held. In 1573, a ship from Holland made five trips from Ipswich to Enkhuizen, each time carrying cargoes of beer. Such traffic seems to have been common, with the expectation at the highest levels of government in the 1560s, that the English would export beer to Holland and Dutch shippers would carry it.[36] The quantities in each instance might not have been large, but the import of beer from England in the 1560s and 1570s is repeatedly mentioned in a variety of Low Countries documents. London appears to have been the typical port of departure and various ports in Holland the destinations.[37] London brewers, operating along the Thames, could ship beer by sea with ease to the Low Countries. Because of access to supplies of coal and grain, and they may have enjoyed certain cost advantages over their counterparts in the big towns of Flanders, Brabant, and Holland. Many London brewers were from the Low Countries, so they knew the market there and they presumably knew how to brew the product that would sell there. It is possible that some of the London breweries were set up and operated in the sixteenth century on the expectation of finding a strong market for their output in a foreign land. London exporters appear to have done well in supplying beer to the armies battling in the Low Countries during the Eighty Years' War. In 1613, London brewers spoke of Dutch traders coming for beer in exchange for grain and other commodities. In 1568, Amsterdam had again reaffirmed maximum prices on English beer so there was some upward pressure on those prices which confirms the ability of English brewers to match in quality the products of their counterparts in many places in Germany and even in Holland.[38]

Mumme sold widely in sixteenth- and seventeenth-century Europe. The legend was that it was a type first brewed by a man named Christian Mumme at Braunschweig in 1492, but there is evidence it was first produced as early as 1425. The story may be a fabrication since a unique beer called Dordrecht *mom* is mentioned as early as 1285. The type certainly proved very durable, *mum* still being a high quality-beer in the twentieth century. In Braunschweig there was a *mom* made for consumption inside the town and a stronger variety made for export to Holland and England called *schiff-mumme* and even English *mum*. It was a seasonal beer, at least in the seventeenth century, with brewing limited to the month of March. It was thick, strong, dark, and flavored with a number of spices which gave it a bitter taste. The bark of fir trees, pimpernel, birch shoots, marjoram, thyme, and fresh eggs among others things have been suggested as the combination of additives, but the exact composition was always kept a secret.[39] The beer traveled well, was very strong, and therefore long lasting, and could even survive voyages to the tropics. It made trips as far afield as India and South Africa in the seventeenth century. Brewers elsewhere imitated Braunschweig practice. By the end of the seventeenth century, brewers in Nijmegen in the eastern part of the Dutch Republic produced the type. In Denmark when in 1623 King Christian IV was forced to rescind his prohibition of imports of beer which he had laid down two years earlier, he retained the restriction on only one type and that was *mom*, so it kept its position as a premium drink and one dangerous in foreign markets.[40]

The other high-quality beer often mentioned which enjoyed wide circulation in northwestern Europe was *Joopen* or *Joopenbier*, a dark, red-brown, sweet, heavy, slow-flowing, and very expensive beer originally from Gdansk but brewed in a number of places in Germany by the sixteenth century. There were as many as thirty variations of *Joopenbier*, including *Preussing*. *Joopenbier* was said to be good for many maladies including bruises and constipation. At the premium price which it commanded, *Joopenbier* had to be thought of as medicine, though the high concentration of nutrients in the thick beer made it more valuable as a drink than even standard double beers.[41] *Joopenbier* was so expensive, made even more so by the high excise taxes placed on it, that it was usually imported into Holland, for example, in small units of less than two liters and rarely by the barrel. Gdansk became in the sixteenth century a principal source of grain shipments to Holland and so adding a few small containers of the high-quality beer to the cargo would have been easy. On the other hand, beer from Einbeck almost never turned up in Holland. The Einbeck product enjoyed success in the face of stiff competition in Germany, but it made few, if any, inroads in the northern Low Countries. The barrier may have been shipping charges which for beers from the interior in Germany were higher than for beers that could make their way to Dutch ports entirely by sea, carried as part of cargoes in other successful and growing trades.

Even though imports were always only a small portion of total beer consumed, governments spent an inordinate amount of time dealing with those beers because they carried higher prices, because they were subject to higher and more varied taxes, and because local brewers always perceived imports as a threat to sales and even more to profits. As the brewing industry in the Low Countries boomed in the fifteenth century and to a lesser degree in England somewhat later, governments set out to improve the classification of beers in order to assess taxation more effectively and equitably. The various names, the definitions based on grain inputs either by weight or type, did not prove effective. Brewers appear to have favored producing a variety of beers under a variety of names. A new name might give them a competitive advantage and a chance that some tax burden somewhere might be reduced because of confusion about what any new name meant. Brewers were in the sixteenth century, after all, still experimenting with ways to make the most out of the new product that was hopped beer. The confusion about the meaning of the names of different types of beer must mirror a complexity in the brewing industry in the sixteenth century. The roots were technical but also economic and political. Government surveillance of brewing, taxation, and regulation, and brewers' efforts to evade taxation and regulation helped to multiply names, and categories thereby increasing the confusion.

Chapter 12
Taxes and Protection

The great flood of legislation on brewing was still to come, but in the first half of the fifteenth century the topics and the pattern for regulation were already clear. Governments would set the size of the brew, the frequency of brewing, the size and marking of the casks, the use of grain in brewing by type and quantity, and the ability to enter the trade. They would also legislate methods for making sure that the regulations on brewing were enforced. That included setting out and, in some cases, controlling the choice of the officials responsible for enforcing the rules. The character and scope of regulation would only grow over time. Town governments showed a consistent interest in controlling the brewing industry in order to retain economic strength and also to guarantee their tax income from the trade. By the middle of the fifteenth century, the structure of the brewing industry was set both in terms of the character of the firms which made up the industry and in terms of relations with governments. That relationship, the need to pay excise taxes and to be accountable at any moment for what was owed, dictated the keeping of extensive records. In addition, brewers had to keep track of a large number of transactions, usually in cash but often by credit, with retailers. Extending credit to alehouse keepers certainly existed in the sixteenth century and most likely well before that. Brewers always and everywhere engaged in many small transactions.[1] They created and maintained many records of various sorts. The trend was an increase in record keeping, and as the scale of brewing rose, so did the administrative effort required of brewers to operate the relatively larger firms. The concentration of the industry in the Renaissance was the most important force, next to government regulation, in shaping brewing, but the difference was more of scale than of kind.

Beer Taxes and Government Income

The most obvious sign of the importance of brewing and of excise taxes was towns' heavy reliance those levies as a source of income. Indirect taxes on alcoholic drinks had existed in some places for a long time, at Nuremberg, for example, beginning in 1253. There the share of town income from taxes on alcoholic drinks varied from a third to a half, a typical pattern. Production taxes on beer rose as a share of town incomes at a number of sites throughout the fifteenth century as did the income from indirect taxes sustained by the brewing industry on its raw materials.[2] Between 1342 and 1390 the town of Deventer, in the northeastern Low Countries, got almost 20 percent of its net income from a tax on beer making, a relatively low figure. At Haarlem, a major exporter, on the other hand, in the mid-fifteenth century, taking all taxes on beer together, the share was around 50 percent, but rose as high as 89 percent in 1437/1438. The sudden and sharp fall in beer production in Haarlem late in the same century was a major contributor to the bankruptcy of the town. At Leiden in the fifteenth century, all excise taxes made up 70 percent to 90 percent of income; in the 1420s and 1430s, between 42 percent and 59 percent of that income from excise taxes came from beer alone. In 1429 the Dordrecht government received almost 15 percent of its income from the beer excise, a figure which dropped slightly to just over 13 percent by 1450.[3] The share was smaller than elsewhere in Holland, perhaps consistent with a town more devoted to trade than to industry. In the southern Low Countries, Bruges in 1391–1392 relied on beer taxes for more than 30 percent of town income. Early in the fifteenth century, for a number of important as well as lesser centers throughout Flanders, an average of some 40 percent of total town income came from beer taxes. At Ghent as late as 1452, taxes on wine accounted for 23 percent of town receipts and beer only 5 percent. In 1465–1466 the tax share from wine had fallen to 18 percent while that for beer was up to 25 percent. Similarly, at Leuven from 1348 to 1570 the proportion of income from the taxes on beer tripled while that of taxes on wine fell by one half. Oddly, the government of Hamburg, the great center of beer export, got only 2 percent of its income from the excise on beer at the end of the fourteenth century. One hundred years later that level had gone up but still only to 8 percent. At Cologne, on the other hand, the share went from 2 percent to almost 23 percent in the same period. The Hamburg figure obscures the importance of brewing to town finances since, for instance, property taxes which fell on breweries and on brewers' equipment were critical to the fiscal health of the town.[4] Even so, it appears Hamburg tried not to burden the industry critical to town prosperity with excise taxes. As late as 1548, the Hamburg authorities had difficulty imposing a tax on beer sales from one citizen to another or charging a surtax for sales in public houses. As a result, the excise on beer brought only a small share of the total revenue in the mid-sixteenth century, making Hamburg exceptional and far different from other towns in much of northern Europe. Reliance on beer taxes was usually much greater and usually rising through the fifteenth and sixteenth centuries (see Table 11).

TABLE 11. SHARE OF TOWN INCOME FROM TAXES ON BEER, FOURTEENTH THROUGH
SEVENTEENTH CENTURY

Year	Town	Share in percentages	Remarks
1370–1387	Hamburg	4.6	Average
1391–1392	Delft	24.6	
1391–1392	Leiden	17	
1399	Leiden	47–53	
1413	Leiden	58	
1426	Leiden	42	
1427	Leiden	53	
1429	Dordrecht	14.8	
1433–1434	Leiden	59	
1437–1438	Haarlem	88.5	
1440–1443	Haarlem	35.1	Average
1449	Leiden	78	
1450	Dordrecht	13.2	
Fifteenth century	Mechelen	50	Approximate average
1452	Ghent	5	
1465–1466	Ghent	24.5	
1465–1496	Hamburg	8.6	Average
1490	Hasselt	33	
1492	Breda	52	
1502	Dordrecht	39.9	
1515	Hasselt	60	
1522	Dordrecht	39.3	
1528–1610	Ghent	41.3	Average
1530–1543	Antwerp	53.7	Average
1549–1560	Hamburg	11.9	Average
Sixteenth century	Leuven	39.3	Average
1552	Amsterdam	55	
1556–1558	Dordrecht	37.8	Average
1567–1568	's-Hertogenbosch	51	Approximate
1556–1560	Haarlem	65	
1575–1600	Lier	30.2	Average
1595–1599	Haarlem	23.3	
1600–1609	Haarlem	27.2	
1610–1612	Dordrecht	28.8	Average
1622	Hasselt	70	

Sources: Bing, *Hamburgs Bierbrauerei*, 308; Eykens, "De brouwindustrie te Antwerpen," 82; Hallema and Emmens, *Het bier en zijn brouwers*, 84–85; Martens, "Bier en stadsfinancien te Hasselt," 243; Soly, "De brouwerijenonderneming van Gilbert van Schoonbeke," 339, 1179–81; Soly and Thys, "Nijverheid in de zuidelijke Nederlanden," 47; Unger, *A History of Brewing in Holland*, 60–61, 69–71.

Towns imposed excise taxes earlier and more completely in the Nether-lands so there the share of town income from beer taxes was more important, if not absolutely critical, to their functioning at all. In the northern Nether-lands in consuming towns (like Amsterdam and Leiden), in producing towns (like Dordrecht and Gouda), and after 1542 for the province as a whole, taxes on beer production and sales made up a very large proportion of government income. Taxes on beer were without question crucial to the financial health of all those governments. The fortunes of Haarlem civic finances, for example, rose and fell with the brewing industry. In good years, like those from 1556 to 1560 the town got close to two-thirds of its income from a combination of all taxes on beer sales and production.[5] There was little change from one hundred years before. In the southern Low Countries at Antwerp, the beer excise was always the chief source of income for the town. The receipts from taxes on beer were typically two to three times those on wine. From 1530 to 1543 any-where from 51 percent to 62 percent of total receipts came from beer taxes, that in the years for which figures survive. In towns where imports were sizeable so too was the share of town income from taxes on those foreign beers. At Ghent, 1528–1529, imported beer supplied 66.3 percent of the income from beer taxes and so by itself was 23.1 percent of the gross. At Liege around 1600, taxes on beer brought up to three times as much as taxes on wine.[6] The shift in the beer border, the growth in brewing and beer drinking in the southern Netherlands by the sixteenth century and rising rates of taxation made brewing central to the fiscal welfare of towns there as it had been in Holland just to the north for a century or more.

In England a more centralized monarchy created a different form and style of taxation. Anglo-Saxon lords received a small portion, called a tolcester, from each batch of ale their tenants made. It was in essence a tax. Local authorities, as in the town of Chester in the late eleventh century, imposed rules on brewers with taxes possibly following. From at least the twelfth cen-tury on, some places had an assize of ale which regulated quality and set the price and measure for selling beer. By early in the thirteenth century, some towns even had an officer called an aletaster to enforce the rules. Ale conners, who probably date from the eleventh century if not before, had similar duties and became more common in more parts of the country over time. Despite the national declaration of the Assize of Bread and Ale, traditionally dated 1266–1267, rules and methods of enforcement were defined by local practice. The regulations, which covered all of England, gave specific directions on how the price of ale was to be calculated, based on the price of grain and deter-mined by a jury at least once a year. The aletasters, the enforcers of the assize, brought offending brewers to court and suggested punishments, most often fines. Since in many cases virtually everyone who brewed was charged with violating the assize, it is possible to see the system of regulation as just another way to tax brewers. Many jurisdictions found taxing brewing to be lucrative, and local taxes remained in place through the Renaissance. Examples of successful taxation throughout the kingdom and in towns on the Continent did not go unnoticed by the English royal government. In 1610 in another effort to raise money for the Crown, King James I tried to get Parliament to agree to a national tax on beer. That failed but he did succeed in 1614 in imposing a fee on London brewers for the malt they used.[7] Any efforts at imposing a general system of taxation on brewing fell apart in the subsequent decades in the struggle between king and Parliament. In 1643 Parliament repeated an ordinance imposing a national excise tax on all beer as it left the brewery, the rate of tax being based on the price of the beer. The system envisaged in the legislation was like the contemporary Dutch one, but the disruption of the Civil War meant that it was never fully implemented.

In sixteenth-century Aberdeen, Scotland, the system of regulation, dating back to the late fourteenth century, was very similar to that in southern Britain. The prices of different classes of ale were fixed annually, though it was possible to have the decision reviewed should circumstances change. The *cunnars* or aletasters tried each barrel separately, preferably on a Sunday, in the open air to be sure there was no collusion or bribery. The *cunnar* decided the price of the ale based on the quality and price of grain within the annually set guidelines. All beer makers were subject to limits on the maximum amount they could brew though the quotas were so high that it is doubtful that many of them ever reached those levels. There were fines for violation of the rules, but, unlike England, it appears the fines were not some veiled license fee for brewing.[8] The Scottish system, though not without tax implications, was like many also designed to assure adequate supplies of drink to townsfolk.

Rates of tax, of course, varied though the tendency was for the rates to rise. The potential for tax income from a prospering brewing industry was not lost on any government. At Nuremberg and elsewhere in Germany, the excise tax in the first half of the fifteenth century was in general only about 5 percent of the price of the beer. By the 1570s it was up to 50 percent. At Hamburg it was significantly less in the mid-fourteenth century but by 1465 it was up to 5 percent of the value. The sixteenth century and its wars took a toll in Hamburg too, and by the 1630s the tax was about 24 percent of the price. The incidence of the tax had increased over time as well. The Antwerp proportion had reached 38 percent of the sale price by 1611. At Hasselt, the excise rose tenfold from the 1490s to the 1610s, stabilized, and then fell a little toward the end of the seventeenth century. It was a pattern typical of much of the Low Countries. Presumably resistance to increases in taxes, like that at Hamburg in the later sixteenth century, was also common.[9]

Towns could also use the excise tax as a mildly and poorly disguised import duty. In cases where imports were few and the local industry easily met demand, there were no special levies on foreign beers. Though this may have been the case in the fifteenth century, by the sixteenth century, levies on imports were common. The argument for higher excise taxes on the consumption of imported beer was that local brewers had already paid levies on production, so having higher consumption excises on imports made competition among beers more equal. A typical case was Leuven where imports beginning in 1547 were taxed at double the rate of beer brewed in the province of Brabant.[10] Imported beers were often luxury items which carried relatively high prices and so were better able to sustain high rates of taxation without undermining sales. Governments recognized that but looked on any decrease in imports, any shift to consumption of locally produced beer, as a positive result.

If towns levied taxes on local producers by the brew, rather than by the barrel sold, then consumers were much less likely to notice the burden. But if the authorities made that shift, it had the potential to create advantages for importers and problems for exporters. For the former, buyers paid less for beer brought in from outside because of lighter sales taxes. For the latter, the tax on the brew fell on all beer whether intended for local consumption or not. In a place like Hamburg, which relied heavily on the export market, the change to charging by the brew rather than the barrel in 1628 generated a controversy and also some erosion in exports because the town government would not or could not, for diplomatic reasons, offer a rebate or drawback on the brewing tax to exporters. Exporting towns tried to use whatever political power they had to get taxes lowered on their products in other towns. In the sixteenth century in general, German brewers lost privileges in foreign ports as brewing expanded in so many towns and as the Hanseatic League lost political clout. In Germany and the Low Countries, the barriers towns erected to imports deflected or decreased the trade in beer. Brewing in Hamburg, and for that matter in a number of traditional export centers, became more and more an enterprise for satisfying the local market.[11]

Town and Countryside

In one obvious case of protection, towns did not encounter any opposition, except from consumers. In Germany, but even more so in the Low Countries, towns made longstanding and repeated efforts to prevent competition from brewers in the nearby countryside (see Figure 18). Drinking outside the walls predated 1450, but the problem, as towns and urban brewers perceived it,

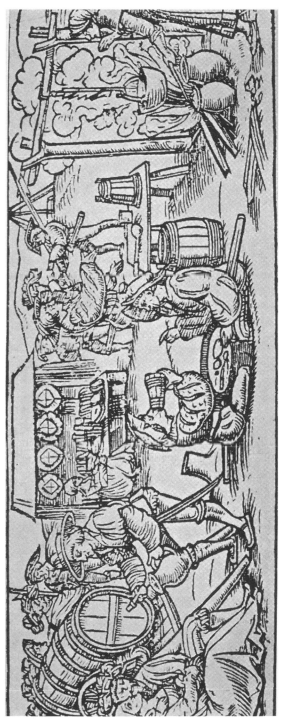

Figure 18. Peasants drinking beer in the countryside, *Lagertreiben*, a woodcut from Livy's *Roman History* published by Schöffer at Mainz in 1523. Reprinted from Hermann Jung, *Bier- Kunst und Brauchtum* (Dortmund: Schropp Verlag, n.d.), 63.

became acute as the fifteenth century wore on. That was in part because rural brewers learned to make better beer that could compete with what their urban counterparts made. Small brewers outside city jurisdictions, and so beyond the reach of tax collectors, offered drinkers a less expensive alternative. Rural producers did not have to pay taxes, and rural property was less expensive as well, so savings of 40 percent or more were possible. As the quality of urban beers went down in the sixteenth century, rural brewers could be more successful. They had direct access to grain supplies, had available labor in the winter months when brewing increased and field work fell dramatically, and had, as always, lower taxes. Brewers in the countryside around Nuremberg in 1577 enjoyed a tax burden half that of their urban counterparts and were not answerable to the enforcers of numerous regulations.[12] A bit farther east in Bohemia, landlords at the same time were restricting access of urban brewers to rural markets, all part of a general move toward creating monopolies which they could then tax. The practice of limiting where peasants could buy beer extended in some cases back into the fifteenth century and not just in Czech lands. By about 1600 levies on brewing apparently made up a significant share of estate incomes. The landlords did have some success since it appears that urban beer production went down in the second half of the sixteenth century in Bohemia and Moravia. The many complaints and court suits indicate rural brewing did make inroads into urban markets in many places, drawing thirsty townsfolk to drinking establishments outside the walls. How large a share of sales country brewers enjoyed is impossible to estimate. The scale of brewing on estates, especially in east central Europe, was always small. However, the ability of urban brewers to gain government support, as well as some sparse tax data and anecdotal evidence, all indicate that brewers in towns everywhere remained relatively much larger producers. Restrictions on sales, like the extensive tax legislation, make it implausible to suggest that there was anything like a free market in beer and, to a certain extent, a free market in brewing grains.

Brewers in a number of Low Countries towns from Groningen to Amsterdam, Bruges, and elsewhere pressed for and got restrictions from their counts in the fifteenth century against commercial brewing in the countryside. They also pressed for and got rulings that any beer or wine drunk near the town had to pay civic excise taxes. In the early sixteenth century, agitation against rural brewers increased until, in 1531, the government of the Low Countries took definite action outlawing any new breweries in the countryside and the presence of any alehouse within six kilometers of a town. The effectiveness of the restrictions was limited. The county did not enforce the law vigorously. Towns found it hard to win judgments in court based on the law so by mid-century it was virtually a dead letter.[13] Towns' rights to limit brewing in nearby villages was not in doubt, but their ability to do so always was. Lords in the countryside resisted the expansion of town power and with that the reach of the urban tax collector. Consumers resisted for more mundane reasons.

Wismar reissued an ordinance in 1572 that declared brewing in the countryside illegal. The law was repeated again in 1621, and as late as 1755, taverns within two miles of the town were required to have their beer brewed in Wismar. It was rural brewing that in the end undermined beer production in the powerful town of Gdansk, and other towns feared they might face the same fate.[14] In the sixteenth century southern Low Countries towns, like Leuven in 1542, obtained legal rulings that specified no brewing would be allowed near the town, except for personal consumption. Brewing in small villages around Leuven had been a source of competition for brewers at least from the early fourteenth century on, and the challenge became greater as local production increased. At Ghent the problem got so bad that in 1598 the town finally prohibited the sale of beer coming from the countryside, but the punishing of rural producers did not stop people from going out of town to drink beer. At Antwerp, despite decades of efforts by the town government, in 1578 there were still no less than thirty-eight breweries in villages and hamlets around the town.[15] In 1561 the county of Brabant considered, apparently very seriously, a regulation which would have stopped country brewers from producing strong beers. The goal was to decrease alcohol consumption while keeping down expenditures for rural workers. Such a measure would also have made it easier to keep their wages down. The maximum price of country-brewed beer was to be fixed along with the maximum time it could be left to ferment. A similar general restriction for all of the Low Countries was considered. The towns of Flanders as well as the States of Brabant and of Utrecht reported favorably on the proposal, but the Dutch Revolt intervened and the idea went no further.[16]

There were no efforts to protect urban brewers from rural competition in England. Towns did not have the jurisdiction or authority to make such demands. Brewers in the countryside were subject to tax through a system similar to that which prevailed in many of the towns. English towns outside of London, and possibly Norwich, were never very large. But the most important reason towns did not act was the constitution, which made taxation primarily a royal matter. The result was that by the sixteenth century, urban brewers were sending their beer to the countryside and undermining rural brewers, even driving some of them out of business.[17] The flow from town to countryside was the inverse of the general trend in central Europe. Levels of tax in towns compared to the countryside on the Continent made the difference.

Fraud and the Administration of Beer Taxes

Excise taxes were never popular, and the one on beer was especially hated. Fraud was commonplace, increasingly so as the tax fell on more and more people. In the early sixteenth century, if not before, tax collectors themselves were suspect and remained suspect over time.[18] Governments, claiming fraud to be common, limited transactions to certain places and times and, above all forbade night-time transactions. They increased penalties for failure to pay tax and increased regulation, making the whole process of paying excise tax more complex. The system of collection varied, but some common features emerged in the course of the fifteenth and sixteenth centuries, with England again being something of an exception.

A series of beer tax reforms in the 1540s at Ghent created an administration similar to that in many other places and offers a good example of what brewers faced. Beginning in 1542, whenever a Ghent brewer set out to brew he had to send a "ticket" to the tax collectors saying how much and what kind of beer he planned to make. The brewer also had to inform the tax collector when he planned to put the beer in casks.[19] Beer for export, which was free of tax, could leave Ghent only if there was a proper ticket from the tax collector saying the beer was for export. From 1543 the tax men had to have a weekly report from each brewery of how much beer was brewed and who got it. Quarterly the recipients of the beer had to report how much beer they got. This allowed the tax collectors to compare reports and see if either buyers or sellers were lying. From 1545 on, brewers had to make a monthly report of how much they exported. Beginning in 1546 a system of receipts was instituted. No publican was allowed to get beer from a brewery without a receipt and the sworn beer porters, the men required by law to transport any beer in the town, were not allowed to move beer until they had seen the receipt. Purchasers had to buy a receipt from the tax man at the excise house or shed before they could get beer from a brewer. So buying a receipt was paying the taxes due. Receipts could be good for a period of time or good only for a specific person and were certainly only good for the stated type and quantity of beer.[20] Brewers could also pay tax if they wanted to initiate a sale. On payment by the brewer, the tax man drew a receipt which he gave to the beer porters who, in turn, would give it, after delivery, to the brewer. The brewer brought all the receipts to the tax man at the end of the week. The excise master would then check those receipts to make sure they corresponded precisely to the receipts issued. If for any reason the brewery could not supply the beer anticipated, then the receipt had to go back to the excise man. At Bruges starting in 1587 each evening the porters had to come to the excise shed in the marketplace to deposit their excise tickets in a chest, and any who failed to supply all tickets and on time got fined.[21]

Beginning in 1569, Ghent brewers were prohibited from getting receipts them-selves, so it was purchasers exclusively who got them. In addition, if brewers wanted to make a different type of beer, they had to move the output of the previous brew into a cellar across the street and store it there until it was sold so that the two types did not get mixed up. The rule was directed against potential fraud by brewers misrepresenting the type of beer sold.

The excise master or his employees had to be available to sell receipts to brewers, publicans, and consumers at specific and widely publicized times of the day.[22] The Reformation apparently generated changes in practices. Sale of receipts on Sunday was eliminated, and opening hours for the excise-tax office were the same for all other days of the week with no variation for saints' days or holidays. In the end, though, in Amsterdam and in much of Holland, the system of receipts and delivery was very similar to that which evolved after some experiment at Ghent. The Dutch Republic codified legislation on beer taxes in 1616, and the law included what, by then, were standard requirements for brewers: to use sworn beer porters, to use excise tickets, to tell the excise man about any beer to be exported, to follow accepted accounting procedures, and for brewers as well as wholesalers and beer porters not to sell at retail.[23] Brewers were to keep a daily record of the receipts received and the tax man, whether town official or tax farmer, was to check it each day as well. Porters had to turn in their receipts each morning to the excise collector. Brewers were prohibited from brewing the thinnest, and therefore tax-free, beer before get-ting special permission from a tax official. Amsterdam was especially careful about the production and delivery of such thin beer, afraid that somehow a brewer would pass off higher-quality beer as tax-free beer.[24] As time went on in Holland, as elsewhere in northern Europe, regulations on all aspects of tax collection became more complex. Each new regulation was presumably designed to stamp out some novel form of tax evasion.

In virtually every town in the Low Countries, the law required that sworn beer porters had to deliver the products of the breweries for a fixed fee. Those men who might be paid by the brewers and customers were ultimately agents of the tax collectors. The emergence of sworn groups of porters in the course of the fifteenth century was a sign of the greater professionalization of the brewing trade and the rising limitations on brewing by ordinary citizens. At Bruges, porters took over the job of moving beer in 1475 when the task was sold off along with other town offices. Brewery workers lost the job of taking beer to houses of clients and were distressed enough about the loss of income to petition the government to revert to earlier practice. They did succeed in having the monopoly of the porters set aside but their success was temporary. By the closing years of the century the town had thirty-six sworn beer porters who bought their jobs for a period of six years. Later the job was to become one for life and was one of the most expensive of the many public positions which were for sale. Rules for beer porters in the Low Countries had precedents in German brewing towns like Wismar where, for example, as early as 1419, brewers were not allowed to give beer porters breakfast or anything to drink in order to prevent any sense of obligation which might lead to collusion. The porters usually used sledges to deliver the beer, though barrows for small quantities were also a possibility. Where it was reasonable, the porters preferred to use flat-bottomed boats which made the task of moving the heavy barrels much easier.[25] They also had to return the barrels to the breweries. The return of their cooperage was a long standing problem for brewers. As they became more conscious of the cost of lost barrels, brewers pressed the porters to help them in getting the cooperage back. A 1559 law for Holland, Zeeland, and Flanders, issued at the instigation of Delft to help its brewers, dealt with protecting, maintaining, and above all retrieving brewers' barrels.[26]

Brewers and publicans in Germany and the Low Countries came under a number of restrictions to guarantee that beer was channeled through the hands of the excise master and sworn porters. Having independent porters decreased the number of people employed by each brewer. English brewers had to keep draymen and stable-workers, but Low Countries brewers had no such problem. They also had no control over the costs of distribution and no flexibility in marketing their beer. The strict separation of beer making, beer transportation, and beer selling, dictated by law in a number of places, such as explicitly in Amsterdam in 1497, was probably one of the most effective devices used to decrease fraud.[27] The mass of regulation on the movement of beer, the marking of barrels of precisely legislated size and shape, the transfer of documentation, and the careful and precise recording of all transactions created a burden for brewers. The partnership of brewers and governments to share the potential profits from making beer shifted in the fifteenth and sixteenth centuries in favor of government. The fiscal needs of states, engaged in more expensive and more frequent wars in the sixteenth century, motivated both rising levels of tax and increasing regulation. The tax burden and the administrative limitations that came with it added to brewers' problems, already acute because of higher grain prices. Brewers found themselves increasingly concerned with legislation to protect them and with legislation that might be detrimental to them. Over time, in the Low Countries especially, relations with government became a more important avenue for brewers' efforts, even more important than investing in a larger scale of production or improving the quality of the product. By the seventeenth century, relations with governments fell under the umbrella of brewers' organizations, their guilds.

Chapter 13

Guilds, Brewery Workers, and Work in Breweries

In fifteenth-century northern Europe, guilds were not the common vehicles for regulating brewing. Associations of brewers had existed for a long time but, compared to groups of other skilled craftsmen in medieval and Renaissance towns, they were very slow to become legally recognized guilds which protected the members and regulated the trade. There was no pressing need for towns or brewers to create guilds.[1] Not having an official organization for brewers was the norm virtually everywhere. Town governments in Hanse towns and the Low Countries or, to some degree, kings in England and France made and enforced the rules for brewing.[2] It was as if brewing and the tax income from it were too important to be left to guilds for supervision. Town governments, which had a deep and abiding interest in the income which came to them from the sale of beer, imposed extensive regulations allowing brewing to remain primarily a free trade. The guilds that did emerge usually had a limited scale and scope. Antwerp may have been an extreme example, but the action of the town indicates clearly the goals of urban authorities. There brewers only had a "nation" forced on them by the town government in 1581. The chief officer of the organization was the treasurer of the town, so nothing could be done without approval from the civic government. Even the selection of brewers to sit as officers of the nation was in the hands of town magistrates.[3] Since guilds were urban institutions their creation meant further assertion of urban control over brewing.[4] The model for legislation of brewers' guild was civic regulation of brewing, not practices with other trades. The function of brewers' organizations as agents of government always predominated over all other considerations.

Many facets of the taxing and regulation of brewing, including brewers' guilds and their rules, became more formal and more strictly specified in the Renaissance. An increasing number of brewers' guilds, or confraternities, received formal recognition over time (see Table 12). It may have had less to do with government efforts to circumscribe brewers' methods of making and selling beer than with offering them a body to represent their case on matters

of regulation to public authorities. The groups that formed in the late sixteenth century and the seventeenth century were more typically social institutions, less concerned with the practice of the trade than with protecting their
declining business through political channels.[5] Brewers' organizations ended
up as lobbying groups which could put their collective case before some superior authority.

Establishment of Brewers' Organizations

The bells of a Brussels church as early as 948 were to be rung by the brewers.
Brewers at Cambrai in the eleventh century had some form of collective discipline and collected funds from members which went to the cathedral chapter.
In the southern Low Countries brewers' groups already existed in the fourteenth century in Bruges, Ghent, Hasselt, Herentals, Leuven, Maastricht,
Mechelen, Namur, as well as in other towns. Where the number of brewers
was small and production was small and overwhelmingly for local consumption, the pace of guild formation was much slower, as at Lier where the brewers were only allowed to form a guild in 1668. Liege brewers had their earlier
rights renewed in 1448 and may have been part of the group of trades which
had struggled for some political authority in the town from at least 1297. The
guild there included not just beer makers but also porters, innkeepers, and
anyone associated with making or distributing beer. Typically those groups
were kept separate but combinations of brewers with other trades appeared in
a number of places.[6] At Leuven a distinction was eventually made inside the
brewers' organization between the large producers and those who also ran
their own taverns, a separation which in the late sixteenth century was common throughout northern Europe. The guild in Leuven got a full set of ordinances in 1568, renewed and revised in 1588, which covered the combination
of grains allowed in making beer, the quantities of beer brewed, the storing of
beer, the price of beer, and, of course, payment of excise. Most of rules directly
or indirectly dealt with taxation.[7] The scope of regulation there was typical of
towns in the region by around 1600.

In north German beer-exporting towns, guilds were rare. Even Lübeck,
where the brewing trade was more strongly organized from the mid-
fourteenth century than elsewhere, did not have a formal brewers' guild with
legal responsibility for the trade. Much later, when German brewers did establish guilds, they always regulated their members less strictly than did other
trade guilds. Wismar, for example, despite repeated petitions in the sixteenth
century, did not even get two officers to look after their affairs until 1594. The
town limited the power of those elders and made them agents of the town, this

TABLE 12. EARLIEST RECORDS OF BREWERS' ORGANIZATIONS IN CERTAIN TOWNS

Date	Town	Remarks
c.1200	London	
1267	Ypres	
1280	Bruges	Renewal of earlier privileges
1340	Delft	Disappeared by 1600, reappeared in the seventeenth century
1342	Newcastle	With the bakers, separate ordinances in 1583
1348	Mechelen	Possibly as early as 1301
Fourteenth century	Haarlem	
1362	Augsburg	
1378	Nuremburg	
1396	Cologne	
1433	Utrecht	Possibly part of a broader trade association from 1304
Fifteenth century	Dortmund	Predates 1400
Fifteenth century	Dusseldorf	Predates 1400
Fifteenth century	Münster	Predates 1400
Fifteenth century	Dordrecht	Disappeared by 1450, new organization established 1583
1448	Liege	Renewal of earlier recognition
1468	Rotterdam	
1500	Gouda	Existed by 1500, disappeared in the sixteenth century
Sixteenth century	Norwich	Existed early in the century
1514	Paris	First full set of regulations awarded 1489, rules by 1268
1521	Oxford	
1543	Southampton	
Sixteenth century	Munich	
Sixteenth century	Maastricht	Some form of organization existed by 1299
1555	Leuven	
1561	Breda	
1574	Leicester	
1575	Winchester	
1578	Northampton	
1579	Exeter	
1586	York	
Seventeenth century	Amersfoort	Probably established post 1580
1600	Elblag	Well established in the seventeenth century
1600	Gdansk	Well established in the seventeenth century
1607	Chester	
1609	Alkmaar	
1609	Hannover	
1624	Lincoln	

TABLE 12. EARLIEST RECORDS OF BREWERS' ORGANIZATIONS IN CERTAIN TOWNS (continued)

Date	Town	Remarks
1658	Amsterdam	Brewers' society, not a true guild
1668	Lier	

Sources: Apeldoorn, "Een onderzoek naar de prijzen van het bier," 2; Balberghe, *De Mechelse bierhandel*, 15–16; Bemmel, *Beschryving der stad Amersfoort*, 2: 774; Bennett, *Ale, Beer, and Brewsters in England*, 48, 50–51, 63, 116; Bruinvis, *De Alkemaarsche bedrijfs- en ambachtsgilden*, 5; Charlie, *L'évolution économique*, 155: Jacob Dirks, *De Noord-nederlandsche gildepenningen*, 171, 214; Goor, *Beschryving der stadt en lande van Breda*, 296–97; Grolsche Bierbrouwerij, *Merckwaerdighe bierologie*, 90; Hoek, "De Gilden van Amersfoort," 4; Hoffmann, *5000 Jahre Bier*, 63–64, 132–33; Kampeter, *Die wirtschaftliche Entwicklung*, 8; Klonder, *Browarnictwo w Prusach królewskich*, 158; Löhdefink, *Die Entwicklung der Brauergilde*, 23–26; Muller Fz., *Schetsen uit de middeleeuwen*, 59, 60–61; Penninck, *Het bier te Brugge*, 9; Schlosser, *Braurechte, Brauer und Braustätten in München*, 11; Siebel, *One Hundred Years of Brewing*, 20; Walford, *Gilds*, 113, 191, 213–14; Wiersum, *De archieven der Rotterdamsche gilden*, 4, IV; Wyffels, *De oorsprong der ambachten*, 71 n. 69; Yntema, "The Brewing Industry in Holland," 224.

in spite of the fact that brewery workers, men and women, had a guild by 1561 and probably much earlier. Hamburg brewers had religious brotherhoods before the Reformation and a society after, but in all cases the functions of the organizations were social at most and regulation of brewing remained in the hands of the town.[8]

In Holland the metropolis, Amsterdam, never had a brewers' guild. In 1613 and again in 1651 officers of the brewers are mentioned but there was apparently no continuing organization and certainly no active institution to regulate and represent brewers. It was only in 1658 that a permanent college or society of brewers was set up, but it was never a real guild. Despite the exceptional case of Amsterdam by the end of the sixteenth century almost all the major brewing towns and some of the less important ones in Holland had guilds.[9] At nearby Middelburg in Zeeland in 1271 when the count granted legal status to a merchant's guild, brewers were listed among tradesmen who could join, but presumably they got swallowed among the wide range of people included in the guild. In France, Paris had a brewers' organization relatively early. French brewers, a group presumably dominated by Paris beer makers, had an organization officially recognized by King Louis IX in 1268, though it probably existed before that date. Paris brewers got their first set of regulations in 1489, and King Louis XII granted a new set of bylaws, giving the organizations guild status, in 1514.[10] In Scotland, in 1596 the brewers in the capital, Edinburgh, created a society, but it was very different from typical guilds anywhere in northern Europe. It became the institution for investment in brewing, owning the reservoir which supplied water and a large common brewhouse.[11]

In England, the capital was exceptional as well. London had some sort of brewers' guild by the end of the eleventh century. In the late twelfth century, there may have been more than one religious or neighborhood organization whose membership was dominated by brewers. One guild of the Virgin and All Saints, Parish of All Hallows London Wall, had as its principal responsibility looking after a chapel in the parish church, but it also had regulations which extended to contractual arrangements with apprentices. By the 1380s it was, it would appear, functioning in some ways like a brewers' guild.[12] Despite the existence of earlier organizations the Brewers' Company, the name for the general organization, was not formally constituted until 1406 and not incorporated by charter until 1438.[13] The society had its own meeting hall and inspectors of the trade selected from among its members. The corporation was to represent ale brewers and the sudden interest in the group's legal status in the first half of the fifteenth century may have been in reaction to the invasion of hopped beer. King Henry VI, in a new and longer charter in 1445, defined the reorganization of the brewers. He continued the grant of officers and the power of corporation members to produce all the customary drinks. The guild had its charter renewed periodically (1558, 1560, 1563, 1579, 1614, 1620, and 1685) often with much the same or even exactly the same language. By the reign of Queen Elizabeth I, the Brewers' Company in London, as it was called, without question included both ale and beer brewers.[14] Over time, and especially from 1579 on, there was a tendency to give more detail in the charters. Reference was invariably made to the 1445 grant of Henry VI as the basis for all subsequent legislation, even down to the 1685 renewal. It was not until the 1563 charter, though, that the guild gained legal status and could sue and be sued. Beginning in 1579 the Crown also made explicit that the guild included all brewers in the city as well as all those in the nearby suburbs and subjected them all to careful supervision.[15]

Brewers of Newcastle were less out of step than Londoners, but they were in the odd position of being in a guild with the bakers by 1342. Putting the two trades together made it easier to administer the Assize of Bread and Ale. The establishment of the organization came very early, but it did not get an ordinance to govern it until 1583. Oxford was also different because it was not the town but the university which gave official recognition to the guild in 1521. The grant stated explicitly that the purpose was to use the institution as a way to keep a better eye on the brewers. When the town tried to bring the guild under its jurisdiction in 1575, the university made sure not to lose control of the brewers' organization. Throughout England a raft of incorporations in the reign of Elizabeth I made brewers' guilds, by the early seventeenth century, as common in England as they were by that late date in much of Germany and the Low Countries.[16]

The Guild Monopoly

Guild members had a monopoly of making beer. Other tradesmen were prohibited from making beer and establishing guilds was often part of a policy depriving citizens of their traditional right to brew. With no apprenticeship requirements or differing status levels limiting entrance to guilds all members were immediately equal, at least in theory. Quite simply there were two ways to become a brewer: by inheritance or by purchase. Even in places where there were guilds the criteria for being a brewer had more to do with capital than with technical skill. Pressure for concentration in the industry, for decreasing the number of breweries and increasing the size of each one, rarely, if ever, came from guilds restricting entry. On the other hand, the absence of a required master status, along with the substantial amount of capital needed to enter and operate in the trade, helped in promoting concentration.[17]

In 1514 the Paris guild did get the right to refuse anyone who wanted to open a brewery, but the brewers' guilds seldom sought or got such direct authority. At Hamburg such a right could not exist since the ability to brew there was tied to the buildings designated as breweries.[18] The general practice in most, if not all towns was to make getting into the guild easier rather than harder. At Liege by the sixteenth century, even the rules against admission of adulterers, concubines, and excommunicants were being relaxed. Bastards could inherit breweries and enter guilds; though it is true that the entry-fine, the fee due on admission and, therefore, the price of entering the trade, for them was 20 percent higher. The entry-fines were fixed arbitrarily and there was potential for abuse. As the sixteenth century wore on, the fees more typically became standardized and unchanging. In a number of towns, there were reductions for natives and for the relatives of guild members or former members. At Ghent from the early fifteenth century to the early sixteenth, new entrants to the brewing trade were often the sons of masters already in the guild. From 1420 to 1449, a full 75 percent of new entrants were masters' sons; by 1510–1539 it was 100 percent.[19] In general, though the trade was open to all, male or female, who had the capital to set up a brewery and wanted to give it a try.

At Wismar the requirement for entry was simply capital. As early as 1399, anyone wishing to become a brewer needed a fixed sum but nothing more. Munich had, at least in the fifteenth century, a limited number of brewers who not only held the right to brew but also the power to grant the right to brew to others. Even though they had the power, they tended to keep the number of practitioners unchanged. There, as was common elsewhere, all brewers had to pay an annual fee to the common organization. Such annual fees kept brewers' organizations solvent and served to separate professional brewers from everyone else. At Haarlem if a member wanted to leave the guild, all he or she had to do was give three months' notice to the guild officers. If a member died, the survivors were to select either the widow or one of the children to assume the vacant membership.[20] At the end of the sixteenth century at Wismar, brewers lost their status if they failed to make beer for twenty consecutive years; it was by no means a stringent requirement. Brewers had to produce beer in their own houses or work for someone else, and like the earlier requirement of a fixed lump of capital, the restriction kept numbers from growing. At Oxford in 1513, brewers lost membership in the guild by not brewing for a year, but joining again was easy. All that was needed was payment of a fixed fee.[21]

Guild membership could mean prohibition from practicing another trade, as in a 1407 Haarlem bylaw. The guild dropped the requirement in 1440, but Hamburg continued to insist that brewers abandon any old trade. Even where restrictions existed, there were usually some options left open to brewers. Big brewers with their own malteries often sold surplus grain to smaller brewers. In Liege some brewers moved into barrel making to guarantee supplies, supplement their incomes, and use time available to them when not making beer.[22] In England from the reign of Henry VIII, however, brewers were prohibited from making beer barrels. It was a job for coopers. For wealthy brewers there were other possible avenues for diversification. Exporters could invest in shares in ships or in production or supply of raw materials like grain or coal. Guilds only extremely rarely prevented members from putting their money in related enterprises and in integrating their business with others.[23]

Internal Guild Administration

The difference between brewers' guilds and guilds of other craftspeople is especially evident in the way legislation evolved and in the form of the organizations. At Paris, the 1489 rules granted by the town gave the brewers all the trappings of a guild. A group of nine men, described as the weightier part of the brewers, asked for and got a set of fifteen regulations on brewing in the city. The requirements covered common topics such as the amount of grain to be used per brew, the proper marking of casks, throwing away bad beer, the appointment of officers who would taste beer to be sure it was of good quality, and the responsibility for brewers to report to a specific higher authority. The earliest rules on brewing in Paris dated back to eight articles of 1268 and covered some of the same topics. A chief of the trade was to keep an eye on the additives used and other brewing practices. That officer had two other men who were to assist him and report to a royal officer in Paris. The thirteenth-century brewers had many of the trappings of a guild except a charter. The organization was disrupted in the Hundred Years' War but was reconstituted in 1435. Competition from foreigners coming into the city to brew led to the request in 1489 for new rules, bylaws the king extended in 1514. They were expanded in 1556 when King Henry II added further limitations on foreigners.[24]

Paris did have a strict legislated hierarchy which set it apart from almost all other brewers' guilds. Under the 1514 regulations an aspiring beer maker had to do an apprenticeship of five years with one of the masters of the trade, serve time as a journeyman, and also produce a masterpiece, a large brew made in front of the guild's officers.[25] In having such requirements, Paris was, if not unique, at least highly exceptional. Munich had a two-year apprenticeship, raised to three years in 1493; on completion of the apprenticeship, the next step was simply to be a worker in the trade. Equally, though, the right to brew could be granted solely on the basis of ownership of property. Bruges had a two-year apprenticeship and then a test brew at the end of the period. Passing the test was a requirement for independent brewers. Lier would impose a similar requirement but not until late in the seventeenth century.[26] In general and despite the exceptions, a formal system of apprenticeship was rare.

Each guild had officers to oversee the business of the organization and to act as the intermediary between members and the town government. The officers were typically selected by a simple process. In the sixteenth century the two officers of the Hasselt guild were chosen by their predecessors. At Antwerp, as at Liege, the membership elected the two deans annually. London brewers elected eight of their members each year to act as inspectors of all matters to do with the trade. At Antwerp the officers' terms were for one year. A second year followed as assistants to the new officers. There was no possibility of being chosen for another term for at least three years. Paris brewers selected, by majority vote, two new men each year to join the third who was carried over from the previous year.[27] The officers acted as the judiciary of the guild and of the brewing trade. They acted as police, ferreting out violations of bylaws. They also acted as judges in cases involving the members and regulations on brewing. In some places, as at Paris, the officers had to taste the product of each brew before it could be put on sale in order to guarantee the quality and type of beer being made. Wismar had a town officer from 1494 who acted as the beer tester and the position remained in place until 1766. Rules to guarantee the openness of brewing went so far at Ghent as to require that the door of the brewery had to be open, or at least not locked, while the brewer worked. At Bruges because of fear of theft, brewers could lock the door but they had to have a bell cord at the door, and when it rang, they had to open the door immediately so that inspectors could see what they were doing.[28]

The guild officers typically had extensive powers. At Antwerp those powers went so far as the ability to dispense excise receipts to specific brewers which, in effect, allowed the officers to decide who could brew. The officers of the Paris guild in 1514 were charged with surveillance of imports, making sure that only good beer was brought into the city. As elsewhere, they were also to see that brewers gave the proper measure and used the proper mark on barrels of standard size.[29] Where there was price legislation, the officers were to see that it was enforced as well. One of their principal tasks was to see that excise taxes were properly paid and administered. The presence of guild officers did not supplant or eliminate the agents or officers of the government and the tax collectors. Often in Germany and England the tester of beer was a town official completely independent of the guild and so of the brewers (see Figure 19).[30] The presence of guild officers did not stop towns from imposing new regulators either. Liege had a governor of the brewers as early as 1302. His status in the fourteenth century is unclear, but by the sixteenth century governors were the chosen officers of the guild. Much later in 1684 the prince-bishop appointed a superintendent, responsible to him, to keep an eye on the governors. At Hasselt there was a town official who went around each morning with a graduated pole and checked the depth of water in the beer kettle. He could confiscate beer improperly made and could even close a brewery.[31]

The more prosperous and successful guilds bought their own house for a meeting site, and the lesser ones used taverns, in rotation, or the hall of another guild. The hall was the largest capital investment a guild could make. In some exceptional cases, such as at Elblag in Poland, the guild owned brewing equipment including kettles. Unlike almost all other brewers' guilds in northern Europe, Elblag had a cooperative organization for managing and financing the trade rather than a group of specialist tradesmen who shared common interests. The London brewers' mistery had their own hall by 1420, recently built in 1406, where guild business was transacted. In fact, they had the hall before they had their guild charter. They paid part of their costs by leasing the hall on occasion to other guilds. The brewers' guild at Mechelen got its first house in 1375, and from 1485 to abolition in 1798 they kept the same building. From 1581 on, the Antwerp brewers' guild used the meeting room in the *waterhuis*, the building erected for distribution of water under Gilbert van Schoonbeke's scheme, while Liege brewers had only one floor of a house, that from 1459, but it served their needs and they kept it apparently as long as their organization survived.[32]

Figure 19. Testing beer in Germany, Linhard Siegel, 1588. Inspectors from the guild or the town government were a common feature in many towns. Reprinted from Hermann Jung, *Bier- Kunst und Brauchtum* (Dortmund: Schropp Verlag, n.d.), 50.

Guild Religious and Social Functions

Brewers' guilds, like most others, had religious origins. The religious functions might not survive the Reformation in Protestant lands but the social functions of the guilds often did. In the fourteenth and fifteenth centuries, brewers' guilds usually had a patron saint or saints and often maintained an altar devoted to the patron. That was the case at Mechelen from the fifteenth century on and at Antwerp in the sixteenth. In both cases, the brewers' altars were devoted to Saint Arnold. An eleventh-century nobleman who became an abbot and bishop at Soissons, Saint Arnold had one miracle attributed to him— making beer by putting his staff in a vat. That was enough to make him the patron saint of brewers in Flanders.[33] In Austria and Bavaria, Saint Florian was a favorite among brewers, but in the northern Netherlands, Saint Martin was more popular. The Amersfoort guild, renewed in 1506, was devoted to God and Mary but got its name from the third patron, Saint George. As late as 1614 and so well after the Reformation, the Amersfoort brewers gave a glass window to the church of St. George, their former patron saint. Haarlem brewers gave glass windows to churches in three towns in the northern Netherlands as thanks for their long patronage.[34] Before the Reformation, presumably, the brewers' guilds participated in the religious processions that marked the calendar, carrying candles which they had to contribute themselves. The late formation of brewers' guilds often freed them from extensive participation in such religious displays. With the Reformation guilds dropped religious functions but the mutual assistance that was part of the religious heritage by no means disappeared.[35] Brewers' guilds typically had provision for the care of sick members and for the burial of deceased members, and some even had sickness or poor funds for their guild brothers and guild sisters. Members and their spouses probably considered the social and religious functions of the guilds the most important aspects of the organizations. The surviving documents of the guilds, however, do not reflect that. Instead the records point to government interest in regulating the trade.

Regulation of Production and Distribution

Guild legislation had much to say about the practice of the trade, about the way beer was made. Kettle size was of concern to sixteenth-century governments, and so rules on kettle size found their way into the paragraphs of guild bylaws. The Paris rules of 1514 even included a rule against having cows, pigs, and birds in breweries because of the chances of corruption and infection of the beer.[36] More common, though, were rules on hours of brewing and times of brewing during the year. Often when the guild got a set of bylaws, it was an opportunity to roll together regulations first laid down by the town and still in force. In some cases the setting up of the guild was an occasion for the town government to create stricter legislation regarding various aspects of the trade.

All kinds of rules found their way into the bylaws of brewers' guilds since they became, when chartered, the vehicle for much of the urban regulation of brewing. Preventing fire was not an uncommon topic. Stockholm made fire prevention the principal force behind brewing regulations in 1557 and 1563. Wooden roofs were outlawed in Hamburg for breweries in the sixteenth century.[37] A tile roof would not catch fire if sparks flew up through the chimney of the brewery. In wooden houses in Hamburg where malt was dried, the oven had to be completely isolated so that it was possible to walk around it. In some towns there was even discussion of moving all breweries to the same district, keeping them close together and, therefore, concentrating the danger from fire. That plan never fully succeeded but brewers often had their businesses close to each other at some place where they had easier access to raw materials like sweet water.[38] By the late sixteenth century, brewers were investing in ways to get more out of their heating fuel, and the furnaces they built gave better control over and containment of fire. That, in turn, decreased the pressure to legislate on matters to do with fire.

Guilds often got the job of making sure brewers used the correct size of barrel.[39] They also, in some cases, took an interest in the proper use of barrels. At Amersfoort in 1610 one of the explanations offered for the deterioration of the brewing industry was the small size of the barrel used. The argument was that the big brewing towns used larger barrels, of a standard size, and so Amersfoort brewers could not compete. In London in 1464, beer brewers themselves approached the town government to fix the number of gallons for barrels of different sizes. Later, King Henry VIII made such regulation kingdom-wide, requiring all coopers to make barrels of the sizes he dictated and no other sizes. The Rostock barrel was the standard that guilds enforced in most north German ports from the late fourteenth century on.[40]. In Holland the Delft beer barrel became something of a standard with regulations requiring use of that size of cask in force through the 1580s and renewed intermittently after that. Brewers were to use their mark to indicate where the beer came from, and at least one guild was to make sure that publicans did not mix beer from different brewers in a barrel.[41]

Guilds often regulated relations of brewers with publicans. Brewers themselves originally retailed beer, but by the sixteenth century they seldom ran their own taverns.[42] The commercialization of brewing and growing scale of operation led many English ale sellers to give up making drinks, as they had commonly in the thirteenth century. They became outlets for the output of common brewers, as happened in London in the fifteenth century and in much of the rest of England in the sixteenth. The licensing of drinking establishments, carried out in England progressively in the sixteenth century, and the regulation of public houses to prevent disorder, carried out in the Low Countries and elsewhere beginning in the fifteenth century, contributed to the separation of brewers and beer sellers. Popular fears about what went on in places where young people, servants, and apprentices gathered were fed by social reformers. It may be that in Protestant countries taverns took on more social functions as the scope of the church became more restricted. Such changes only fed anxiety about drinking establishments as hotbeds of nonconformity and political conspiracy. It was well known, at least among moralists, that pubs bred crime, debauchery, excess, and social and political disruption. Efforts to control taverns by systems of licensing, even in England where national legislation was most fully developed, were not highly successful. But even if the rules could not contain behavior in pubs, they could influence the relations between brewers and publicans by generating greater specialization by both.[43]

Relations between brewers and publicans usually turned on questions of credit. Brewers allowed deferred payment to them by retailers and that gave richer brewers a distinct advantage. Guilds often had rules making it difficult and very public for tavern owners to change suppliers so that big producers would not use their financial resources as a lever to poach customers from other brewers. In tough times, publicans often turned to brewers for financial help and since brewers needed outlets for their beer, they were often willing to accommodate. In bad times, undercapitalized publicans simply could not pay for their beer and that usually meant smaller brewers were forced into bankruptcy. The result was a series of regulations in brewers' guilds and, also from town governments, on publican debt held by brewers. A typical provision was like that of a 1571 Oxford ordinance which made illegal a brewer's selling beer to a tippler or huckster who was in debt to another brewer. Complaints came from brewers about late payment or nonpayment of debt and from publicans about failure to supply beer on time. Publicans were said to try to bribe brewers and bargain down the prices they paid for beer. At Wismar the solution was to insert beer brokers between sellers and buyers, so there were no direct dealings between publicans and brewers.[44] That extreme solution was rarely tried, so brewers' guilds often were left to adjudicate disputes between brewers and their principal customers.

Civic governments in many places relied heavily on oaths to guarantee the reliability of guild officers and citizens. Oaths given by brewers, their employees, publicans, and beer porters were to insure that the many regulations of the trade were followed. The guild officers often got the task of administering those declarations. The requirement that brewers had to swear they would abide by the rules dated back to the fourteenth century in Germany, for example at Nuremberg. They were a common feature of guild and civic regulation of brewing in the Low Countries in the sixteenth century. The use of oaths was widespread but effectiveness was always in doubt. The repetition of oaths, often annually, suggests that authorities were worried they might not work. The many complaints about brewers and violations of rules by them suggest that authorities had reason to worry.

Brewery Workers

Brewers' guilds regulated labor relations in the trade. Divisions in the work force among the owner, chief of brewing, and employees became more common as brewers invested in related trades and the scale of brewing operations increased. The experts in charge of operations tried to distance themselves from the manual laborers over time. The skilled leader, through the fifteenth century usually the brewer, was in charge of three or four men and women, each with specific a task to perform and at a specific wage per brew. The workers in a large brewing center like Hamburg formed a sizeable group, a potential source of social unrest. Hamburg laid down regulations in the sixteenth century trying to control the behavior of brewery workers who, at least in the previous century, numbered in the hundreds. Opportunities for advancement were few. Workers did not have the capital to own a brewery, and the growing scale of the industry put such a possibility even further out of reach. At Paris they were even prevented from becoming partners in breweries since the guild laid down the law that master brewers could enter agreements only with other masters. In London partnerships of owners became more common. In 1574 four of London's largest breweries were owned and operated by partners, but in 1580 the guild said no brewer could be in more than one partnership at a time.[45] Perhaps because they worked in small units, even by the standards of the day, or perhaps because they often worked with the brewer and members of his family, brewery workers did not develop a strong or strict distinction between the wealthy owner and the dependent worker. The split between owner and worker did occur in other trades, but brewing, outside of large centers like Hamburg, Paris, or London, retained much of the form and organization of a medieval craft.[46]

Guilds were typically strict about preventing brewers from recruiting the workers of their fellow guild members. Towns and brewers were interested in keeping wages from being bid up.[47] The family nature of the enterprise, at least through the fifteenth and much of the sixteenth century, made workers' changing breweries less likely. Recruiting workers in some open competition on a daily or weekly basis seems to have been almost unheard of, Oxford in 1571 being a rare exception. Though in mid-sixteenth-century England an apprentice brewer fell into the brewing kettle at work and drowned, working in a brewery was by contemporary standards not dangerous.[48] It was, however, arduous. Temperatures were high, humidity very high, and often there was a good deal of muscle power needed to transfer solids or liquids or to stir some thick solution. Work was not only seasonal but sporadic. At least in bigger breweries there was a chance of some consistency in the frequency of work. Beer porters worked more regularly but had to move heavy casks and also had to be available at specific times and places almost every day of the year. At Bruges porters were allowed a pint of beer before and after they delivered each barrel of beer, so there were some compensations.[49]

The labor required to man the brewing industry was large, not because of the number of employees per brewery but because of the number of breweries. The work force of each unit remained essentially static through the fifteenth and sixteenth centuries, even if the scale of output per brewery on average rose. A brewery could be run by as few as three individuals, and even the largest of breweries probably did not have more than a dozen workers. Around 1600, each brewery at Antwerp would have had about ten employees of whom two or three would have been women, often young women, and some eight would have been called *knechten*, servants, or simply workers, with the implication that they were more than just laborers but certainly less than skilled masters. Numbers in Germany at the same time appear to have been somewhat lower. Hamburg brewers in the sixteenth century limited the number of *knechten* who could work in a brewery to four. To that crew would have been added one or two women. At Wismar a regulation of 1570 suggested that the brewery was to be run by a master *knecht*, and he would have a staff of five, including two women.[50] At Frankfurt am Main in 1594, where the brewing industry was growing rapidly with the movement southward of the beer border, regulations required breweries have a master and no more than eight other workers, of which one would be an apprentice. In the fifteenth century, as in the sixteenth, in Germany, north and south, and in the Netherlands, north or south, breweries were typically operated by a brewer or brewster, sometimes with an assistant brewer or brewster, a chief of the *knechten*, a few *knechten* but rarely more than four or five, and two or three younger women.[51] Sporadic and seasonal work meant that many in the breweries were underemployed. Over time, as the scale and income for each brewery increased, there was a tendency toward greater specialization, members of the team getting specific jobs and the master brewer became more of a businessman and less of a technician.

The sharp separation between owner and workers that was a feature of the textile industry never existed in brewing. Brewing essentially represented the exact antithesis of practices in the textile industry in the thirteenth and fourteenth centuries. Growth in size of firms and scope of operations over the long term had an effect, but even as late as the seventeenth century brewing was hardly beyond the stage of nucleated workshops. Labor costs were always a small portion of total costs for brewers, perhaps in the range of 10 to 12 percent of the total. The scale of operations made relations between the master and workers more intimate. Often some, if not all, of the workers were family members. Wives and children received no wages. Changes in other workers' wages had small effects on profits so brewers typically saw little gain in forcing down the compensation of those in the brewery. Equally they saw no need to increase those wages. The owner of the brewery was over time less likely to be the operator of the brewery. A skilled worker, knowledgeable but without the necessary capital, could take on the day-to-day operation, aided by apprentices or young brewery workers. The skilled worker was often the wife of the owner and could be the brewer, her husband merely acting for her in legal matters.[52] In addition to the manager, there were men responsible for handling the barrels, placing them in storage or handing them on to beer porters. Their numbers increased when brewers stopped producing exclusively for local and immediate consumption and produced hopped beer for sale some time later or at some distance away.

In England there were more employees for the same levels of production because regulation created different requirements. A 1636 estimate of costs indicated that a London beer brewer had twenty-two workers, a figure much higher than was common on the Continent. The English brewer had three clerks, a master brewer, an underbrewer, four men for handling barrels, a stoker, a miller, two coopers, six draymen, two stableworkers, and a hog man. The numbers were about double the bigger Dutch breweries of the day and even greater than the larger breweries of late eighteenth-century Holland. The English figure included eight men responsible for delivery, the draymen and the stableworkers, personnel not needed in a Low Countries brewery since sworn professional beer porters took beer from the brewery to customers. The hog man and miller were also individuals that many Continental breweries would not have had, contracting that work to others. Even without counting those men, and they were typically men, the English brewery still had a large crew compared to contemporary standards in the Low Countries. The regulations which separated tasks within brewing, creating a sharp divide between making beer, shipping beer, and serving or selling beer, gave breweries in the Low Countries, and probably Germany, smaller crews. That made the share of costs attributable to labor smaller and so less critical to profitability. With transport jobs, ones almost invariably held by men, moved out of the brewery and with most of the other tasks such as brewer, underbrewer, and clerk open to and often held by women the share of the work force in the brewery that was female on the Continent was likely to be significantly higher than in England (see Figure 20).[53]

There were, of course, many other workers who relied on brewing for their livelihood and on whom brewing relied for its continued prosperity. Coopers found themselves in some cases working in the brewery itself, supplying the operation directly and exclusively as in the 1636 English case. Brewers needed many barrels and their concern about getting them back from customers indicates how important they were to profitability. In many towns in the Low Countries and Germany, coopers were organized in a separate guild; that is, if their numbers were large enough, and they worked independently and not exclusively for one brewer. Brewers bought the services of a number of other tradesmen including millers, smiths, carpenters, and bricklayers. The beer porters owed their jobs to the legal restrictions on delivery of beer. There were shippers who counted on carrying raw materials to and finished products from breweries. All those individuals formed an additional share of the work force that depended on beer making. It is impossible to estimate what share of the urban labor force relied on brewing indirectly other than to say it was sizeable but less than the percentage working directly in the industry.

Women and Brewing

In the countryside, even before urban brewing developed, "As a supplementary source of income, brewing was often relegated to women, who found that its amenability to home production matched well with their other domestic responsibilities."[54] Women were so commonly mentioned in records of brewing that it appears they typically made beer for home consumption, and when they had extra they sold it. Such rural brewing for sale was common where, in England, every other household brewed for sale at some time or other. Though brewing was a domestic chore primarily done by women, the tendency, especially in towns, was for the job to be done by couples with both husband and wife taking a role in producing the beer. That development would occur in England after 1350 and accelerate in the fifteenth century. In the early fourteenth century, where women did the brewing or where couples shared the task of brewing, women were the ones usually responsible. Over time, men took on more of the public role in brewing, a development most obvious in the larger towns.[55] The process that reached England in the fifteenth century was one already well under way in the Low Countries and possibly in north

Figure 20. Brewer's maid pulling a cart with beer barrels back to the brewery to be filled again. Woodcut from a series by A. Müller, *Der Danziger Frawen und Jungfrawn gebreuchliche Zierheit und Tracht*, 1601. Reprinted from Hermann Jung, *Bier- Kunst und Brauchtum* (Dortmund: Schropp Verlag, n.d.), 67.

German port towns one or even two centuries before. Women were so important to making beer that in a number of Holland towns in the middle of the thirteenth century governments placed a limit on the quantity of beer for which a man could be responsible. Presumably the woman—usually his wife—was responsible for the rest. Women could operate on their own making beer in Germany as in England. A woman produced beer under contract for a church in Cologne in the early thirteenth century, while another sold weak beer to a wide variety of customers at Duisberg. A chronicler thought them worthy of note because both of them, thanks to their honesty and devotion, were spared along with their houses and brewing equipment when fires swept those towns.[56]

In the fourteenth and fifteenth centuries, the role of women in brewing was critical, though not always equal to that of men. When brewing was a household operation and the brewer and his family made beer for sale to the neighborhood, then wives, husbands, and children worked side by side with a limited division of tasks. Equally, women operated their own breweries, as at Strasbourg in the fourteenth century where some 25 percent of brewers were women. In England, "In 1300, brewing was a ubiquitous trade that required little specialized skill or equipment, conferred minimal trade identity, and offered only small profits. As such, it was accessible to women, and compared to the other, even more limited economic options of women, it was a good trade for them."[57] So, compared to other options, commercial brewing was a favorable one for women. Brewing also opened some legal roles for women which were typically closed to them. In England women could be and were aletasters, government officials, even though they were usually excluded from holding any public office. As the urban industry grew, through increasing production but even more significantly through growing output of the individual firm, the number of women and especially the number of single women declined. Within marriages there was also, it would appear, some shift in responsibilities though when, how, and to what extent is extremely difficult to identify.[58]

In London in the first half of the fifteenth century some 30 percent of members of the brewers' guild were women, most of those married to men who were brewers but a number operating on their own. In 1500 only 7 percent of members were women, and those few remaining were widows of late members. Women were excluded from guild office and so seem to have taken little interest in the operation of the organization, probably to their detriment. At least in the fifteenth century, women brewers in London could be members of the guild, an option not open to women in virtually all other trades. As husbands took over more of the management of the brewing enterprise and more of the public face of the operation, women disappeared from the records into the shadows of their husbands.[59] "By 1600, brewing in many places had been transformed into a specialized trade that required training and investment, conferred social prestige and gild status, and offered considerable profits. As such, it had ceased to be a trade of women and had become a trade of men. Brewing had prospered; brewsters had faded away."[60] Though this may have been true in England, in Aberdeen, Scotland, through the sixteenth century, the trade was still dominated by women. In Aberdeen in 1509, all 152 brewers in the town were women, most being the wives of citizens but twenty-nine were listed in their own right and so ran breweries on their own.[61] The dramatic decline of village and small-scale brewing that happened in England may have come sooner on the Continent. Also the ownership of breweries by men on the Continent may have preceded the change in England. The pattern of employment of women in the trade on the Continent, in Holland for example, seems to have been very different from that in England.

Breweries in the Low Countries often had a *comptoirmeyd*, a female clerk responsible for keeping track of outgoing beer and keeping records for the authorities. Women, called *wringsters*, were usually responsible for mashing, moving the malt around in the mash tun with large, long rakes and oar-like paddles. The vessel held a mixture with a consistency of thick dough, so the work was much harder than stirring the wort. Those rakes and long-handled forks, also used to manipulate the grain, were common equipment of the brewery and even symbols of the trade. In sixteenth-century Antwerp, breweries had on average some seven to eight *gesellen*, that is male workers, and two to three women being paid wages. Both the total number and ratio of male to female employees stayed rather stable until some time in the eighteenth century.[62] In Scandinavia mashing appears to have been ordinarily reserved for women. Women, called *brouwsters*, usually oversaw the boiling of the wort with hops. A mid-sixteenth-century writer on the north, Olaus Magnus, said that baking and brewing were the most exalted of tasks left to women. That was true at home but at courts, monasteries, and in larger households much of the work was in the hands of men.[63] While women in England and Scandinavia may have found it harder to be brewers in the fifteenth and sixteenth centuries, women in the Low Countries noticed little change in their involvement in most aspects of the beer trade, at least into the early years of the seventeenth century. Women could inherit breweries and continued to receive and operate them through the eighteenth century.

Widows had the option, under most guild regulations, to carry on with the breweries of their late husbands. The guild usually required no payment, and a widow could practice the trade immediately. In Nuremberg in 1579 a full seven of the forty-nine breweries were operated by widows. The fact that brewing had no specific technical requirements and demanded no demonstrable skills for the equivalent of master status worked to the advantage of women. An appeal to the Munich town government in 1599 to exclude widows from the trade—on the basis of a claim that women could not acquire the learned art of brewing—fell on deaf ears and women continued to inherit breweries.[64] Strangely enough, the structure of brewing, where capital took on greater importance, gave some women, those with capital, an opportunity to act as independent businesswomen. Anna Janssens, born in Antwerp in the first quarter of the sixteenth century, inherited three breweries after the death of her husband. Not only did she continue to operate them, she also went to court to make sure that they would stay open despite privileges granted to others. She bought another brewery in 1563 and then contracted with a man to operate it for her. A decade later she had built another brewery, so at one point she was operating at least four.[65] Though the scale and scope of her investments in brewing were unique, Anna Janssens was by no means the only woman to own and operate brewing enterprises in the sixteenth and seventeenth centuries.

Fewer women were operating their own breweries through the late Middle Ages and the Renaissance but many remained connected with beer by running their own taverns. The alewife was a common figure in England from the high Middle Ages at least, and perhaps earlier. Women are also mentioned among the operators of pubs from the early thirteenth century in Denmark. Women worked in inns and taverns in the towns of Germany and ran taverns in conjunction with their breweries. In Denmark in the course of the fifteenth century women were excluded from the serving of imported beer. The restriction limited both the quality of their clientele and their potential profits. In that regard Danish tavern keepers were different from those in the Low Countries and in England, but all of them shared the need to secure a supply of beer from a brewer. The task became harder as the industry became ever more professional and specialized.[66] In England even as making beer came more and more into the hands of larger firms which were typically dominated by men, retail sales remained very much in the hands of women. The greater regulation of making and selling beer as well as the tax regimen of the sixteenth and seventeenth centuries tended to make the handling of beer a task for those perceived as responsible citizens. That usually meant men. Still by the sixteenth century in England, it was widows who dominated in the operation of small alehouses.[67]

Women who sold beer were long a subject of complaint and even a source for derision. Alewives appear in a number of works in the late Middle Ages and the Renaissance as unscrupulous, corrupt, and disgusting. The operators of taverns were always suspect in northern Europe because of the problems of drunkenness and disorder which the establishments generated, so the women who ran them had bad reputations. That may have deterred some women from being engaged in brewing and beer selling. More important factors in making those trades a place for men were the growing scale of brewing estab- lishments, the growing capital requirements in all aspects of the trade, and the more extensive and careful government regulation. Women, nonetheless, still made beer at home. Domestic brewing never disappeared and even as late as 1680 at Bruges there were 425 private brew kettles with capacities varying between 680 and 1,350 liters.[68] The oldest and simplest form of production continued side by side with later stages of development. Legislation typically prevented the older forms from competing with the more complex. The trends in urban regulation made it all but impossible for women's domestic beer making to challenge seriously commercial brewers.

Consolidation and Governments

Expansion in output, bigger and better equipment, greater stores of raw mate- rials, and finished goods waiting for shipment and sale combined to make breweries valuable properties. In Antwerp in 1584 of thirty-nine breweries thirty-four belonged to the highest category of property tax. The owners of breweries, the brewers themselves often became rich. Because of capital requirements, they often started out rich. King Christian II of Denmark, for example, in 1522 insisted that brewers be chosen from among only the most prosperous citizens. [69] The consolidation that increased the value of breweries and raised brewers' incomes also decreased their number. The total of brewers and of people working in brewing in northern Europe was falling or stable in the sixteenth and early seventeenth centuries. The decline in membership in brewers' guilds, or just in the number of people making beer, was another result of consolidation. There was apparently an increase in the productivity of labor in brewing as the number of workers per brewery stayed much the same or rose slightly while output rose more. The productivity gains appear to have been in the brewing itself, rather than in malting or grinding grain. Brew- ing technology enjoyed only limited flexibility. Even with the trend toward consolidation, there were limitations on how big breweries could get and also on how small they could be and still survive. Technology placed limitations on the industry but so, too, did government regulation.

Guilds were a late addition in the array of vehicles for the regulation of brewing. Other government legislation predated and postdated the guilds. Towns had rules outside the guilds, enforced by their own officers, even where there were guilds. The legislation of guilds reveals only part of the framework within which brewers worked. The lack of development of brewers' guilds, the brewers' limited interest in them, can in part be explained by the presence of rules and restrictions made by government beyond the scope of the guilds. Guilds were urban institutions and so did not replace or abrogate regulations laid down by higher authorities. In Germany that rarely mattered, but in the Low Countries counts could be critical in matters of regulation, and in England the king could claim and in some case even impose ultimate authority. Regulations beyond those of the guilds were often to do with collecting excise taxes. The rules were directed as much to the tax farmers as to the producers and dispensers of beer. Methods or forms of enforcement were complex, increasingly bureaucratic, and a source of ever lengthier legislation. As with all other trades, brewers' guilds were the products of civic governments and were agents of those governments for the regulation of the craft. But unlike other trades, brewers' guilds were more likely to suffer intervention by town officials, and members were subject to and answerable to other authorities which could supersede the powers of the guilds. Town authorities in much of northern Europe could tax brewers, inspect what they did, force them to continue to brew, and prohibit them their trade. For governments, brewers were tradespeople but they were also public servants supplying a necessity for the welfare and even survival of their fellow townsfolk.

Brewers' guilds in the seventeenth century eventually became advocates for the members rather than regulators. The number of brewers' guilds increased as did the scope of guild agitation. The principal tasks and goals of guilds remained, but they expanded their political activity. Brewers' guilds could never act as cartels in the way guilds in other trades did. They were cartels in that all producers joined together and limited access to the market to themselves. Guild members competed for shares of the market. They could, and in some cases did, act jointly to improve supplies of raw materials including, most commonly, water. However, it was on matters of technology where they parted company with most other trades that had similar guild structures. Brewers and their guilds could not regulate the methods used. They could not chose or even insist on standards of technical knowledge for admission to the trade. They could not collectively or individually make choices about methods used in making beer. The restrictions set down by governments at various levels on price, on the proportions of raw materials used, the size of the kettle, even the location of the fire in breweries were so extensive that innovation was not possible without lengthy discussion and appeal. The discussion was not with brewers but with politicians, and the considerations were to only a limited degree commercial. In other guilds, the limitations on entry, the requirements of technical knowledge, the forum for the exchange of information, and the ability to cooperate and even go into partnership with other skilled craftsmen could promote technical improvement.[70] In brewing the overwhelming importance of capital to finance the purchase of raw materials, to buy and maintain equipment, and to lend to retailers combined with the intrusion of government in virtually every aspect of the trade kept guilds from acting to promote technical advance. For brewers in northern Europe in the late Middle Ages and the Renaissance, government regulation created a highly circumscribed commercial and industrial life. That was true for the owners of breweries, for those who directed operations in the breweries, and for those who worked in them. Often they were the same people. Brewers found themselves sharply confined. The limitations made brewers incapable, at least in some parts of northern Europe, from responding to challenges from new alternative drinks. The failure to contend with competition often meant contraction and even decline for brewing in the closing years of the Renaissance.

Chapter 14

Epilogue: The Decline of Brewing

The consolidated, relatively capital-intensive beer brewing industry of the seventeenth century was firmly established as an integral feature of the economy and of the social life of northern Europe. Drinking ale, beer, or mead had a long history which stretched back far beyond the Middle Ages. But it was in the twelfth and thirteenth centuries that urbanization led to specialization and first allowed commercial brewers to thrive. Men and mostly women still made ale at home, but for the first time in Europe there was the possibility of making a living producing the drink. The presence of a number of people with relatively higher incomes living close together meant that there was a market for beer. After the first period of development, preparation of a market, came the second, perfecting of the use of hops in making beer. How and when that happened remains obscure, but the exports from Bremen, then Hamburg and other north German Hanse ports after 1200 are a sure sign of the production of large quantities of durable hopped beer. The spread of hopped beer was followed by the spread of the technology of making hopped beer. That third phase took much longer. The process depended on the presence of a market for the new good, one often prepared by imports from northern Germany. It also depended on minimum levels of income and urbanization as well as on government action. It was in the era of adoption of hopped-beer brewing that the importance of government regulation to the industry became obvious. That role would increase over time as brewing passed through a fourth period, that of adjusting existing techniques to the production of the new type of drink and adjusting the drink to the tastes of consumers. That acclimatization to local conditions was followed by a fifth period where brewers throughout northern Europe could produce hopped beer of consistent quality and in quantities to satisfy the existing demand. The process began with the success in thirteenth-century Bremen and Hamburg and was carried on in Holland, Brabant, Flanders, England, Prussia, Scandinavia, and then Bavaria through the fifteenth and into the sixteenth century. The outcomes were an ability throughout northern Europe to make hopped beer and a mature brewing industry. With that maturity came innovation, not in the product, but in ways of making it. Brewers found that they could reduce costs most effectively by increasing investment and the scale of production. The sixth phase of process innovation created the industry of the seventeenth century with, relatively, a small and declining number of breweries each with about the same number of employees. In the course of that change, small brewers, those who made beer infrequently or just for their own consumption and that of a few neighbors, disappeared. The bigger brewers with access to capital for investment in equipment and for extending credit and with access to wider markets were able to smother their little competitors. Again, governments found themselves a part of the process. With few exceptions, the authorities, whether urban, royal or at any level between those two extremes, opted to allow, if not actively support, the growth of relatively big breweries. The greater political power of the more prosperous brewers, reflected in their ever increasing presence in civic governments in the sixteenth and seventeenth centuries, often made the choice a simple one.

The pace of change in brewing, which had been by standards of the Middle Ages intense in the thirteenth, fourteenth, and fifteenth centuries, slowed in the Renaissance. The dramatic demographic and social changes of the fourteenth and fifteenth centuries contributed to the rapid transformation of brewing, to the adoption and spread of the technology of making beer with hops. The sixteenth and early seventeenth centuries saw an elaboration and consolidation of the earlier development. The trends toward commercialization of the production and distribution of beer, toward specialization with a few producers supplying the entire market, and toward professionalization with brewers becoming full-time producers of beer and abandoning other employment continued and intensified. The production and consumption of beer also continued to spread. Adding hops won new customers for beer first in Germany and then in the Low Countries. In England, the eastern Baltic, and Scandinavia beer only had to win over mead and ale drinkers; in the southern Low Countries and in central and southern Germany, it had to battle wine. The movement of the beer border southward started in Brabant and Flanders in the fourteenth century, but the process did not stop there. Hopped beer went up the valley of the Rhine and into Bavaria where already by the mid-fifteenth century it had won many converts. Combined with the use of a distinctive type of yeast, brewers in both Bohemia and Bavaria were able to erode the market for wine in the course of the sixteenth century and bring the beer border somewhere near to the Alps, very far south of where it was in the thirteenth century. They had accomplished what English brewers were able to accomplish in the fifteenth century, taking advantage of high wine prices and relatively low beer prices. By 1600, the scope of the region where beer was the preferred or a very popular drink stretched from somewhere around Paris north through much of the British Isles, the Low Countries, all of Germany

Figure 21. Still life, 1627, Pieter Claesz (1597–1661). Though beer was still the standard drink on tables in Holland in the early seventeenth century, it made only sporadic appearances in still life paintings showing food. Courtesy of The Putnam Foundation, Timken Museum of Art, San Diego, California.

and Scandinavia, and even into Bohemia and parts of Poland and Lithuania. The mature industry had established itself over a wide geographic area and had put down deep roots in traditional areas of beer consumption. Brewers in 1600, or at least those that had survived, had extensive networks for the retail sale of their beer and had productive relations with government authorities. They could settle back and feel some confidence about the future in light of the long-term success of brewing over the previous three centuries. Beer consumption in Europe per person may have reached its highest historic level around 1600 (see Figure 21). It was just at that point that trouble appeared on the horizon for brewing and beer drinking.

The First Problem: Import Substitution

Brewers faced a series of increasingly substantial challenges to their prosperity and even their survival beginning in the early seventeenth century, and those challenges became ever more serious as time when on. The first problem they faced was created by the successful spread of hopped brewing. As the making of the new type of beer reached more parts of Europe, the need to import hopped beer disappeared. What had been export markets became sources of competition first for brewers in the Hanse ports and then successively for Dutch brewers, and Brabantine brewers, and brewers in towns in the interior in Germany.[1] Improvements in ways of making beer or in the distribution of beer might mitigate the loss of sales overseas, but the result in some great export centers like Hamburg, Gouda, Haarlem, and Delft was a decline in production.

The fall in beer exports from north German ports had already begun in the fifteenth century. Competition from other producers meant that traditional markets for north German beer in the Low Countries and England disappeared, followed in the sixteenth century by ones in Scandinavia, followed in the seventeenth by markets in the Baltic.[2] The king of Sweden set up a brewery around 1540 with the sole intention of replacing imported beer. By 1600, almost half of the imports to the five largest Swedish towns came from ports around the North Sea and not from Wismar and Rostock, the German towns which were the traditional suppliers. In the fifteenth century, beer from Holland, Gouda, and Delft found buyers in the *ratskellers* of north Germany. Shippers and merchants from Holland made inroads in a number of places which had been traditional export markets for the Hanse towns. Political maneuvering and the balance of forces in the north worked to the advantage of the Dutch, at least through the sixteenth century. Despite competition, Hamburg remained the principal producer and exporter of beer in north Germany through the seventeenth century, but the local industry, due to the loss of export markets, did not grow at the pace of total beer consumption in northern Europe.[3]

In the major Dutch exporting towns of the northern Netherlands, towns like Gouda and Delft, the decline in beer production was dramatic starting around 1600. There families of entrepreneurs who had invested in beer making and became prosperous—especially in the 1580s and 1590s in the wake of the rapid economic growth after the first stages of the Dutch Revolt—found themselves by the 1630s and 1640s selling off their assets and turning their attention elsewhere. Towns in the Dutch Republic in the seventeenth century saw beer output fall. The exception was Haarlem but brewing contracted even there after about 1650.[4] The authorities and entrepreneurs in the southern Low Countries were among the first to attack the problem of imports by developing their own hopped beer brewing industries. The cities of Flanders, such as Ghent and Bruges, which had been major importers of hopped beer first from Germany and then from Holland, turned gradually in the sixteenth century to their own or to hopped beer produced in one of the rural centers in Flanders or Brabant. Changing political circumstances, import substitution, and falling real incomes in the sixteenth century meant a collapse in the market for the middle range of beers produced in Dutch towns. The success of Antwerp in developing a stable supply of good water for brewing translated into greater beer production and at the same time fewer imports and sizeable exports. Alternate suppliers of hopped beer in a number of different towns made customers more bold. They negotiated for higher quality or lower prices from their suppliers, whoever those suppliers were.[5]

In England the process of replacing beer from exporters like Hamburg and Holland with beer from home took slightly longer, but by the second half of the sixteenth century, the effect was unmistakable. By that time consumers had almost completely accepted hopped beer, with a small minority still preferring ale. The spread of the cultivation of hops in England, replacing imported hops from the Low Countries, and the interest in improving the quality indicated a strong and growing market for the beer additive. Not only did English brewers replace imports, by the mid-sixteenth century they competed effectively in international markets, even exporting beer directly to Holland. London and small ports like Rye, Winchelsea, and Poole developed an export trade. London alone exported more than 4,300,000 liters of beer in 1591 going to north Germany, the Low Countries and France. English beer was free of excise tax and despite efforts in 1580 and 1586 to impose a small levy on each barrel, it was not until 1643 that anything like the impost on each barrel which prevailed in all of Holland was charged to English brewers.[6] Lighter taxation and, in general, lighter regulation gave English beer an obvious advantage. Access to large quantities of coal, a fuel source which could be used to make beer thanks to investment in furnaces, could translate into an advantage for English brewers. Amsterdam's regulation of the import of English beer indicates that the beer had developed a loyal following and showed that the town a transport center for German beer up to the mid-fifteenth century and for beer from Haarlem, Gouda, and Amersfoort from then on—was becoming something of a transfer point for English beer. Certainly the drink had a market in the Netherlands and northern Germany, and at the end of the sixteenth century, it found a market as far away as Elblag in the Baltic.[7]

Tendencies in export markets to shelter growing local hopped-beer production hurt exporters from the Hanse towns and later Holland as well. Already in the fifteenth century, the decline of the political power of the Hanseatic League meant the organization was less and less able to stem the growth of protectionist legislation in many places. That had serious and increasingly adverse effects on beer exports. The pattern became more prevalent over time. Scotland, to guard its own industry, outlawed the import of foreign beer in 1625. Beer from the Baltic was one of the principal targets, though the effect of the embargo is open to question.[8] The protectionist tendencies in smaller towns in the Low Countries and northern Germany restricted access to nearby markets. The vigorous attack on rural brewing in villages near towns, common among beer exporting towns and their brewers in the sixteenth century, could in part be explained by the clear sense of loss of valuable export markets.[9] Towns and brewers in exporting towns could do little to change the legislation in distant markets, but at least they could try to change the rules in places close by. The attack on rural brewing was part of a more general development of lobbying governments for support in the wake of what were, in many places, increasingly difficulties times for brewing.

The Second Problem: Competition from Wine and Brandy

When incomes rose more people could buy beer, but rising incomes also meant more people could buy wine. One of the reasons for the continuity of beer sales was the high cost of wine. Well-paid workers in Ghent in the 1570s had to part with at least a third of their daily wage for a liter of wine, but for a twentieth of that wage they could get a liter of good beer. Wine was always expensive and so not a consumption good for common laborers. In much of northern Europe it was the well-to-do who drank wine which left people of middling income as beer drinkers.[10] Many people in that middle range took on different drinking habits through the seventeenth century. Rising incomes in Holland allowed consumers to buy more beer, but many took the opportunity to buy wine. The same Dutch traders who brought salt back from the ports of the French Atlantic coast promoted the production of wine in southwestern France so that they would have another good to add to their cargoes of the traditional export. They took the wine to the Low Countries and then farther east. The volume of wine shipped into the Baltic, often in Dutch vessels, rose markedly from about 1617 on. The total volume of wine traded internationally remained small compared to total production, but the rise in commerce in wine made the drink available in more places. In addition, the greater use of bottles for wine and the development of the corkscrew around 1700 made it easier to get, keep, and drink wine.[11] The price differential between beer and wine narrowed in the seventeenth and eighteenth centuries, thanks in part to faster increases in taxes on beer than taxes on wine. Already in 1586 the Lier wage laborer could buy only one-seventh as much beer as his grandfather had been able to buy a half century before.[12] When seventeenth-century brewers complained about shifts in taste, they tended to talk about the drinking of wine in place of drinking beer. At one Jesuit establishment, in the Brabant town of Bergen-op-Zoom, expenditure on beer from 1640 to 1770 remained a constant 11 percent of the total expenditure, but in the same period spending on wine rose from 13 percent to 34 percent of total payments.[13] The shift indicates a change in drinking habits which worked to the detriment of beer. Wine making became more concentrated in areas of high-quality production over time. While the relative price of wine had risen in northern Germany in the sixteenth century, the shift in relative prices changed direction in the seventeenth, so wine began to replace at least higher-quality beers, even in Hamburg. In the mid-seventeenth century the price differential in southern Germany began to work to the advantage of beer, and production rose rapidly in Bavaria where drinkers turned away from wine. In an odd reversal of the historic pattern, beer in the eighteenth century became the most popular drink in southern Germany, and wine made some limited gains in the north.[14]

Wine, however, was not as great a threat in the short and long term as another product from French coastal districts, brandy. Brandy was distilled there in part to recycle otherwise undrinkable wine and in part to decrease volume of the drink. Shipping the alcohol in a smaller package sharply decreased transport costs. Italians made brandy as far back as the thirteenth century. By the fourteenth century it was an export good. In 1332 some was sent to Paris. In the Middle Ages the drink was almost exclusively used for medicinal purposes, so consumption levels were extremely low. In the sixteenth century a number of books appeared, usually associated with medicine, explaining how to make brandy. The result was a spread of distilleries to a number of places. In 1588 Amsterdam, Rotterdam, Hoorn, and Enkhuizen, among other Holland towns, had people distilling wine to make brandy. By that date, production was not limited to places like Cognac and Armagnac on the southwest coast of France. Such "heated wine" as it was called in Dutch was already subject to an excise tax at Amsterdam in 1504. The volume consumed was great enough even at the start of the sixteenth century to attract the attention of tax collectors in the northern Low Countries. The periodic renewal of such taxes shows it was sold to a much wider market.[15] Brandy was increasingly a viable alternative to higher-quality beers and so attacked the most profitable part of the brewers' market. Volumes were small in the sixteenth century but would only grow, especially as shippers from Holland carried more brandy eastward to Germany and into the Baltic to fill their holds. The spread of distilling was not a threat just because it meant a loss of market for beer. In Holland, distillers produced their own brandy from all kinds of materials, including beer, so some brewers gave up the trade to take up making the competing drink.[16]

The Third Problem: Competition from Spirits

An even more serious long-term threat to brewing came from distilled gin, first in the form of *genever*, or Geneva gin, with its distinctive juniper flavoring.

Distilled spirits radically changed European drinking habits in the seventeenth and eighteenth centuries and led to serious problems for brewers especially in the Low Countries and in northeastern Europe. Already in 1552 an author, probably from Brussels, described in detail how to distill and urged the addition of juniper, *geneverhout*, because of the medicinal benefits. Brandy distilling created the necessary technology, expertise, equipment, and market for the new drink. *Genever* was made from malt, oats, rye, wheat, or barley, but originally it may have been made from distilling wine. Distillers could make gin from any sort of grain and of any quality; often they chose the lowest. Quality of raw materials hardly mattered. Few if any people in the sixteenth century made a distinction between gin and brandy, but from the seventeenth century on producers, drinkers, and tax collectors treated them differently. Gin was not a drink for the well-to-do who stayed with wine and brandy. Students stayed with beer. Gin was an alternative for laborers, beginning with its introduction to a wider market in the late sixteenth and early seventeenth century. Retail sales of beer and spirits remained separate, at least in England and at least until the late seventeenth century. Pub owners seemed little interested in selling the stronger drink.[17]

Genever production in the seventeenth century rose briskly, first in Holland and then in England. In Holland distilling started its rapid increase in the 1640s. Expansion of gin production in Holland predated that in England but by the end of seventeenth century the gap was closing. After 1700, output continued to climb throughout northern Europe. Schiedam, the great center of Dutch gin making, had just 10 distilleries at most in the 1670s and 34 in 1700, but the number was up to 121 by 1730. The level of output grew even faster than the number of distilleries since there was a tendency toward a larger scale of production. While Dutch and other northern European drinkers had learned and understood the advantages of spirits by as much as a century before the English, the rapid change in habits was more striking among them. In England in 1696, the government charged excise tax on 4,500,000 liters of distilled spirits, but in 1751 the figure was more than seven times as great, 32,000,000 liters. Growth was at a compound rate of almost 5 percent, impressive even by twenty-first-century standards. The rise came in part because of the introduction of London dry gin, a type separated from *genever* by small differences in production methods. London dry gin appeared only at the start of the eighteenth century but enjoyed rapidly growing sales in the 1720s and 1730s. The rise came in part because of changes in taxation policy which lowered gin prices. London alone in 1736 had 7,044 gin shops, or one house in every six in the city.[18] Dutch *genever* producers were concentrated in major and minor ports, exporting gin throughout northern Europe and to America. The great majority of those Schiedam distillers relied on sales to foreign markets. In 1771 only 15 percent of total output in Holland was sold at home, a fact somewhat comforting for Dutch brewers but of no help to brewers in towns in Germany, Scandinavia, and ports on the Baltic. The success of distilled spirits in general depended on its lower price for a volume of alcohol equal to that found in beer. Spirits took up much less space for the same quantity of alcohol. Spirits could also last longer than beer. Those considerations were especially important on board ship. Through the eighteenth century, European navies, one after the other, replaced their beer ration with spirits.[19]

It was with laborers and the poor that spirits found their greatest popularity and so formed the greatest threat to beer. In the seventeenth century, but more so through the eighteenth, whisky in various forms became the staple drink of peasants and of the urban poor in Ireland, England, Germany, the Low Countries, and even in the towns of the Low Countries which had long been the preserve of beer. At Berlin in the 1780s, for example, consumption of distilled drinks, which meant schnapps, was twenty four liters per person per year. The alcohol intake was comparable to levels of beer drinking in the sixteenth century, but consumers of distilled drink took in fewer calories, vitamins, and minerals than they would have if they had drunk beer. That was one reason for the complaints about the consumption of spirits. It was also a reason why distilling did not enjoy the "moral legitimacy" that brewing did, at least in Holland.[20] It was also the reason for the serious concern about the deterioration of society in England in the early eighteenth century, expressed graphically in William Hogarth's diptych of *Gin Lane* as a place of debauchery and the destruction of the family and public order compared to *Beer Street* where all is peaceful and both people and society are healthy (see Figure 22).

In about 1688, the brewers of Leiden in explaining why their trade had fallen on hard times, said that tradesmen, skilled laborers, now spent their evenings and days in gin shops, spending their money to the detriment of themselves and their families, and most important, as far as they were concerned, to the detriment of the brewing industry.[21] The competition from *genever*, London dry gin, schnapps, and whisky began the decline of brewing in much of northern Europe. Yet by the eighteenth century, the battered brewing industry faced a new danger in the form of tropical drinks which offered even more alternatives to beer.

The Fourth Problem: Competition from Tropical Drinks

Coffee, tea, and cocoa each started as an exotic beverage brought from far away. In the sixteenth and much of the seventeenth century, they were hard to find and used almost exclusively for medicinal purposes. First it was apothe-

Figure 22. *Gin Lane* (*above*) and *Beer Street* (*facing page*), by William Hogarth. Two prints from 1751 "calculated to reform some of the reigning vices peculiar to the lower class of people." Reprinted from Stuart Barton and R. A. Curtis, *The Genius of William Hogarth* (Worthing, Sussex: Apollo Press, 1972), 58–59.

BEER STREET.

Beer, happy Produce of our Isle
  Can sinewy Strength impart,
And wearied with Fatigue and Toil
  Can chear each manly Heart.

W. Hogarth.

Labour and Art upheld by Thee
  Successfully advance,
We quaff THY balmy Juice with Glee
  And Water leave to France.

Publish'd according to Act of Parliament Feb. 1. 1751.

Genius of Health, thy grateful Taste
  Rivals the Cup of Jove,
And warms each English generous Breast
  With Liberty and Love.

Price 1.ˢ

caries who sold the drinks because of their reputed healing powers. By the 1640s and 1650s, coffeehouses appeared which, along with the new drink, sold tobacco as well as newspapers. That made them, by about 1700, places for well-to-do businessmen to gather, that despite warnings in popular tracts in the 1670s about the dangers to men's potency from spending time in coffeehouses instead of drinking beer. It was not until the middle of the eighteenth century that coffee gained widespread acceptance. The shift to coffee occurred first among the well-to-do and later among a broader spectrum of the population as the price fell rapidly after midcentury. Prices collapsed as the trade in coffee and in tea boomed. From 1750 to 1800, the price of coffee went down about 80 percent. Tea prices fell even faster, by 95 percent. Even with the price reductions, tea and coffee still cost much more than an equal quantity of beer.[22] Increased consumption of tropical beverages came sooner in northwestern Europe. There commercial contact with the Indies, both the East and West, made the drinks available sooner, in greater quantities, and at lower prices. The tropical drinks had become such a normal part of daily life in Holland that already from 1691 coffee, tea, and cocoa joined beer in being subject to excise tax. The threat to brewing from the trio of new beverages was serious. By the tax year 1707–1708 in Amsterdam the tax on tea and coffee brought in more than twice what the tax on brewing yielded.[23] By the end of the century, the excise tax on coffee, tea, and cocoa brought in more than the tax on beer for the province of Holland.

Brewers in the eighteenth century were hurt by the fall in the incomes of poorer consumers who, as a result, could not afford to drink as much beer. Brewers still had to carry heavy tax burdens, inherited from the sixteenth century, which other drinks had yet to assume. If that was not enough, the brewing industry was crippled by rising grain prices from the 1750s on. Competition from spirits limited beer sales. Increasingly easy access to coffee and tea threatened other established markets for the brewers. By the opening years of the nineteenth century, the competition left the brewing industry, outside of a few isolated regions, a shadow of what it was in the Renaissance.

The Reaction of Brewers

The long-term dangers from gin and other drinks did not seem serious in 1600 or even 1620 or 1650. Beer was a standard component of the everyday diet of most people in northern Europe. Its production was important to the economy of towns from northern Poland to northern France and throughout the British Isles. Confidence in the beneficial powers of the drink for humans was shared throughout northern Europe and especially, but not exclusively, by

Dutchmen—that is if stories about Dutch drinking habits are to be believed. At the seventeenth-century Danish royal court beer was also considered good enough for sick and wounded horses and dogs.[24] Brewing survived from the late fifteenth century to the early decades of the seventeenth with few apparent scars. There were fewer brewers. Small brewers, which included almost all women except those who were successors of their late husbands, had disappeared from the trade. Surviving firms were bigger and more robust with bigger kettles, more efficient plants, and the potential for making better beer. The organization of production in the brewery and the methods of production were much the same in 1650 as in 1450. Though the scale of production might have risen, the number of workers in each brewery remained more or less constant over the two centuries. Even in the late seventeenth century—though the growth in the size of kettles continued and, if anything, at a faster pace—there were no factories in the true sense, no use of inanimate power from wind or water to do the work. Fossil fuels in some places like London and a few other English and Dutch towns might have supplied the necessary heat, but it was the muscles of people and horses that made beer. Breweries remained, even with larger kettles and cellars for storage of the finished product little more than workshops.[25] In only rare cases, if at all, had brewing moved beyond the stage of nucleated workshops which it had reached in the high Middle Ages. A very few breweries might have begun to look like manufactories but in much of northern Europe, where brewing was in decline, there was no possibility of moving beyond late medieval forms of organization.

By the second half of the seventeenth century, it was clear that the zenith of production and employment in brewing had passed. The signs of decline were more obvious in Holland and in some towns in northern Germany than they were in England or Bavaria or the southern Low Countries. No matter the variation, the trend in brewing was, throughout virtually all of northern Europe, in the same direction. The growth, expansion, and dissemination of a new type of beer leading to investment in brewing which had been typical of the fourteenth and fifteenth centuries was from around 1600 on reversed.

It is all too easy to blame governments, as many did in the seventeenth century, for the problems of the brewing industry. A number of other forces worked to the detriment of beer sales and production. However, the limitations set by various jurisdictions, the requirements laid down, created extra burdens for doing business and, more particularly, made difficult any experimentation to find alternative ways of dealing with the problems brewing faced. The fact that brewers found themselves going to government, lobbying various jurisdictions for help, indicated the depth of the problems that brewing confronted. High grain prices in the sixteenth century had forced brewers to lower the quality of their beer. The leveling off of grain prices in the 1620s and 1630s may have given brewers a chance to improve quality. That was certainly the case after 1650 in Lier for example. It appears to have been true in England as well. Complaints were made there in 1617 that brewers were using more grain to make their beer than provided for in the regulations and that the strong drink was causing a greater frequency of drunkenness.[26] Even if brewers did make better beer, it did not prove to be enough to reverse the decline in the industry. Beer was subject to ever increasing tax burdens, the rise starting in the fifteenth century and continuing almost invariably in the same direction through the eighteenth century. In the sixteenth century direct taxes on brewing already raised the price of beer from 15 to 35 percent, and there were, in addition, taxes on the raw materials and their preparation in many places. In 1564 at Lier taxes were about 50 percent of the price of beer but about a century later in 1668 they were 79 percent and in 1698 they were 86.4 percent.[27] The problems of brewing became so acute that finally in the eighteenth century governments stopped increasing the burden on beer. By then, in most parts of northern Europe, the change in policy came too late for the industry.

After about 1730 and only in a rapidly growing and prosperous London, in Bavaria, and in some small towns in the southern Low Countries did brewers find a way to overcome the adversity created by prevailing technology, regulation, taxation, competition, and changing tastes. Technical advances in England and Bavaria made possible a revival of brewing on an impressive scale. New types of beer, in England porter and in Bavaria pilsner, came on the market and attracted a new clientele. The different kind of yeast Bavarian brewers used in making pilsner was lighter and clearer so more suited to drinking from glasses. The porter of London brewers was a dark strong beer first made in 1722. Porter cost 25 percent less than ordinary beer, it kept longer and even got better over time because the alcohol content rose. Moreover, less care was needed in handling it since it was relatively more stable than other types of beer. Since it could tolerate higher temperatures, brewers of porter could make it throughout most of the year, suspending production only between mid-June and the beginning of September. That added almost a month to the brewing season and, fortunately for the brewers, at a time of the year when sales were typically robust. Porter brewers used soft rather than hard water, less but drier and darker malt scorched a little, and more hops. Given rising taxes on malt in England, that helped to control costs. London porter breweries grew beyond any previously known scale. In 1748 the twelve largest London houses produced 62,678,000 liters of strong beer, 42 percent of the total for the capital, but for the year 1759–1760 they produced 86,000,000 liters and by 1786–1787 over 160,000,000 liters, a figure dwarfing levels of the Middle Ages. One effect of the gigantic scale was that London porter brewers became industrialists of a different type from any seen before anywhere.[28]

In the southern Low Countries, there were isolated cases of towns overcoming the general trend of decline. Output at Leuven increased fourfold from 1650 to 1785. At the later date, 80 percent of beer produced was sold outside the town. Brewers found export markets despite competition from rural breweries and new drinks. Leuven brewers reaped the benefits of new paved roads and then new waterways to reach larger markets. They took an active role in getting governments to maintain canals and keeping them open. They certainly appreciated that their ability to extend the market depended directly on cheap transportation. In the case of Lier, the government dropped regulation of inputs in beer making and opened the door to making a different type of beer which proved successful in export markets. It was the brewers themselves who developed the new type in the absence of government constraint. The village of Hoegaarden was a small enclave able to evade supervision by any authority and so, by the closing years of the eighteenth century, Hoegaarden exported some 3,250,000 liters to the neighboring Austrian Netherlands alone. That number was small, however, compared to contemporary Brussels production which reached over 23,000,000 liters per year in the 1770s. Brewers in Brussels took advantage, as did London brewers, of growing population.[29] Those few cases of success in the seventeenth and eighteenth centuries, however, were the anomalies.

Despite falling grain prices through the second half of the seventeenth century, the decline in brewing continued. In the eighteenth century when grain prices began to rise again, the situation only became worse. Brewers and governments, with a few exceptions, failed to understand, confront, or find solutions to the problems that faced them. By 1650, the first era of prosperity for European brewing was over. The period had been marked by growth in output, concentration of the industry, and improvement in the social and political status of brewers. It was marked by expansion not only of breweries but also in the geographical area where beer was produced and consumed. The beer border had moved inexorably west and south out of the traditional region of beer drinking in north Germany to reach the eastern Baltic, the Low Countries, northern France, and ultimately southern Germany and Bohemia. At times beer even threatened an invasion of northern Italy. After 1650, with few exceptions, the trend was reversed. The late seventeenth century and the eighteenth century, outside of Bavaria and England and, to some degree, the southern Low Countries, proved overall to be bad times for brewers and for brewing. The entire apparatus of control and regulation set up by tax collectors, regularly extended and elaborated over the previous two centuries, gave brewers a burden they could not sustain when faced with rising raw-materials costs and alternatives both in the use of their capital and equipment and in drinks that consumers could choose.

The age of prosperity was over by 1650, but there would be another one. Scientific advances in eighteenth-century England (such as the use of the thermometer) were the start of a long series of developments which came to fruition in Bavaria, Austria, Denmark and later in Holland, Brabant, and England in the late nineteenth century. Mechanization and the use of steam engines to help with the heavy work was followed by the introduction of refrigeration, which made possible control of the environment in breweries. The developments came at the same time as research on yeast which, combined with other advances, made it possible to produce a consistent and reliable pilsner beer of high quality and competitive price. With an improved product which brewers could distribute along ever improving transportation networks and the invasion of the brewery by chemists who put the process of making beer more than ever on a scientific basis there was to be another age of prosperity with beer production and consumption spreading throughout the entire year and throughout the entire world. Beginning in the late nineteenth century there was to be a second brewing boom. It was an industry very different from its counterpart of the era of growth and prosperity in the Middle Ages and the Renaissance, a boom which had been created by another technical innovation: the use of hops in the making of beer.

Appendix
On Classification and Measurement

There are many different ways of classifying beers, for example, by percentage of alcohol, by the protein content of the final product, by the raw materials used, by the brewing method used, and by the price. The names applied to beer are often not helpful since their use changed over time or the name had a specific purpose not always relevant to separating one type from all others (See Chapter 11). It is possible to measure the amount of material loose in the water before fermentation and use that as the basis for distinction. If, for example, a liter of liquid weighs 1.045 kilograms before fermentation, then it is said to be of 4.5 degrees. This measure of original gravity, called OG, the specific gravity at the beginning of fermentation, will not necessarily be proportional to alcohol content. Few beers fall below 1.030 OG, that is below 3.0 degrees. In some places beer is rated by the amount of sugar in the liquid. The grams of sugar for each 100 grams of wort are reported as Balling degrees, after the celebrated professor from Prague, Carl Balling, known for his work on brewing after 1837. If measurement is at a temperature of 17.5°C. then it is Balling degrees and Plato degrees if measurement is at 20°C. Alcohol content can be measured by weight or by volume. Both are reported in percentages. Measuring by weight gives a lower figure since alcohol weighs less than water.[1] The development of the saccharometer in the eighteenth century and its increasing use in the nineteenth century made it possible to measure alcohol content and so gave governments a new basis on which to tax beer, and for that matter, all alcoholic beverages. The inability to measure alcohol content with any accuracy at all was at the base of most government problems with the brewing industry, its taxation and regulation.

Quantities of beer are measured in barrels. Barrel size varied over time and among jurisdictions. Though subject to regulation and surveillance by town officials and subject to efforts at standardization, there were always inconsistencies. Even when a group of towns would agree to regional standards, measurement was not highly accurate nor was control over coopers. There was, as well, the potential for fraud. The great variations in the quantity of liquid contained in what was called a barrel, especially before the seventeenth century, make measuring the activity of the brewing industry difficult.

A barrel in Hamburg in the fourteenth century, a *fass*, contained 175 liters of beer.[2] All estimates for Hamburg beer production and shipment are based on that measure, the Hamburg barrel being larger than the barrel in use in many other jurisdictions. For other towns in north Germany, figures are reported directly or estimates are based on a barrel smaller than the Hamburg one and closer to the barrel in use in Holland in the sixteenth century. Various words in forms of Low German were applied to the container including *vat* or *ton* or *tun*. Barrel, on the other hand, came from French, possibly through the use of containers in the Bordeaux wine trade though there the tun was also used to describe the cylindrical container.

The barrel in Holland varied between 100 and 160 liters. Distinctions were made in some cases between the *smalvat*, of about 124 liters, and the *grofvat* or *volle ton*, about 155 liters. There were variations from town to town before the drive to standardize the barrel succeeded, more or less, by the early seventeenth century. The Haarlem barrel or vat was 88–91 *mengelen* or about 113 liters and so smaller than the sixteenth-century Amsterdam barrel of 155 liters.[3] Smaller divisions existed including half barrels, quarter barrels, and eighth barrels. Governments did not like smaller units since their use reduced the accuracy of taxation. Brewers did not especially like them since more wood and more cooper's time was needed to make two half barrels instead of one full barrel. For the sake of uniformity and to avoid confusion, the Dutch barrel is assumed to be 120 liters up to and through the sixteenth century. That choice yields a tendency to overestimate by a small percentage figures for the fifteenth century while being consistent or, in some cases, understating the figures for the sixteenth. For all figures from the seventeenth century the standard barrel of 155 liters is assumed for the northern Netherlands. Dutch pubs served beer by the *kan* between 1.4 liters and almost 2 liters. The publican could also sell by the smaller, though not that much smaller, *mengel*, and by the definitely smaller *pint* of 0.50–0.65 liters.

The Antwerp *ame* was 148.75 liters.[4] The *ame* or *aam* was usually divided into four *anker*, and each *anker* had 16 *stoop* so there were 62 *stoop* for each *aam*. A *mengel* was one-half of a *stoop* or could be equated with 2 pints. In Denmark in the seventeenth century, beer was measured by *laest* of 12 *fade*. The *fade* or *ton*, that is the barrel, in turn was made up of 120 *potter*. That would give a figure of about 116 liters for the barrel. The Danish beer *laest* was 1,394 liters, the largest measure used for beer. It was never a single unit. Having barrels even of 100 liters presented problems of loading and of transport. With the much larger barrels, for example, in Hamburg at 175 liters, the problems must have been considerable.

In England by the sixteenth century a barrel of ale, that is made without hops, was 32 gallons while a barrel of beer, made with hops was 36 gallons.

The gallon is the imperial one of 4.45 liters which made the ale barrel 144 liters and the beer barrel 162 liters. The relatively large size of the beer barrel, approaching the Hamburg *fass*, may reflect production directed in some degree toward export markets. There were four firkins to the barrel, no matter its size, and two firkins, that is half a barrel, equaled a kilderkin in England.[5]

An English quarter of barley is 448 pounds or 203.6 kilograms, while a quarter of malt is 336 pounds or 152.7 kilograms.[6] The English quarter of eight bushels is also 290.94 liters or alternately 100 liters of grain is equal to 2.75 bushels. The specific gravity of wheat was between 0.70 and 0.85 so the figures can be converted from volume to weight.[7] Throughout, again for the sake of consistency, a standard conversion of 0.80 is used for all grains, accepting the small percentage error introduced by using the single figure.

Notes

Chapter 1

1. Louis Pasteur, *Studies on Fermentation: The Diseases of Beer, Their Causes, and the Means of Preventing Them. A Translation, Made with the Author's Sanction, of "Études sur la biere," with Notes, Index and Original Illustrations by Frank Faulkner, author of "The Art of Brewing", etc. and D. Constable Robb* (London: Macmillan, 1879), 1.

2. Patrice Debré, *Louis Pasteur* (Paris: Flammarion, 1994), 270–76.

3. J. S. Hough, *The Biotechnology of Malting and Brewing* (Cambridge: Cambridge University Press, 1985), 3.

4. A. Lynn Martin, *Alcohol, Sex, and Gender in Late Medieval and Early Modern Europe* (Basingstoke: Palgrave, 2001), 2.

5. Martin, *Alcohol, Sex, and Gender*, 5; Jessica Warner, "Before there was 'alcoholism': Lessons from the Medieval experience with Alcohol," *Contemporary Drug Problems* 20 (1992): 409–10, 413–17, 422–23.

6. Hough, *The Biotechnology of Malting and Brewing*, 4–5.

7. Jean De Clerck, *A Textbook of Brewing*, trans. Kathleen Barton-Wright, 2 vols. (London: Chapman and Hall, 1957–58), 151–58, 181–82, 192, 197; Hough, *The Biotechnology of Malting and Brewing*, 21–23, 26–38.

8. De Clerk, *A Textbook of Brewing*, 217–18.

9. De Clerck, *A Textbook of Brewing*, 249–50; Hough, *The Biotechnology of Malting and Brewing*, 54, 56–7.

10. Herbert Langer, "Das Braugewerbe in den deutschen Hansestädten der frühen Neuzeit," in Konrad Fritze, Eckard Müller-Mertens, Johannes Schildhauer, eds., *Hansische Studiën IV Gewerbliche Produktion und Stadt-Land-Beziehungen, Abhandlungen zur Handels- und Sozialgeschichte*, 18 (Weimar: Hermann Böhlaus Nachfolger, 1979), 71, 74; Peter Mathias, "Agriculture and the Brewing and Distilling Industries in the Eighteenth Century," *Economic History Review*, 2nd series 5 (1952): 250–53, 257; Raymonde Monnier, *Un bourgeois sans-culotte: Le général Santerre suivi de l'art du brasseur* (Paris: Publications de la Sorbonne, 1989), 123; Friedrich Techen, "Das Brauwerk in Wismar," *Hansisches Geschichtsblätter* 21 (1915): 328–30.

11. De Clerck, *A Textbook of Brewing*, 302–4; Hough, *The Biotechnology of Malting and Brewing*, 85–86; M. G. Royston, "Wort Boiling and Cooling," in W. P. K. Findlay, ed., *Modern Brewing Technology* (London: Macmillan, 1971), 60–66.

12. R. G. Ault and R. Newton, "Spoilage Organisms in Brewing," in W. P. K. Findlay, ed., *Modern Brewing Technology* (London: Macmillan, 1971), 183; Hough, *The Biotechnology of Malting and Brewing*, 108–10.

13. De Clerck, *A Textbook of Brewing*, 361–64, 390–97, 403; Pasteur, *Studies on Fermentation*, 222.

14. De Clerck, *A Textbook of Brewing*, 363, 428–31, 447; Hough, *The Biotechnology of Malting and Brewing*, 137–38, 142–47; Royston, "Wort Boiling and Cooling," 80; C. Anne Wilson, *Food and Drink in Britain from the Stone Age to Recent Times* (London: Constable, 1973), 45.

15. Odd Nordlund, *Brewing and Beer Traditions in Norway: The Social Anthropological Background of the Brewing Industry* (Oslo: Universitetsforlaget, 1969).

16. Nordlund, *Brewing and Beer Traditions in Norway*, preface, 158, 283.

17. Matti Räsänen, *Von Halm zum Fass. Die volkstümlichen alkoholarmen Getreidegetränke in Finnland* (Helsinki: Suomen muinaismuistoyhdistys, 1975), 12–13.

18. A. Bömer, ed., "Eine Vagantenliedersammlung des 14. Jahrhunderts in de Scholssbibliothek zu Herdringend (Kr. Arnsberg)," *Zeitschrift für deutsches Altertum und deutsche Litteratur* 49 (1908): 161–238; W. T. Marchant, *In Praise of Ale or Songs, Ballads, Epigrams, and Anecdotes Relating to Beer, Malt and Hops with some curious Particulars concerning Ale-Wives and Brewers Drinking-Clubs and Customs* (London: George Redway, 1888).

19. E. Wiersum, *De archieven der Rotterdamsche gilden* (Rotterdam: Wed. P. van Waesberge en Zoon, 1926), 4.

20. Jacques C. van Loenen, *De Haarlemse brouwindustrie voor 1600* (Amsterdam: Universiteitspers, 1950), 24–25.

21. Judith M. Bennett, *Ale, Beer, and Brewsters in England: Women's Work in a Changing World, 1300–1600* (New York: Oxford University Press, 1996), 21; René van Santbergen, *Les bons métiers des meuniers, des boulangers et des brasseurs de la cité de Liège* (Liege: Faculté de philosophie et lettres, 1949), 45.

22. D. P. S. Peacock, *Pottery in the Roman World: an Ethnoarchaeological Approach* (London: Longman, 1982), 8.

23. Richard G. Wilson, "The British Brewing Industry Since 1750," in Lesley Richmond and Alison Turton, eds., *The brewing industry A guide to historical records* (Manchester: Manchester University Press, 1990), 1.

24. Peacock, *Pottery in the Roman World*, 8.

25. Judith M. Bennett, "The Village Ale-Wife: Women and Brewing in Fourteenth-Century England," in Barbara Hanawalt, ed., *Women and Work in Preindustrial Europe* (Bloomington: Indiana University Press, 1986), 23–24; Bennett, *Ale, Beer, and Brewsters in England*, 18–21.

26. Peacock, *Pottery in the Roman World*, 9.

27. Louis F. Hartman, and A.L. Oppenheim, "On Beer and Brewing Techniques in Ancient Mesopotamia According to the 23rd Tablet of the Series HAR.ra = hubullu," *Supplement to the Journal of the American Oriental Society* 10, issued with vol. 70, no. 4 (Baltimore: American Oriental Society, 1950), 12.

28. Peacock, *Pottery in the Roman World*, 10.

29. Peacock, *Pottery in the Roman World*, 9–11.

Chapter 2

1. Robert I. Curtis, *Ancient Food Technology* (Leiden: Brill, 2001), 184, 210–11.

2. Curtis, *Ancient Food Technology*, 105–6; M. Hoffmann, *5000 Jahre Bier* (Nuremberg: Verlag Hans Carl, 1956), 17–19; Rudolph H. Michel, Patrick E. McGovern, and Virginia R. Badler, "Chemical Evidence for Ancient Beer," *Nature* 360, no. 6399 (5

November 1992): 24; Wolfgang Röllig, *Das Bier im alten Mesopotamien* (Berlin: Gesellschaft für die Geschichte und Bibliographie des Brauwesens E.V., 1970), 19, 33, 38; Richard L. Zettler and Naomi F. Miller, "Searching for Wine in the Archaeological Record of Ancient Mesopotamia of the Third and Second Millennia B. C.," in Patrick E. McGovern, Stuart J. Fleming, and Solomon H. Katz, eds., *The Origins and Ancient History of Wine* (Luxembourg: Gordon and Breach Publishers, 1995), 123.

3. Assyrians, for example, used beer as a medium for the onion they consumed as a drug to treat dryness of the eyes. Al-Kindī, *The Medical Formulary of Aqrābādhīn of Al-Kindī*, trans. Martin Levey (Madison: University of Wisconsin Press, 1966), 230.

4. Marten Stol, "Beer in Neo-Babylonian Times," in Lucio Milano, ed., *Drinking in Ancient Societies: History and Culture of Drinks in the Ancient Near East*, papers of a symposium held in Rome, May 17–19, 1990 (Padua: Sargon, 1994), 179.

5. Phyllis P. Bober, *Art, Culture, and Cuisine: Ancient and Medieval Gastronomy* (Chicago: University of Chicago Press, 1999), 63–64; Curtis, *Ancient Food Technology*, 213; Marvin A. Powell, "Metron Ariston: Measure as a Tool for Studying Beer in Ancient Mesopotamia," in Lucio Milano, ed., *Drinking in Ancient Societies: History and Culture of Drinks in the Ancient Near East*, papers of a symposium held in Rome, May 17–19, 1990 (Padua: Sargon, 1994); Röllig, *Das Bier im alten Mesopotamien*, 22, 33, 45–48, 52–56, 64–66, 75.

6. Curtis, *Ancient Food Technology*, 88, 184; Zettler and Miller, "Searching for Wine," 123–25, 131.

7. Curtis, *Ancient Food Technology*, 116, 132; Hoffmann, *5000 Jahre Bier*, 21–23.

8. Curtis, *Ancient Food Technology*, 215–17; Powell, "Metron Ariston," 95, 97–99. Mesopotamians used vessels with holes to drain vegetable matter into a collecting vessel when they made beer with dates, the vessel having a unique name related to the word for squeezing. Stol, "Beer in Neo-Babylonian Times," 170–71, 155–57.

9. Curtis, *Ancient Food Technology*, 242; Hartman and Oppenheim, "On Beer and Brewing Techniques in Ancient Mesopotamia," 7–12, 16; Röllig, *Das Bier im alten Mesopotamien*, 21–26; Stol, "Beer in Neo-Babylonian Times," 155–57, 161–67.

10. Bober, *Art, Culture and Cuisine*, 64–65; Curtis, *Ancient Food Technology*, 217–19.

11. Curtis, *Ancient Food Technology*, 106, 217 n. 72, 219; Hartman and Oppenheim, "On Beer and Brewing Techniques in Ancient Mesopotamia," 6, 13–15, 23; Frank A. King, *Beer Has a History* (London: Hutchinson's Scientific and Technical Publications, 1947), 11; Räsänen, *Von Halm zum Fass*, 78–84; Röllig, *Das Bier im alten Mesopotamien*, 23–39.

12. Curtis, *Ancient Food Technology*, 249; Grolsche Bierbrouwerij, *Merckwaerdighe Bierologie zijnde het verhaal van een plezierige bierreis door meer dan vijftig eeuwen elk op zijn of haar manier beleefd door een geschiedschriftster en een reclameman, een tekenaar en een oudheidkundige, een bronnenspeurder en een genealoog* (Amsterdam: Uitgeverij Van Lindonk, 1966), 14–18; Hoffmann, *5000 Jahre Bier*, 26; Powell, "Metron Ariston," 104–18; Röllig, *Das Bier im alten Mesopotamien*, 33.

13. Curtis, *Ancient Food Technology*, 106; Hartman and Oppenheim, "On Beer and Brewing Techniques in Ancient Mesopotamia," 12; King, *Beer Has a History*, 11; Räsänen, *Von Halm zum Fass*, 68; Delwen Samuel, "Brewing and Baking," in Paul T. Nicholson and Ian Shaw, eds., *Ancient Egyptian Materials and Technology* (Cambridge: Cambridge University Press, 2000), 540; Martini Schoockii [Martinus Schookhuis], *Liber de Cervisia. Quo Non modo omnia ad Cerealem potum pertinentia comprehend-*

umtur, sed varia quoque Problemata, Philosophica & Philologica, discutiuntur; Simul incidentes quædam Authorum antiquorum loca illustrantur (Groningen: Francisci Bronchortsii, 1661), 18.

14. Hoffmann, *5000 Jahre Bier*, 23–25, 31–34.

15. Curtis, *Ancient Food Technology*, 132–37. For a good recent translation of the description by Zosimus see Max Nelson, *Beer in Greco-Roman Antiquity* (Ph.D. diss., University of British Columbia, 2001).

16. Curtis, *Ancient Food Technology*, 137–38; Samuel, "Brewing and Baking," 540–56; Delwen Samuel, "Investigation of Ancient Egyptian Baking and Brewing Methods by Correlative Microscopy," *Science* 273 (26 July 1996): 488–90.

17. The proximity of the two trades in illustrations as well as in sites investigated by archeologists has fed the notion that brewers used bread in making beer. Curtis, *Ancient Food Technology*, 108, 127–29, 137, 214.

18. Bober, *Art, Culture, and Cuisine*, 41–42; Curtis, *Ancient Food Technology*, 139; Samuel, "Brewing and Baking," 556–57, 569.

19. Curtis, *Ancient Food Technology*, 211 n. 58; Stol, "Beer in Neo-Babylonian Times," 158.

20. Curtis, *Ancient Food Technology*, 294; Pasteur, *Studies on Fermentation*, 1; H. Stopes, *Malt and Malting: An Historical, Scientific, and Practical Treatise, showing, as clearly as existing knowledge permits, What Malt Is, and How to Make It* (London: F. W. Lyon, 1885), 4.

21. John Compton-Davey, "Some Evidence of Brewing in Roman Times," *The Journal of the Brewery History Society* 80 (Summer 1995): 7; King, *Beer Has a History*, 12; Samuel, "Brewing and Baking," 538; Stopes, *Malt and Malting*, 4–5; C. Anne Wilson, *Food and Drink in Britain from the Stone Age to recent times* (London: Constable, 1973), 231; D. Gay Wilson, "Plant Remains from the Graveney Boat and the Early History of *Humulus lupulus L.* in W. Europe," *New Phytologist* 75 (1975): 639.

22. For example, the emperor Julian (361–63) called beer a barbarian drink, something he may have come across in his years in Gaul. He asked why wine was scented with nectar but beer smelled like a goat. Compton-Davey, "Some Evidence of Brewing in Roman Times," 4–5, 12–13; Curtis, *Ancient Food Technology*, 370; Raymond van Uytven, "Bier und Brauer in Brabant und Flandern: Ein Blick auf sechs Jahrhunderte Konsum-geschichte," in Fritz Langensiepen, ed., *Bierkultur an Rhein und Maas* (Bonn: Bouvier Verlag, n. d.), 2.

23. Egyptian brewers may possibly have cured grains in ovens, but the evidence is unclear. Karl-Ernst Behre, "The History of Beer Additives in Europe: A Review," *Vegetation History and Archeobotany* 8 (1999): 35; Compton-Davey, "Some Evidence of Brewing in Roman Times," 10–12; Curtis, *Ancient Food Technology*, 115, 132, 370–71.

24. R. J. Forbes, "Food and Drink," in C. Singer et al., eds., *A History of Technology* (Oxford: Clarendon Press, 1956), 2: 136.

25. C. E. Fell, "Old English *Beor*," *Leeds Studies in English* 8 (1975): 89; Wilson, "Plant Remains from the Graveney Boat," 640.

26. Curtis, *Ancient Food Technology*, 363; Peter Garnsey, *Food and Society in Classical Antiquity* (Cambridge: Cambridge University Press, 1999), 67, 118; Grolsche Bierbrouwerij, *Merckwaerdighe Bierologie*, 34; Hoffmann, *5000 Jahre Bier*, 36–37; Léo Moulin, "Bière, houblon et cervoise," *Bulletin de l'académie royale de langue et de littérature françaises* 59 (1981): 111–12; Nelson, *Beer in Greco-Roman Antiquity*, 60; J. E. Siebel et al., eds., *One Hundred Years of Brewing A Complete History of the Progress Made in*

the *Art, Science and Industry of Brewing in the World, Particularly During the Nineteenth Century: Historical Sketches and Views of Ancient and Modern Breweries: Lives and Portraits of Brewers of the Past and Present*, supplement to *The Western Brewer*, 1903 (Chicago: H. S. Rich, 1903; reproduced Evansville, Ind.: Unigraphic, 1973), 12; Edmond Urion and Frédéric Eyer, *La bière Art et tradition* (Paris: Librairie Istra, 1968), 19, 25–27.

27. Hoffmann, *5000 Jahre Bier*, 17–18, 42–43, 53; Schoockii, *Liber de Cervisia*, 23; Tacitus, *Germania*, in H. Mattingly, trans., *Tacitus on Britain and Germany* (Harmondsworth: Penguin, 1948), 119–20.

28. H. Blink, "Geschiedenis en verbreiding van de bierproductie en van den bierhandel," *Tijdschrift voor economische geographie* 10 (1914): 98; Hoffmann, *5000 Jahre Bier*, 42–44, 51; Räsänen, *Von Halm zum Fass*, 107–8; Harald Thunæus, *Ölets historia i Sverige* (Stockholm: Almqvist & Wiksell, 1968–70), 13.

29. Mead may also have been just beer with honey added to increase the fermentable sugar but that is doubtful. Honey would certainly have increased the alcohol content and improved the taste of beer. That was the experience of early European settlers of New England among many others. Sanborn C. Brown, *Wines and Beers of Old New England: A How-To-Do-It History* (Hanover: University Press of New England, 1978), 15–16.

30. Maria Dembinska, *Food and Drink in Medieval Poland: Rediscovering a Cuisine of the Past*, trans. Magdalena Thomas, revised and adapted by William Woys Weaver (Philadelphia: University of Pennsylvania Press, 1999), 80–83; Fell, "Old English *Beor*," 81; Niels Lund, ed., *Two Voyagers at the Court of King Alfred: The ventures of Othere and Wulfstan together with the Description of Northern Europe from the Old English Orosius* (York: William Sessions, 1984), 23.

31. The standard ingredients were ale, honey and powdered pepper but a fourteenth-century recipe has both fine wort and honey mixed with the ale and then flavored with small quantities of cinnamon, pepper, cloves, and ginger, clearly something far removed from simple mead and something not commonly made. See Wilson, *Food and Drink in Britain*, 374–75. A 1543 Polish mead recipe called for 4.5 kilograms of honey, 10.1 kilograms of water, and 0.45 kilograms of hops. The water-honey mixture was heated and then the hops, already boiled in water, were put in a sack, and the sack was then introduced into the honey-water mixture after it had cooled. At the same time, the mead maker added beer yeast and then let the drink ferment. A 1613 herbal recommended adding fennel, and other recipes suggested pepper, cloves, and cinnamon. See Dembinska, *Food and Drink in Medieval Poland*, 82.

32. Wilhelm Abel, *Stufen der Ernährung: Eine historische Skizze* (Göttingen: Vandenhoeck & Ruprecht, 1981), 20–21; Anon., *The Goodman of Paris (Le Ménagier de Paris) A Treatise on Moral and Domestic Economy by A Citizen of Paris c. 1393*, trans., intro., and notes Eileen Power (London: Folio Society, 1992), 192–93; Terence Scully, *The Art of Cookery in the Middle Ages* (Woodbridge: Boydell and Brewer, 1995), 154–55.

33. Blink, "Geschiedenis en verbreiding van de bierproductie," 98–99; Hoffmann, *5000 Jahre Bier*, 53; Ann Hagen, *A Second Handbook of Anglo-Saxon Food and Drink Production and Distribution* (Hockwold cum Wilton, Norfolk: Anglo-Saxon Books, 1995), 217, 233–34; King, *Beer Has a History*, 13; Wilson, *Food and Drink in Britain*, 366.

34. In Innocent's case the comment was on beer consumption. William Dunn Macray, *Chronicum abbotiæ de Evesham AD Annum 1418* (London: Longman, Green, Longman, Roberts, and Green, 1863), 189; Charles Henry Cook, *The Curiosities of Ale*

and Beer: An Entertaining History by John Bickerdyke [pseudonym] (New York: Scribner & Welford, 1886), 408; Fell, "Old English *Beor*," 85; Hagen, *A Second Handbook of Anglo-Saxon Food*, 209, 212–14, 247; King, *Beer Has a History*, 16.

35. Anglo-Saxon brewers may also have used oats in some cases, as in the Orkneys, to generate a more intoxicating drink. Hagen, *A Second Handbook of Anglo-Saxon Food*, 24. Incidentally the term *cervesarius*, meaning a brewer, only appears for the first time in the reign of Edgar though even there it can be interpreted in different ways and does not turn up in the ancient world. Hagen, *A Second Handbook of Anglo-Saxon Food*, 205; Nelson, *Beer in Greco-Roman Antiquity*, 60; H. A. Monckton, *A History of English Ale and Beer* (London: Bodley Head, 1966), 33–39; Stopes, *Malt and Malting*, 6; Wilson, "Plant Remains from the Graveney Boat," 640, 645.

36. J. Deckers, "Recherches sur l'histoire des brasseries dans la region mosane au moyen âge," *Le Moyen Âge Revue d'histoire et de philologie* 76 nos. 3–4 (1970): 448.

37. Nordlund, *Brewing and Beer Traditions in Norway*, 283.

38. Fell, "Old English *Beor*," 86–88; Bruce E. Gelsinger, *Icelandic Enterprise: Commerce and Economy in the Middle Ages* (Columbia: University of South Carolina Press, 1981), 14; Nordlund, *Brewing and Beer Traditions in Norway*, 36; Thunæus, *Ölets historia i Sverige*, 42–46.

39. W. C. Ackersdyck, "Het regt van de gruit," *Verhandelingen van de maatschappij der Nederlandsche letterkunde te Leiden* 32 (1819): 187; Jehan Charlie, *L'évolution économique de la brasserie françaises* (Paris: V. Giard & E. Briere, 1909), 3–4; G. Doorman, *De middeleeuwse brouwerij en de gruit* (The Hague: Martinus Nijhoff, 1955), 15. Among the many translations of the *Capitulare de Villis* the one in *Introduction to Contemporary Civilization in the West*, 3rd edition (New York: Columbia University Press, 1960), 326–34, is relatively recent and based directly on the text in the *Monumenta Germaniae Historica: Leges* II (1883), vol. 1.

40. Deckers, "Recherches sur l'histoire des brasseries," 448–51; Hagen, *A Second Handbook of Anglo-Saxon Food*, 217; Hoffmann, *5000 Jahre Bier*, 53; Langer, "Das Braugewerbe in den deutschen Hansestädten," 65; Frederick William Salem, *Beer: Its History and Its Economic Value as a National Beverage* (Springfield, Mass.: Clark W. Bryan Company, 1880; reprint New York: Arno Press, 1972), 18; Siebel, *One Hundred Years of Brewing*, 16.

41. Hoffmann, *5000 Jahre Bier*, 45; Walter Horn and Ernest Born, *The Plan of St. Gall: A Study of the Architecture and Economy of, and Life in a Paradigmatic Carolingian Monastery* (Berkeley: University of California Press, 1979), 2, 259; Moulin, "Bière, houblon et cervoise," 113–14, 145–46; Ildefons Poll, *Das Brauwesen des Klosters Prüsening* (Berlin: Gesellschaft für die Geschichte und Bibliographie des Brauwesens E.V., 1936), 35.

42. Horn and Born, *The Plan of St. Gall*, 2: 261.

43. Hagen, *A Second Handbook of Anglo-Saxon Food*, 225; Hildegard von Bingen, *Heilkunde Das Buch von dem Grund und Wesen und der Heilung der Krankheiten*, trans. and ed. Heinrich Schipperges (Salzburg: Otto Müller Verlag, 1957), 191–92, 194–95, 233.

44. In seventeenth-century England the brewery and bakehouse were usually near the laundry too. Pamela Sambrook, *Country House Brewing in England 1500–1900* (London: Hambledon, 1996), 26–27. At about the same time as the St. Gall Plan was drawn up there were four presumably similar brewhouses on the royal domain of Annapes, on the borders of Flanders and Artois. It may be that they, like the St. Gall Plan breweries, were designed for and used to make different kinds of beer. Doorman,

De middeleeuwse brouwerij en de gruit, 47; Hagen, *A Second Handbook of Anglo-Saxon Food*, 208; Horn and Born, *The Plan of St. Gall*, 1: 8, 249–61, 2: 222–35, 254–57, and 3: 67; Aloys Schulte, "Vom Grutbiere: Eine Studie zur Wirtschafts- und Verfassungsgeschichte," *Annalen des historischen Vereins für den Niederrhein* 85 (1908): 132.

45. Horn and Born, *The Plan of St. Gall*, 1: 303, 2: 261, 264, and 3: 105.

46. A monastery at Canterbury in England had a similar arrangement. Bennett, *Ale, Beer, and Brewsters in England*, 17; Moulin, "Bière, houblon et cervoise," 115; Nordlund, *Brewing and Beer Traditions in Norway*, 57–58.

47. Caesarius of Heisterbach, *The Dialogue on Miracles*, trans. H. von E. Scott and C. C. Swinton Bland (New York: Harcourt, Brace, 1929), 1: 379, 2: 185–86.

48. H. D'Arbois de Jubainville, "De la nourriture des cisterciens principalement à Clairvaux au XIIe et au XIIIe Siècle," *Bibliothèque de l'ecole des Chartes* 19 (1858): 273–75; Heinrich Fichtenau, *Living in the Tenth Century Mentalities and Social Orders*, trans. Patrick J. Geary (Chicago: University of Chicago Press, 1991), 212–13, 225.

49. Wolf Bing, *Hamburgs Bierbrauerei vom 14. bis zum 18. Jahrhundert*, Dissertation zur Erlangung der Doctorwürde der philosophischen Fakultät der Universität Leipzig, 1907, *Zeitschrift des Vereins für Hamburgischen Geschichte* 14 (1909): 221; Deckers, "Recherches sur l'histoire des brasseries," 457; Schulte, "Vom Grutbiere," 120. In 1324 the count of Holland prohibited making *gruit* without a grant from him which suggests that people in the countryside used the additive in the region and probably had for some time. Doorman, *De middeleeuwse brouwerij en de gruit*, 16.

50. Doorman, *De middeleeuwse brouwerij en de gruit*, x; H. Ebbing and V. T. van Vilsteren, "Van gruiters, gruitketels en gruithuizen: Over en typisch middeleeuws fenomeen," in R. E. Kistemaker and V. T. van Vilsteren, eds., *Bier! Geschiedenis van een volksdrank* (Amsterdam: De Bataafsche Leeuw, 1994), 21–22, 27.

51. Deckers, "Recherches sur l'histoire des brasseries," 181–84; Doorman, *De middeleeuwse brouwerij en de gruit*, 4–6, 10, 17; Th. E. Jensma, "Bronnen tot de geschiedenis van het recht van de gruit in het graafschap Holland, het bisdom Utrecht en het hertogdom Gelre," *Verslagen en mededeelingen tot uitgaaf der bronnen van het oud-vaderlansch recht* 12 (1960): 167; Schulte, "Vom Grutbiere," 121, 123–25. The suggestion has been made that the word *gruit* referred to small sand-like *grof* grains of the additive, and so it has been equated with fermented grain or with malt, that is with the essential raw materials of brewing. Another, and almost certainly incorrect view, is that *gruit* was a plant with a number of distinctive species. Another explanation was that *gruit* was a combination of grains and had some role in aiding yeast in the process of fermentation. This was in part because of confusion over calling the additive *fermentum*, a word which may have had a different meaning in the Middle Ages from that of fermentation which it bore in classical Latin. J. De Hullu, "Iets over de gruit," *Bijdragen voor vaderlandsche geschiedenis en oudheidkunde*, 3rd series, 10 (1899): 114–15; W. De Vries, "Enige opmerkingen naar aanleiding van de Zutphense gruit," *Tijdschrift voor rechtsgeschiedenis* 28 (1960): 59–60; Wilson, "Plant Remains from the Graveney Boat," 643. *Fermentum*, a word often connected with yeast, was also used as a term having to do with brewing in general. W. Jappe Alberts, "Bijdrage tot de geschiedenis der accijnzen te Arnhem in de middeleeuwen," *Tijdschrift voor geschiedenis* 64 (1951): 338; C. van de Kieft, "Gruit en ban," *Tijdschrift voor geschiedenis* 77 (1964): 158; S. Muller Fz., *Schetsen uit de middeleeuwen* (Amsterdam: S. L. van Looy, 1900), 59, no. 3.

52. De Hullu, "Iets over de gruit," 118; Jensma, "Bronnen tot de geschiedenis van het recht van de gruit," 167.

53. Joseph Deckers, "Gruit et droit de gruit: Aspects techniques et fiscaux de la fabrication de la bière dans la région mosane au moyen âge," *Handelingen van het XLIe Congres te Mechelen 3-6-IX-1970* (1971): 188; Doorman, *De middeleeuwse brouwerij en de gruit*, 27–31; G. Doorman, *Techniek en octrooiwezen in hun aanvang* (The Hague: Martinus Nijhoff, 1953), 76; Nordlund, *Brewing and Beer Traditions in Norway*, 216, 222–23, 226.

54. A. Hallema and J. A. Emmens, *Het bier en zijn brouwers. De geschiendenis van onze oudste volksdrank* (Amsterdam: J. H. DeBussy, 1968), 29; Moulin, "Bière, houblon et cervoise," 117; Schulte, "Vom Grutbiere," 130; Nordlund, *Brewing and Beer Traditions in Norway*, 126, 132–34, 144, 158–159, 173–93, 217–19, 225–26.

55. English brewers still used some of those additives even in the late Middle Ages, that is along with spices like cinnamon and nutmeg. The Europeans who made their way to New England in the seventeenth century used sage, wormwood, and myrtle but not *gruit*. Their principal additive and bittering agent instead was ground ivy. Brown, *Wines and Beers of Old New England*, 65; Deckers, "Gruit et droit de gruit," 184–88; Deckers, "Recherches sur l'histoire des brasseries," 459–60; Hagen, *A Second Handbook of Anglo-Saxon Food*, 212; Schulte, "Vom Grutbiere," 129; Wilson, *Food and Drink in Britain*, 373; Wilson, "Plant Remains from the Graveney Boat," 643.

56. Doorman, *De middeleeuwse brouwerij en de gruit*, 14–15; Jozef Penninck, *Het Bier te Brugge: Geschiedenis en Folklore* (Bruges: Heemkundige Kring Maurits van Coppenolle Sint-Andries, 1963), 4.

57. William H. TeBrake, *Medieval Frontier Culture and Ecology in Rijnland* (College Station, Texas: Texas A&M University Press, 1985), 126–28.

58. The grant of 999 is the first mention of the term. Moulin, "Bière, houblon et cervoise," 112 n. 6. Following the emperors, kings, such as Hakon VI of Norway, treated the distribution of *pors* in the same way, as a regalian right. Nordlund, *Brewing and Beer Traditions in Norway*, 216.

59. Ackersdyck, "Het regt van de gruit," 188, 190; Deckers, "Gruit et droit de gruit," 188–89; Doorman, *De middeleeuwse brouwerij en de gruit*, vi, 3–6, 12–14; Kieft, "Gruit en ban," 164.

60. Deckers, "Gruit et droit de gruit," 189–91; Deckers, "Recherches sur l'histoire des brasseries," 463–65; Doorman, *De middeleeuwse brouwerij en de gruit*, 8–10; Kieft, "Gruit en ban," 159–68; Schulte, "Vom Grutbiere," 132, 135; De Vries, "Enige opmerkingen naar aanleiding van de Zutphense gruit," 60–62, 66–69.

61. Deckers, "Gruit et droit de gruit," 191–93.

62. Erik Aerts, "De Zuidnederlandse brouwindustrie tijdens het Ancien Régime. Status quaestionis van het onderzoek," *Handelingen XXXIII der Koninklijke Zuidnederlandse Maatschappij voor Taal- en Letterkunde en Geschiedenis* (1979): 20; Deckers, "Gruit et droit de gruit," 188; Nordlund, *Brewing and Beer Traditions in Norway*, 60; Poll, *Das Brauwesen des Klosters Prüsening*, 35.

63. Horn and Born, *The Plan of St. Gall*, II, 264; Ildefons Poll, *Des Brauwesen des Benediktinerklosters Metten* (Berlin: Gesellschaft für die Geschichte und Bibliographie des Brauwesens E.V., 1937), 9, 19–26; Poll, *Das Brauwesen des Klosters Prüsening*, 13–14, 37.

64. Doorman, *De middeleeuwse brouwerij en de gruit*, 38; Hoffmann, *5000 Jahre Bier*, 81–83.

65. Friedrich M. Illert, "Geschichte der Wormser Brauereien von ihren Anfängen bis zum Gegenwert," *Der Wormsgau Zeitschrift des Altertumsvereins und der städtischen*

Kulturinstitute, Beiheft 14 (Worms: Verlag Stadtbibliothek Worms, 1954), 1–2; Urion and Eyer, *La bière: Art et tradition,* 30.

66. Irena Ciesla, "Taberna Wczesnośredniowieczna na ziemiach polskich," *Studia Wczesnośredniowieczne* 4 (1958): 222.

67. Hallema and Emmens, *Het bier en zijn brouwers,* 82; Hoffmann, *5000 Jahre Bier,* 84; Urion and Eyer, *La bière: Art et tradition,* 46.

Chapter 3

1. Blink, "Geschiedenis en verbreiding van de bierproductie," 104; J. L. Van Dalen, *Geschiedenis van Dordrecht* (Dordrecht: C. Morks Czn., 1931–33). 1: 389; Deckers, "Gruit et droit de gruit," 190; A. H. Klop, "De Amersfoortse brouwneringen tot de 19e eeuw" (unpublished doctoraal scriptie, economisch-historisch seminarium, University of Amsterdam, #104, 1935), 6; Frederick William Maitland, *Domesday Book and Beyond: Three Essays in the Early History of England* (Cambridge: Cambridge University Press, 1897), 439; Santbergen, *Les Bons Métiers des Meuniers,* 44; Urion and Eyer, *La bière: Art et tradition,* 28.

2. Bennett, *Ale, Beer, and Brewsters in England,* 16–20; Nordlund, *Brewing and Beer Traditions in Norway,* 15.

3. Bennett, "The Village Ale-Wife," 23–26; Bennett, *Ale, Beer, and Brewsters in England,* 19–20; Deckers, "Recherches sur l'histoire des brasseries," 463, 469.

4. Hagen, *A Second Handbook of Anglo-Saxon Food,* 214; Nordlund, *Brewing and Beer Traditions in Norway,* 263–74.

5. Bing, *Hamburgs Bierbrauerei,* 214; Deckers, "Recherches sur l'histoire des brasseries," 451–52.

6. Bing, *Hamburgs Bierbrauerei,* 264; Deckers, "Recherches sur l'histoire des brasseries," 477; Hallema and Emmens, *Het bier en zijn brouwers,* 65.

7. J. A. Faber, H. A. Diederiks, and S. Hart, "Urbanisering, industrialisering en milieuaantasting in Nederland in de periode van 1500 tot 1800," *A.A.G. Bijdragen* 18 (1973): 263–65; L. F. Salzman, *English Industries of the Middle Ages,* new edition, enlarged and illustrated (1913; London: H. Pordes, 1964), 291.

8. Bennett, *Ale, Beer, and Brewsters in England,* 4, 15; Peter Clark, *The English Alehouse A Social History 1200–1830* (London: Longman, 1983), 28; Monckton, *A History of English Ale and Beer,* 47–54; H. A. Monckton, *A History of the English Public House* (London: Bodley Head, 1969), 20.

9. Clark, *The English Alehouse,* 20–21; King, *Beer Has a History,* 22; Monckton, *A History of English Ale and Beer,* 41.

10. Bing, *Hamburgs Bierbrauerei,* 259, 272; Doorman, *De middeleeuwse brouwerij en de gruit,* vii, 36, 49.

11. Even as late as the beginning of the nineteenth century in some villages in Friesland in the Netherlands, there were public brewhouses where housewives from the district could bring their grain for making beer. Erik Aerts, *Het bier van Lier De economische ontwikkeling van de bierindustrie in een middelgrote Brabantse stad (eind 14de–begin 19de eeuw),* Verhandelingen van de koninklijke academie voor wetenschappen, letteren en schone kunsten van België, klasse der letteren, jaargang 58, 1996, no. 161 (Brussels: Paleis der Academiën, 1996), 148–49, 162; Penninck, *Het bier te Brugge,* 10.

12. Doorman, *De middeleeuwse brouwerij en de gruit,* 54, 56–58; Loenen, *De Haar-*

lemse brouwindustrie voor 1600, 26; Räsänen, *Von Halm zum Fass*, 36; Techen, "Das Brauwerk in Wismar," 333; V. T. van Vilsteren, "De oorsprong en techniek van het brouwen tot de 14de eeuw," in R. E. Kistemaker and V. T. van Vilsteren, eds., *Bier! Geschiedenis van een volksdrank* (Amsterdam: De Bataafsche Leeuw, 1994), 14–19.

13. The troughs were long, narrow, and shallow, possibly made from hollowed out trees. Doorman, *De middeleeuwse brouwerij en de gruit*, x–xi, 48, 53–54.

14. Margery Kempe, *The Book of Margery Kempe*, trans. A. Windeatt (London: Penguin, 1985), 44.

15. De Vries, "Enige opmerkingen naar aanleiding van de Zutphense gruit," 62–64; Doorman, *De middeleeuwse brouwerij en de gruit*, 16; Kieft, "Gruit en ban," 165; Pennick, *Het bier te Brugge*, 4; Raymond van Uytven, *Stadsfinanciën en stadsekonomie te Leuven van de XIIe tot het einde der XVIe eeuw* (Brussels: Paleis der Academiën, 1961), 314.

16. Ackersdyck, "Het regt van de gruit," 198–200; Paul Heinrich Kampeter, *Die wirtschaftliche Entwicklung des Rheinisch-westfälischen Brauerei-Gewerbes unter besonderer Berücksichtigung des bergischen Landes* (Giessen, 1925), 10; Schulte, "Vom Grutbiere," 133–36.

17. Tax farming was not always straightforward and simple. Arnhem in the eastern Netherlands, for example, made its way to tax farming in a long and circuitous way. It was only in 1345 that the bishop sold his right of collecting a *gruit* tax even though the town as early as 1315 had already received the right to collect a tax on *gruit* from the count of Gelderland. The town government was able to set rates and deal with all matters to do with collection of the count's tax. In exchange the count got a fee, usually a lump sum to cover twenty-five years at a time. The town then sold the right to collect the tax to the person or persons willing to give them the highest lump sum. Alberts, "Bijdrage tot de geschiedenis der accijnzen te Arnhem," 335–37, 344–45; Jensma, "Bronnen tot de geschiedenis van het recht van de gruit," 194.

18. At Saint Trond, which got *gruitrecht* in 1045 from the bishop of Metz, there was an agent of the monastery, a *grutarius*, mentioned already in the twelfth century. Deckers, "Recherches sur l'histoire des brasseries," 466.

19. The *gruyter* may have also dried components of *gruit*. Records for the *gruithuis* at Wesel show expenses for peat which are higher than would seem to be needed just to heat the building, so some of the energy could have gone to preparing the various herbs or even toward making malt. Doorman, *De middeleeuwse brouwerij en de gruit*, 35; Ebbing and Vilstern, "Van gruiters, gruitketels en gruithuizen," 24–27.

20. Bing, *Hamburgs Bierbrauerei*, 220; Rudolph Häpke, *Brügges Entwicklung zum mittelalterlichen Weltmarkt* (Berlin: Karl Curtius, 1908), 94.

21. Ackersdyck, "Het regt van de gruit," 186; Jan Alleblas, "Nieuw leven in een oud brouwerij? Geschiedenis en toekomst van De Sleutel," *Kwartaal & teken van Dordrecht Gemeentelijke archiefdienst Dordrecht*, 9, no. 2 (1983): 1; De Hullu, "Iets over de gruit," 116–17; Doorman, *De middeleeuwse brouwerij en de gruit*, 32, 93.

22. Bing, *Hamburgs Bierbrauerei*, 242–43; De Vries, "Enige opmerkingen naar aanleiding van de Zutphense gruit," 67; Doorman, *De middeleeuwse brouwerij en de gruit*, 37.

23. It was impossible to impose such a tax in the countryside though it was tried by a family who owned the tax in the northern part of Holland and in Westfriesland in the fourteenth century. Jensma, "Bronnen tot de geschiedenis van het recht van de gruit," 179.

24. Uytven, *Stadsfinanciën en stadsekonomie te Leuven*, 315.

25. De Vries, "Enige opmerkingen naar aanleiding van de Zutphense gruit," 65–66; Uytven, *Stadsfinanciën en stadsekonomie te Leuven*, 324; J. De Wal, "Accijnsbrief van Haarlem in 1274 door Floris V verleend of ontworpen," *Werken van de maatschapij van Nederlandse letterkunde te Leiden*, new series vol. 7, no. 2 (1856): 166; Carlos Wyffels, *De oorsprong der ambachten in Vlaanderen en Brabant* (Brussels: Paleis der Academiën, 1951), 101–2.

26. Hans Enss, *Die Anfänge der Bier-Zeise unter dem Deutschen Orden Ein Beitrag zur Geschichte der Preussischen Accise* (Königsberg: Buch- und Steindruckerei von Otto Kümmel, 1908), 7; Techen, "Das Brauwerk in Wismar," 217.

27. Charlie, *L'Évolution économique*, 4–6; Kampeter, *Die wirtschaftliche Entwicklung*, 3; Salem, *Beer*, 19–20.

28. Frans van Mieris, *Groot Charterboek der Graven van Holland, van Zeeland en heeren van Vriesland* (Leiden: Pieter van der Eyk, 1753–56), 1: 234, 481.

29. Bing, *Hamburgs Bierbrauerei*, 267; Hans Schlosser, *Braurechte, Brauer und Braustätten in München: Zur Rechts- und Sozialgeschichte des spätmittelalterlichen Brauwesens* (Elsbach am Main: Verlag Rolf Grener, 1981), 4.

30. J. G. Theodor Grässe, *Bierstudien* (Dresden: R. v. Zahn's Verlag, 1872), 26; Schlosser, *Braurechte Brauer und Braustätten in München*, 8–11, 22; Werner Schultheiss, *Brauwesen und Braurechte in Nürnberg bis zum Beginn des 19. Jahrhunderts*, Nürnberger Werkstücke zur Stadt- und Landesgeschichte, Schriftenreihe des Stadtarchivs Nürnberg (Nuremberg, 1978), 23: 4–6; Siebel, *One Hundred Years of Brewing*, 18; Gerald Stefke, *Ein städtisches Exportgewerbe des Spatmittelaters in seiner Entfaltung und ersten Blüte Untersuchungen zur Geschichte der Hamburger Seebrauerei des 14. Jahrhunderts* (Hamburg, 1979), 19–22.

31. Bing, *Hamburgs Bierbrauerei*, 257–67; Techen, "Das Brauwerk in Wismar," 294–95.

32. Loenen, *De Haarlemse brouwindustrie*, 11; Muller Fz., *Schetsen uit de middeleeuwen*, 65–66; Salzman, *English Industries of the Middle Ages*, 288.

33. Joh. C. Breen, "Aanteekeningen uit de geschiedenis der Amsterdamsche nijverheid, II bierbrouuwerijen," *Nederlands fabrikaat Maandblad der vereniging Nederlands fabrikaat* (1921): 75; Jos. Martens, "Bier en stadsfinancien te Hasselt, 16e en 17e eeuw," *Gemeente krediet van Belgie, driemaandelijke tijdschrift*, vol. 30, no. 118 (1976): 250; J. P. W. Philipsen, "De Amsterdamsche Brouwnijverheid tot het Einde der Zestiende Eeuw" (Unpublished doctoraal scriptie, economisch-historisch seminarium, University of Amsterdam, 1937), 8–9.

34. G. A. Leiden, Archieven van de Gilden: #191, 37 [1616]; Cornelis Cau, Simon van Leeuwen, Jacobus Paulus and Isaac Scheltus, eds., *Groot Placaatboek vervattende de Placaaten, Ordonnantien en Edicten van den Hoog Mog. Heeren Staaten Generaal der Vereenigde Nederlanden . . .* (The Hague: Hillebrandt Jacobus van Wouw, Jacobus, Paulus and Isaac Scheltus, 1658–1770), 1:1715–1716, LV; 3: 938–39; Richard J. Yntema, "The Brewing Industry in Holland, 1300–1800: A Study in Industrial Development" (Ph.D. diss., University of Chicago, 1992), 20, 20 n.43.

35. Wilson, *Food and Drink in Britain*, 383.

36. Schultheiss, *Brauwesen und Braurechte in Nürnberg*, 4; H. L. Werneck, "Brauwesen und Hopfenbrau in Oberösterreich von 1100–1930," *Jahrbuch 1937 Gesellschaft für die Geschichte und Bibliographie des Brauwesens E.V.* (Berlin, 1937): 50.

37. Bennett, *Ale, Beer, and Brewsters in England*, 43–51; Clark, *The English Ale-*

house, 11, 20–21, 28; Hagen, *A Second Handbook of Anglo-Saxon Food*, 208; King, *Beer Has a History*, 20; Monckton, *A History of the English Public House*, 19–26.

38. Bing, *Hamburgs Bierbrauerei*, 280, 282–83.

39. In addition to selling beer Polish tavern keepers usually brewed it, increasing the variety of activity in the tavern and expanding the scale. Ciesla, "Taberna Wczesno-średniowieczna na ziemiach polskich," 222–25; Irena Rabecka, "The Early Medieval Tavern in Poland," *Kwartalnik Historii Kultury Materialnej* 10, nos. 1–2 (1962), Fascicule supplémentaire *Ergon*, 3: 372–75.

40. Bing, *Hamburgs Bierbrauerei*, 213–214; De Vries, "Enige opmerkingen naar aanleiding van de Zutphense gruit," 68; Walter Prevenier and Wim Blockmans, *The Burgundian Netherlands* (Cambridge: Cambridge University Press, 1986), 83–86; Salzman, *English Industries of the Middle Ages*, 287–88.

41. Stopes, *Malt and Malting*, 6.

42. Peacock, *Pottery in the Roman World*, 8–9.

Chapter 4

1. Wilson, "Plant Remains from the Graveney Boat," 640.

2. The Talmud mentions an aromatic plant the Babylonians used as an additive in the making of beer when the Jews were in Mesopotamia. It was possibly, but by no means certainly, hops. Hoffmann, *5000 Jahre Bier*, 27; King, *Beer Has a History*, 12; Urion and Eyer, *La bière: Art et tradition*, 40.

3. Bober, *Art Culture and Cuisine*, 207–8; Grolsche Bierbrouwerij, *Merckwaerdighe bierologie*, 43; Nelson, *Beer in Greco-Roman Antiquity*, 141–42.

4. The 1581 translation of John of Damascus appears, at least with hops, to rely more on the Arab pharmacologist Masawaih al-Mardini (d. 1015) than on the original. Wilson, "Plant Remains from the Graveney Boat," 638–39.

5. Bober, *Art, Culture, and Cuisine*, 207–8; Horn and Born, *The Plan of St. Gall*. 1: 261–63; Nelson, *Beer in Greco-Roman Antiquity*, 142–43, 368–72; Wilson, "Plant Remains from the Graveney Boat," 644–55.

6. Johann Beckmann, *A Concise History of Ancient Institutions, Inventions and Discoveries in Science and Mechanic Art: Abridged and translated from "Beyträge zur Geschichte der Erfindungen . . ." with Various Important Additions* (London: G. & W. B. Whittaker, 1823), 1: 306; Behre, "The History of Beer Additives in Europe," 39–40; Karl-Ernst Behre, "Untersuchungen des botanischen Materials der frühmittelalterlichen Siedlung Haithabu (Ausgrabung 1963–1964)," in K. Schietzel, ed., *Berichte über die Ausgrabungen in Haithabu* (Neumünster: Karl Wachholtz Verlag, 1969), 2: 33; George Clinch, *English Hops: A History of Cultivation and Preparation For the Market From the Earliest Times* (London: McCorquodale, [1919]), 64; Doorman, *De middeleeuwse brouwerij en de gruit*, 39–40; Hagen, *A Second Handbook of Anglo-Saxon Food*, 211; Kampeter, *Die wirtschaftliche Entwicklung*, 10; Moulin, "Bière, houblon et cervoise," 120; Vilsteren, "De oorsprong en techniek van het brouwen," 14; Wilson, "Plant Remains from the Graveney Boat," 627–37, 645–46.

7. Though the use of hops in beer may have been limited there is extensive evidence of continued use of the plant to help with various maladies. Hildegard of Bingen, much later in 1179, thought hops induced melancholia in the user and so preferred ash leaves as a treatment. Behre, "The History of Beer Additives in Europe," 44; Deckers,

"Gruit et droit de gruit," 186–87; Doorman, *De middeleeuwse brouwerij en de gruit*, 40; Hagen, *A Second Handbook of Anglo-Saxon Food*, 209–11; Moulin, "Bière, houblon et cervoise," 121, 124–27.

8. Moulin, "Bière, houblon et cervoise," 120; Nordlund, *Brewing and Beer Traditions in Norway*, 203, 210; Räsänen, *Von Halm zum Fass*, 147; Thunæus, *Ölets historia i Sverige*, 1: 67; Werneck, "Brauwesen und Hopfenbrau," 57, 82.

9. Though hops could grow rather far south in Europe, there are no finds south of the Alps which confirms that brewing and especially brewing of higher-quality hopped beer did not succeed. Even into the Renaissance the region remained dominated by wine. Behre, "The History of Beer Additives in Europe," 38–41.

10. Deckers, "Recherches sur l'histoire des brasseries," 461; Moulin,"Bière, houblon et cervoise," 127; Schultheiss, *Brauwesen und Braurechte in Nürnberg*, 3.

11. Ashurst, "Hops and Their Use in Brewing," 31–32, 55; Deckers, "Gruit et droit de gruit," 186; Doorman, *De middeleeuwse brouwerij en de gruit*, 17; Pasteur, *Studies on Fermentation*, 16–17, 21.

12. Ashurst, "Hops and Their Use in Brewing," 32–34.

13. Ashurst, "Hops and Their Use in Brewing," 51; De Clerck, *A Textbook of Brewing*, 54, 69, 321–24; Hough, *The Biotechnology of Malting and Brewing*, 75.

14. Filtering using twigs was traditional Norwegian practice. Doorman, *De middeleeuwse brouwerij en de gruit*, vi, x–xi, 53, 63; Hough, *The Biotechnology of Malting and Brewing*, 87–88; Nordlund, *Brewing and Beer Traditions in Norway*, 227–28; Loenen, *De Haarlemse brouwindustrie*, 26; Räsänen, *Von Halm zum Fass*, 146.

15. Behre, "The History of Beer Additives in Europe," 36, 39, 41–42; Ciesla,"Taberna Wczesnośredniowieczna na ziemiach polskich," 225; Moulin, "Bière, houblon et cervoise," 145–47.

16. Hans Huntemann, *Das deutsche Braugewerbe vom Ausgang des Mittelalters bis zum Beginn der Industriealisierung: Biererzeugung—Bierhandel—Bierverbrauch* (Nuremberg: Verlag Hans Carl, 1971), 9; Loenen, *De Haarlemse brouwindustrie*, 70–71; H. J. Smit, *De opkomst van den handel van Amsterdam, onderzoekingen naar de economische ontwikkeling der stad tot 1441* (Amsterdam: A. H. Kruyt, 1914), 31.

17. Schultheiss, *Brauwesen und Braurechte in Nürnberg*, 3; Techen, "Das Brauwerk in Wismar," 318–22; Thunæus, *Ölets historia i Sverige*, 1: 71–72.

18. Bing, *Hamburgs Bierbrauerei*, 210, 217–18, 242–43; J. Bracker, "Hopbier uit Hamburg Het verhaal van een middeleeuwse succes-formule," in R. E. Kistemaker and V. T. van Vilsteren, eds., *Bier! Geschiedenis van een volksdrank* (Amsterdam: De Bataafsche Leeuw, 1994), 28; August Löhdefink, *Die Entwicklung der Brauergilde der Stadt Hannover zur heutigen Erwerbsgesellschaft (Ein Beitrag zur Lehre von den Unternehmungen)* (Hannover: Eulemannsche Buchdrukerei, 1925), 8–9; Techen, "Das Brauwerk in Wismar," 264–66, 299.

19. Bing, *Hamburgs Bierbrauerei*, 212; Doorman, *De middeleeuwse brouwerij en de gruit*, 5, 18; A. van der Poest Clement, "De bierbrouwerijen van Gouda in middeleeuwn en 16e eeuw" (Ph. D. diss., incomplete, 1959), G. A. Gouda, 37; Lydia Niehoff, "*Bierproduktion und Bierkonsum in der Stadt Bremen vom 17. bis zum 19. Jahrhundert*" (Dissertation zur Erlangung des akademischen Grades eines Doktors der Wirtschafts- und Sozialwissenschaften der Universität Bremen, 1996), 1.

20. Bing, *Hamburgs Bierbrauerei*, 237; Niehoff, "*Bierproduktion und Bierkonsum*," 10; G. Frhr. von der Ropp, Dietrich Schäfer, Gottfried Wentz et. al., eds., *Hanserecesse Die Recesse und Andere Akten der Hansetage* (Leipzig: Verlag von Duncker und Humblot and Böhlau Verlag, 1870–1970), 2: 82 n. 4.

21. Frisian traders may have reexported some of that Hamburg beer to England. F. C. Berkenvelder, "Frieslands handel in de late middeleeuwen," *Economisch-historisch jaarboek* 29 (1963): 138–40, 143–45, 153, 156; Hallema and Emmens, *Het bier en zijn brouwers*, 75; Techen, "Das Brauwerk in Wismar," 201–2; G. A. Hoorn: #481[2879].

22. The terms for the two groups were *braxatores de Ammelstredamme* and *braxatores de Stauria* respectively.

23. Bing, *Hamburgs Bierbrauerei*, 222–23, 243–44; Konstantin Höhlbaum, Karl Kunze, Walther Stein *et al.*, eds., *Hansisches Urkundenbuch* (Halle, Weimar, and Leipzig: Verlag der Buchhandlung des Waisenhauses and Verlag von Duncker und Humblot, 1876–1916), 4: 332–35 [1384]; Smit, *De opkomst van den handel van Amsterdam*, 100; Stefke, *Ein städtisches Exportgewerbe*, 119–22; W. Stieda, "Das Böttcherei-Gewerbe in Alt-Rostock," *Beiträge zur Geschichte der Stadt Rostock*, vols. 1 and 2 (1895): 30.

24. Imports to Amsterdam 1352–1354 were 31,319 barrels in 105 ships. The seemingly large number of vessels can be explained only by their bringing more than just beer. In 1364 the figure was 17,514 barrels, that in 98 ships. For 1365–1366 it was 39,316 barrels. A quantity of beer avoided the toll collector but the exact quantity unaccounted for is not known. Bracker, "Hopbier uit Hamburg" 29; Huntemann, *Das deutsche Braugewerbe*, 14–15; Smit, *De opkomst van den handel van Amsterdam*, 37–39, 89; Stefke, *Ein Städtisches Exportgewerbe*, 63–78, 129–31, xlvi–l.

25. The income in 1343 was more than 15 percent of the income from the count's district of Amstelland. It went down 40 percent in 1344 but that was still 2.5 percent of all the money collected by the count. The absolute figure was considerably higher by 1368. F. Ketner, *Handel en scheepvaart van Amsterdam in de vijftiende eeuw* (Leiden: E.J. Brill, 1946), 4; Smit, *De opkomst van den handel van Amsterdam*, 29–31, 34, 115; Richard W. Unger, *A History of Brewing in Holland 900–1900 Economy, Technology, and the State* (Leiden: E. J. Brill, 2001), 32.

26. There are problems with the Hamburg records since the size of the barrel, the *fud*, which was the unit of tax is not certain. Still those records do show exports of 9,144.5 *fuder* of beer of which 4,262, or 47 percent, went to Amsterdam. Philippe Dollinger, *La Hanse* (Paris: Éditions Montaigne, Aubier, 1964), 275; Smit, *De opkomst van den handel van Amsterdam*, 48; H. J. Smit, "De Registers van den biertol te Amsterdam," *Historisch genootschap te Utrecht, Bijdragen en mededelingen* 38 (1917): 3–7; Stefke, *Ein städtisches Exportgewerbe*, 88–90, 95, 117–18 ; Unger, *A History of Brewing in Holland*, 28.

27. Bing, *Hamburgs Bierbrauerei*, 250–52; Smit, *De opkomst van den handel van Amsterdam*, 39–44, 91, 103, 107; Unger, *A History of Brewing in Holland*, 28–29.

28. The grant at Stavoren, for example, dated from 1358. Incidentally Netherlands merchants were in Hamburg for some time even before the growth of the beer trade and possibly before there were Hamburg merchants in the Low Countries. There were Alkmaar traders there by 1287, Kampen and Harderwijk visitors by around 1280, and Enkhuizeners in 1307. Bracker, "Hopbier uit Hamburg," 28; Ernst Daenell, *Die Blütezeit der deutschen Hanse* (Berlin: Georg Reimer, 1905), 1: 266–67; Ernst Daenell, "Holland und die Hanse im 15. Jahrhundert," *Hansische Geschichtsblätter* 9 (1903): 10–11; Stefke, *Ein städtisches Exportgewerbe*, 79–83, li–liv; Smit, *De opkomst van den handel van Amsterdam*, 30.

29. H. Ebbing, "Bier op transport De binnenvaart door Holland en de ontwikkeling van de Hollandse brouwnijverheid tot 1500," in R. E. Kistemaker and V. T. van Vilsteren, eds., *Bier! Geschiedenis van een volksdrank* (Amsterdam: De Bataafsche

Leeuw, 1994). 44; Ketner, *Handel en scheepvaart van Amsterdam*, 5; Unger, *A History of Brewing in Holland*, 29.

30. Daenell, *Die Blütezeit der deutschen Hanse*, 2: 408–411; P. H. J. van der Laan, *Oorkondenboek van Amsterdam tot 1400* (Amsterdam: N. Israel, 1975), 522; Smit, *De opkomst van den handel van Amsterdam*, 45; Smit, "De Registers van den biertol te Amsterdam," 6–7; Gerald Stefke, "Die Hamburger Zollbücher von 1399/1400 und '1418' Der Werkzoll im 14. und Frühen 15. Jahrhundert und die Ausfuhr von Hamburger Bier über See im Jahre 1417," *Zeitschrift des Vereins für Hamburgische Geschichte*, 69 (1983): 20–21, 23–25; Unger, *A History of Brewing in Holland*, 29.

31. Stefke, "Die Hamburger Zollbücher," 23; W. S. Unger, ed., *De tol van Iersekeroord, documenten en rekeningen 1321–1572* (The Hague: Martinus Nijhoff, 1939), 165, 179.

32. Huntemann, *Das deutsche Braugewerbe*, 46; Rolf Sprandel, *Das Hamburger Pfundzollbuch von 1418* (Cologne: Böhlau Verlag, 1972), 57–58; Stefke, "Die Hamburger Zollbücher," 23, 28–33.

33. Abel, *Stufen der Ernährung*, 21; Huntemann, *Das deutsche Braugewerbe*, 11–12, 14–15, 18, 38–39.

34. Dollinger, *La Hanse*, 59, 282–83; Carlos Wyffels and J. De Smet, *De rekeningen van de stad Brugge (1280–1319)*, vol. 1, 1280–1302 (Brussels: Paleis der Academiën, 1965), 1: 571.

35. Bing, *Hamburgs Bierbrauerei*, 229; Höhlbaum et al., *Hansisches Urkundenbuch*, 1: #1279 [1298]; Albert Schouteet, *Regesten op de oordkonden van het stadsbestuur van Brugge*, vol. 1, 1089–1300 (Brussels: Koninklijke Bibliotheek, 1973), #441 [1298]; V. C. C. J. Pinkse, "Het Goudse kuitbier, Gouda's welveren in de late middeleeuwen, 1400–1568," *Gouda zeven eeuwen stad* (19 July 1972): 113–14.

36. Höhlbaum, et al., *Hansisches Urkundenbuch*, 5: #133, #150; J. F. Niermeyer, ed., *Bronnen voor de economische geschiedenis van het Beneden-Maasgebied. Eerste deel: 1104–1399* (The Hague: Martinus Nijhoff, 1968), #462; Ropp et al., *Hanserecesse*, 2: #184, 3: #444, #445, 4: #39; Raymond van Uytven, "Het bierverbruik en de sociaal-economische toestand in het Brugse Vrije in de zestiende eeuw," *Handelingen van het genootschap voor geschiedenis gesticht onder de benaming "Societé d'emulation" te Brugge*, 131 (1994): 7–8.

37. Stefke, *Ein städtisches Exportgewerbe*, 123, 127–28, 131.

38. H. J. Smit, ed., *Bronnen tot de geschiedenis van den handel mit Engeland, Schotland, en Ierland, 1150–1585* (The Hague: Martinus Nijhoff, 1928, 1942, 1950), 1: #805; George Warner, ed., *The Libelle of Englyshe Polycye: A Poem on the Use of Sea-Power, 1436* (Oxford: Clarendon Press, 1921), 15–16.

39. Berkenvelder, "Frieslands Handel in de late Middeleeuwen," 166–67; Bing, *Hamburgs Bierbrauerei*, 226; Höhlbaum et al., *Hansisches Urkundenbuch*, 5: #585, #698.

40. Lydia Niehoff, "Bremer Bier im Baltikum oder 'Lieffländer brawen auch gute Biere' Eine Suche nach Bremer Brauprodukten im Ostseeraum" (unpublished essay, 1995), 2–15.

41. Abel, *Stufen der Ernährung*, 22; Bing, *Hamburgs Bierbrauerei*, 224–25, 235–36, 245–47, 284; Dollinger, *La Hanse*, 141, 275; Schlosser, *Braurechte Brauer und Braustätten*, xvi, 83–89.

42. Behre, "The History of Beer Additives in Europe," 42; Techen, "Das Brauwerk in Wismar," 176–77, 182, 188–89; Curt Weibull, *Lübeck och Skånemarknaden: Studier i Lübecks pundtullsböcker och pundtullskvitton 1368–1369 och 1398–1400* (Lund: Berlingska Boktryckeriet, 1922), 26–27, 51–80.

43. Gelsinger, *Icelandic Enterprise*, 183; Huntemann, *Das deutsche Braugewerbe*, 13–19.

44. Techen, "Das Brauwerk in Wismar," 324–27, 182–83.

45. Bing, *Hamburgs Bierbrauerei*, 225; Huntemann, *Das deutsche Braugewerbe*, 47, 53, 59–60; Loenen, *De Haarlemse brouwindustrie*, 78; Johannes Schildhauer, "Der Seehandel Danzigs im 16. Jahrhundert und die Verlagerung des Warenverkehrs im Nord- und Mitteleuropäischen Raum," *Jahrbuch für Wirtschaftsgeschichte* 3 (1970): 159–60; Techen, "Das Brauwerk in Wismar," 269–71, 314, 335–36, 150, 186, 193–96; Thunæus, *Ölets historia i Sverige*, 1: 162, 259, 271.

46. Bing, *Hamburgs Bierbrauerei*, 239–40, 253; Stefke, *Ein städtisches Exportgewerbe*, 27–35, 50, 67–68.

47. Bing, *Hamburgs Bierbrauerei*, 267, 280; Bracker, "Hopbier uit Hamburg," 28–29; Hoffmann, *5000 Jahre Bier*, 63–64, 132–33; Huntemann, *Das deutsche Braugewerbe*, 39.

48. Bing, *Hamburgs Bierbrauerei*, 244–47, 253–55, 262, 271–72; Stefke, *Ein städtisches Exportgewerbe*, 46–49, 51–53, 129–31.

49. Bing, *Hamburgs Bierbrauerei*, 212, 236, 241–42, 247–49, 255–62; Bracker, "Hopbier uit Hamburg," 32.

50. Huntemann, *Das deutsche Braugewerbe*, 41–42.

51. Niehoff, "Bremer Bier im Baltikum," 11–14.

52. On the frequency of brewing see below, Table 10. Techen, "Das Brauwerk in Wismar," 275, 279–82, 291–95; 335–37, 347–49, 205.

53. Bing, *Hamburgs Bierbrauerei*, 236; Techen, "Das Brauwerk in Wismar," 352, 163.

54. Langer, "Das Braugewerbe in den deutschen Hansestädten," 69.

Chapter 5

1. J. A. van Houtte, *An Economic History of the Low Countries, 800–1800* (New York: St. Martin's, 1977), 68; P. Tim H. Unwin, *Wine and the Vine: An Historical Geography of Viticulture and the Wine Trade* (London: Routledge, 1991), 175–76.

2. Abel, *Stufen der Ernährung*, 20–21.

3. Bömer, "Eine Vagantenliedersammlung," 174, 199–202; Elizabeth Revell, ed., *The Later Letters of Peter of Blois* (Oxford: Oxford University Press, 1993), #31; Scully, *The Art of Cookery*, 152, 179, 233.

4. Bernard van Rijswijk, *Geschiedenis van het Dordtsche stapelrecht* (The Hague: Martinus Nijhoff, 1900), 20, 36; Stefke, *Ein städtisches Exportgewerbe*, xxiii–xxxiv, 58–60; W. S. Unger, "De economische ontwikkeling van Middelburg voor den Bourgondischen tijd," *Archief uitgegeven door het Zeeuwsch genootschap der wetenschappen* (1918): 59.

5. J. F. Niermeyer, "Dordrecht als handelsstad in de tweede helft van de veertiende eeuw," *Bijdragen voor vaderlandsche geschiedenis en oudheidkunde*, 8th series, 3 (1942): 200–201; Unger, *A History of Brewing in Holland*, 33.

6. Huntemann, *Das deutsche Braugewerbe*, 16, 22–25, 55–56; Moulin, "Bière, houblon et cervoise," 116; Scully, *The Art of Cookery*, 143; Stefke, *Ein städtisches Exportgewerbe*, xli–xlv.

7. A Flemish writer in 1441 explicitly said that drinking beer was a status symbol

and there are other sources from the fifteenth and also the sixteenth century which support that conclusion. Moulin, "Bière, houblon et cervoise," 134, 137–38; Jan Craeybeckx, *Un grand commerce d'importation: Les vins de France aux anciens Pays-Bas (XIIIe–XVIe siècle)* (Paris: Services d'edition et du vente des publications de l'education, 1958), 2; Margery Kirkbride James, *Studies in the Medieval Wine Trade*, E. M. Veale, ed. (Oxford: Clarendon Press, 1971), 9, 28–33, 38, 55–56; Yves Renouard, "Les transformations économiques et sociales," in Charles Higounet, ed., *Histoire de Bordeaux*, vol. 3, *Bordeaux sous les rois d'Angleterre* (Bordeaux: Fédération historique du Sud-Ouest, 1965), 423–33.

8. On the movement of the beer border south into Flanders and Bavaria, see below, chapter 7. Herman van der Wee, *The Growth of the Antwerp Market and the European Economy in the Fifteenth and Sixteenth Centuries* (The Hague: Martinus Nijhoff, 1963), 1: 294.

9. Uytven,"Bier und Brauer in Brabant und Flandern," 3; Uytven, *Stadsfinanciën en stadsekonomie te Leuven*, 335–36.

10. It is that tax which generated data on Hamburg exports to the Low Countries as reported above, pp. 61–63. Doorman, *De middeleeuwse brouwerij en de gruit*, 25; Laan, *Oorkondenboek van Amsterdam*, #16, #129, #522; Smit, *De opkomst van den handel van Amsterdam*, 31–34, 37–40, 45–49, 89–92, 103, 115; for a general discussion of the development of brewing in Holland in the late Middle Ages see Unger, *A History of Brewing in Holland*, 26–68.

11. Dirck van Bleyswijck, *Beschryvinge der stadt Delft* (Delft: Arnold Bon, 1667), 695–96.

12. Ackersdyck, "Het regt van de gruit," 194; Urion and Eyer, *La bière: Art et tradition*, 6, 29, 35.

13. Fell, "Old English *Beor*," 76–79, 81, 86–91; Hagen, *A Second Handbook of Anglo-Saxon Food*, 150, 204–7; Else Roesdahl, *Viking Age Denmark*, trans. Susan Morgeson and Kirsten Willams (London, British Museum, 1982), 120.

14. Moulin, "Bière, houblon et cervoise," 130, 143.

15. De Boer, *Graaf en grafiek*, 274; Raymond De Roover, "Les comptes communaux et la comptabilité communale à Bruges au XIVe siècle: Finances et comptabilité urbaines Du XIIIe au XVIe siècle," *Colloque international Blakenberge 6-9-IX-1962* (Blankenberge: Pro Civitate, 1964), 94, 100–101; Doorman, *De middeleeuwse brouwerij en de gruit*, 18–20, 50–51.

16. Already in 1363 the town of Deventer exchanged letters with a number of towns such as Amsterdam and Amersfoort about the use of hops. Doorman, *De middeleeuwse brouwerij en de gruit*, 37; Uytven, *Stadsfinanciën en stadsekonomie te Leuven*, 315.

17. L. P. L. Pirenne and W. J. Formsma, *Koopmensgeest te 's-Hertogenbosch in de vijftiende en zestiende eeuw: Het kasboek van Jaspen van Bull 1564–1568* (Nijmegen: N.V. Centrale Drukkerij, 1962), 36–37; A. Swartelé, "Iets over de geschiedenis van het bier in de Nederlanden," *Fermentatio* 3 (1961): 123.

18. Cau, van Leeuwen, and Scheltus, eds., *Groot Placaatboek*, 1: 1202–5; De Boer, *Graaf en grafiek*, 279; P. C. M. Hoppenbrouwers, *Een middeleeuwse samenleving: Het Land van Heusden (ca. 1360—ca. 1515)* (Wageningen: Afdeling Agrarische Geschiedenis, Landbouwuniversiteit, 1992), 255–60; Pinkse, "Het Goudse kuitbier," 120; Raymond van Uytven, "Oudheid en middeleeuwen," in J. H. van Stuijvenberg, ed., *De economische geschiedenis van Nederland* (Groningen: Wolters-Noordhoff, 1977), 40.

19. Clement, "De bierbrouwerijen van Gouda," 56; De Boer, *Graaf en grafiek*,

283–84; Florike Egmond,"De strijd om het dagelijks bier brouwerijen, groothandel in bier en economische politiek in de noordelijke nederlanden tijdens de zestiende eeuw," in C. Lesger and L. Noordegraaf, eds., *Ondernemers en bestuurders: Economie en politiek in de noordelijke Nederlanden in de late middeleeuwen en vroegmoderne tijd* (Amsterdam: Nederlands Economisch Historisch Archief, 1999), 159; Hallema and Emmens, *Het bier en zijn brouwers*, 65; Loenen, *De Haarlemse brouwindustrie*, 20; J. Schouten, *Gouda vroeger en nu* (Bussum: Fibula-van Dishoeck, 1969), 67.

20. Loenen, *De Haarlemse brouwindustrie*, 55, 59, 64–65; A. Houwen,"De Haarlemsche brouwerij 1575–1600" (Unpublished doctoraal scriptie, economisch-historisch seminarium, University of Amsterdam, 1932), 27; Pinkse, "Het Goudse kuitbier," 91; see also Unger, *A History of Brewing in Holland*, 73–86.

21. Uytven, "Het bierverbruik," 7–10.

22. Alberts, "Bijdrage tot de geschiedenis der accijnzen," 334, 338–44; W. Jappe Alberts and H. P. H. Jansen, *Welvaart in wording* (The Hague: Martinus Nijhoff, 1964), 143; Clement, "De bierbrouwerijen van Gouda," 57, 203–4; De Hullu, "Iets over de gruit," 114–24; H. G. Hamaker, ed., *De rekeningen der grafelijkheid van Holland onder het Henegouwsche Huis* (Utrecht: Kemink en Zoon, 1875–78), 2: 19, 125.

23. The *gruit* tax held on in a number of places for a long time. It disappeared at Leiden only after 1501. Alkmaar and Amsterdam paid the monarch lump sums for the right to collect the tax only in 1559. Even into the eighteenth century's-Hertogenbosch levied a *gruit* tax, and it was not finally abolished entirely until the end of the Dutch Republic in 1798. Ackersdyck, "Het regt van de gruit," 196–200; Dick E. H. De Boer, "Delft omstreeks 1400," in Ineke Spander and R. A. Leeuw, eds., *De stad Delft cultuur en maatschappij tot 1572* (Delft: Stedelijk museum het Prinsenhof, 1979), 96; Doorman, *De middeleeuwse brouwerij en de gruit*, 20; Jensma, "Bronnen tot de geschiedenis van het recht," 168, 176; H. van Noordkerk, *Handvesten ofte Privilegien ende Octroyen; mitsgaders Willekeuren, Costumen, ordonnantien en Handelingen der Stad Amstelredam . . .*, vol. 1 (Amsterdam: Hendrik van Waesberge, Salomon en Petrus Schouten, 1748), 185–86.

24. Richard W. Unger, "Technical Change in the Brewing Industry in Germany, the Low Countries, and England in the Late Middle Ages," *The Journal of European Economic History*, 21 (1992): 296–99; Unger, *A History of Brewing in Holland*, 41–50.

25. Alberts and Jansen, *Welvaart in wording*, 134 n. 6; Bleyswijck, *Beschryvinge der stadt Delft*, 697–699.

26. Huntemann, *Das deutsche Braugewerbe*, 14.

27. N. H. L. van den Heuvel, *De ambachtsgilden van's-Hertogenbosch voor 1629* (Utrecht: Kemink en Zoon N.V., 1946), 413–14; Loenen, *De Haarlemse brouwindustrie*, 10–11; De Wal, "Accijnsbrief van Haarlem in 1274," 172–74, 176–87.

28. See below, Chapter 12.

29. King, *Beer Has a History*, 41.

30. The Dordrecht rules set limits on the number of brews that a brewer could produce and included requirements for payment of a producers' tax. Dalen, *Geschiedenis van Dordrecht*, 1: 390; Doorman, *De middeleeuwse brouwerij en de gruit*, 89; Loenen, *De Haarlemse brouwindustrie*, 74–75.

31. Hallema and Emmens, *Het bier en zijn brouwers*, 133; K. Heeringa,, ed. *Rechtsbronnen der stad Schiedam* (The Hague: Martinus Nijhoff, 1904), 247–48.

32. Unger, "Technical Change in the Brewing Industry," 293–300.

33. William H. TeBrake, *Medieval Frontier: Culture and Ecology in Rijnland* (College Station, Texas: Texas A&M University Press, 1985), 185.

34. H. P. H. Jansen, "Holland's Advance," *Acta historiae Neerlandicae* 10 (1978): 16.

35. Jansen, "Holland's Advance," 6, 12, 16–17; M. M. Postan, "The Trade of Medieval Europe: The North," in M. M. Postan and E. E. Rich, eds., *The Cambridge Economic History of Europe* (Cambridge: Cambridge University Press, 1952), 2: 122, 251–56.

36. Loenen, *De Haarlemse brouwindustrie*, 76–77; Smit, *De opkomst van den handel van Amsterdam*, 161, 184–85, 193–94, 223, 317–18; Techen, "Das Brauwerk in Wismar," 200.

37. Ketner, *Handel en scheepvaart van Amsterdam*, 124–25; Smit, *De opkomst van den handel van Amsterdam*, 225.

38. Clement, "De bierbrouwerijen van Gouda," 40–41; Huntemann, *Das deutsche Braugewerbe*, 12–13, 20; Pinkse, "Het Goudse kuitbier," 114, 121.

39. Alberts and Jansen, *Welvaart in wording*, 135–36; Berkenvelder, "Frieslands handel," 168, 176–84; Houtte, *An Economic History of the Low Countries*, 93.

40. Nordlund, *Brewing and Beer Traditions in Norway*, 204; Prevenier and Blockmans, *The Burgundian Netherlands*, 83.

41. The man was Antonio de Beatis in his *Journey of Cardinal Luigi d'Aragona*; Corran, *A History of Brewing*, 44.

42. Peacock, *Pottery in the Roman World*, 9.

Chapter 6

1. In the case of the bishop of Liege and Utrecht it took the intervention of Emperor Charles IV to get a lower tax on hopped beer and so guarantee its success. As late as 1351 at Bruges in Flanders a woman was fined for selling hopped beer at her pub because she was avoiding the tax on *gruit*. Moulin, "Bière, houblon et cervoise," 122; Bing, *Hamburgs Bierbrauerei*, 220–21; Corran, *A History of Brewing*, 44; Santbergen, *Les bons métiers des meuniers*, 108–9, 167, 289–90; Siebel, *One Hundred Years of Brewing*, 32; Raymond van Uytven, "Haarlemmer hop, Goudse kuit en Leuvense Peterman," *Arca Lovaniensis jaarboek 1975* 4 (1975): 336.

2. Ackersdyck, "Het regt van de gruit," 195–96; Michel van der Eycken, *Geschiedenis van Diest* (Diest: Stadsbestuur Diest, 1980), 58–60; Heuvel, *De ambachtsgilden van 's-Hertogenbosch*, 413; Penninck, *Het Bier te Brugge*, 5; Prevenier and Blockmans, *The Burgundian Netherlands*, 87–88; Schulte, "Vom Grutbiere," 140–41; Wee, *The Growth of the Antwerp Market*, 1: 228.

3. Bing, *Hamburgs Bierbrauerei*, 221; Doorman, *De middeleeuwse brouwerij en de gruit*, 40; Schulte, "Vom Grutbiere," 141

4. Corran, *A History of Brewing*, 43; Doorman, *De middeleeuwse brouwerij en de gruit*, 18, 80; Poll, *Das Brauwesen des Klosters Prüsening*, 37–38; Uytven, "Haarlemmer hop," 336.

5. Aerts, "De Zuidnederlandse brouwindustrie," 17; Eycken, *Geschiedenis van Diest*, 60; Pinkse, "Het Goudse kuitbier," 112.

6. Bing, *Hamburgs Bierbrauerei*, 227–28; Clement, "De bierbrouwerijen van Gouda," 33; Höhlbaum et al., *Hansisches Urkundenbuch*, 5: #16; Huntemann, *Das deutsche Braugewerbe*, 18.

7. Ropp et al., *Hanserecesse*, 4: #134.

8. W. S. Unger, "Twee rekeningen van den invoer van Hollandsch bier te Duinkerke uit de XIVe eeuw," *Annales de la société d'émulation de Bruges* 72 (1929): 1.

9. Bing, *Hamburgs Bierbrauerei*, 219, 227–28; Clement, "De bierbrouwerijen van Gouda," 37–38; Pinkse, "Het Goudse kuitbier," 113.

10. Aerts, *Het bier van Lier*, 150; Prevenier and Blockmans, *The Burgundian Netherlands*, 87; Uytven, "Haarlemmer hop," 339, 341.

11. Bing, *Hamburgs Bierbrauerei*, 227; Unger, "Twee rekeningen," 2–4; Uytven, "Haarlemmer hop," 335–36, 340; Uytven,"Oudheid en middeleeuwen," 39; Raymond van Uytven, "Stages of Economic Decline: Late Medieval Bruges," in J.-M. Duvosquel and E. Thoen, eds., *Studia in honorem Adriaan Verhulst* (Ghent, 1995), 259–69, reprinted in Raymond van Uytven, *Production and Consumption in the Low Countries, 13th–16th Centuries* (Aldershot: Ashgate, 2001), V: 254; Wee, *The Growth of the Antwerp Market*, 1: 228–29.

12. Ropp at al., *Hanserecesse*, 2nd series, 1: #482.

13. Höhlbaum, et al., *Hansisches Urkundenbuch*, 9: 320–21, 414–20, 436–37, 441–42.

14. Ropp et al., *Hanserecesse*, 5: #243.

15. Bing, *Hamburgs Bierbrauerei*, 230–33; Daenell, *Die Blütezeit der deutschen Hanse*, 1: 383; P. A. Meilink, "Rekening van het Lastgelt in Amsterdam, Waterland en het Noorderkwartier van Holland in 1507," *Bijdragen en mededeelingen van het historisch genootschap* 44 (1923): 188, 202–3; Unger, *A History of Brewing in Holland*, 59.

16. Raymond van Uytven, "Bestaansmiddelen," *Arca Louvaniensis jaarboek* 7 (1978): 153–54; Uytven, "Haarlemmer hop," 338–40; Wee, *The Growth of the Antwerp Market*, 1: 268–269.

17. Karl O. Herz,"Tabernaemontanus on Sixteenth-Century Beer," *Wallerstein Laboratories Communications* 27 (1964): 112.

18. Aerts, *Het bier van Lier*, 140–44; Jozef van Balberghe, *De Mechelse bierhandel-geschiedenis-folklore-dialekt* (Antwerp: Boekuil en Karveel-uitgaven, 1945), 19; Wee, *The Growth of the Antwerp Market*, 1: 229.

19. Uytven,"Bier und Brauer," 8; Uytven, *Stadsfinanciën en stadsekonomie te Leuven*, 314–15; Uytven, "Bestaansmiddelen," 154; Raymond van Uytven, *De drankcultuur in de zuidelijke Nederlanden tot de XVIIIde eeuw: Drinken in het verleden: Tentoonstelling ingericht door het stadsbestuur van Leuven , 9 juni–5 augustus, 1973* (Leuven: Stadsbestuur Leuven, 1973), 32–33.

20. Loenen, *De Haarlemse brouwindustrie*, 45; Pinkse, "Het Goudse kuitbier," 114, 128; Uytven, "Bestaansmiddelen," 154; Uytven, *De drankcultuur in de zuidelijke Nederlanden*, 32–33.

21. Uytven, *Stadsfinanciën en stadsekonomie te Leuven*, 313.

22. Aerts, *Het bier van Lier*, 20, 39–40, 44–45, 59, 84, 151–53, 156, 161–63, 166–67.

23. Hugo Soly,"De economische betekenis van de zuidnederlandse brouwindustrie in de 16e eeuw. Problematie," *Handelingen van het Colloquium over de economische geschiedenis van België. Behandelingen van de Bronnen en Problematiek* (Brussels: Archives Générale du Royaume, 1972), 101–4; Uytven, "Bier und Brauer," 8.

24. Paul De Commer, "De brouwindustrie te Ghent, 1505–1622," *Handelingen der Maatschappij voor geschiedenis en oudheidkunde te Gent*, new series, 35 (1981): 109 and 37 (1983): 129–38; Prevenier and Blockmans, *The Burgundian Netherlands*, 88, 95; Uytven, "Haarlemmer hop," 339–42.

25. P. Rickard, *Britain in Medieval French Literature 1100–1500* (Cambridge: Cam-

bridge University Press, 1956), 169–70; James Caigie Robertson, ed., *Materials for the History of Thomas Becket, Archbishop of Canterbury* (London: Longman and Co. et al., 1877), 3: 29–30.

26. Bennett, *Ale, Beer, and Brewsters in England*, 43–44.

27. Clark, *The English Alehouse*, 31–32; Monckton, *A History of English Ale and Beer*, 66; Salzman, *English Industries of the Middle Ages*, 294–95.

28. For examples of shipments of beer see H. J. Smit, ed., *Bronnen tot de geschiedenis van den handel mit Engeland, Schotland en Ierland, 1150–1585*, (The Hague: Martinus Nijhoff, 1928), 1: #576–577, #589, #603, #724, #732, #736, #782, #842, #859.

29. Smit, *Bronnen*, 1: #867, #908, #1257.

30. Nelly Johanna Martina Kerling, *Commercial Relations of Holland and Zeeland with England from the late 13th Century to the Close of the Middle Ages* (Leiden: E. J. Brill, 1954), 110–11, 114, 216–20; Unger, *A History of Brewing in Holland*, 59–60.

31. Bennett, *Ale, Beer, and Brewsters in England*, 79–82, 86, 95, 144; Clinch, *English Hops*, 66; Doorman, *De middeleeuwse brouwerij en de gruit*, 40–41; Salzman, *English Industries of the Middle Ages*, 29.

32. Corran, *A History of Brewing*, 46; King, *Beer Has a History*, 55; Salzman, *English Industries of the Middle Ages*, 296–98.

33. Corran, *A History of Brewing*, 53–55; Salzman, *English Industries of the Middle Ages*, 285, 295, 297; Alison Sim, *Food and Feast in Tudor England* (London: Sutton, 1997), 57.

34. Bennett, *Ale, Beer, and Brewsters in England*, 79–80; Corran, *A History of Brewing*, 53–55; F. G. Emmison, *Tudor Food and Pastimes* (London: Ernest Benn, 1964), 56; Salzman, *English Industries of the Middle Ages*, 285, 295, 297.

35. Clark, *The English Alehouse*, 97; Salzman, *English Industries of the Middle Ages*, 299; Sambrook, *Country House Brewing*, 133; Sim, *Food and Feast*, 47, 50.

36. James L. Bolton, ed., *The Alien Communities of London in the Fifteenth Century: The Subsidy Rolls of 1440 and 1483–4* (Stamford: Richard III & Yorkist History Trust in association with Paul Watkins, 1998), 19, 79–80; Corran, *A History of Brewing*, 54; Salzman, *English Industries of the Middle Ages*, 297–98.

37. The beer barrel was 36 gallons, the ale barrel 32. The barrels were far from water tight, so there was always loss due to leakage. A brewer's dozen was not 12 but anywhere from 13 to 15 barrels in England to compensate buyers for that loss. Corran, *A History of Brewing*, 44, 54; King, *Beer Has a History*, 53; Salzman, *English Industries of the Middle Ages*, 290; Sim, *Food and Feast*, 56;

38. On the Brewers' Company in London see below, Chapter 13. Bennett, *Ale, Beer, and Brewsters in England*, 88; Frederick W. Hackwood, *Inns, Ales, and Drinking Customs of Old England* (London: T. Fisher Unwin, 1910), 83; Monckton, *A History of English Ale and Beer*, 96–97.

39. Alberts and Jansen, *Welvaart in wording*, 114–15, 250; G. Asaert, *De Antwerpse scheepvaart in de XVe eeuw (1394–1480) Bijdrage tot de economische geschiedenis van de stad Antwerpen* (Brussels: Paleis der Academiën, 1973), 263–64, 304; Hallema and Emmens, *Het bier en zijn brouwers*, 35, 62; Niermeyer, "Dordrecht als handelsstad," 9–11; Pinkse, "Het Goudse kuitbier," 120.

40. Bennett, *Ale, Beer, and Brewsters in England*, 90; Clark, *The English Alehouse*, 101–2; Monckton, *A History of English Ale and Beer*, 67; Sim, *Food and Feast*, 50.

41. Clark, *The English Alehouse*, 97; Corran, *A History of Brewing*, 57–59; Kerling,

Commercial Relations, 115–16; Gervase Markham, *The English Housewife: Containing the inward and outward virtues which ought to be in a complete woman; as her skill in physik, cookery, banqueting-stuff, distillation, perfumes, wool, hemp, flax, dairies, brewing, baking and all other things belonging to a household*, ed. Michael R. Best (1615; Montreal: McGill-Queen's University Press, 1986), 206.

42. On the consumption of mead in the eastern Baltic see above, Chapter 2. Dembinska, *Food and Drink in Medieval Poland*, 78, 83; Scully, *The Art of Cookery*, 153–54; A. G. Preobrazhensky, *Etymological Dictionary of the Russian Language* (New York: Columbia University Press, 1951).

43. David Christian, *"Living Water" Vodka and Russian Society on the Eve of Emancipation* (Oxford: Clarendon, 1990), 22–23, 227; Dembinska, *Food and Drink in Medieval Poland*, 78–79; Powell, "Metron Ariston," 91–92; Räsänen, *Von Halm zum Fass*, 84; Richard W. Unger, "Beer in Eastern Europe in the Middle Ages," in Balazs Nagy and Marcell Sebok, eds., . . . *The Man of many Devices, Who Wandered Full Many Ways . . . Festschrift in Honor of Janos M. Bak* (Budapest: Central European University Press, 1999), 294–302.

44. See above, Chapter 4. For example drinkers in western Norway and especially around Bergen even at the end of the twentieth century still preferred beer with a relatively large quantity of hops. That taste presumably is a result of German imports into Bergen which had to be heavily hopped to maintain quality during the sea voyage from Wismar or other Wendish towns. Nordlund, *Brewing and Beer Traditions in Norway*, 203–4, 210, 216–17, 225–26; Räsänen, *Von Halm zum Fass*, 37, 134, 147, 269; Thunæus, *Ölets historia i Sverige*, 1: 122–43, 185–86.

45. Kristof Glamann, "Beer and Brewing in Pre-Industrial Denmark," *The Scandinavian Economic History Review* 10 (1962): 134–35; Kristof Glamann, *Jacobsen of Carlsberg, Brewer and Philanthropist*, trans. Geoffrey French (Copenhagen: Glydendal, 1991), 23–24.

46. Gelsinger, *Icelandic Enterprise*, 170–71; Huntemann, *Das deutsche Brauegewerbe*, 30–32, 37–38; Stefke: *Ein Städtisches Exportgewerbe*, 47–49; Techen, "Das Brauwerk in Wismar," 307, 315–16; Richard W. Unger, "The Trade in Beer to Medieval Scandinavia," *Deutsches Schiffahrtsarchiv* 11 (1988): 249–58.

Chapter 7

1. The comment about the renown of English beer is from Fynes Moryson in 1617. Not everything he said was reliable. Corran, *A History of Brewing*, 65–66; Fynes Moryson, *Itinerary* (London, 1617), in Frederick J. Furnivall, ed., *Harrison's Description of England in Shakspere's[sic] Youth* (London: Chatto and Windus, 1908), 263–64, 269.

2. On literary evidence for the movement of the beer border and prices of beer relative to wine, see above, Chapter 5. Grässe, *Bierstudien*, 28; Emil Struve, *Die Entwicktung des bayerischen Braugewerbes in neunzehnten Jahrhundert* (Leipzig: Verlag von Duncker & Humblot, 1893), 12–13.

3. Abel, *Stufen der Ernährung*, 51–53; Huntemann, *Das deutsche Braugewerbe*, 37–38, 47, 56, 69–70; Poll, *Des Brauwesen des Benediktinerklosters Metten*, 52.

4. Aerts, "De Zuidnederlandse brouwindustrie," 23; De Commer, "De Brouwindustrie te Ghent," 93–94, 144; Eycken, *Geschiedenis van Diest*, 199; Uytven, "Het bierv-

erbruik en de sociaal-economische toestand," 30; Wee, *The Growth of the Antwerp Market*, 1: 294, 2: 301.

5. Erik Aerts, "De bibliografie van de Zuidnederlandse biernijverheid tot omstreeks 1800: Een aanvulling," *Handelingen XXXVII der koninklijke zuidnederlandse maatschappij voor taal- en letterkunde en geschiedenis* (1983): 8–9.

6. Heinrich Huber, "Altbayerische Vorschriften über das Biersudwesen," *Brauwelt Zeitschrift für das gesamte brauwesen*, 99 (1959): 438; Schlosser, *Braurechte, Brauer und Braustätten in München*, xvi, 85–99, 95–96.

7. Grässe, *Bierstudien*, 29; Hoffmann, *5000 Jahre Bier*, 71; Kampeter, *Die wirtschaftliche Entwicklung*, 14.

8. Moryson, *Itinerary*, 262–63.

9. Corran, *A History of Brewing*, 57–58; Monckton, *A History of English Ale and Beer*, 96.

10. There was a blatant case in Leiden in 1622. G. A. Leiden, Archieven van de Gilden: #197; Aerts, *Het bier van Lier*, 44; De Commer, "De brouwindustrie te Ghent," 107–9, 112; Hallema and Emmens, *Het bier en zijn brouwers*, 140.

11. Aerts, *Het bier van Lier*, 52–53; Erik Aerts and Eddy Put, "Jezuïetenbier: Bierhistorische beschouwingen bij een brouwhandleiding uit 1627," *Volkskunde* 93, no. 2 (1992): 108–9.

12. De Commer, "De brouwindustrie te Ghent," 102–3.

13. J. G. van Dillen, *Bronnen tot de geschiedenis van het bedrijfsleven en het gildewezen van Amsterdam [1512–1632]* (The Hague: Martinus Nijhoff, 1929), 1:#240; Noordkerk, *Handvesten ofte Privilegien ende Octroyen*, 181; Philipsen, "De Amsterdamsche brouwnijverheid," 15; Techen,"Das Brauwerk in Wismar," 219; E. M. A. Timmer, "Grepen uit de geschiedenis der Delftsche brouwnering," parts 1 and 2, *De Economist* (1920): 420; Jan Wagenaar, *Amsterdam in zyne opkomst, aanwas, Geschiedenissen, voorregten, koophandel, Gebouwen, kerkenstaat, schoolen, schutterye, Gilden en Regeeringe* (Amsterdam: Isaak Tirion, 1760–68), 2: 460.

14. The prize for hitting the stuffed popinjay the group used as a target was also a bonus of beer. G. van der Feijst, *Geschiedenis van Schiedam* (Schiedam: Interbook International, 1975), 36–37, 50, 67, 69, 225; Unger, *A History of Brewing in Holland*, 72.

15. W. S. Unger, ed., *Bronnen tot de geschiedenis van Middelburg* (The Hague: Martinus Nijhoff, 1923–1931), 3: #443 [before 1512], #447 [1512], #590, 2 [1541], #753 [1558].

16. For example Corran, *A History of Brewing*, 61–64; Emmison, *Tudor Food and Pastimes*, 56–57.

17. Josef Janáček, "Pivoarniectví v Českych Královských Městech V 16. Století," *Rozpravy Československe Akademie Věd Ročník* 69—Sešit 1 (Prague: Nakladetelství Československí Akademie Věd, 1959), 76; Langer, "Das Braugewerbe in den deutschen Hansestädten," 69. Also see below, Chapter 12.

18. Emmison, *Tudor Food and Pastimes*, 57.

19. See above, Table 1. Bing, *Hamburgs Bierbrauerei*, 215–16, 234–36, 239, 278, 301; Huntemann, *Das deutsche Braugewerbe*, 18, 59.

20. Langer, "Das Braugewerbe in den deutschen Hansestädten," 68.

21. Hoffmann, *5000 Jahre Bier*, 59, 73, 128; Huntemann, *Das deutsche Braugewerbe*, 19, 51–52; Siebel, *One Hundred Years of Brewing*, 20.

22. Huntemann, *Das deutsche Braugewerbe*, 11, 48.

23. Yntema, "The Brewing Industry in Holland," 58–60; Richard J. Yntema, "Een

kapitale nering: De brouwindustrie in Holland tussen 1500 en 1800," in R. E. Kistem-aker and V. T. van Vilsteren, eds., *Bier! Geschiedenis van een volksdrank* (Amsterdam: De Bataafsche Leeuw, 1994), 73.

24. Hugo Soly, "De brouwerijenonderneming van Gilbert van Schoonbeke (1552–1562)," *Revue belge de philolgie et d'histoire*, 46 (1968): 346; Unger, *A History of Brewing in Holland*, 74; Uytven, "Het bierverbruik en de sociaal-economische toestand," 12, 17; Uytven, "Haarlemmer hop," 340–41.

25. H. Halbertsma, *Zeven eeuwen Amersfoort* (Amersfoort: Veenendaal, 1959), 43, 49; W. F. N. van. Rootselaar, *Amersfoort, Sprokkelingen* (Amersfoort: B. Blankenberg en Zoon, 1898–1899), no. LXXI.

26. J. A. Faber, *Drie eeuwen Friesland: Economische en sociale ontwikkelingen van 1500 tot 1800* (Wageningen: Afdeling agrarische geschiedenis, Landbouwhogeschool, 1972), 244, 438.

27. Sa Leuven, Oud Archief: #2991; Uytven, "Bestaansmiddelen," 155, 157; Uytven, *Stadsfinanciën en stadsekonomie te Leuven*, 326–28.

28. Eycken, *Geschiedenis van Diest*, 199; Heuvel, *De ambachtsgilden van 's-Hertogenbosch*, 416–17.

29. On output at Lier see above, Chapter 6; Aerts, *Het bier van Lier*, 161, tables 3, 4, 8.

30. De Commer, "De brouwindustrie te Ghent," 82, 118, 123–24; Uytven, "Het bierverbruik en de sociaal-economische toestand," 12, 24–25; Uytven, "Stages of Economic Decline," 265.

31. On the different types of beer made, see below, Chapter 9.

32. De Commer, "De Brouwindustrie te Ghent," 116–18, 121–22; Uytven, "Het bierverbruik en de sociaal-economische toestand," 15, 30.

33. On capital investment in the supply of water for Antwerp brewers see below, Chapter 10. Soly, "De brouwerijenonderneming van Gilbert van Schoonbeke," 345, 347, 1187, 1198; Hugo Soly, *Urbanisme en kapitalisme te Antwerpen in de 16de eeuw: De stedebouwkundige en industriële ondernemingen van Gilbert van Schoonbeke* (Antwerp: Gemeentekrediet van Belgie, historische uitgaven pro civitate, series in 8⁰, no. 47, 1977), 312.

34. Corran, *A History of Brewing*, 64–65; King, *Beer Has a History*, 57; Stopes, *Malt and Malting*, 10.

35. Bennett, *Ale, Beer, and Brewsters in England*, 90; Monckton, *A History of English Ale and Beer*, 98.

36. In villages in the southern Low Countries with about 1,000 residents in the fifteenth and sixteenth centuries there would have been 25–30 brewers. In the big towns like Mechelen and Leuven by the middle of the fifteenth century there were about 150 brewers, the majority being small operators not brewing even once per week. Uytven, "Bier und Brauer," 10. That changed over time with numbers of brewers falling and output rising. Bennett, *Ale, Beer, and Brewsters in England*, 46–47.

37. De Commer, "De bouwindustrie te Ghent," 125, 127.

38. Andrzej Klonder,"Rachunki cechu browarników Starego Miasta Elblaga jako źródo do badán nad produkcją piwa w XVI–XVII w," *Kwartalnik Historii Kultury Materialnej* 28 (1980): 203.

39. On the frequency of brewing at Wismar, see below, Chapter 10. Techen, "Das Brauwerk in Wismar," 270.

40. Bing, *Hamburgs Bierbrauerei*, 265–66, 296–97.

Chapter 8

1. Abel, *Stufen der Ernährung*, 23; Loenen, *De Haarlemse brouwindustrie*, 52–56.

2. Aerts, *Het bier van Lier*, 91; Raymond van Uytven, "The Consumption of Domestic and Foreign Wines in Brabant in the Sixteenth Century," English trans. by Raymond van Uytven of "Het verbruik van land- en vreemde wijnen in Brabant gedurende de 16e eeuw," *De Brabantse folklore* 167 (1965): 299–337, reprinted in Raymond van Uytven, *Production and Consumption in the Low Countries, 13th–16th Centuries* (Aldershot: Ashgate, 2001), XIII, 14–15. In 1835–1846 in Brabant beer consumption was at 255 liters per person per year but that figure had fallen to 221 for all of Belgium by 1900 and by the 1930s for all of Belgium the rate of beer consumption was around 180 liters.

3. The consumption figure of more than nineteen liters per day or above 7,000 liters per year for each canon of St. Paul's in London in the thirteenth century is certainly too high. Bennett, *Ale, Beer, and Brewsters in England*, 17; Dembinska, *Food and Drink in Medieval Poland*, 80; Christopher Dyer, *Standards of Living in the Later Middle Ages: Social Change in England c. 1200–1520* (Cambridge: Cambridge University Press, 1989), 64, 114; Maitland, *Domesday Book and Beyond*, 440.

4. Clark, *The English Alehouse*, 24–26; Martin, *Alcohol, Sex, and Gender*, 20.

5. Soly, "De Brouwerijenonderneming van Gilbert van Schoonbeke," 349–50. In 1382, 1412–1413, 1421, and the 1550s independent sources indicate that all members of the households on country estates received about four to five liters per day. Each person did not drink that much, some of it being handed on to family members or assistants. Martin, *Alcohol, Sex, and Gender*, 29; Sambrook, *Country House Brewing in England*, 228. 1,660 liters per person per year which translates to more than four liters each day for an English country house in the 1540s does seem extreme, but there is a solid basis for the estimate. A level somewhere near half that, that is about a liter per meal per person, from 1478 seems more likely. Corran, *A History of Brewing*, 61–64; Emmison, *Tudor Food and Pastimes*, 57–58; C. M. Woolgar, *The Great Household in Late Medieval England* (New Haven: Yale University Press, 1999), 127.

6. Glamann, "Beer and Brewing in Pre-Industrial Denmark," 130; Nordlund, *Brewing and Beer Traditions in Norway*, 57–58; Thunæus, *Ölets historia i Sverige*, 1: 119.

7. C. S. L. Davies, "Les rations alimentaires de l'armée et de la marine anglaise au XVIe siècle," *Annales ESC* 18, (1963): 139; Konrad Pilgrim, "Der Durst auf den Weltmeeren Das Problem der Versorgung des Seeleute mit Getränken im 16., 17. und 18. Jahrhundert," *Jahrbuch 1969 Gesellschaft für die Geschichte und Bibliographie des Brauwesens E. V.* (Berlin, 1969): 81.

8. Aerts and Put, "Jezuïetenbier," 120–22; Bennett, *Ale, Beer, and Brewsters in England*, 93; Davies, "Les rations alimentaires," 139–40; Glamann, "Beer and Brewing in Pre-Industrial Denmark," 129; Klonder, *Browarnictwo w Prusach królewskich*, 160; Pilgrim, "Der Durst auf den Weltmeeren," 81.

9. Räsänen, *Von Halm zum Fass*, 37; Thunæus, *Ölets historia i Sverige*, 1: 170.

10. J. R. Bruijn, "Voeding op de staatse vloot," *Spiegel historiael* 2 (March 1967): 175–80; H. G. Schultze-Berndt, "Noch einmal: Von Durst auf dem Weltmeeren," *Jahrbuch 1974 Gesellschaft für Geschichte und Bibliographie des Brauwesens E. V.* (Berlin, 1973): 107; Yntema, "The Brewing Industry in Holland," 91–92.

11. Fourteenth-century Poland knew a beer soup, made with cheese and eggs, and good enough to be on the menu at royal feasts. The *Zupa Piwna z Brybdza, lub Caseata*

was by no means unique and there were many other recipes of the late Middle Ages that included beer among the ingredients. Dembinska, *Food and Drink in Medieval Poland*, 159.

12. Abel, *Stufen der Ernährung*, 24; Huntemann, *Das deutsche Braugewerbe*, 60; Klonder, *Browarnictwo w Prusach królewskich*, 160.

13. Aerts, *Het bier van Lier*, 86–90; Uytven, "Het bierverbruik en de sociaal-economische toestand," 31–32; Raymond van Uytven, "The Consumption of Domestic and Foreign Wines in Brabant," 14.

14. Martin, *Alcohol, Sex, and Gender*, 7.

15. Craeybeckx, *Un grand commerce d'importation*, 4–8, 11, 19, 40–41.

16. By the second half of the fifteenth century almost no wine was drunk at Lier even though the town was very close to the Brabant wine-producing area. In 1458–60 the average of per capita wine consumption was 8 liters per person per year. It rose to 9 liters in 1473 but was down to just 7.6 in 1474. Aerts, *Het bier van Lier*, 158–61; Uytven, "The Consumption of Domestic and Foreign Wines in Brabant," 13.

17. In Sint Truiden, for example, from 1500 to 1579 the price of wine went up some fivefold while from 1500 to 1580 the price of the cheapest beer only doubled. Uytven, "Bier und Brauer," 5–6. Flanders, in part due to shipments overland from France and down the Rhine through Dordrecht, always had higher levels of wine consumption than Brabant or Holland which were certainly within the beer region. Uytven, "L'approvisionnement des villes des anciens Pays-Bas," 98–99; Uytven, "The Consumption of Domestic and Foreign Wines in Brabant," 13.

18. Uytven, "The Consumption of Domestic and Foreign Wines in Brabant," 27.

19. Klonder, *Browarnictwo w Prusach królewskich*, 160; Richard W. Unger, "Beer, Wine and Land Use in the Late Medieval Low Countries," *Bijdragen tot de Geschiedenis* 81 (1998): 335–36; Warner, "Before There Was 'Alcoholism'," 414–15.

20. Galbert of Bruges, *The Murder of Charles the Good Count of Flanders*, trans. and ed. James Bruce Ross (New York: Columbia University Press, 1950), 84–88.

21. Kampeter, *Die wirtschaftliche Entwicklung*, 5; Henry S. Lucas, "The Great European Famine of 1315, 1316, and 1317," *Speculum* 5 (1930): 371; Nordlund, *Brewing and Beer Traditions in Norway*, 138; Stefke, *Ein städtisches Exportgewerbe*, 20–26; Stopes, *Malt and Malting*, 8.

22. In the same vein, in 1425 Groningen prohibited brewers from using rye, possibly as part of a policy of keeping that grain for bread making. Additionally and for no obvious reason, the town also prohibited brewers from using their own malt, and no one was allowed to make malt from grain that belonged to someone from outside the town. Albertus Telting, ed., *Stadboek van Groningen* (The Hague: Martinus Nijhoff, 1886), 73. Clark, *The English Alehouse*, 169; Clement, "De bierbrouwerijen van Gouda," 54; Loenen: *De Haarlemse brouwindustrie*, 60–61.

23. The government reissued instructions for closing unnecessary taverns in 1594 and 1595 in the wake of harvest failures. In 1627 the English Parliament talked about brewers using excessive quantities of barley which might better have been used for bread. In 1630–31 when famine struck, the royal government closed a number of drinking establishments because of grain shortages. Clark, *The English Alehouse*, 167, 172. King, *Beer Has a History*, 65; W. S. Unger, *De levenmiddelenvoorziening der Hollandsche steden in de middeleeuwen* (Amsterdam: A. H. Kruyt, 1916), 71–73.

24. Glamann, "Beer and Brewing in Pre-Industrial Denmark," 137–38; Huntemann, *Das deutsche Braugewerbe*, 75; Soly, "De brouwerijenonderneming van Gilbert van Schoonbeke," 1189.

25. Niehoff, "Bierproduktion und Bierkonsum," 170; Niehoff, "Bremer Bier im Baltikum," 11.

26. Dyer, *Standards of Living*, 58.

27. Bennett, *Ale, Beer, and Brewsters in England*, 18, 20–23, 85–86; Martin, *Alcohol, Sex, and Gender*, 33.

28. Uytven, "L'approvisionnement des villes des anciens Pays-Bas," 91.

29. The figure of 20 kilograms/100 liters of beer is probably closer to the right number than a higher number from a sixteenth-century Antwerp statement. M. A. W. Gerding, *Vier Eeuwen Turfwinning: De verveningen in Groningen, Friesland, Drenthe en Overijssel tussen 1550 en 1950* (Wageningen: Afdeling Agrarische Geschiedenis, Land-bouwuniversiteit, 1995), 320; Soly, "De brouwerijenonderneming van Gilbert van Schoonbeke," 1190; Uytven, "Oudheid en middeleeuwen," 40. See W. J. Diepeveen, *De Vervening in Delfland en Schieland tot het einde der Zestiende Eeeuw* (Leiden: Eduard IJdo, N. V., 1950), 111–14 for statistics on Delft.

30. Jan De Vries, *The Dutch Rural Economy in the Golden Age, 1500–1700* (New Haven: Yale University Press, 1974), 202, 204; Faber, *Drie eeuwen Friesland*, 294–95; Gerding, *Vier Eeuwen Turfwinning*, 115–20, 129–32.

31. G. A. Haarlem, Archief van het Brouwersgilde: #19; Doorman, *Techniek en octrooiwezen*, 75; Unger, *A History of Brewing in Holland*, 100–103.

32. Techen, "Das Brauwerk in Wismar," 333–35.

33. Buijs, "De Bierbrouwer," 29; Hoekstra, "Het Haarlems brouwersbedrijf," 16–17; Richard W. Unger, "Energy Sources for the Dutch Golden Age: Peat, Wind and Coal," *Research in Economic History* 9 (1984): 232.

34. Alberts and Jansen, *Welvaart in wording*, 96; Buijs, "De Bierbrouwer," 29.

35. Eykens, "De brouwindustrie te Antwerpen," 95; Kerling, *Commercial Relations*, 122; Jean Lejeune, *La formation du capitalisme moderne dans la principauté de Liège au XVIe siècle* (Liège: Faculté de philosophie et lettres, 1939), 172, 252.

36. Wilhelm Abel, *Agricultural Fluctuations in Europe from the thirteenth to the twentieth centuries*, trans. Olive Ordish (London: Methuen, 1980), 138; Leo Noordegraaf, *Hollands welvaren? Levenstandaard in Holland 1450–1650* (Bergen (NH): Octavo, 1985), 170–83.

37. A. E. Dingle, "Drink and Working-Class Living Standards in Britain, 1870–1914," *Economic History Review* 25 (1972): 617.

38. Clark, *The English Alehouse*, 32–34, 40–44; Dyer, *Standards of Living*, 198–99.

39. Soly, "De economische betekenis," 115–16; Wee, *The Growth of the Antwerp Market*, 3: 86–87.

Chapter 9

1. Anon., *Kellermaistereij: Grüntlicher bericht/wie man alle wein/Teutscher und Welcher landen/vor allen zufallen beweren* (n. p., 1539), chapter 20; Corran, *A History of Brewing*, 50–53; Hubert Ermisch and Robert Wuttke, eds. *Haushaltung in Vorwerken: Ein landwirtschaftliches Lehrbuch aus der Zeit des Kurfürsten August von Sachsen* (Leipzig: B. G. Teubner, 1910), 33; Klemens Löffler,"Die altesten Bierbücher," *Archiv für Kultur-Geschichte* 7 (1909): 5; Salem, *Beer, Its History*, 36.

2. Some of the treatments for beer were similar to those suggested for wine in the early fourteenth century by a professor of medicine at Montpellier. He called for the

addition of all kinds of nuts, herbs, and spices from almonds to honey, sage, caraway seeds, sugar, and saffron. Each was designed to deal with a specific problem, and he gave variants on the additives if one did not work. Arnaldus de Villanova, *The earliest printed book on wine / by Arnald of Villanova . . . now for the first time rendered into English and with an historical essay by Henry E. Sigerist, with facsimile of the original edition, 1478* (New York : Schuman's, 1943), 28–31.

3. Grolsche Bierbrouwerij, *Merckwaerdighe bierologie*, 84.

4. He urged the drinking of warm beer for the sake of good health and to prevent toothache, cough, rheumatism, and other ailments. The book went through a number of editions and was still in print in 1724. Anon. [R. D.], *Warme Beere, or A Treatise Wherein is declared by many reasons that Beere so qualitied is farre more wholsome than that which is drunk cold With a continuation of such objections that are saide against it; published for the preservation of health* (Cambridge: Richard Overton, 1641).

5. Löffler, "Die altesten Bierbücher," 6–8; Schulte, "Vom Grutbiere," 126–27; Stopes, *Malt and Malting*, 9.

6. Herz, "Tabernaemontanus on Sixteenth-Century Beer," 111–13.

7. Löffler, "Die altesten Bierbücher," 5–12.

8. Ermisch and Wuttke, *Haushaltung in Vorwerken*, xix–xxi, 32–34, 93–94; Markham, *The English Housewife*, 205–8.

9. Aerts and Put, "Jezuïetenbier," 94–102.

10. Buijs, "De Bierbrouwer," 45.

11. See also Chapter 8. On kettle sizes in later years see below Table 8. Buijs, "De Bierbrouwer," 14–15; Langer, "Das Braugewerbe in den deutschen Hansestädten," 70.

12. Buijs, "De Bierbrouwer," 18; William Harrison, *A Description of England*, in *Lothrop Withington, Holingshed's Chronicles*, intro. by F. J. Furnivall (London: Walter Scott, 1876), 101; Langer, "Das Braugewerbe in den deutschen Hansestädten," 71; John U. Nef, "The Progress of Technology and the Growth of Large-Scale Industry in Great Britain, 1540–1640," in E. M. Carus-Wilson, ed., *Essays in Economic History*, (London: Edward Arnold, 1954), 1: 99; Sambrook, *Country House Brewing*, 35–36.

13. Buijs, "De Bierbrouwer," 19–20; G. Doorman, *Octrooien voor uitvindingen in de Nederlanden uit de 16e–18e eeuw* (The Hague: Martinus Nijhoff, 1940), 143.

14. Clark, *The English Alehouse*, 31.

15. For the maltery, there were as well as the usual rakes and shovels, leaden cisterns for water, a leaden cistern for steeping, a fan for cooling, and haircloth to be used under the malt in the kiln while drying. King, *Beer Has a History*, 55; Monckton, *A History of English Ale*, 77.

16. Loenen, *De Haarlemse brouwindustrie*, 27–28; Sambrook, *Country House Brewing*, 33–34, 51–52.

17. The brewer in the country house used a spade, large oar-like paddles, large ladles, large tubs for carrying water, small tubs for keeping yeast, and some baskets. For fixed equipment he had one mashing tun and one wort barrel, a copper kettle, a cooler which was made of wood like the barrels, a fermenting vat, and leaden troughs. Emmison, *Tudor Food and Pastimes*, 56; Loenen, *De Haarlemse brouwindustrie*, 28–29; Penninck, *Het bier te Brugge*, 9; Uytven, "Bier und Brauer," 11.

18. Bennett, *Ale, Beer, and Brewsters in England*, 100–101; Poll, *Des Brauwesen des Benediktinerklosters Metten*, 41.

19. De Commer, "De Brouwindustrie te Ghent," 100; Hoffmann, *5000 Jahre Bier*, 60.

20. Buijs, "De Bierbrouwer," 38–39; Doorman, *De middeleeuwse brouwerij en de gruit*, 40; Martens, "Bier en stadsfinancien te Hasselt," 249.

21. For example, permitted hours for brewing at Delft were 6:00 a.m. to 7:00 p.m. from 1 March to 1 October; in February and October from 8:00 a.m. to 7:00 p.m., and from 1 November to 31 January they were 6:00 a.m. to only 3:30 p.m. Beer could not go into casks before 11:00 a.m., no matter the month. From 1616 and probably before, Sunday brewing, though not malting, was permitted but subject to very strict limitations. G. A. Delft, Eerst Afdeling: #1922, 4, 5; Unger, *A History of Brewing in Holland*, 120–21.

22. Bing, *Hamburgs Bierbrauerei*, 251–22; Hallema and Emmens, *Het bier en zijn brouwers*, 77; Niehoff, "Bremer Bier im Baltikum," 14; Techen, "Das Brauwerk in Wismar," 335–36.

23. Clark, *The English Alehouse*, 104; Harrison, *A Description of England*, 98–99; Techen, "Das Brauwerk in Wismar," 309–10.

24. Doorman, *De middeleeuwse brouwerij en de gruit*, 45–46, 50–51; Hoffmann, *5000 Jahre Bier*, 111–13; Hough, *The Biotechnology of Malting and Brewing*, 122–24; Pasteur, *Studies on Fermentation*, 7–10; Poll, *Des Brauwesen des Benediktinerklosters Metten*, 30, 52.

25. Corran, *A History of Brewing*, 47.

26. Doorman, *De middeleeuwse brouwerij en de gruit*, 51.

27. March beers got better with age and so were kept for a time as they matured. In some cases, drinkers would even try some tricks to speed the process of maturation and so get a higher alcohol content. Huber, "Altbayerische Vorschriften," 437; Sim, *Food and Feast in Tudor England*, 51, 56.

28. Bracker, "Hopbier uit Hamburg," 29; Doorman, *De middeleeuwse brouwerij en de gruit*, 50; Eykens, "De brouwindustrie te Antwerpen," 85–86.

29. Sambrook, *Country House Brewing*, 114, 120; Uytven, "Bier und Brauer," 19.

30. Klonder, *Browarnictwo w Prusach królewskich*, 160; Klonder, "Rachunki cechu browarników Starego Miasta Elbląga," 206; Techen, "Das Brauwerk in Wismar," 291–92.

31. ARa, Papiers de l'état et de l'audience: 1665/1.

32. Ebbing and Vilsteren, "Van gruiters, gruitketels en gruithuizen," 25; Mathias, "Agriculture and the Brewing and Distilling Industries," 249.

33. Uytven, "Het bierverbruik en de sociaal-economische toestand," 13.

34. Harrison, *A Description of England*, 99, 102.

35. Buijs, "De Bierbrouwer," 9, 34, 38; Harrison, *A Description of England*, 100–101; Herz, "Tabernaemontanus on Sixteenth-Century Beer," 112.

36. Nordlund, *Brewing and Beer Traditions in Norway*, 220–21. North German brewers kept on using *gruit* since it was as late as the eighteenth century that governments, like that of Hannover in 1723, prohibited the use of bog myrtle in making beer.

37. Behre, "The History of Beer Additives in Europe," 43.

38. Aerts and Put, "Jezuïetenbier," 116; Penninck, *Het bier te Brugge*, 11; Scully, *The Art of Cookery in the Middle Ages*, 14 n. 6; Techen, "Das Brauwerk in Wismar," 343–44.

39. Behre, "The History of Beer Additives in Europe," 35; Doorman, *De middeleeuwse brouwerij en de gruit*, 44; Loenen, *De Haarlemse brouwindustrie*, 30.

40. The practice was still known in the twentieth century. Hough, *The Biotechnology of Malting and Brewing*, 99, 104, 129. Buijs, "De Bierbrouwer," 46–47; Nordlund,

Brewing and Beer Traditions in Norway, 238–55; Pasteur, *Studies on Fermentation*, 22, 25, 149, 183, 186–87, 221.

41. Pasteur, *Studies on Fermentation*, 223–25, 337–38; Salzman, *English Industries of the Middle Ages*, 293–94.

42. In some districts in Norway in the twentieth century where traditional methods were presumably highly durable, yeast that went to the bottom clearly was the preferred choice of home brewers. If a brewer was not sure about how lively his yeast might be, perhaps through lack of use for some time, he would often blend it with yeast from a neighbor. Those making weaker beers might just leave the wort to ferment, counting on airborne yeasts to get the process started. Räsänen, *Von Halm zum Fass*, 158; Corran, *A History of Brewing*, 46–47; Schultheiss, *Brauwesen und Braurechte*, 13, 16.

43. Ermisch and Wuttke, *Haushaltung in Vorwerken*, 32; Pasteur, *Studies on Fermentation*, 348.

44. Buijs, "De Bierbrouwer," 46; Doorman, *De middeleeuwse brouwerij en de gruit*, 44–45; Loenen, *De Haarlemse brouwindustrie*, 30.

45. Bing, *Hamburgs Bierbrauerei*, 212; Schultheiss, *Brauwesen und Braurechte*, 17; Techen, "Das Brauwerk in Wismar," 347.

46. Hallema and Emmens, *Het bier en zijn brouwers*, 137; Philipsen, "De Amsterdamsche brouwnijverheid," 8; Wilson, *Food and Drink in Britain*, 374.

47. Andrew Boorde writing in England in the first half of the sixteenth century said that ale, made without hops, should be at least five days old before it was drunk. Before that, he claimed, it was unwholesome. Salzman, *English Industries of the Middle Ages*, 285.

48. In English country houses by the late sixteenth century beer was left for a year or even two before being served, at least to noblemen. The servants and other household members would drink a weaker beer usually kept for only about a month before serving. Harrison, *A Description of England*, 93–94.

49. Hoffmann, *5000 Jahre Bier*, 60; Schlosser, *Braurechte, Brauer und Braustätten*, 83–92; Schultheiss, *Brauwesen und Braurechte*, 4–7.

50. Bennett, *Ale, Beer, and Brewsters in England*, 4; King, *Beer Has a History*, 23–24; Monckton, *A History of English Ale and Beer*, 47–54; Salzman, *English Industries of the Middle Ages*, 286–90, 292–93.

51. Bennett, *Ale, Beer, and Brewsters in England*, 107; Doorman, *De middeleeuwse brouwerij en de gruit*, 88.

52. Clement, "De bierbrouwerijen van Gouda," 74–75; Eycken, *Geschiedenis van Diest*, 60; Uytven, *Stadsfinanciën en stadsekonomie te Leuven*, 316.

53. At Utrecht when the price of wheat rose dramatically in 1491, brewers were prohibited from using it and instead had to substitute oats. Muller Fz., *Schetsen uit de middeleeuwen*, 62 n. 1.

54. Sa Leuven: #11592, fol. 1–14 [1568]; Bing, *Hamburgs Bierbrauerei*, 293–94; Bleyswijck, *Beschryvinge der stadt Delft*, 711–13.

55. For example, by malting their grain for a shorter period of time, it was said in 1586, brewers in Wismar could get more beer from the same quantity of grain than brewers in nearby Rostock. Techen, "Das Brauwerk in Wismar," 308.

56. Bruce M. S. Campbell, James A. Galloway, Derek Keene, and Margaret Murphy, *A Medieval Capital and Its Grain Supply: Agrarian Production and Distribution in the London Region c. 1300* (Belfast: The Queen's University and London: Centre for

Metropolitan History, Institute of Historical Research, University of London, 1993), 25; Wilson, *Food and Drink in Britain*, 373.

57. Behre, "The History of Beer Additives in Europe," 35; Herz, "Tabernaemontanus on sixteenth-century beer," 112; Löffler, "Die altesten Bierbücher," 6–7.

58. Bruce M. S. Campbell, *English Seigniorial Agriculture, 1250–1450* (Cambridge: Cambridge University Press, 2000), 243–45; Dyer, *Standards of Living in the Later Middle Ages*, 57.

59. Huntemann, *Das deutsche Braugewerbe*, 30–31; Wee, *The Growth of the Antwerp Market*, 2: 32, 392–93.

60. Corran, *A History of Brewing*, 47; Hoffmann, *5000 Jahre Bier*, 96; Schultheiss, *Brauwesen und Braurechte*, 21; Werneck, "Brauwesen und Hopfenbrau," 84.

61. Janáček, "Pivoarniectví v Čæskych Královských Městech v 16. Století," 75.

62. Huntemann, *Das deutsche Braugewerbe*, 61–62.

63. Doorman, *De middeleeuwse brouwerij en de gruit*, 62; Harrison, *A Description of England*, 100.

64. Aerts, *Het bier van Lier*, 102, 299; Bennett, *Ale, Beer, and Brewsters in England*, 17; Hoffmann, *5000 Jahre Bier*, 96; Uytven, "Bestaansmiddelen," 154–55; Uytven, "De Leuvense bierindustrie," 325.

65. In 1593 the town set new requirements for the composition of beer to stem the fall in quality, but the effort does not appear to have succeeded since even more drastic measures were taken in 1619. Eykens, "De brouwindustrie te Antwerpen," 87–88, 94; Soly, "De economische betekenis," 105–7.

66. Dembinska, *Food and Drink in Medieval Poland*, 78–79.

67. Aerts and Put, "Jezuïetenbier," 112–15, 127–29.

68. Techen, "Das Brauwerk in Wismar," 276–77.

69. Y. S. Brenner, "The Inflation of Prices in Early Sixteenth Century England," *Economic History Review* 14 (1961): 226, 230–32, 239.

70. In the late seventeenth century, Lier brewers turned the pattern of degrading beer around and followed the other option. Instead of following the well-established tradition of watering down their beer they began to make thicker and heavier and stronger beer with a higher alcohol content. The *caves* beer as it was called with not much hops and a little bit of wheat to give it a fresh taste, became popular and the foundation of a thriving export industry. In the second half of the seventeenth century, grain prices fell which gave Lier and all other brewers more flexibility and it is not surprising that some experimented with making stronger beer. Aerts, *Het bier van Lier*, 173, 175–77, 195–98; De Commer, "De brouwindustrie te Ghent," 91.

71. Schultheiss, *Brauwesen und Braurechte*, 23; Techen, "Das Brauwerk in Wismar," 339–40.

72. Monckton, *A History of English Ale and Beer*, 69; Santbergen, *Les bons métiers*, 108–9, 167, 289–90.

73. Bing, *Hamburgs Bierbrauerei*, 255–56.

74. G. A. Leiden, Archieven van de Gilden: #184, #185; Schultheiss, *Brauwesen und Braurechte*, 39.

75. DuPlessis, *Lille and the Dutch Revolt*, 124 n. 12. At Coventry in England in 1513, the town required brewers to continue to make beer no matter how high the price of grain might be. Monckton, *A History of English Ale and Beer*, 94–95. There were similar requirements set at Oxford as early as 1434. Salzman, *English Industries of the Middle Ages*, 293.

76. King, *Beer Has a History*, 68; Techen, "Das Brauwerk in Wismar," 206–7.

77. DuPlessis, *Lille and the Dutch Revolt*, 123; Salzman, *English Industries of the Middle Ages*, 296; Techen, "Das Brauwerk in Wismar," 209.

78. De Commer, "De brouwindustrie te Ghent," 85, 88–90; Soly, "De brouwerij-enonderneming van Gilbert van Schoonbeke," 343; Unger, *Bronnen tot de Geschiedenis van Middelburg*, 3: #781.

79. Bennett, *Ale, Beer, and Brewsters in England*, 22–23.

80. Corran, *A History of Brewing*, 56; Harrison, *A Description of England*, 102.

81. Huntemann, *Das deutsche Braugewerbe*, 28, 34; Muller Fz., *Schetsen uit de Middeleeuwen*, 63; Soly, "De economische betekenis," 115; Hugo Soly, "Nijverheid en kapitalisme te Antwerpen in de 16e eeuw," *Studia historica Gandensia* 193 (1975): 348.

82. Huntemann, *Das deutsche Braugewerbe*, 41–42, 71–72; Langer, "Das Brauge-werbe in den deutschen Hansestädten," 72.

Chapter 10

1. Langer, "Das Braugewerbe in den deutschen Hansestädten," 79; Soly, "De eco-nomische betekenis," 107–11; Soly, "Nijverheid en kapitalisme," 345; Uytven, *Stadsfi-nanciën en stadsekonomie te Leuven*, 336.

2. Bennett, *Ale, Beer, and Brewsters in England*, 50–52.

3. Soly, "De economische betekenis," 105. There were advantages to concentra-tion. Governments saw bringing brewers together as a way to isolate or at least localize the fire danger created by the industry, localize the pollution from the smoke gener-ated, and also bring together the pigs, a serious source of pollution as were all animals in towns which brewers often raised on the spent grains from mashing. The practice of raising pigs on draff then was common among domestic, estate, and commercial brewers. Langer, "Das Braugewerbe in den deutschen Hansestädten," 71, 74; Sim, *Food and Feast in Tudor England*, 48–49; Techen, "Das Brauwerk in Wismar," 328–30.

4. Corran, *A History of Brewing*, 31; Schultheiss, *Brauwesen und Braurechte in Nürn-berg*, 56.

5. Mieczyslaw Grabowski and Georg Schmitt, "'Und das Wasser fliesst in Röh-ren' Wasserversorgung und Wasserkünste in Lübeck,"*Archaeologie des Mittelalters und Bauforschung im Hanseraum: Eine Festschrift für Guenter P. Fehring* (Rostock: Konrad Reich Verlag, 1993), 217–19; Guenter P. Fehring. *The Archaeology of Medieval Germany: An Introduction* (London: Routledge, 1991), 209. I am grateful to Mark Peterson for information about the Lübeck water supply system.

6. Ian Donnachie, *A History of the Brewing Industry in Scotland* (Edinburgh: John Donald, 1979), 2; Unger, *A History of Brewing in Holland*, 166–69, 298–302.

7. In the 1530s output was about 10,500,000 liters per year, but the annual average was some 25,500,000 liters per year from 1558 to 1563 and climbed to 45,000,000 liters per year by the early 1580s. As late as 1542–1543, Antwerp imported over 11,500,000 liters of beer a year. In the 1550s Antwerp began to export beer largely to nearby markets and especially to those in Zeeland. In twelve months in 1559–1560 Antwerp sent out a little over 3,000,000 liters of beer. Soly, "De brouwerijenonderneming van Gilbert van Schoonbeke," 346–47, 352–57, 360–63, 367–74, 1166–76, 1182–86, 1194–95, 1200, 1203; Soly, *Urbanisme en kapitalisme*, 288–307, 310–19.

8. There production rose from about 8,000,000 liters in 1482 to 16,000,000 in

1580, about a third of the Antwerp figures. Soly, "De brouwerijenonderneming van Gilbert van Schoonbeke," 347–49, 355–74, 1187, 1198; Soly, *Urbanisme en kapitalisme*, 294, 307, 312; Soly and Thys, "Nijverheid in de zuidelijke Nederlanden," 47.

9. Buijs, "De Bierbrouwer," 19–20; De Clerck, *A Textbook of Brewing*, 312–13.

10. Unger, *A History of Brewing in Holland*, 174–82.

11. Dillen, *Bronnen tot de geschiedenis van het bedrijfsleven*, 1: #18–9; Doorman, *De middeleeuwse brouwerij en de gruit*, 48–49.

12. Loenen, *De Haarlemse brouwindustrie*, 87; Soly, "De economische betekenis," 111–13.

13. Nordlund, *Brewing and Beer Traditions in Norway*, 59; Thunæus, *Ölets historia i Sverige*, 1: 141.

14. Doorman, *De middeleeuwse brouwerij en de gruit*, 65; Huntemann, *Das deutsche Braugewerbe*, 10–12.

15. Huntemann, *Das deutsche Braugewerbe*, 10, 75; Niehoff, "Bierproduktion und Bierkonsum," 170–71; Langer, "Das Braugewerbe in den deutschen Hansestädten," 70–71; Techen, "Das Brauwerk in Wismar," 333.

16. Doorman, *De middeleeuwse brouwerij en de gruit*, 49, 61.

17. Aerts, *Het bier van Lier*, 94, 185.

18. Around 1585 Coventry had thirteen common brewers whose average production of about 4,500 litres per week in the weeks they brewed. Leicester had five large common brewers who dominated output in the town at the same time. Bennett, *Ale, Beer, and Brewsters in England*, 48–49, 115–16; Clark, *The English Alehouse*, 106–7; Stopes, *Malt and Malting*, 10.

19. Techen, "Das Brauwerk in Wismar," 337, 339–40.

20. Brasseurs de bière de le ville de Paris, *Articles contenent les statuts et Ordonnances des Maitres Jurez* (16 March 1730), 7.

21. Leo Noordegraaf, "Betriebsformen und Arbeitsorganisation im Gewerbe der nördlichen Niederlande, 1400–1800," in Konrad Fritze, Eckhard Müller-Mertens, Johannes Schildhauer, eds., *Hansische Studien IV: Gewerbliche Produktion und Stadt-Land-Beziehungen Abhandlungen zur Handels- und Sozialgeschichte*, 18 (Weimar: Verlag Hermann Böhlaus Nachfolger, 1979), 54–64.

22. The distinction, established already by the fourteenth century in Hamburg, between brewers for the home market and brewers for export was not the same as regulations which divided brewers along lines of the total beer they produced. However, often in Hamburg and in other north German towns, the brewers who made for export were typically the bigger producers. See Chapter 4 above on Hamburg regulations. Langer, "Das Braugewerbe in den deutschen Hansestädten," 72–73.

23. Emmison, *Tudor Food and Pastimes*, 57; Harrison, *A Description of England*, 100–101; J. A. Ten Cate, "Verslag van een onderzoek naar de geschiedenis van het Amsterdamse brouwersbedrijf in de 17e eeuw" (Unpublished doctoraal scriptie, economisch-historisch seminarium, University of Amsterdam, #118, 1940), 2.

24. Bing, *Hamburgs Bierbrauerei*, 257–59; De Commer, "De Brouwindustrie te Ghent," 127–28, 145; Uytven, *Stadsfinanciën en stadsekonomie*, 326.

25. Glamann, "Beer and Brewing in Pre-Industrial Denmark," 133; Soly, "De economische betekenis," 113–44.

26. Santbergen, *Les bons métiers*," 66–69, 236–37; Uytven, "Bier und Brauer," 12.

27. Prevenier and Blockmans, *The Burgundian Netherlands*, 178; Schultheiss, *Brauwesen und Braurechte in Nürnberg*, 69; Techen, "Das Brauwerk in Wismar," 269.

28. In the second half of the sixteenth century a wave of local ordinances prohibited English food suppliers from brewing their own beer. The new rules in places as varied as Wallingford, Stratford, Norwich, Gloucester, Taunton, Shrewsbury, and Marlborough forced those people to buy from common brewers. The regulations may reflect less a desire to control the trade and more the great political influence which brewers enjoyed in English towns. Clark, *The English Alehouse*, 107.

29. Bennett, *Ale, Beer, and Brewsters in England*, 50–51; Doorman, *De middeleeuwse brouwerij en de gruit*, 54; Huntemann, *Das deutsche Braugewerbe*, 77–78.

30. Aerts, *Het bier van Lier*, 97–101; Uytven, "Bier und Brauer," 13.

Chapter 11

1. Langer, "Das Braugewerbe in den deutschen Hansestädten," 79; Techen, "Das Brauwerk in Wismar," 145.

2. Glamann, "Beer and Brewing," 135–36; Uytven, "Bier und Brauer," 18.

3. Abel, *Stufen der Ernährung*, 23.

4. Eycken, *Geschiedenis van Diest*, 60.

5. Schultheiss, *Brauwesen und Braurechte in Nürnberg*, 6, 18–20, 84–86. Other towns had similar divisions. In late fourteenth-century Lübeck, the distinction was among *dickeber*, *penningber*, and *stopbier* with the last only sold in taverns. In the next century the division in Hannover was threefold among a strong, a thin, and a cellar beer with the last name possibly having more to do with the age of the beer than its strength. At Hamburg the distinction around 1500 was beer, middle beer, and then some lesser beers. Techen, "Das Brauwerk in Wismar," 148.

6. The healing qualities of beer from Dordrecht were hailed by at least one writer. Abel, *Stufen der Ernährung*, 22; Hallema and Emmens, *Het bier en zijn brouwers*, 74.

7. Bracker, "Hopbier uit Hamburg," 32; Hallema and Emmens, *Het bier en zijn brouwers*, 124; Huntemann, *Das deutsche Braugewerbe*, 12; Räsänen, *Von Halm zum Fass*, 37; Thunæus, *Ölets historia i Sverige*, 1: 121; C. Verlinden, and J. Craeybeckx, *Prijzen- en lonenpolitiek in de Nederlanden in 1561 en 1588–1589: Onuitgegeven adviezen, ontwerpen en ordonnanties* (Brussels: Koninlijke Belgische academie, koninklijke commissie voor geschiedenis, 1962), 85.

8. Niehoff, "Bremer Bier im Baltikum," 15.

9. The word for the type of beer gave rise to *godalier* or *goudalier* which meant a drunken and dissolute person, at least by the fifteenth century. It was often used referring to Englishmen who from the thirteenth century on enjoyed a reputation in France for being heavy drinkers. Rickard, *Britain in Medieval French Literature*, 167–69; Scully, *The Art of Cookery*, 153. The reputation extended further afield and had a long history. See above, Chapter 2.

10. Doorman, *De middeleeuwse brouwerij en de gruit*, 66–67; Moulin, "Bière, houblon et cervoise," 113; Siebel, *One Hundred Years of Brewing*, 697.

11. Corran, *A History of Brewing*, 40; Sambrook, *Country House Brewing*, 110.

12. Aerts, *Het bier van Lier*, 46–47; 155–56, 189, 195–96; Aerts and Put, "Jezuïetenbier," 116–17, 124; Eykens, "De brouwindustrie te Antwerpen," 85–86; Soly, "De brouwerijenonderneming van Gilbert van Schoonbeke," 342.

13. De Commer, "De brouwindustrie te Ghent," 85. Ghent brewers, presumably with the full agreement of government, did suspend the production of luxury beers on

occasion for a year or two because grain costs were so high and all agreed making more of the low quality beer was the correct use of expensive raw material.

14. De Commer, "De brouwindustrie te Ghent," 89, 95, 115–18, 121–23, 142.

15. De Commer, "De brouwindustrie te Ghent," 84.

16. Under the 1441 English assize, which included beer as well as ale, double *kuit* or coyt cost one-third more than single and while the price of single coyt was fixed the price of double varied with the price of grain. Wilson, *Food and Drink in Britain*, 375; L. F. Salzman, *English Life in the Middle Ages* (Oxford: Oxford University Press, 1921), 293–94; Uytven, "Bier und Brauer," 18.

17. G. A. Veere: #311, fols. 100v–102r; Soly, "De brouwerijenonderneming van Gilbert van Schoonbeke," 342.

18. In 1552 in London there were two beers, single and double, the latter being twice the price of the former. Perversely the same quantity of grain yielded just 89 percent more single beer than double beer so single gave greater value. Corran, *A History of Brewing*, 69; Monckton, *A History of English Ale and Beer*, 106–7. Doble-doble was presumably the best product to come out of breweries though there were other drinks like huffcap and in the seventeenth century stingo which might have claimed that honor. Martin, *Alcohol, Sex, and Gender* 30; Wilson, *Food and Drink in Britain*, 377.

19. Dembinska, *Food and Drink in Medieval Poland*, 80; Hallema and Emmens, *Het bier en zijn brouwers*, 76, 80; Soly and Thys, "Nijverheid in de zuidelijke Nederlanden," 47; Unger, *Bronnen tot de geschiedenis van Middelburg*, 3: 553.

20. Hallema and Emmens, *Het bier en zijn brouwers*, 76; Huntemann, *Das deutsche Braugewerbe*, 12, 57; Uytven, "L'approvisionnement des villes des anciens Pays-Bas," 91.

21. Bing, *Hamburgs Bierbrauerei*, 254–55; Eykens, "De brouwindustrie te Antwerpen," 86; Techen, "Das Brauwerk in Wismar," 153–54.

22. One exception was the Utrecht government which in an unusual move in 1468 prohibited the production of thin beer in order to force consumers to turn to thick, heavy beer which carried a higher price and with it a higher tax burden. Elevated excises on imported beers made it hard for customers to find alternatives. Muller Fz., *Schetsen uit de middeleeuwen*, 66. In Ghent a 1360 ordinance required brewers who used to make low-quality beer to continue, and in 1366 they could get permission to make beer of the highest quality only if they kept on making middle and poor quality beer. Uytven, "L'approvisionnement des villes des anciens Pays-Bas," 91.

23. G. A. Amsterdam, Gilden Archieven: #1669, 29, 1–2. It was sold both to shippers for sailors to drink and to shipbuilders in Amsterdam. Posthumus, *De Uitvoer van Amsterdam*, 33. See above, Chapter 7.

24. G. A. Delft, Eerste Afdeling: #950; Timmer, "Uit de nadagen der Delftsche brouwnering," 312.

25. Thunæus, *Ölets historia i Sverige*, 1: 121.

26. Aerts, *Het bier van Lier*, 84; De Commer, "De brouwindustrie te Ghent," 102, 106, 132; Uytven, "Bestaansmiddelen," 156; Uytven, *Stadsfinanciën en stadsekonomie*, 332.

27. There was a long history of levies on imported Hamburg beer in Flanders. See above, Chapter 6. Bing, *Hamburgs Bierbrauerei*, 231–32.

28. See Chapter 4, above. Techen, "Das Brauwerk in Wismar," 182–89; Unger, *A History of Brewing in Holland*, 249–58.

29. Bracker, "Hopbier uit Hamburg," 32; Siebel, *One Hundred Years of Brewing*, 28.

30. Bing, *Hamburgs Bierbrauerei*, 285–88.

31. See Chapter 7, above. Langer, "Das Braugewerbe in den deutschen Hansestädten," 67; Victor Lauffer, "Danzigs Schiffs- und Waarenverkehr am Ende des XV. Jahrhunderts." *Zeitschrift des Westpreussischen Geschichtsvereins* 33 (1894): 28; Techen, "Das Brauwerk in Wismar," 163–64.

32. Langer, "Das Braugewerbe in den deutschen Hansestädten," 67; Löffler, "Die altesten Bierbücher," 7; Techen, "Das Brauwerk in Wismar," 160–62.

33. Kathleen Kish, "Celestina Speaks Dutch—in the Sixteenth Century Spanish Netherlands," in John S. Miletich, ed., *Hispanic Studies in Honor of Alan D. Deyermond A North American Tribute* (Madison: Hispanic Seminary of Medieval Studies, 1986), 171–82.

34. Balberghe, *De Mechelse bierhandel*, 54–56; Soly, "De brouwerijenonderneming van Gilbert van Schoonbeke," 1188; P. H. Winkelman, ed., *Nederlandse rekeningen in de tolregisters van Koningsbergen, 1588–1602: Bronnen voor de geschiedenis van de Nederlandse Oostzeehandel in de zeventiende Eeuw* (The Hague: Martinus Nijhoff, 1971), 1: 18 March 1589, 9 April 1602.

35. Unger, *De Tol van Iersekeroord, passim*.

36. Smit, *Bronnen tot de geschiedenis van den handel*, 1: #2002, 2: #1060, #1062, #1103, #1231.

37. Smit, *Bronnen tot de geschiedenis van den handel*, for example 2: #967, #1033, #1080, #1105, #1137, #1210.

38. Clark, *The English Alehouse*, 106; Dillen, *Bronnen tot de geschiedenis van het bedrijfsleven*, 1: #555, 556.

39. Dalen, *Geschiedenis van Dordrecht*, 1: 389; Grolsche Bierbrouwerij, *Merckwaerdighe Bierologie*, 52–53; Hoffmann, *5000 Jahre Bier*, 71–72; Techen, "Das Brauwerk in Wismar," 148–50.

40. Grässe, *Bierstudien*, 40–42; Pilgrim, "Der Durst auf den Weltmeeren," 86; Techen, "Das Brauwerk in Wismar," 186.

41. Corran, *A History of Brewing*, 48–49; Grässe, *Bierstudien*, 35; Hallema and Emmens, *Het bier en zijn brouwers*, 122; Hoffmann, *5000 Jahre Bier*, 72; Siebel, *One Hundred Years of Brewing*, 29.

Chapter 12

1. Clark, *The English Alehouse*, 102–3; Peter Mathias, "Brewing archives: their nature and use," in Lesley Richmond and Alison Turton, eds., *The brewing industry A guide to historical records* (Manchester: Manchester University Press, 1990), 26–27; Peter Mathias, *The Brewing Industry in England, 1700–1830* (Cambridge: Cambridge University Press, 1959), 28–30.

2. Huntemann, *Das deutsche Braugewerbe*, 25–26, 44, 56, 79–80; Schultheiss, *Brauwesen und Braurechte in Nürnberg*, 100–101, 106.

3. G. A. Dordrecht, De Grafelijke Tijd 1200–1572: #433, #436; Loenen, *De Haarlemse brouwindustrie*, 12–13.

4. Aerts, "De Zuidnederlandse brouwindustrie," 14–15, 23; Craeybeckx, *Un grand commerce d'importation*, 8; De Roover, "Les comptes communaux," 94; Doorman,

Techniek en octrooiwezen, 27, 100–101; Huntemann, *Das deutsche Braugewerbe*, 44–45; Loenen, *De Haarlemse brouwindustrie*, 10–17; Schulte,"Vom Grutbiere," 137; Soly, "De brouwerijenonderneming van Gilbert van Schoonbeke," 339–40; Uytven, *Stadsfinanciën en stadsekonomie te Leuven*, 313.

5. G. A. Haarlem, Thesauriersrekeningen: #136–140, #175–184; Hallema and Emmens, *Het bier en zijn brouwers*, 42–43, 45, 54.

6. De Commer, "De brouwindustrie te Ghent," 106, 110; Lejeune, *La formation du capitalisme moderne*, 107–8, 121; Soly, "De brouwerijenonderneming van Gilbert van Schoonbeke," 339–40.

7. Bennett, *Ale, Beer, and Brewsters in England*, 99–101; Clark, *The English Alehouse*, 28; Monckton, *A History of English Ale*, 113–14.

8. Nicholas Mayhew, "The Status of Women and the Brewing of Ale in Medieval Aberdeen," *Review of Scottish Culture* 10 (1966–67): 17–18. On the Continent brewers often did not reach the maximum possible levels of output. See above, Chapter 10 and table 10.

9. Bing, *Hamburgs Bierbrauerei*, 306; Eykens, "De brouwindustrie te Antwerpen," 87; Huntemann, *Das deutsche Braugewerbe*, 35–36, 66–68; Martens, "Bier en stadsfinancien te Hasselt," 247.

10. Uytven, *Stadsfinancien en stadsekonomie te Leuven*, 332.

11. Bing, *Hamburgs Bierbrauerei*, 239, 287–88, 307.

12. Doorman, *De middeleeuwse brouwerij en de gruit*, 24–25; Huntemann, *Das deutsche Braugewerbe*, 50–51; Verlinden and Craeybeckx, *Prijzen- en lonenpolitiek*, 142.

13. Noordkerk, *Handvesten ofte Privilegien ende Octroyen*, 18, 171–72; Philipsen, "De Amsterdamsche brouwnijverheid," 12; P. Scheltema, *Inventaris van het Amsterdamsche archief* (Amsterdam: Stads-Druckkerij, 1866–1874), 1: 76–77; Uytven, "Het bierverbruik en de sociaal-economische toestand," 22; Unger, *A History of Brewing in Holland*, 182–89; Wagenaar, *Amsterdam in zyne opkomst*, 8: 227.

14. Langer, "Das Braugewerbe in den deutschen Hansestädten," 70; Techen, "Das Brauwerk in Wismar," 174.

15. De Commer, "De brouwindustrie te Ghent," 87, 103; Soly, "De brouwerijenonderneming van Gilbert van Schoonbeke," 1202; Uytven, "Bestaansmiddelen," 155–56; Uytven, *Stadsfinanciën en stadsekonomie te Leuven*, 329–30.

16. Verlinden and Craeybeckx, *Prijzen- en lonenpolitiek*, 53–64, 78, 84, 96, 102–3, 113.

17. Bennett, *Ale, Beer, and Brewsters in England*, 50–51, 80–81.

18. W. F. H. Oldewelt, "De Hollandse imposten en ons beeld van de conjunctuur tijdens de Republiek," *Jaarboek Amstelodamum* 47 (1955): 55; Unger, *De tol van Iersekeroord*, 106.

19. Amsterdam, as a number of other towns in the Low Countries, had similar requirements with heavy penalties for failure to comply, as early as 1497. J. C. Breen, *Rechtsbronnen der stad Amsterdam* (The Hague: Martinus Nijhoff, 1902), 1497, 18; Philipsen, "De Amsterdamsche brouwnijverheid," 13–14.

20. Receipts at Ghent had a life of one day while at Amsterdam they were good for fourteen days, and were renewable on permission of the excise collector. The flexibility helped to avoid trouble. Noordkerk, *Handvesten ofte Privilegien ende Octroyen*, 177–79 [1586].

21. Penninck, *Het bier te Brugge*, 20.

22. If the brewer sold more beer than he reported, then he was liable for tax on

any excess. There was also the danger of a fine for violating the rules. On Ghent, see De Commer, "De Brouwindustrie te Ghent," 97–100. At Hoorn in Holland, for example, the hours were from 8 a.m. to 11 a.m. and from 1 p.m. to 4 p.m. with no variation for time of the year. G. A. Hoorn: #305 [1611].

23. G. A. Leiden, Archieven van de Gilden: #191, 22–34, 39–43, #198; Cau, van Leeuwen, and Scheltus, eds., *Groot Placaatboek*, 1: 1708–15 [1632], 2048–59.

24. Noordkerk, *Handvesten ofte Privilegien ende Octroyen*, 177–79 [1586]; Timmer, *De generale brouwers van Holland*, 9–10.

25. Dillen, *Bronnen tot de geschiedenis van het bedrijfsleven*, 1: #441 [1558], #514 [1564]; Penninck, *Het bier te Brugge*, 17–18; Techen, "Das Brauwerk in Wismar," 279–80.

26. Bleyswijck, *Beschryvinge der stadt Delft*, 726–27. In the late seventeenth and eighteenth century, Dutch brewers became almost obsessed with getting their barrels back. Unger, *A History of Brewing in Holland*, 264, 306–12.

27. Bennett, *Ale, Beer, and Brewsters in England*, 91; Breen, *Rechtsbronnen der stad Amsterdam*, 1497, 14.

Chapter 13

1. Noordegraaf, "Betriebsformen und Arbeitsorganisation," 64; Soly, "Nijverheid en kapitalisme," 345–46.

2. Philipsen, "De Amsterdamsche brouwnijverheid," 1–2, 5; Siebel, *One Hundred Years of Brewing*, 19.

3. Amsterdam, for example, never had a brewers' guild, but by 1437 there was a guild for the beer porters so towns were willing to use guilds to regulate some aspects of brewing. I. H. van Eeghen, *Inventarissen der archieven van de gilden en van het brouwerscollege* (Amsterdam: Stadsdruckkerij, 1951), 21; Eykens, "De brouwindustrie te Antwerpen," 82–83; Soly, "De economische betekenis," 112.

4. Janáček, "Pivoarniectví v Českych Královských Městech v 16. Století," 75; Löhdefink, *Die Entwicklung der Brauergilde*, 29, 36.

5. Langer, "Das Braugewerbe in den deutschen Hansestädten," 75.

6. Aerts, *Het bier van Lier*, 110, 113–15; Émile Coornaert, *Les corporations en France avant 1789*, 2nd ed. (Paris: Les Éditions ouvrières, 1968), 49, 57–58; Santbergen, *Les bons métiers*, 56–57, 63, 99.

7. On divisions between production and retailing see above, Chapter 12. Sa Leuven, #11592, Archive de la nation des brasseurs: 1–14, 69–79; Uytven, *Stadsfinanciën en stadsekonomie te Leuven*, 329.

8. Bing, *Hamburgs Bierbrauerei*, 269–71; Techen, "Das Brauwerk in Wismar," 268, 275.

9. On brewers' guilds in Holland before 1620 see Unger, *A History of Brewing in Holland*, 199–221; Breen, "Aanteekeningen uit de geschiedenis," 75; Eeghen, *Inventarissen der archieven*, 127; Philipsen, "De Amsterdamsche brouwnijverheid," 1–2; Willem van Ravesteyn, Jr., *Onderzoekingen over de economische en sociale ontwikkeling van Amsterdam gedurende de 16de en het eerste kwart der 17de Eeuw* (Amsterdam: S. L. Van Looy, 1906), 162.

10. Brasseurs de bière de le ville de Paris, *Articles contenent les statuts*, 1; Charlie,

L'évolution économique, 155; Moulin, "Bière, houblon et cervoise," 118; Unger, "De economische ontwikkeling van Middelburg," 46–48.

11. Donnachie, *A History of the Brewing Industry*, 2. On investment in water supplies in general see above, Chapter 10.

12. PRO: C 47/46/471, C 47/42/206; H. F. Westlake, *The Parish Guilds of Mediæval England* (London: Society for the Propagation of Christian Knowledge, 1919), 27, 185, 238. I am indebted to Caroline Barron for pointing out the source to me.

13. London Guildhall, MS. 5425; Bennett, *Ale, Beer, and Brewsters in England*, 62; King, *Beer Has a History*, 38, 42, 46; Salzman, *English Industries of the Middle Ages*, 295; Sylvia L. Thrupp, "A Survey of the Alien Population of England in 1440," *Speculum* 32 (1957): 265–67.

14. London Guildhall, MSS. 5425, 5427, 5428; Hackwood, *Inns, Ales, and Drinking Customs*, 82; King, *Beer Has a History*, 64.

15. London Guildhall, MSS. 5426–5429, 5432; Bennett, *Ale, Beer, and Brewsters in England*, 62; Corran *A History of Brewing*, 64–65, 88; King, *Beer Has a History*, 64–65.

16. Clark, *The English Alehouse*, 107.

17. On concentration, see above, Chapter 10. Noordegraaf, "Betriebsformen und Arbeitsorganisation," 60.

18. Brasseurs de bière de le ville de Paris, *Articles contenent les statuts*, 13; Bing, *Hamburgs Bierbrauerei*, 267.

19. Prevenier and Blockmans, *The Burgundian Netherlands*, 164; Santbergen, *Les bons métiers*, 93, 100–103, 108–11.

20. Loenen, *De Haarlemse brouwindustrie*, 83–85, 109; Schlosser, *Braurechte, Brauer und Braustätten*, 25–26, 84; Techen, "Das Brauwerk in Wismar," 281.

21. Techen, "Das Brauwerk in Wismar," 283, 286, 298–99; Walford, *Gilds*, 213.

22. Bing, *Hamburgs Bierbrauerei*, 268; Loenen, *De Haarlemse Brouwindustrie*, 94; Santbergen, *Les bons métiers*, 170.

23. A 1438 Amsterdam regulation, for instance, suggests that some brewers there dealt in grain. Unger, *De Levenmiddelenvoorziening*, 67–68. Hamburg in 1459 took the somewhat unusual step of outlawing grain dealing by brewers. The rule was presumably to inhibit concentration in the industry. Bing, *Hamburgs Bierbrauerei*, 249; Langer, "Das Braugewerbe in den deutschen Hansestädten," 73–74.

24. Charlie, *L'évolution économique*, 4–9, 153–63; Urion and Eyer, *La bière*, 29, 35.

25. Brasseurs de bière de le ville de Paris, *Articles contenent les statuts*, 2, 12, 14.

26. Liege oddly had a category of apprentice but no apprenticeship was required of aspiring brewers through the fourteenth, fifteenth, and sixteenth centuries. Santbergen, *Les bons métiers*, 138–139. Aerts, *Het bier van Lier*, 112; Penninck, *Het bier te Brugge*, 10; Schlosser, *Braurechte, Brauer und Braustätten*, 22, 35, 93–94.

27. Brasseurs de Bière de le Ville de Paris, *Articles contenent les statuts*, 17 [1514]; Eykens, "De brouwindustrie te Antwerpen," 83; King, *Beer Has a History*, 46; Martens, "Bier en stadsfinancien te Hasselt," 255; Santbergen, *Les bons métiers*, 198.

28. Charlie, *L'évolution économique*, 155–63; De Commer, "De Brouwindustrie te Ghent," 100; Penninck, *Het bier te Brugge*, 14–5; Techen, "Das Brauwerk in Wismar," 348–49.

29. Brasseurs de bière de le ville de Paris, *Articles contenent les statuts*, 5, 8; Eykens, "De brouwindustrie te Antwerpen," 84.

30. For example, at Nuremberg by the fifteenth century a city *braumeister*

responsible to the town government made sure that the ordinance on beer making was followed. He got assistance and also greater scope for his authority as time passed. Schultheiss, *Brauwesen und Braurechte in Nürnberg*, 59–60. Hamburg beginning in the fifteenth century had a town official in the harbor testing export beer. See above, Chapter 4. English ale conners who dated from the eleventh century or aletasters from the early thirteenth century were similar independent government agents. See above, Chapter 12.

31. Martens, "Bier en stadsfinancien te Hasselt," 249; Santbergen, *Les bons métiers*, 197.

32. Balberghe, *De Mechelse bierhandel*, 15–16; Eykens, "De brouwindustrie te Antwerpen," 98–99; King, *Beer Has a History*, 46–48; Klonder, "Rachunki cechu browarników Starego Miasta Elbląga," 210; Monckton, *A History of English Ale*, 72; Santbergen, *Les bons métiers*, 186.

33. Balberghe, *De Mechelse bierhandel*, 17–18; Eykens, "De brouwindustrie te Antwerpen," 85; Penninck, *Het bier te Brugge*, 15–6.

34. Bemmel, *Beschryving der stad Amersfoort*, 2: 774; Halbertsma, *Zeven eeuwen Amersfoort*, 42–43; Loenen, *De Haarlemse brouwindustrie*, 39; Rootselaar, *Amersfoort 777–1580*, 2: 174.

35. Bing, *Hamburgs Bierbrauerei*, 276–77.

36. Brasseurs de Bière de la Ville de Paris, *Articles contenent les statuts*, 6–7.

37. Bing, *Hamburgs Bierbrauerei*, 263; Thunæus, *Ölets historia i Sverige*, 1: 152.

38. Hoekstra, "Het Haarlems brouwersbedrijf," 10; Soly, *Urbanisme en kapitalisme*, 288–97.

39. G. A. Dordrecht, Archief van de Gilden: #930, 35 [1614]; G. A. Vlissingen, Archieven der Gilden: #134, 6 [1598].

40. On the English act of Parliament of 1531 establishing the size of beer and ale barrels, see above, Chapter 6 and on standard barrels in north Germany see above, Chapter 4. Monckton, *A History of English Ale*, 68–69; Rootselaar, *Amersfoort, Sprokkelingen*, XCVI.

41. Pieter Hendrik Engels, *De belastingen en de geldmiddelen van den aanvang der Republiek tot op heden* (Utrecht: Kemink en Zoon, 1862), 61; Walford, *Gilds*, 212.

42. In some places it was even illegal for them to do so, as at Lier and at Southampton from 1478 on and at Ghent after 1579. Bennett, *Ale, Beer, and Brewsters in England*, 46; De Commer, "De brouwindustrie te Ghent," 94. In other cases those who brewed for their own pubs could sell only their own beer and were separated legally from those who sold on an open market, as at Leuven. Uytven, "Bestaansmiddelen," 156–57. On divisions between producers and retailers, see Chapter 12.

43. Bennett, *Ale, Beer, and Brewsters in England*, 20–21, 40–41, 45–47, 106–7; Clark, *The English Alehouse*, 145–66; A. T. van Deursen, *Plain Lives in a Golden Age Popular Culture, Religion and Society in Seventeenth-Century Holland*, trans. Maarten Ultee (Cambridge: Cambridge University Press, 1991), 102, 106; W. G. D. Murray, "Oud-Rotterdamsch kroegleven," *Rotterdamsche jaarboekje*, 5th series, 2 (1944): 40–78.

44. Bing, *Hamburgs Bierbrauerei*, 282–83; Soly, "De economische betekenis," 111; Techen, "Das Brauwerk in Wismar," 169–73; Walford, *Gilds*, 212.

45. Liege may have been a little more lenient on that matter. Bennett, *Ale, Beer, and Brewsters in England*, 89; Bing, *Hamburgs Bierbrauerei*, 273–76; Brasseurs de bière de la ville de Paris, *Articles contenent les statuts*, 11; Langer, "Das Braugewerbe in den deutschen Hansestädten," 75–78; Santbergen, *Les bons métiers*, 160.

46. Aerts, "De Zuidnederlandse brouwindustrie," 14; Noordegraaf, "Betriebsformen und Arbeitsorganisation," 63.

47. Langer, "Das Braugewerbe in den deutschen Hansestädten," 79.

48. Emmison, *Tudor Food*, 57; Walford, *Gilds*, 213.

49. Penninck, *Het bier te Brugge*, 20.

50. Bing, *Hamburgs Bierbrauerei*, 275; Eykens, "De brouwindustrie te Antwerpen," 96; Soly, "De brouwerijenonderneming van Gilbert van Schoonbeke," 1191; Techen, "Das Brauwerk in Wismar," 276.

51. Hoffmann, *5000 Jahre Bier*, 96–97; N. W. Posthumus, *De uitvoer van Amsterdam 1543–1545* (Leiden: E. J. Brill, 1971), 33.

52. Bennett, *Ale, Beer, and Brewsters in England*, 60–70, 113; Soly, "Nijverheid en kapitalisme," 346–51.

53. PRO: SP 16/341/124; Bennett, *Ale, Beer, and Brewsters in England*, 91. I am grateful to Judith Bennett for supplying me with a transcription of the document in the Public Records Office.

54. Bennett, "The Village Ale-Wife," 22.

55. Bennett, *Ale, Beer, and Brewsters in England*, 18–19, 24–27, 43–59.

56. Caesarius of Heisterbach, *The Dialogue on Miracles*, 2: 65, 198–99; Doorman, *De middeleeuwse brouwerij en de gruit*, 51–52.

57. Bennett, *Ale, Beer, and Brewsters in England*, 145.

58. Bennett, *Ale, Beer, and Brewsters in England*, 35–36, 60–61, 149, 166–68; Urion and Eyer, *La Bière*, 33.

59. Bennett, *Ale, Beer, and Brewsters in England*, 61–63, 70–73.

60. Bennett, *Ale, Beer, and Brewsters in England*, 145.

61. Mayhew, "The Status of Women," 16–17.

62. R. Bijlsma, *Rotterdams welvaren 1550–1650* (The Hague: Martinus Nijhoff, 1918), 104; Uytven, "Bier und Brauer," 12.

63. Grethe Jacobsen, "Women's Work and Women's Role: Ideology and Reality in Danish Urban Society," *Scandinavian Economic History Review* 31 (1983): 4; Thunæus, *Ölets historia i Sverige*, 1: 122–25.

64. Brasseurs de bière de la ville de Paris, *Articles contenent les statuts*, 15; Houwen, "De Haarlemsche brouwerij," 38; Merry E. Wiesner, *Working Women in Renaissance Germany* (New Brunswick, N.J.: Rutgers University Press, 1986), 128–29, 190–91. In sixteenth-century England, it was as successors of their late husbands that women were the heads of brewing firms. Bennett, *Ale, Beer, and Brewsters in England*, 57.

65. Hugo Soly, "De Antwerpse onderneemster Anna Janssens en de economische boom na de vrede van Cateau-Cambrésis (1559)," *Bijdragen tot de geschiedenis* 52 (1969): 142–62.

66. Jacobsen, "Women's Work," 17–18; Wiesner, *Working Women*, 127, 129.

67. Bennett, *Ale, Beer, and Brewsters in England*, 56.

68. Judith M. Bennett, "Work in Progress: Misogyny, Popular Culture, and Women's Work," *History Workshop a journal of socialist and feminist historians* 31 (spring, 1991): 168–87; Bennett, *Ale, Beer, and Brewsters in England*, 123–40; Penninck, *Het bier te Brugge*, 12.

69. Glamann, "Beer and Brewing," 133; Soly, "Nijverheid en kapitalisme," 345 n. 60.

70. Richard W. Unger, *Dutch Shipbuilding Before 1800: Ships and Guilds* (Assen: Van Gorcum, 1978), 78–82.

Chapter 14

1. Unger, "Technical Change in the Brewing Industry," 281–313.

2. Brewers in Rostock and Gdansk already in the sixteenth century began to export beer westward. The figures rose sharply so that in the 1580s Rostock was shipping out something close to 1,500,000 liters of beer each year, Dutch consumers taking about 10 percent of the volume. So Rostock beer displaced Hamburg and Bremen beer. Huntemann, *Das deutsche Braugewerbe*, 19, 53; Niehoff, "Bremer Bier im Baltikum," 21.

3. Daenell, *Die Blütezeit der deutschen Hanse*, 2: 386–88; Dollinger, *La hanse*, 243, 300, 366, 438; Langer, "Das Braugewerbe in den deutschen Hansestädten," 67, 70; Thunæus, *Ölets historia i Sverige*, 1: 127, 259.

4. R. Bijlsma, "De opkomst van Rotterdams koopvaardij," *Bijdragen voor vaderlandsche geschiedenis en oudheidkunde*, 5th series, 1 (1913): 78–81; Unger, *A History of Brewing in Holland*, 222–44.

5. G. A. Veere: #311, fol. 97v–98r [1541].

6. Corran, *A History of Brewing*, 65–66; King, *Beer Has a History*, 56; Monckton, *A History of English Ale*, 45, 98.

7. On comments on the popularity of English beer in 1617, see above, Chapter 7. F. B. M. Tangelder, *Nederlandse rekeningen in de pontolregisters van Elbing, 1585–1602* (The Hague: Martinus Nijhoff, 1972), 1596; Ter Gouw, *Geschiedenis van Amsterdam*, 3: 254.

8. Donnachie, *A History of the Brewing Industry*, 3.

9. J. F. Niermeyer, *De wording van onze volkshuishouding. Hoofdlijnen uit de economische geschiedenis der noordelijke Nederlanden in de middeleeuwen* (The Hague: N. V. Servire, 1946), 98.

10. De Commer, "De brouwindustrie te Ghent," 83, 91–94; Soly, "De economische betekenis," 103; Ten Cate, "Verslag van een onderzoek," 17; Th. F. Wijsenbeek-Olthuis, "Ondernemen in moeilijke tijden: Delftse bierbrouwers en plateelbakkers in de achttiende eeuw," *Economisch- en sociaal-historisch jaarboek* 44 (1982): 70.

11. Jean Maurice Bizière, "The Baltic Wine Trade," *Scandinavian Economic History Review* 20 (1972): 121–26, 132; Monckton. *A History of English Ale*, 142–43.

12. Falling real incomes contributed to the decline in laborers' beer-buying power. Aerts, *Het bier van Lier*, 180.

13. Aerts and Put, "Jezuïetenbier," 112.

14. Abel, *Stufen der Ernährung*, 51–53; Bing, *Hamburgs Bierbrauerei*, 314.

15. For example at Amsterdam, see Dillen, *Bronnen tot de Geschiedenis*, I, #478 [1561].

16. Pieter Jan Dobbelaar, *De branderijen in Holland tot het begin der negentiende eeuw* (Rotterdam: N. V. Nijgh & van Ditmar's Uitgevers-Mij., 1930), 10–20, 250; Pieter Hendrik Engels, *De geschiedenis der belastingen in Nederland, van de vroegste tijden tot op heden mit eenen beknopten inhoud der tegenwoordig in werking zijnde belastingwetten* (Rotterdam: H. A. Kramers, 1848), 97–98.

17. Clark, *The English Alehouse*, 96; Dobbelaar, *De branderijen in Holland*, 265–66.

18. Dobbelaar, *De branderijen in Holland*, 26–27, 59, 65; King, *Beer Has a History*, 97; Monckton, *A History of English Ale*, 66. On the rapid rise of gin consumption in general, see Jessica Warner, *Craze Gin and Debauchery in an Age of Reason* (New York: Four Walls Eight Windows, 2002), 100–103.

19. Bruijn, "Voeding op de staatse vloot," 178–80.

20. Abel, *Stufen der Ernährung*, 57; Patrick Lynch and John Vaizey, *Guinness's Brewery in the Irish Economy 1759–1876* (Cambridge: Cambridge University Press, 1960), 49; Simon Schama, *The Embarrassment of Riches: An Interpretation of Dutch Culture in the Golden Age* (New York: Alfred A. Knopf, 1987), 191.

21. G. A. Leiden, Archieven van de Gilden: #232.

22. J. G. van Dillen, "De achttiende eeuw," *Tijdschrift voor geschiedenis* 61 (1948): 27; Huntemann, *Das deutsche Braugewerbe*, 114–15; Martin, *Alcohol, Sex, and Gender*, 43–44; Monckton, *A History of English Ale*, 132–33; Timmer, *De generale brouwers*, 78–81; Wijsenbeek-Olthuis, "Ondernemen in moeilijke tijden," 70.

23. R. Beeldsnyder, *Verslag van een Onderzoek naar de Ontduiking van de Voornaamste Imposten te Amsterdam gedurende 1701 t/m 1710 (wijn, bier, brandewijn, gemaal, turf, zeep, boter, zout)* (n.p., n.d.), 5–6.

24. Deursen, *Plain Lives in a Golden Age*, 100–101; Glamann, "Beer and Brewing," 128; Klonder, *Browarnictwo w Prusach królewskich*, 157.

25. Klonder, *Browarnictwo w Prusach królewskich*, 159; Peacock, *Pottery in the Roman world*, 9–10.

26. Aerts, *Het bier van Lier*, 197; King, *Beer Has a History*, 72.

27. Aerts, *Het bier van Lier*, 59, 186–87; Uytven, "Bier und Brauer," 18.

28. King, *Beer Has a History*, 91; Lynch and Vaizey, *Guinness's Brewery*, 38–39; Mathias, "Agriculture and the Brewing and Distilling Industries," 250 n. 1; Mathias, *The Brewing Industry in England*, xxviii, 6, 10, 14, 18, 23, 26; Monckton, *A History of English Ale*, 144.

29. Aerts, *Het bier van Lier*, 105, 198; Houtte, *An Economic History of the Low Countries*, 255; Uytven, "Bier und Brauer," 9; Raymond van Uytven,"De scheepstrafiek tussen Leuven en Mechelen in de zeventiende en achttiende eeuw," *Acta geographica Lovaniensis* 34 (1994): 619–24.

Appendix

1. Hough, *The Biotechnology of Malting and Brewing*, 5; Jansen, "Holland's Advance," 23–24.

2. Huntemann, *Das deutsche Braugewerbe*, 14–15.

3. Doorman, *De middeleeuwse brouwerij en de gruit*, 63; Loenen, *De Haarlemse bouwindustrie*, 58.

4. Doorman, *De middeleeuwse brouwerij en de gruit* , 63.

5. Bennett, *Ale, Beer, and Brewsters in England*, xv.

6. De Clerck, *A Textbook of Brewing*, 1: 587; Hough, *The Biotechnology of Malting and Brewing*, 161.

7. Doorman, *Techniek en octooiwezen in hun aanvang*, 61

Bibliography

Abel, Wilhelm. *Agricultural Fluctuations in Europe from the Thirteenth to the Twentieth Centuries.* Trans. Olive Ordish. London: Methuen and Co. Ltd., 1980.
———. *Stufen der Ernährung: Eine historische Skizze.* Göttingen: Vandenhoeck & Ruprecht, 1981.
Ackersdyck, W. C. "Het regt van de gruit." *Verhandelingen van de maatschappij der Nederlandsche letterkunde te Leiden* 32 (1819): 177–202.
Aerts, Erik. "De bibliografie van de Zuidnederlandse biernijverheid tot omstreeks 1800. Een aanvulling." *Handelingen XXXVII der koninklijke Zuidnederlandse maatschappij voor taal- en letterkunde en geschiedenis* (1983): 5–12.
———. *Het bier van Lier. De economische ontwikkeling van de bierindustrie in een middelgrote Brabantse stad (eind 14de-begin 19de eeuw).* Verhandelingen van de koninklijke academie voor wetenschappen, letteren en schone kunsten van België, klasse der letteren, jaargang 58, 1996, no. 161. Brussels: Paleis der Academiën, 1996.
———. "De Zuidnederlandse brouwindustrie tijdens het Ancien Régime: Status quaestionis van het onderzoek." *Handelingen XXXIII der koninklijke Zuidnederlandse maatschappij voor taal- en letterkunde en geschiedenis* (1979): 5–34.
Aerts, Erik, and Eddy Put. "Jezuïetenbier: Bierhistorische beschouwingen bij een brouwhandleiding uit 1627." *Volkskunde* 93, no. 2 (1992): 94–133.
Alberts, W. Jappe. "Bijdrage tot de geschiedenis der accijnzen te Arnhem in de middeleeuwen." *Tijdschrift voor geschiedenis* 64 (1951): 333–48.
Alberts, W. Jappe and H. P. H. Jansen. *Welvaart in wording.* The Hague: Martinus Nijhoff, 1964.
Al-Kindī. *The Medical Formulary of Aqrābādhin of Al-Kindī.* Trans. Martin Levey. Madison: University of Wisconsin Press, 1966.
Alleblas, Jan. "Nieuw leven in een oud brouwerij? Geschiedenis en toekomst van De Sleutel." *Kwartaal & teken van Dordrecht Gemeentelijke archiefdienst Dordrecht* 9, no. 2 (1983): 1–25.
Anon. "Capitulare de villis." In *Introduction to Contemporary Civilization in the West*, 3rd ed. New York: Columbia University Press, 1960.
Anon. *De droghe, natte, ende langhe maten, als van coorenhaver, wijn, bier, harijne, zaut, peck, terre, smecolen, asschen, ende hoppe. . . .* Ghent: Joos Lambrecht, 1545.
Anon. *The Goodman of Paris (Le ménagier de Paris): A Treatise on Moral and Domestic Economy by a Citizen of Paris c. 1393.* Trans. Eileen Power, intro. and notes. London: The Folio Society, 1992.
Anon. *Kellermaistereij: Grüntlicher bericht/wie man alle wein/Teutscher und Welcher landen/vor allen zufallen beweren. . .* N.p., 1539.
Anon. *An Ordinance of the Lords and Commons Assembled in Parliament Shewing That all Brewers of Beere, Ale, Cider or Perry, shall pay the Excise imposed by a former Ordinance of Parliament before the delivering upon paine of forfeiting double the value of the said Commoditie . . . 17 Oct. 1643.* London: John Wright, 1643.

Anon. [R. D.]. *Warme Beere, or A Treatise Wherein is declared by many reasons that Beere so qualitied is farre more wholsome than that which is drunk cold With a continuation of such objections that are saide against it; published for the preservation of health*. Cambridge: Richard Overton, 1641.

Apeldoorn, C. G. L. "Een onderzoek naar de prijzen van het bier en andere gegevens met het bier verband houdende, op het stedelijk archief te Maastricht." Unpublished doctoraal scriptie, economisch-historisch seminarium, University of Amsterdam, #69, n.d.

D'Arbois de Jubainville, H. "De la nourriture des cisterciens principalement à Clairvaux au XIIe et au XIIIe siècle." *Bibliothèque de l'école des Chartes* 19 (1858): 271–82.

Arnaldus de Villanova. *The earliest printed book on wine / by Arnald of Villanova . . . now for the first time rendered into English and with an historical essay by Henry E. Sigerist, with facsimile of the original edition, 1478*. New York: Schuman's, 1943.

Arnold, Richard. *Chronicle (Customs of London)*. Reprint of the 1st edition with the additions included in the 2nd. London: Harding and Wright, 1811.

Asaert, G. *De Antwerpse scheepvaart in de XVe eeuw (1394–1480): Bijdrage tot de economische geschiedenis van de stad Antwerpen*. Verhandelingen van de koninklijke academie voor wetenschappen, letteren en schone kunsten van België, klasse der letteren, jaargang 25, no. 72. Brussels: Paleis der Academiën, 1973.

Ashurst, P. R. "Hops and Their Use in Brewing." In W. P. K. Findlay, ed., *Modern Brewing Technology*. London: Macmillan, 1971.

Ault, R. G., and R. Newton. "Spoilage Organisms in Brewing." In W. P. K. Findlay, ed., *Modern Brewing Technology*. London: Macmillan Press, 1971.

Balberghe, Jozef van. *De Mechelse bierhandel-geschiedenis-folklore-dialekt*. Antwerp: Boekuil en Karveel-uitgaven, 1945.

Barton, Stuart, and R. A. Curtis. *The Genius of William Hogarth*. Worthing, Sussex: Apollo Press, 1972.

Beckmann, Johann. *A Concise History of Ancient Institutions, Inventions and Discoveries in Science and Mechanic Art: Abridged and translated from "Beyträge zur Geschichte der Erfindungen" . . . with Various Important Additions*. 2 vols. London: G. & W.B. Whittaker, 1823.

Beeldsnyder, R. *Verslag van een Onderzoek naar de Ontduiking van de Voornaamste Imposten te Amsterdam gedurende 1701 t/m 1710 (wijn, bier, brandewijn, gemaal, turf, zeep, boter, zout)*. N.p., n.d.

Behre, Karl-Ernst. "The History of Beer Additives in Europe—A Review." *Vegetation History and Archeobotany* 8 (1999): 35–48.

Behre, Karl-Ernst. "Untersuchungen des botanischen Materials der frühmittelalterlichen Siedlung Haithabu (Ausgrabung 1963–1964)." In K. Schietzel, ed., *Berichte über die Ausgrabungen in Haithabu*. Vol. 2. Neumünster: Karl Wachholtz Verlag, 1969.

Bemmel, Abraham van. *Beschryving der stad Amersfoort. . . .* 2 vols. Utrecht: Henrikes Spruyt, 1760.

Bennett, Judith M. *Ale, Beer, and Brewsters in England: Women's Work in a Changing World, 1300–1600*. New York: Oxford University Press, 1996.

———. "The Village Ale-Wife: Women and Brewing in Fourteenth-Century England." In Barbara Hanawalt, ed., *Women and Work in Preindustrial Europe*. Bloomington: Indiana University Press, 1986.

———. "Work in Progress: Misogyny, Popular Culture, and Women's Work." *History Workshop a journal of socialist and feminist historians* 31 (Spring 1991): 166–87.

Berkenvelder, F. C. "Frieslands handel in de late middeleeuwen." *Economisch-historisch jaarboek* 29 (1963): 136–87.

Bijlsma, R. "De opkomst van Rotterdams koopvaardij," *Bijdragen voor vaderlandsche geschiedenis en oudheidkunde*, 5th series, no. 1 (1913): 56–87.

———. *Rotterdams welvaren 1550–1650*. The Hague: Martinus Nijhoff, 1918.

———. "Rotterdams welvaren in den Spaanschen tijd." *Rotterdamsch jaarboekje* 8 (1910): 75–100.

Bing, Wolf. *Hamburgs Bierbrauerei vom 14. bis zum 18. Jahrhundert*. (Dissertation zur Erlangung der Doctorwürde der philosophischen Fakultät der Universität Leipzig.) In *Zeitschrift des Vereins für Hamburgischen Geschichte* 14 (1909): 209–332.

Bizière, Jean Maurice. "The Baltic Wine Trade." *Scandinavian Economic History Review* 20 (1972): 121–32.

Bleyswijck, Dirck van. *Beschryvinge der stadt Delft*. Delft: Arnold Bon, 1667.

Blink, H. "Geschiedenis en verbreiding van de bierproductie en van den bierhandel." *Tijdschrift voor economische geographie* 10 (1914): 96–106.

Bober, Phyllis P. *Art, Culture, and Cuisine: Ancient and Medieval Gastronomy*. Chicago: University of Chicago Press, 1999.

Bömer, A., ed. "Eine Vagantenliedersammlung des 14. Jahrhunderts in de Schlossbibliothek zu Herdringend (Kr. Arnsberg)." *Zeitschrift für deutsches Altertum und deutsche Litteratur* 49 (1908): 161–238.

Bolton, James L., ed. *The Alien Communities of London in the Fifteenth Century The Subsidy Rolls of 1440 and 1483–4*. Stamford: Richard III & Yorkist History Trust in association with Paul Watkins, 1998.

Bracker, J. "Hopbier uit Hamburg Het verhaal van een middeleeuwse succes-formule." In R. E. Kistemaker and V. T. van Vilsteren, eds., *Bier! Geschiedenis van een volksdrank*. Amsterdam: De Bataafsche Leeuw, 1994.

Brasseurs de bière de le ville de Paris. Articles contenent les statuts et Ordonnances des Maitres Jurez. 16 March 1730.

Breen, Joh. C. "Aanteekeningen uit de geschiedenis der Amsterdamsche nijverheid, II bierbrouwerijen." *Nederlands fabrikaat Maandblad der vereniging Nederlands fabrikaat* (1921): 75–76.

Breen, J. C. *Rechtsbronnen der stad Amsterdam*. The Hague: Martinus Nijhoff, 1902.

Brenner, Y. S. "The Inflation of Prices in Early Sixteenth-Century England." *Economic History Review* 14 (1961): 225–39.

Brown, Sanborn C. *Wines and Beers of Old New England: A How-To-Do-It History*. Hanover, N.H.: University Press of New England, 1978.

Brugmans, H. *Amsterdam in de zeventiende eeuw*. Vol. 2, *Handel en nijverheid te Amsterdam in de 17e eeuw*. The Hague: W. P. van Stockum & Zoon, 1904.

Bruijn, J. R. "Voeding op de staatse Vloot." *Spiegel historiael*, 2 (March 1967): 175–83.

Bruinvis, C. W. *De Alkemaarsche bedrijfs- en ambachtsgilden*. Haarlem: J. W. DeWaard, 1906.

Buijs, Jakobus. "De Bierbrouwer of Volledige Beschrijving van het Brouwer der Bieren; Midsgaders van het Mouten der Graane, tot het Brouwen van Bier Gebruikt Wordende." In *Volledige Beschrijving van Alle Konsten, Ambachten, Handwerken, Fabrieken, Trafieken, Derzelver Werkhiuzen, Gereedschappen, enz. ten deele overgenomen uit de Beroemdste Buitenlandsche Werken . . . Zestiende Stuk*. Dordrecht: A. Blussé en Zoon, 1799.

Caesarius of Heisterbach. *The Dialogue on Miracles*. Trans. H. von E. Scott and C. C. Swinton Bland. 2 vols. New York: Harcourt, Brace, 1929.

Campbell, Bruce M. S. *English Seigniorial Agriculture, 1250–1450*. Cambridge: Cambridge University Press, 2000.

Campbell, Bruce M. S., James A. Galloway, Derek Keene, and Margaret Murphy. *A Medieval Capital and Its Grain Supply: Agrarian Production and Distribution in the London Region c. 1300*. Belfast: The Queen's University and London: Centre for Metropolitan History, Institute of Historical Research, University of London, 1993.

Cau, Cornelis, Simon van Leeuwen, Jacobus, Paulus and Isaac Scheltus, eds. *Groot Placaatboek vervattende de Placaaten, Ordonnantien en Edicten van den Hoog Mog. Heeren Staaten Generaal der Vereenigde Nederlanden*. . . . 7 vols. The Hague: Hillebrandt Jacobus van Wouw, Jacobus, Paulus and Isaac Scheltus, 1658–1770.

Charlie, Jehan. *L'évolution économique de la brasserie françaises*. Paris: V. Giard & E. Briere, 1909.

Christian, David. *"Living Water" Vodka and Russian Society on the Eve of Emancipation*. Oxford: Clarendon Press, 1990.

Ciesla, Irena. "Taberna Wczesnośredniowieczna na ziemiach polskich." *Studia Wczesnośredniowieczne* 4 (1958): 159–225.

Clark, Peter. *The English Alehouse A Social History, 1200–1830*. London: Longman, 1983.

Clement, A. van der Poest. "De Bierbrouwerijen van Gouda in middeleeuwn en 16e eeuw." Ph.d. diss., incomplete, 1959, G. A. Gouda.

Clinch, George. *English Hops: A History of Cultivation and Preparation for the Market from the Earliest Times*. London: McCorquodale, [1919].

Compton-Davey, John. "Some Evidence of Brewing in Roman Times." *The Journal of the Brewery History Society* 80 (1995): 4–13.

Cook, Charles Henry. *The Curiosities of Ale and Beer: An Entertaining History by John Bickerdyke*. New York: Scribner & Welford, 1886.

Coornaert, Émile. *Les corporations en France avant 1789*. 2nd ed. Paris: Les éditions ouvrières, 1968.

Corran, H. S. *A History of Brewing*. Newton Abbot: David and Charles, 1975.

Couquerque, L. M. Rollin, and A. Meerkamp van Embden. *Rechtsbronnen der stad Gouda*. The Hague: Martinus Nijhoff, 1917.

Craeybeckx, Jan. *Un grand commerce d'importation: Les vins de France aux anciens Pays-Bas (XIIIe-XVIe siècle)*. Paris: Service d'Édition et du Vente des Publications de l'Education, 1958.

Curtis, Robert I. *Ancient Food Technology*. Technology and Change in History, vol. 5. Leiden: Brill, 2001.

Daenell, Ernst. *Die Blütezeit der deutschen Hanse*. 2 vols. Berlin: Georg Reimer, 1905.

———. "Holland und die Hanse im 15. Jahrhundert." *Hansische Geschichtsblätter* 9 (1903): 3–41.

Dalen, J. L. van. *Geschiedenis van Dordrecht*. 2 vols. Dordrecht: C. Morks Czn., 1931–33.

Davies, C. S. L. "Les rations alimentaires de l'armée et de la marine anglaise au XVIe siècle." *Annales ESC* 18 (1963): 139–41.

De Boer, Dick E. H. "Delft omstreeks 1400." In Ineke Spander and R. A. Leeuw, eds., *De stad Delft: cultuur en maatschappij tot 1572*. Delft: Stedelijk museum het Prinsenhof, 1979.

———. *Graaf en grafiek Sociale en economische ontwikkelingen in het middeleeuwse 'Noorholland' tussen ±1345 em ±1415*. Leiden: NRP, 1978.

Debré, Patrice. *Louis Pasteur*. Paris: Flammarion, 1994.

Deckers, Joseph. "Gruit et droit de gruit: Aspects techniques et fiscaux de la fabrication de la bière dans la région mosane au moyen âge." *Handelingen van het XLIe congres te Mechelen 3-6-IX-1970* (1971): 181–93.

———. "Recherches sur l'histoire des brasseries dans la region mosane au moyen âge." *Le moyen âge Revue d'histoire et de philologie* 76, nos. 3–4 (1970): 445–91.

De Clerck, Jean. *A Textbook of Brewing*. Trans. Kathleen Barton-Wright. 2 vols. London: Chapman and Hall Ltd., 1957–58. Originally publ. in French, 1948.

De Commer, Paul. "De brouwindustrie te Ghent, 1505–1622." *Handelingen der maatschappij voor geschiedenis en oudheidkunde te Gent*, new series, 35 (1981): 81–114 and 37 (1983): 113–71.

De Hullu, J. "Iets over de gruit." *Bijdragen voor vaderlandsche geschiedenis en oudheidkunde*, 3rd series 10 (1899): 114–24.

Dembinska, Maria. *Food and Drink in Medieval Poland : Rediscovering a Cuisine of the Past*. Trans. Magdalena Thomas, revised and adapted by William Woys Weaver. Philadelphia: University of Pennsylvania Press, 1999.

De Roover, Raymond. "Les comptes communaux et la comptabilité communale à Bruges au XIVe siècle: Finances et comptabilité urbaines du XIIIe au XVIe siècle." *Colloque international Blakenberge 6–9-IX-1962*. Blankenberge. Pro Civitate, 1964.

Deursen, A. T. van. *Plain Lives in a Golden Age: Popular Culture, Religion and Society in Seventeenth-Century Holland*. Trans. Maarten Ultee. Cambridge: Cambridge University Press, 1991.

De Vries, Jan. *The Dutch Rural Economy in the Golden Age, 1500–1700*. New Haven: Yale University Press, 1974.

De Vries, W. "Enige opmerkingen naar aanleiding van de Zutphense gruit." *Tijdschrift voor rechtsgeschiedenis* 28 (1960): 59–69.

De Wal, J. "Accijnsbrief van Haarlem in 1274 door Floris V verleend of ontworpen." *Werken van de maatschapij van Nederlandse letterkunde te Leiden*, new series 7/2 (1856): 159–87.

Diepeveen, W. J. *De vervening in Delfland en Schieland tot het einde der zestiende eeuw*. Leiden: Eduard IJdo, N. V., 1950.

Dillen, J. G. van. "De achttiende eeuw." *Tijdschrift voor geschiedenis* 61 (1948): 16–30.

———. *Bronnen tot de geschiedenis van het bedrijfsleven en het gildewezen van Amsterdam [1512–1632]*. 3 vols. Rijks geschiedkundige publicatiën, 69, 78, 133. The Hague: Martinus Nijhoff, 1929–74.

Dingle, A. E. "Drink and Working-Class Living Standards in Britain, 1870–1914." *Economic History Review* 25 (1972): 608–22.

Dirks, Jacob. *De Noord-nederlandsche Gildepenningen*. 2 vols. and plates. Haarlem: De Erven F. Bohn, 1878.

Dobbelaar, Pieter Jan. *De branderijen in Holland tot het begin der negentiende eeuw*. Rotterdam: N. V. Nijgh & van Ditmar's Uitgevers-Mij., 1930.

Doehaerd, Renée. "Bierhandel van Brabantsche kooplieden met Nederland in de 14e eeuw." *Handelingen van de koninklijke kring voor oudheidkunde, letteren en kunst van Mechelen* 50 (1946): 84–89.

Dollinger, Philippe. *La hanse*. Paris: Éditions Montaigne, Aubier, 1964.

Donnachie, Ian. *A History of the Brewing Industry in Scotland*. Edinburgh: John Donald, 1979.

Doorman, G. *De middeleeuwse brouwerij en de gruit*. The Hague: Martinus Nijhoff, 1955.

————. *Octrooien voor uitvindingen in de Nederlanden uit de 16e-18e eeuw.* The Hague: Martinus Nijhoff, 1940.

————. *Techniek en octrooiwezen in hun aanvang.* The Hague: Martinus Nijhoff, 1953.

DuPlessis, Robert S. *Lille and the Dutch Revolt: Urban Stability in an Era of Revolution, 1500–1582.* Cambridge: Cambridge University Press, 1991.

Dyer, Christopher. *Standards of Living in the Later Middle Ages: Social Change in England c. 1200–1520.* Cambridge: Cambridge University Press, 1989.

Ebbing, H. "Bier op transport: De binnenvaart door Holland en de ontwikkeling van de Hollandse brouwnijverheid tot 1500." In R. E. Kistemaker and V. T. van Vilsteren, eds., *Bier! Geschiedenis van een volksdrank.* Amsterdam: De Bataafsche Leeuw, 1994.

Ebbing, H., and V. T. van Vilsteren. "Van gruiters, gruitketels en gruithuizen: Over en typisch middeleeuws fenomeen." In R. E. Kistemaker and V. T. van Vilsteren, eds., *Bier! Geschiedenis van een volksdrank.* Amsterdam: De Bataafsche Leeuw, 1994.

Eeghen, I. H. van. "De brouwerij de Hooiberg." *Jaarboek van het genootschap Amstelodamum* 58 (1958): 46–97.

————. *Inventarissen der archieven van de gilden en van het brouwerscollege.* Amsterdam: Stadsdruckkerij, 1951.

Egmond, Florike. "De strijd om het dagelijks bier brouwerijen, groothandel in bier en economische politiek in de noordelijke Nederlanden tijdens de zestiende eeuw." In C. Lesger and L. Noordegraaf, eds., *Ondernemers en bestuurders: Economie en politiek in de noordelijke Nederlanden in de late middeleeuwen en vroegmoderne tijd.* Amsterdam: Nederlands Economisch Historisch Archief, 1999.

Emmison, F. G. *Tudor Food and Pastimes.* London: Ernest Benn, 1964.

Engels, Pieter Hendrik. *De belastingen en de geldmiddelen van den aanvang der Republiek tot op heden.* Utrecht: Kemink en Zoon, 1862.

————. *De geschiedenis der belastingen in Nederland, van de vroegste tijden tot op heden mit eenen beknopten inhoud der tegenwoordig in werking zijnde belastingwetten.* Rotterdam: H. A. Kramers, 1848.

Enss, Hans. *Die Anfänge der Bier-Zeise unter dem Deutschen Orden: Ein Beitrag zur Geschichte der Preussischen Accise.* Königsberg: Buch- und Steindruckerei von Otto Kümmel, 1908.

Ermisch, Hubert and Robert Wuttke, eds. *Haushaltung in Vorwerken: Ein landwirtschaftliches Lehrbuch aus der Zeit des Kurfürsten August von Sachsen.* Leipzig: B. G. Teubner, 1910.

Eycken, Michel van der. *Geschiedenis van Diest.* Diest: Stadsbestuur Diest, 1980.

Eykens, M. J. "De brouwindustrie te Antwerpen, 1585–1700." *Bijdragen tot de geschiedenis, bijzonderlijk van het aloude hertogdom Brabant* 56 (1973): 80–101.

Faber, J. A. *Drie eeuwen Friesland. Economische en sociale ontwikkelingen van 1500 tot 1800.* Wageningen: Afdeling Agrarische Geschiedenis, Landbouwhogeschool, 1972.

Faber, J. A., H. A. Diederiks, and S. Hart. "Urbanisering, industrialisering en milieuaantasting in Nederland in de periode van 1500 tot 1800." *A. A. G. Bijdragen* 18 (1973): 251–71.

Fehring, Guenter P. *The Archaeology of Medieval Germany: An Introduction.* London: Routledge, 1991.

Feijst, G. van der. *Geschiedenis van Schiedam.* Schiedam: Interbook International, 1975.

Fell, C. E. "Old English *Beor*." *Leeds Studies in English* 8 (1975): 76–95.

Fichtenau, Heinrich. *Living in the Tenth Century Mentalities and Social Orders.* Trans. Patrick J. Geary. Chicago: University of Chicago Press, 1991.

Forbes, R. J. "Food and Drink." In C. Singer et al., eds. *A History of Technology.* Vol. 2. Oxford: Clarendon Press, 1956.

Galbert of Bruges. *The Murder of Charles the Good Count of Flanders.* Trans. and ed. James Bruce Ross. New York: Columbia University Press, 1950.

Garnsey, Peter. *Food and Society in Classical Antiquity.* Cambridge: Cambridge University Press, 1999.

Gelsinger, Bruce E. *Icelandic Enterprise: Commerce and Economy in the Middle Ages.* Columbia: University of South Carolina Press, 1981.

Gerding, M. A. W. *Vier Eeuwen Turfwinning: De verveningen in Groningen, Friesland, Drenthe en Overijssel tussen 1550 en 1950.* Wageningen: Afdeling Agrarische Geschiedenis, Landbouwuniversiteit, 1995.

Glamann, Kristof. "Beer and Brewing in Pre-Industrial Denmark." *Scandinavian Economic History Review* 10 (1962): 128–40.

———. *Jacobsen of Carlsberg, Brewer and Philanthropist.* Trans. Geoffrey French. Copenhagen: Glydendal, 1991.

Goor, Thomas Ernst van. *Beschryving der stadt en lande van Breda.* The Hague: Jacobus van den Kieboom, 1744.

Grabowski, Mieczyslaw and Georg Schmitt. "'Und das Wasser fliesst in Röhren' Wasserversorgung und Wasserkünste in Lübeck." In *Archaeologie des Mittelalters und Bauforschung im Hanseraum: Eine Festschrift für Guenter P. Fehring.* Rostock: Konrad Reich Verlag, 1993.

Grässe, J. G. Theodor. *Bierstudien.* Dresden: R. v. Zahn's Verlag, 1872.

Grolsche Bierbrouwerij. *Merckwaerdighe bierologie zijnde het verhaal van een plezierige bierreis door meer dan vijftig eeuwen elk op zijn of haar manier beleefd door een geschiedschrijfster en een reclameman, een tekenaar en een oudheidkundige, een bronnenspeurder en een genealoog.* Amsterdam: Uitgeverij Van Lindonk, 1966.

Hackwood, Frederick W. *Inns, Ales, and Drinking Customs of Old England.* London: T. Fisher Unwin, 1910.

Hagen, Ann. *A Second Handbook of Anglo Saxon Food and Drink Production and Distribution,* Hockwold cum Wilton, Norfolk: Anglo-Saxon Books, 1995.

Halbertsma, H. *Zeven Eeuwen Amersfoort.* Amersfoort: Veenendaal, 1959.

Hallema, A. and J. A. Emmens. *Het bier en zijn brouwers: De geschiedenis van onze oudste volksdrank.* Amsterdam: J. H. DeBussy, 1968.

Hamaker, H. G., ed. *De rekeningen der grafelijkheid van Holland onder het Henegouwsche huis.* 3 vols. Utrecht: Kemink en Zoon, 1875–78.

Häpke, Rudolph. *Brügges Entwicklung zum mittelalterlichen Weltmarkt.* Berlin: Karl Curtius, 1908.

Harrison, William. *A Description of England.* In *Lothrop Withington, Holingshed's Chronicles.* Intro. by F. J. Furnivall. London: Walter Scott, 1876.

Hartman, Louis F. and A. L. Oppenheim. "On Beer and Brewing Techniques in Ancient Mesopotamia According to the 23rd Tablet of the Series HAR.ra = hubullu." *Supplement to the Journal of the American Oriental Society* 10, issued with vol. 70, no. 4. Baltimore: American Oriental Society, 1950.

Heeringa, K., ed. *Rechtsbronnen der stad Schiedam,* Oude vaderlandsche rechtsbronnen, 2nd series, no. 6. The Hague: Martinus Nijhoff, 1904.

Helbig, Jean. *Les vitraux médiévaux conservés en Belgique, 1200–1500.* Brussels: Imprimerie Weissenbruch, 1961.

Herz, Karl O. "Tabernaemontanus on Sixteenth-Century beer." *Wallerstein Laboratories Communications* 27 (1964): 111–13.

Heuvel, N. H. L. van den. *De ambachtsgilden van 's-Hertogenbosch voor 1629.* Utrecht: Kemink en Zoon N. V., 1946.

Hildegard von Bingen. *Heilkunde Das Buch von dem Grund und Wesen und der Heilung der Krankheiten.* Trans. and ed. Heinrich Schipperges. Salzburg: Otto Müller Verlag, 1957.

Hoek, B. van der. "De gilden van Amersfoort." Unpublished doctoraal scriptie, economisch-historisch seminarium, University of Amsterdam, #144, 1938.

Hoekstra, P. "Het Haarlems Brouwersbedrijf in de 17e eeuw." Unpublished doctoraal scriptie, economisch-historisch seminarium, University of Amsterdam, 1935.

Hoffmann, M. *5000 Jahre Bier.* Nuremberg: Verlag Hans Carl, 1956.

Höhlbaum, Konstantin, Karl Kunze, Walther Stein et al., eds. *Hansisches Urkundenbuch,* vols. 1–11. Halle, Weimar, and Leipzig: Verlag der Buchhandlung des Waisenhauses and Verlag von Duncker und Humblot, 1876–1916.

Hoppenbrouwers, P. C. M. *Een middeleeuwse samenleving Het Land van Heusden (ca. 1360—ca. 1515).* Wageningen: Afdeling Agrarische Geschiedenis, Landbouwuniversiteit, 1992.

Horn, Walter and Ernest Born. *The Plan of St. Gall: A Study of the Architecture and Economy of, and Life in a Paradigmatic Carolingian Monastery.* 3 vols. Berkeley: University of California Press, 1979.

Hough, J. S. *The Biotechnology of Malting and Brewing.* Cambridge: Cambridge University Press, 1985.

Houtte, J. A. van. *An Economic History of the Low Countries 800–1800.* New York: St. Martin's, 1977.

———. *Economische en sociale geschiedenis van de lage landen.* Zeist: W. De Haan N.V., 1964.

Houwen, A. "De Haarlemsche brouwerij 1575–1600." Unpublished doctoraal scriptie, economisch-historisch seminarium, University of Amsterdam, 1932.

Huber, Heinrich. "Altbayerische Vorschriften über das Biersudwesen." *Brauwelt Zeitschrift für das gesamte Brauwesen* 99 (1959): 437–39.

Huizinga, Johan, ed. *Rechtsbronnen der stad Haarlem.* The Hague: Martinus Nijhoff, 1911.

Huntemann, Hans. *Das deutsche Braugewerbe vom Ausgang des Mittelalters bis zum Beginn der Industriealisierung: Biererzeugung—Bierhandel—Bierverbrauch.* Nuremberg: Verlag Hans Carl, 1971.

Illert, Friedrich M. "Geschichte der Wormser Brauereien von ihren Anfängen bis zum Gegenwert." *Der Wormsgau Zeitschrift des Altertumsvereins und der städtischen Kulturinstitute* Beiheft 14. Worms: Verlag Stadtbibliothek Worms, 1954.

Jacobsen, Grethe. "Women's Work and Women's Role: Ideology and Reality in Danish Urban Society." *Scandinavian Economic History Review* 31 (1983): 3–20.

James, Margery Kirkbride. *Studies in the Medieval Wine Trade.* Ed. E. M. Veale. Oxford: The Clarendon Press, 1971.

Janáček, Josef. "Pivoarniectví v Českych Královských Městech v 16. Století." *Rozpravy Československe Akademie Ve/akd Ročník* 69—Sešit 1. Prague: Nakladetelství Československí Akademie Věd, 1959.

Jansen, H. P. H. "Holland's Advance. *Acta Historiae Neerlandicae* 10 (1978): 1–19.

Jensma, Th. E. "Bronnen tot de geschiedenis van het recht van de gruit in het graafschap Holland, het bisdom Utrecht en het hertogdom Gelre." *Verslagen en mede-deelingen tot uitgaaf der bronnen van het oud-vaderlansch recht* 12 (1960): 167–215.

Jung, Hermann. *Bier- Kunst und Brauchtum.* Dortmund: Schropp Verlag, [n.d.].

Kampeter, Paul Heinrich. *Die wirtschaftliche Entwicklung des rheinisch-westfalischen Brauerei-Gewerbes unter besonderer Berücksichtigung des bergischen landes.* Giessen, 1925.

Kempe, Margery. *The Book of Margery Kempe.* Trans. B. A. Windeatt. London: Penguin, 1985.

Kerling, Nelly Johanna Martina. *Commercial Relations of Holland and Zeeland with England from the Late 13th Century to the Close of the Middle Ages.* Leiden: E.J. Brill, 1954.

Ketner, F. *Handel en scheepvaart van Amsterdam in de vijftiende eeuw.* Leiden: E. J. Brill, 1946.

Kieft, C. van de. "Gruit en ban." *Tijdschrift voor geschiedenis* 77 (1964): 158–68.

King, Frank A. *Beer Has a History.* London: Hutchinson's Scientific and Technical Publications, 1947.

Kish, Kathleen. "Celestina Speaks Dutch—in the Sixteenth Century Spanish Netherlands." In John S. Miletich, ed., *Hispanic Studies in Honor of Alan D. Deyermond: A North American Tribute.* Madison: Hispanic Seminary of Medieval Studies, 1986.

Klonder, Andrzej. *Browarnictwo w Prusach królewskich [2 Połowa XVI–XVII W.].* Polska akademia nauk instytut historii kultury materialnej. Warsaw: Zakład narodowy imienia Ossolińskich Wydawnictwo Polskiej Akademii Nauk, 1983.

———. "Rachunki cechu browarników Starego Miasta Elbląga jako zrodo do badán nad produkcją piwa w XVI–XVII w." *Kwartalnik historii kultury materialnej* 28 (1980): 201–10.

Klop, A. H. "De Amersfoortse Brouwneringen tot de 19e eeuw." Unpublished doctoraal scriptie, economisch-historisch seminarium, University of Amsterdam, #104, 1935.

Laan, P. H. J. van der. *Oorkondenboek van Amsterdam tot 1400.* Amsterdam: N. Israel, 1975.

Langer, Herbert. "Das Braugewerbe in den deutschen Hansestädten der frühen Neuzeit." In Konrad Fritze, Eckard Müller-Mertens, Johannes Schildhauer, eds., *Hansische Studien IV Gewerbliche Produktion und Stadt-Land-Beziehungen, Abhandlungen zur Handels- und Sozialgeschichte*, 18. Weimar: Hermann Böhlaus Nachfolger, 1979.

Lauffer, Victor. "Danzigs Schiffs- und Waarenverkehr am Ende des XV. Jahrhunderts." *Zeitschrift des Westpreussischen Geschichtsvereins* 33 (1894): 1–44.

Lejeune, Jean. *La formation du capitalisme moderne dans la principauté de Liège au XVIe siècle.* Bibliothèque de la faculté de philosophie et lettres de l'université de Liège 87. Liege: Faculté de philosophie et lettres, 1939.

Lemoine, Serge, and Bernard Marchand. *Les peintres et la bière Painters and Beer.* Preface by Pierre-Jean Rémy. Paris: Éditions d'art Somogy, 1999.

Loenen, Jacques C. van. *De Haarlemse bouwindustrie voor 1600.* Amsterdam: Universiteitspers, 1950.

Löffler, Klemens. "Die altesten Bierbücher." *Archiv für Kultur-Geschichte* 7 (1909): 5–12.

Löhdefink, August. *Die Entwicklung der Brauergilde der Stadt Hannover zur heutigen*

Erwerbsgesellschaft (Ein Beitrag zur Lehre von den Unternehmungen). Hannover: Eulemannsche Buchdruckerei, 1925.

Lucas, Henry S. "The Great European Famine of 1315, 1316, and 1317." *Speculum* 5 (1930): 343–77.

Lund, Niels, ed. *Two Voyagers at the Court of King Alfred. The ventures of Othere and Wulfstan together with the Description of Northern Europe from the Old English Orosius.* York: William Sessions, 1984.

Lynch, Patrick, and John Vaizey. *Guinness's Brewery in the Irish Economy, 1759–1876.* Cambridge: Cambridge University Press, 1960.

Macray, William Dunn. *Chronicum abbatiæ de Evesham AD Annum 1418.* London: Longman, Green, Longman, Roberts and Green, 1863.

Maitland, Frederick William. *Domesday Book and Beyond: Three Essays in the Early History of England.* Cambridge: Cambridge University Press, 1897.

Marchant, W. T. *In Praise of Ale or Songs, Ballads, Epigrams, and Anecdotes Relating to Beer, Malt and Hops with some curious Particulars concerning Ale-Wives and Brewers Drinking-Clubs and Customs.* London: George Redway, 1888.

Markham, Gervase. *The English Housewife: Containing the inward and outward virtues which ought to be in a complete woman; as her skill in physik, cookery, banqueting-stuff, distillation, perfumes, wool, hemp, flax, dairies, brewing, baking and all other things belonging to a household.* Ed. Michael R. Best. 1615; reprint, Montreal: McGill-Queen's University Press, 1986.

Martens, Jos. "Bier en stadsfinancien te Hasselt, 16e en 17e eeuw." *Gemeente krediet van België, Driemaandelijke tijdschrift* 30, no. 118 (1976): 243–56.

Martin, A. Lynn. *Alcohol, Sex, and Gender in Late Medieval and Early Modern Europe.* Basingstoke: Palgrave, 2001.

Mathias, Peter. "Agriculture and the Brewing and Distilling Industries in the Eighteenth Century." *Economic History Review* 5 (1952): 249–57.

———. "Brewing archives: their nature and use." In Lesley Richmond and Alison Turton, eds., *The brewing industry A guide to historical records.* Manchester and New York: Manchester University Press, 1990.

———. *The Brewing Industry in England 1700–1830.* Cambridge: Cambridge University Press, 1959.

Mayhew, Nicholas. "The Status of Women and the Brewing of Ale in Medieval Aberdeen." *Review of Scottish Culture* 10 (1966–67): 16–21.

Meilink, P. A. "Rekening van het lastgelt in Amsterdam, Waterland en het Noorderkwartier van Holland in 1507." *Bijdragen en mededeelingen van het historisch genootschap* 44 (1923): 187–230.

Michel, Rudolph H., Patrick E. McGovern, and Virginia R. Badler. "Chemical Evidence for Ancient Beer." *Nature* 360, no. 6399 (5 November 1992): 24.

Mieris, Frans van. *Groot Charterboek der Graven van Holland, van Zeeland en heeren van Vriesland.* 4 vols. Leiden: Pieter van der Eyk, 1753–56.

Monckton, H. A. *A History of English Ale and Beer.* London: The Bodley Head, 1966.

———. *A History of the English Public House.* London: The Bodley Head, 1969.

Monnier, Raymonde. *Un bourgeois sans-culotte: Le général Santerre suivi de l'art du brasseur.* Paris: Publications de la Sorbonne, 1989.

Moryson, Fynes. *Itinerary* (London, 1617). In Frederick J. Furnivall, ed., *Harrison's Description of England in Shakspere's[sic] Youth.* London: Chatto and Windus, 1908.

Moulin, Léo. "Bière, houblon et cervoise." *Bulletin de l'académie royale de langue et de littérature françaises* 59 (1981): 111–48.

Muller Fz., S. *Schetsen uit de middeleeuwen*. Amsterdam: S. L. van Looy, 1900.

Murray, W. G. D. "Oud-Rotterdamsch kroegleven." *Rotterdamsche Jaarboekje*, 5th series, no. 2 (1944): 40–78.

Nef, John U. "The Progress of Technology and the Growth of Large-Scale Industry in Great Britain, 1540–1640." In E. M. Carus-Wilson, ed., *Essays in Economic History*. Vol. 1. London: Edward Arnold, 1954.

Nelson, Max. "Beer in Greco-Roman Antiquity." Ph.D. diss., University of British Columbia, 2001.

Niehoff, Lydia. "Bierproduktion und Bierkonsum in der Stadt Bremen vom 17. bis zum 19. Jahrhundert." Dissertation zur Erlangung des akademischen Grades eines Doktors der Wirtschafts- und Sozialwissenschaften der Universität Bremen, 1996.

———. "Bremer Bier im Baltikum oder 'Liefländer brawen auch gute Biere': Eine Suche nach Bremer Brauprodukten im Ostseeraum." Unpublished essay, 1995.

Niermeyer, J. F., ed. *Bronnen voor de economische geschiedenis van het Beneden-Maas-gebied. Eerste deel: 1104–1399*. Rijks geschiedkundige publicatiën 127. The Hague: Martinus Nijhoff, 1968.

———. "Dordrecht als handelsstad in de tweede helft van de veertiende eeuw." *Bijdragen voor vaderlandsche geschiedenis en oudheidkunde*, 8th series, 3 (1942): 1–36, 177–222; 4 (1943): 86–113, 145–68.

———. *De wording van onze volkshuishouding. Hoofdlijnen uit de economische geschiedenis der noordelijke Nederlanden in de middeleeuwen*. The Hague: N. V. Servire, 1946.

Noordegraaf, Leo. "Betriebsformen und Arbeitsorganisation im Gewerbe der nördlichen Niederlande, 1400–1800." In Konrad Fritze, Eckhard Müller-Mertens, and Johannes Schildhauer, eds., *Hansische Studien IV Gewerbliche Produktion und Stadt-Land-Beziehungen, Abhandlungen zur Handels- und Sozialgeschichte*, 18. Weimar: Verlag Hermann Böhlaus Nachfolger, 1979.

———. *Hollands welvaren? Levensstandaard in Holland 1450–1650*. Bergen (NH): Octavo, 1985.

Noordkerk, H. van. *Handvesten ofte Privilegien ende Octroyen; mitsgaders Willekeuren, Costumen, ordonnantien en Handelingen der Stad Amstelredam*. Vol. 1. Amsterdam: Hendrik van Waesberge, Salomon en Petrus Schouten, 1748.

Nordlund, Odd. *Brewing and Beer Traditions in Norway: The Social Anthropological Background of the Brewing Industry*. Oslo: Universitetsforlaget, 1969.

Oldewelt, W. F. H. "De Hollandse Imposten en Ons Beeld van de Conjunctuur Tijdens de Republiek." *Jaarboek Amstelodamum* 47 (1955): 48–80.

Pächt, Otto, and J. J. G. Alexander. *Illuminated Manuscripts in the Bodleian Library Oxford*. Vol. 3, *British, Irish and Icelandic Schools*. Oxford: Clarendon Press, 1973.

Pasteur, Louis. *Studies on Fermentation: The Diseases of Beer, Their Causes, and the Means of Preventing Them. A Translation, Made with the Author's Sanction, of "Études sur la biere," with Notes, Index and Original Illustrations by Frank Faulkner, author of "The Art of Brewing," etc. and D. Constable Robb*. London: Macmillan, 1879.

Peacock, D. P. S. *Pottery in the Roman World: An Ethnoarchaeological Approach*. London: Longman, 1982.

Peeters, F. A. H. Introduction. In combined facsimile edition of W. van Lis, *Brouw-*

kunde of verhandeling van het voornaamste dat tot een brouwery en moutery en het brouwen en mouten behoort; alsmede een korte beschryving van het bier and J. Buys, De bierbrouwer. Tilburg: F. A. H. Peeters, 1986.

Penninck, Jozef. Het bier te Brugge Geschiedenis en folklore. Bruges: Heemkundige kring Maurits van Coppenolle Sint-Andries, 1963.

Philipsen, J. P. W. "De Amsterdamsche Brouwnijverheid tot het Einde der Zestiende Eeuw." Unpublished doctoraal scriptie, economisch-historisch seminarium, University of Amsterdam, 1937.

Pilgrim, Konrad. "Der Durst auf den Weltmeeren Das Problem der Versorgung des Seeleute mit Getränken im 16., 17. und 18. Jahrhundert." Jahrbuch 1969 Gesellschaft für die Geschichte und Bibliographie des Brauwesens E. V. Berlin, 1969.

Pinkse, V. C. C. J. "Het Goudse kuitbier, Gouda's welveren in de late middeleeuwen, 1400–1568." Gouda zeven eeuwen stad (19 July 1972): 91–128.

Pirenne, L. P. L., and W. J. Formsma. Koopmensgeest te 's-Hertogenbosch in de vijftiende en zestiende eeuw Het kasboek van Jaspen van Bull, 1564–1568. Nijmegen: N.V. Centrale Drukkerij, 1962.

Poll, Ildefons. Des Brauwesen des Benediktinerklosters Metten. Berlin: Gesellschaft für die Geschichte und Bibliographie des Brauwesens E. V., 1937.

———. Das Brauwesen des Klosters Prüsening. Berlin: Gesellschaft für die Geschichte und Bibliographie des Brauwesens E. V., 1936.

Postan, M. M. "The Trade of Medieval Europe: the North." In M. M. Postan and E. E. Rich, eds., The Cambridge Economic History of Europe. Vol. 2. Cambridge: Cambridge University Press, 1952.

Posthumus, N. W. De uitvoer van Amsterdam, 1543–1545. Leiden: E. J. Brill, 1971.

Powell, Marvin A. "Metron Ariston: Measure As a Tool for Studying Beer in Ancient Mesopotamia." In Lucio Milano, ed., Drinking in Ancient Societies: History and Culture of Drinks in the Ancient Near East. Papers of a symposium, Rome, May 17–19, 1990. Padua: Sargon, 1994.

Preece, I. A. The Biochemistry of Brewing. Edinburgh: Oliver & Boyd, 1954.

Preobrazhensky, A. G. Etymological Dictionary of the Russian Language. New York: Columbia University Press, 1951.

Prevenier, Walter and Wim Blockmans. The Burgundian Netherlands. Cambridge: Cambridge University Press, 1986.

Rabecka, Irena. "The Early Medieval Tavern in Poland." Kwartalnik Historii Kultury Materialnej 10, nos. 1–2 (1962), Fascicule supplémentaire Ergon, 3: 372–75.

Räsänen, Matti. Von Halm zum Fass. Die volkstümlichen alkoholarmen Getreidegetränke in Finnland. Helsinki, Suomen muinaismuistoyhdistys, 1975.

Ravesteyn, Willem van, Jr. Onderzoekingen over de economische en sociale ontwikkeling van Amsterdam gedurende de 16de en het eerste kwart der 17de eeuw. Amsterdam: S. L. Van Looy, 1906.

Renouard, Yves. "Les transformations économiques et sociales." In Charles Higounet, ed., Histoire de Bordeaux. Vol. 3, Bordeaux sous les rois d'Angleterre. Bordeaux: Fédération historique du Sud-Ouest, 1965.

Revell, Elizabeth, ed. The Later Letters of Peter of Blois. Oxford: Oxford University Press, 1993.

Rickard, P. Britain in Medieval French Literature, 1100–1500. Cambridge: Cambridge University Press, 1956.

Rijswijk, Bernard van. Geschiedenis van het Dordtsche stapelrecht. The Hague: Martinus Nijhoff, 1900.

Robertson, James Caigie, ed. *Materials for the History of Thomas Becket, Archbishop of Canterbury.* Vol. 3. London: Longman, 1877.

Roesdahl, Else. *Viking Age Denmark.* Trans. Susan Morgeson and Kirsten Willams. London: British Museum Publications Ltd., 1982..

Röllig, Wolfgang. *Das Bier im alten Mesopotamien.* Berlin: Gesellschaft für die Geschichte und Bibliographie des Brauwesens E. V., 1970.

Rootselaar, W. F. N. van. *Amersfoort, 777–1580.* 2 vols. Amersfoort: B. Blankenberg en Zoon, 1878.

———. *Amersfoort, Sprokkelingen.* 2 vols. Amersfoort: B. Blankenberg en Zoon, 1898–99.

Ropp, G. Frhr. von der, Dietrich Schäfer, Gottfried Wentz et al., eds. *Hanserecesse: Die Recesse und andere Akten der Hansetage.* 4th series. Leipzig: Verlag von Duncker und Humblot and Böhlau Verlag, 1870–1970.

Royston, M. G. "Wort Boiling and Cooling." In W. P. K. Findlay, ed., *Modern Brewing Technology.* London: Macmillan Press, 1971.

Salem, Frederick William. *Beer, Its History and Its Economic Value as a National Beverage.* Springfield, Mass.: Clark W. Bryan Company, 1880; rpt. New York: Arno Press Inc., 1972.

Salzman, L. F. *English Industries of the Middle Ages.* 1913. New edition, enlarged and illustrated. London: H. Pordes, 1964.

———. *English Life in the Middle Ages.* Oxford: Oxford University Press, 1921.

Sambrook, Pamela. *Country House Brewing in England, 1500–1900.* London: Hambledon Press, 1996.

Samuel, Delwen. "Brewing and Baking." In Paul T. Nicholson and Ian Shaw, eds., *Ancient Egyptian Materials and Technology.* Cambridge: Cambridge University Press, 2000.

———. "Investigation of Ancient Egyptian Baking and Brewing Methods by Correlative Microscopy." *Science* 273 (26 July 1996): 488–90.

Santbergen, René van. *Les bons métiers des meuniers, des boulangers et des brasseurs de la cité de Liege.* Liège: Faculté de Philosophie et Lettres, 1949.

Schade, Werner. *Die Malerfamilie Cranach.* Dresden: VEB Verlag der Kunst, 1974.

Schama, Simon. *The Embarrassment of Riches: An Interpretation of Dutch Culture in the Golden Age.* New York: Alfred A. Knopf, 1987.

Scheltema, P. *Inventaris van het Amsterdamsche archief.* 3 vols. Amsterdam: Stadsdruckkerij, 1866–74.

Schildhauer, Johannes. *The Hanse History and Culture.* Trans. Katherine Vanovitch. Leipzig: Edition Leipzig, 1985.

———. "Der Seehandel Danzigs im 16. Jahrhundert und die Verlagerung des Warenverkehrs im Nord- und Mitteleuropäischen Raum." *Jahrbuch für Wirtschaftsgeschichte* 3 (1970): 155–78.

Schlosser, Hans. *Braurechte, Brauer und Braustätten in München: Zur Rechts- und Sozialgeschichte des spätmittelalterlichen Brauwesens.* Elsbach am Main: Verlag Rolf Grener, 1981.

Schoockii, Martini [Martinus Schookhuis]. *Liber de Cervisia. quo Non modo omnia ad Cerealem potum pertinentia comprehendumtur, sed varia quoque Problemata, Philosophica & Philologica; discutiuntur; Simul incidentes quædam Authorum antiquorum loca illustrantur.* Groningen: Francisci Bronchortsii, 1661.

Schouteet, Albert. *Regesten op de oordkonden van het stadsbestuur van Brugge.* Vol. 1, *1089–1300.* Brussels: Koninklijke Bibliotheek, 1973.

Schouten, J. *Gouda, vroeger en nu.* Bussum: Fibula-van Dishoeck, 1969.

Schulte, Aloys. "Vom Grutbiere: Eine Studie zur Wirtschafts- und Verfassungsge-schichte." *Annalen des historischen Vereins für den Niederrhein* 85 (1908): 118–46.

Schultze-Berndt, H. G. "Noch einmal: Von Durst auf den Weltmeeren." *Jahrbuch 1974 Gesellschaft für Geschichte und Bibliographie des Brauwesens E. V.* Berlin, 1973.

Schultheiss, Werner. *Brauwesen und Braurechte in Nürnberg bis zum Beginn des 19. Jahrhunderts.* Nürnberger Werkstücke zur Stadt- und Landesgeschichte. Schriftenreihe des Stadtarchivs Nürnberg. Vol. 23. Nuremberg: Stadtarchiv, 1978.

Scot, Reginald. *A Perfite Platforme of a Hoppe Garden.* London: Henrie Denham, 1574. Facsimile Da Capo Press Amsterdam: Theatrum Orbis Terrarum, 1973.

Scully, Terence. *The Art of Cookery in the Middle Ages.* Woodbridge: Boydell and Brewer, 1995.

Sedlmeyr, Fritz. *Die "prewen" Münchens seit 1363 biz zur Aufhebung der Lehensverleihung durch den Landesfürsten (1814).* Ed. Lore Grohsmann. Nuremberg: Verlag Hans Carl, 1969.

Siebel, J. E., et al., eds. *One Hundred Years of Brewing: A Complete History of the Progress Made in the Art, Science, and Industry of Brewing in the World, Particularly During the Nineteenth Century: Historical Sketches and Views of Ancient and Modern Breweries: Lives and Portraits of Brewers of the Past and Present.* Supplement to *The Western Brewer.* Chicago: H. S. Rich, 1903. Reprint, Evansville, Ind.: Unigraphic, 1973.

Sim, Alison. *Food and Feast in Tudor England.* London: Sutton Publishing, 1997.

Smit, H. J., ed. *Bronnen tot de geschiedenis van den handel mit Engeland, Schotland en Ierland, 1150–1585.* 2 vols. Rijks geschiedkundige publicatiën 65, 66, 86, 91. The Hague: Martinus Nijhoff, 1928, 1942, 1950.

Smit, H. J. *De opkomst van den handel van Amsterdam, onderzoekingen naar de economische ontwikkeling der stad tot 1441.* Amsterdam: H. Kruyt, 1914.

———. "De Registers van den biertol te Amsterdam." *Historisch genootschap te Utrecht, Bijdragen en mededelingen* 38 (1917): 1–97.

Soly, Hugo. "De Antwerpse onderneemster Anna Janssens en de economische boom na de vrede van Cateau-Cambrésis (1559)." *Bijdragen tot de geschiedenis* 52 (1969): 139–64.

———. "De brouwerijenonderneming van Gilbert van Schoonbeke (1552–1562)." *Revue belge de philolgie et d'histoire* 46 (1968): 337–92, 1166–1204.

———. "De economische betekenis van de Zuidnederlandse brouwindustrie in de 16e eeuw. Problematie." *Handelingen van het colloquium over de economische geschiedenis van België. Behandelingen van de bronnen en problematiek.* Brussels: Archives Générale du Royaume, 1972.

———. "Nijverheid en kapitalisme te Antwerpen in de 16e eeuw." *Studia historica Gandensia* 193 (1975): 331–52.

———. *Urbanisme en kapitalisme te Antwerpen in de 16de eeuw: De stedebouwkundige en industriële ondernemingen van Gilbert van Schoonbeke.* Antwerp: Gemeentekrediet van Belgie, historische uitgaven pro civitate, series in 8⁰, no. 47, 1977.

Soly, Hugo, and A. K. L. Thys. "Nijverheid in de zuidelijke Nederlanden." *Algemene Geschiedenis der Nederlanden.* Vol. 6. Haarlem: Fibula-van Dishoeck, 1979.

Soutendam, J. *Keuren en ordonnantiën der stad Delft van den aanvang der XVIe eeuw tot het jaar 1536.* Delft: J. H. Molenbroek, 1870.

Sprandel, Rolf. *Das Hamburger Pfundzollbuch von 1418.* Cologne: Böhlau Verlag, 1972.

Stefke, Gerald. "Die Hamburger Zollbücher von 1399/1400 und '1418': Der Werkzoll im 14. und frühen 15. Jahrhundert und die Ausfuhr von Hamburger Bier über See im Jahre 1417." *Zeitschrift des Vereins für Hamburgische Geschichte* 69 (1983): 1–33.

————. *Ein Städtisches Exportgewerbe des Spätmittelaters in seiner Entfaltung und ersten Blüte Untersuchungen zur Geschichte der Hamburger Seebrauerei des 14. Jahrhunderts.* Hamburg, 1979.

Stieda, W. "Das Böttcherei-Gewerbe in Alt-Rostock." *Beiträge zur Geschichte der Stadt Rostock* 1/2 (1895): 29–52.

Stol, Marten. "Beer in Neo-Babylonian Times." In Lucio Milano, ed., *Drinking in Ancient Societies: History and Culture of Drinks in the Ancient Near East.* Papers of a symposium held in Rome, May 17–19, 1990. Padua: Sargon, 1994.

Stopes, H. *Malt and Malting: An Historical, Scientific, and Practical Treatise, showing, as clearly as existing knowledge permits, What Malt Is, and How to Make It.* London: F. W. Lyon, 1885.

Struve, Emil. *Die Entwicktung des bayerischen Braugewerbes in neunzehnten Jahrhundert.* Leipzig: Verlag von Duncker & Humblot, 1893.

Swartelé, A. "Iets over de geschiedenis van het bier in de Nederlanden." *Fermentatio* 3 (1961): 107–25.

Tacitus. *Germania, Tacitus on Britain and Germany.* Trans. H. Mattingly. Harmondsworth: Penguin, 1948.

Tangelder, F. B. M. *Nederlandse rekeningen in de pontolregisters van Elbing, 1585–1602.* The Hague: Martinus Nijhoff, 1972.

TeBrake, William H. *Medieval Frontier Culture and Ecology in Rijnland.* College Station: Texas A&M University Press, 1985.

Techen, Friedrich. "Das Brauwerk in Wismar." *Hansisches Geschichtsblätter* 21 (1915): 263–352; 22 (1916):145–224.

Telting, Albertus, ed. *Stadboek van Groningen.* The Hague: Martinus Nijhoff, 1886.

Ten Cate, J. A. "Verslag van een onderzoek naar de geschiedenis van het Amsterdamse brouwersbedrijf in de 17e eeuw." Unpublished doctoraal scriptie, economisch-historisch seminarium, University of Amsterdam, #118, 1940.

Ter Gouw, J. *Geschiedenis van Amsterdam.* 8 vols. Amsterdam: Scheltema & Holkema, 1879.

Thrupp, Sylvia L. "A Survey of the Alien Population of England in 1440." *Speculum* 32 (1957): 262–73.

Thunæus, Harald. *Ölets historia i Sverige.* 2 vols. Stockholm: Almqvist & Wiksell, 1968–70.

Timmer, E. M. A. *De generale brouwers van Holland: Een bijdrage tot de geschiedenis der brouwnering in Holland in de 17de, 18de en 19de Eeuw.* Haarlem: Kleynenberg, 1918.

————. "Grepen uit de geschiedenis der Delftsche brouwnering." Parts 1 and 2. *De economist* (1920): 358–72 and 415–29.

————. "Uit de nadagen der Delftsche brouwnering." *De economist* (1916): 740–73.

Unger, Richard W. "Beer in Eastern Europe in the Middle Ages." In Balazs Nagy and Marcell Sebok, eds., . . . *The Man of many Devices, Who Wandered Full Many Ways . . . Festschrift in Honor of Janos M. Bak.* Budapest: Central European University Press, 1999.

————. "Beer, Wine, and Land Use in the Late Medieval Low Countries." *Bijdragen tot de Geschiedenis* 81 (1998): 329–37.

————. *Dutch Shipbuilding Before 1800: Ships and Guilds.* Assen: Van Gorcum, 1978.

————. "Energy Sources for the Dutch Golden Age: Peat, Wind and Coal." *Research in Economic History* 9 (1984): 221–53.

————. *A History of Brewing in Holland, 900–1900 Economy, Technology and the State.* Leiden: E. J. Brill, 2001.

————. "Technical Change in the Brewing Industry in Germany, the Low Countries, and England in the Late Middle Ages." *The Journal of European Economic History* 21 (1992): 281–313.

————. "The Trade in Beer to Medieval Scandinavia." *Deutsches Schiffahrtsarchiv* 11 (1988): 249–58.

Unger, W. S., "De economische ontwikkeling van Middelburg voor den Bourgondischen tijd," *Archief uitgegeven door het Zeeuwsch genootschap der wetenschappen.* (1918): 43–104.

————. *De levensmiddelenvoorziening der Hollandsche steden in de middeleeuwen.* Amsterdam: A.H. Kruyt, 1916.

————. "Twee rekeningen van den invoer van Hollandsch bier te Duinkerke uit de XIVe eeuw," *Annales de la société d'emulation de Bruges* 72 (1929): 1–4.

Unger, W. S., ed. *Bronnen tot de geschiedenis van Middelburg.* 3 vols. Rijks geschiedkundige publicatiën 54, 61 and 75. The Hague: Martinus Nijhoff, 1923–31.

————, ed. *De tol van Iersekeroord, documenten en rekeningen 1321–1572.* Rijks geschiedkundige publicatiën, kleine series 29. The Hague: Martinus Nijhoff, 1939.

Unwin, P. Tim H. *Wine and the Vine: An Historical Geography of Viticulture and the Wine Trade.* London: Routledge, 1991.

Urion, Edmond, and Frédéric Eyer. *La bière: Art et tradition.* Paris: Librairie Istra, 1968.

Uytven, Raymond van. "L'approvisionnement des villes des anciens Pays-Bas au moyen âge." *Flaran* 5 (1983): 75–116. Reprinted in Raymond van Uytven, *Production and Consumption in the Low Countries, 13th-16th Centuries.* Aldershot: Ashgate, 2001, XI.

————. "Bestaansmiddelen." *Arca Louvaniensis jaarboek* 7 (1978):129–94.

————. "Bier und Brauer in Brabant und Flandern: Ein Blick auf sechs Jahrhunderte Konsum-geschichte." In Fritz Langensiepen, ed., *Bierkultur an Rhein und Maas.* Bonn: Bouvier Verlag, n.d.

————. "Het bierverbruik en de sociaal-economische toestand in het Brugse Vrije in de zestiende eeuw." *Handelingen van het genootschap voor geschiedenis gesticht onder de benaming "Societé d'emulation" te Brugge* 131 (1994): 5–34. English translation, "Beer Consumption and the Socio-Economic Situation in the Franc of Bruges in the Sixteenth Century." In Raymond van Uytven, *Production and Consumption in the Low Countries, 13th-16th Centuries.* Aldershot: Ashgate, 2001, XII.

————. "The Consumption of Domestic and Foreign Wines in Brabant in the Sixteenth Century." English trans. by Raymond van Uytven of "Het verbruik van land- en vreemde wijnen in Brabant gedurende de 16e eeuw." *De Brabantse Folklore* 167 (1965): 299–337. Reprinted in Raymond van Uytven, *Production and Consumption in the Low Countries, 13th-16th Centuries.* Aldershot: Ashgate, 2001, XIII.

————. *De drankcultuur in de zuidelijke Nederlanden tot de XVIIIde eeuw. Drinken in het verleden: Tentoonstelling ingericht door het stadsbestuur van Leuven, 9 juni–5 augustus, 1973.* Leuven: Stadsbestuur Leuven, 1973.

————. "Haarlemmer hop, Goudse kuit en Leuvense Peterman." *Arca Lovaniensis jaarboek 1975* 4 (1975): 334–51.

————. "De Leuvense bierindustrie in de XVIIIe eeuw." *Bijdragen voor de geschiedenis der Nederlanden* 16 (1961): 193–227.

————. "Oudheid en middeleeuwen." In J. H. van Stuijvenberg, ed., *De economische geschiedenis van Nederland.* Groningen: Wolters-Noordhoff, 1977.

————. "De scheepstrafiek tussen Leuven en Mechelen in de zeventiende en achttiende eeuw." *Acta geographica Lovaniensis* 34 (1994): 617–25.

————. *Stadsfinanciën en stadsekonomie te Leuven van de XIIe tot het einde der XVIe eeuw.* Brussels: Paleis der Academiën, 1961.

————. "Stages of Economic Decline: Late Medieval Bruges." In J.-M. Duvosquel and E. Thoen, eds., *Studia in honorem Adriaan Verhulst.* Ghent: Snoeck-Ducaju, 1995. Reprinted in Raymond van Uytven, *Production and Consumption in the Low Countries, 13th-16th Centuries.* Aldershot: Ashgate, 2001, V.

Vandenbroeke, C. *Agriculture et alimentation.* Ghent: Centre belge d'histoire rurale, 1975.

Verlinden, C., and J. Craeybeckx. *Prijzen- en lonenpolitiek in de Nederlanden in 1561 en 1588–1589. Onuitgegeven adviezen, ontwerpen en ordonnanties.* Brussels: Koninlijke Belgische academie, koninklijke commissie voor geschiedenis, 1962.

Vilsteren, V. T. van. "De oorsprong en techniek van het brouwen tot de 14de eeuw." In R. E. Kistemaker and V. T. van Vilsteren, eds., *Bier! Geschiedenis van een volksdrank.* Amsterdam: De Bataafsche Leeuw, 1994.

Wagenaar, Jan. *Amsterdam in zyne opkomst, aanwas, Geschiedenissen, voorregten, koophandel, Gebouwen, kerkenstaat, schoolen, schutterye, Gilden en Regeeringe.* 18 vols. Amsterdam: Isaak Tirion, 1760–68.

Walford, Cornelius. *Gilds: Their Origin, Constitution, Objects, and Later History.* New and enlarged edition. London: George Redway, 1888.

Warner, George, ed. *The Libelle of Englyshe Polycye: A Poem on the Use of Sea-Power, 1436.* Oxford: The Clarendon Press, 1921.

Warner, Jessica. "Before There Was "Alcoholism": Lessons from the Medieval Experience with Alcohol." *Contemporary Drug Problems* 20 (1992): 409–29.

————. *Craze Gin and Debauchery in an Age of Reason.* New York: Four Walls Eight Windows, 2002.

Wee, Herman van der. *The Growth of the Antwerp Market and the European Economy in the Fifteenth and Sixteenth Centuries.* 3 vols. The Hague: Martinus Nijhoff, 1963.

Wee, Herman van der. "De handelsbetrekkingen tussen Antwerpen en de noordelijke Nederlanden tijdens de 14e, 15e en 16e eeuw." *Bijdragen voor de geschiedenis der Nederlanden* 20 (1965–66): 267–85.

Weibull, Curt. *Lübeck och Skånemarknaden. Studier i Lübecks pundtullsböcker och pundtullskvitton 1368–1369 och 1398–1400.* Lund: Berlingska Boktryckeriet, 1922.

Werneck, H. L. "Brauwesen und Hopfenbrau in Oberösterreich von 1100–1930." *Jahrbuch 1937 Gesellschaft für die Geschichte und Bibliographie des Brauwesens E.V.* Berlin, 1937.

Westlake, H. F. *The Parish Guilds of Mediæval England.* London: Society for the Propagation of Christian Knowledge, 1919.

Wiersum, E. *De archieven der Rotterdamsche gilden.* Rotterdam: Wed. P. van Waesberge en Zoon, 1926.

Wiesner, Merry E. *Working Women in Renaissance Germany.* New Brunswick, N. J.: Rutgers University Press, 1986.

Wijsenbeek-Olthuis, Th. F. "Ondernemen in moeilijke tijden: Delftse bierbrouwers en plateelbakkers in de achttiende eeuw." *Economisch- en sociaal-historisch jaarboek* 44 (1982): 65–78.

Wilson, C. Anne. *Food and Drink in Britain from the Stone Age to Recent Times.* London: Constable, 1973.

Wilson, D. Gay. "Plant Remains from the Graveney Boat and the Early History of *Humulus lupulus L.* in W. Europe." *New Phytologist* 75 (1975): 627–48.

Wilson, Richard G. "The British Brewing Industry Since 1750." In Lesley Richmond and Alison Turton, eds., *The Brewing Industry: A Guide to Historical Records.* Manchester: Manchester University Press, 1990.

Winkelman, P. H., ed. *Nederlandse rekeningen in de tolregisters van Koningsbergen, 1588–1602: Bronnen voor de geschiedenis van de Nederlandse Oostzeehandel in de zeventiende eeuw.* Vol. 1. Rijks geschiedkundige publicatiën 133. The Hague: Martinus Nijhoff, 1971.

Woolgar, C. M. *The Great Household in Late Medieval England.* New Haven: Yale University Press, 1999.

Wyffels, Carlos. *De oorsprong der ambachten in Vlaanderen en Brabant.* Brussels: Paleis der Academiën, 1951.

Wyffels, Carlos, and J. De Smet. *De rekeningen van de stad Brugge (1280–1319).* Vol. 1, *1280–1302.* Brussels: Paleis der Academiën, 1965.

Yntema, Richard J. "The Brewing Industry in Holland, 1300–1800: A Study in Industrial Development." Ph.D. diss., University of Chicago, March 1992.

———. "Een kapitale nering: De brouwindustrie in Holland tussen 1500 en 1800." In R. E. Kistemaker and V. T. van Vilsteren, eds., *Bier! Geschiedenis van een volksdrank.* Amsterdam: De Bataafsche Leeuw, 1994.

Zettler, Richard L., and Naomi F. Miller. "Searching for Wine in the Archaeological Record of Ancient Mesopotamia of the Third and Second Millennia B. C." In Patrick E. McGovern, Stuart J. Fleming, and Solomon H. Katz, eds., *The Origins and Ancient History of Wine.* Luxembourg: Gordon and Breach, 1995.

Index